The Evolution of Cognition

The Vienna Series in Theoretical Biology
Gerd B. Müller, Günter P. Wagner, and Werner Callebaut, editors

The Evolution of Cognition, edited by Cecilia Heyes and Ludwig Huber, 2000

The Evolution of Cognition

edited by Cecilia Heyes and Ludwig Huber

A Bradford Book
The MIT Press
Cambridge, Massachusetts
London, England

This book was set in Times New Roman by Asco Typesetters, Hong Kong, and was printed and bound in the United States of America.

Library of Congress Cataloging-in-Publication Data
The evolution of cognition / edited by Cecilia Heyes and Ludwig Huber.
      p.   cm. — (Vienna series in theoretical biology)
  Includes bibliographical references and index.
  ISBN 0-262-08286-1 (pbk. : alk. paper)
  1. Genetic psychology. 2. Psychology, Comparative. I. Heyes, Cecilia M. II. Huber, Ludwig, 1950–   III. Series.
  BF701.E598 2000
  156′.3—dc21

99-046217

Contents

Biology promises to the leading science in this century. As in all other sciences, progress in biology depends on interactions among empirical research, theory building, and modeling. But whereas the techniques and methods of descriptive and experimental biology have dramatically evolved in recent years, generating a flood of highly detailed empirical data, the integration of these results into useful theoretical frameworks has lagged behind. Biological research is currently much driven by pragmatic and technical considerations and remains less guided by theory than other fundamental sciences. As a consequence, theory-driven research into some of the major open questions of biology, such as the origin and organization of organismal form, the relationship between development and evolution, or the biological bases of cognition and mind, has been impeded. This series intends to help fill such conceptual gaps by promoting the discussion and formulation of new theoretical concepts in the biosciences.

Theoretical biology has important roots in the experimental biology movement that formed in the early decades of twentieth century Vienna. Paul Weiss and Ludwig von Bertalanffy were among the first to use the term "theoretical biology" in a modern scientific context. Their usage of the expression was not limited to mathematical formalization, as is often the case today, but rather applied to a general theoretical foundation of biology. This synthetic endeavor aimed at connecting the laws underlying the organization, metabolism, development, and growth of organisms. It included understandably little of population, ecological, molecular, and even evolutionary theory, which today represent the major connective concepts in biology. In addition to these, a successful integrative theoretical biology must encompass relevant aspects of computational biology, semiotics, and cognition, and should have continuities with a modern philosophy of the sciences of natural systems. It is this tradition of a comprehensive, cross-disciplinary integration of theoretical concepts that the present series intends to return to the center of biological research. The name "Vienna Series" is reflective of the location of initiating discussion meetings for the series and commemorates the seminal work of the aforementioned founding scientists.

The series is spawned by the yearly "Workshops in Theoretical Biology" held at the Konrad Lorenz Institute for Evolution and Cognition Research near Vienna, Austria. The Konrad Lorenz Institute is a private institution, closely associated with the University of Vienna. It fosters research projects, seminars, workshops, and symposia on all aspects of theoretical biology, with an emphasis on the developmental, evolutionary, and cognitive sciences. The workshops, each organized by leading experts in their fields, concentrate on new conceptual advances originating in these disciplines, and are meant to facilitate the formulation of integrative, cross-disciplinary theoretical models. Volumes on emerging topics of crucial theoretical importance not directly related to any of the workshops will also be included in the series. The series editors welcome suggestions for workshops or book projects on new theoretical advances in the biosciences.

Gerd B. Müller, University of Vienna, Konrad Lorenz Institute
Günter P. Wagner, Yale University, Konrad Lorenz Institute
Werner Callebaut, Limburg University Center, Konrad Lorenz Institute

Preface

The Konrad Lorenz Institute for Evolution and Cognition Research (KLI) devoted its 1998 Altenberg Workshop in Theoretical Biology to "The Evolution of Cognition"—a theme that lies at the core of the KLI's scientific aims. The workshop was held exactly 25 years after publication of Lorenz's book *Die Rückseite des Spiegels*. This book first appeared in 1973 (translation published as *Behind the Mirror* in 1977, London: Methuen), the year in which Lorenz retired and earned the Nobel Prize. It summarized the results of his long inquiry into the "natural history of human knowledge."

The themes and structure of the present volume are introduced in chapter 1. The book arose from the 1998 Altenberg workshop, and could also be said to be about "the natural history of human knowledge." However, the subject matter of this book is now more commonly known as "evolutionary psychology." Owing to the distinction, professionalism, and hard work of the contributors, this book is better integrated and more authoritative than is typical of conference volumes. It provides an overview of contemporary research on the phylogenetic, ontogenetic, and cultural evolution of cognition.

The workshop was held in the beautiful Lorenz mansion outside Vienna, where Konrad Lorenz grew up and spent the latter years of his life. His home is one of the cradles of ethology and evolutionary epistemology. The sessions took place in Lorenz's spacious library, and the conversation continued, through lunch and well into the evenings, in the "winter dining room," "the hall," and under the nut tree in the gardens. It is a pleasure to acknowledge the assistance of the KLI, in particular General Secretary Dr. Adolf Heschl, Chairman Prof. Gerd Müller, and the former chairman and founder of the KLI, Prof. Rupert Riedl. It was he who invited us to organize the workshop and to edit the book, and who provided invaluable support and encouragement throughout the process. We wish to express our sincere gratitude to the sponsors of the KLI for their generous financial support.

We are also very grateful for the help of the KLI's secretary, Ulrike Kühn; LH's secretary, Mag. Maria Nausch, who assisted in the editorial work; and CH's collaborators, Fiona Campbell and Elizabeth Ray, who perfected the English in the manuscripts from German-speaking contributors. Our particular thanks go to the students of the Department of Theoretical Biology at the University of Vienna, who helped out with so many practical details of the workshop; and to the Bauer family of Hotel Marienhof, who made the participants welcome in the Vienna Woods. Finally, it has been a pleasure to work with Michael Rutter of The MIT Press, whose enthusiasm for the series and the present volume provided continuous encouragement.

I ORIENTATIONS

1 Evolutionary Psychology in the Round

Cecilia Heyes

When I first encountered the term "evolutionary psychology," I thought it referred to the study of how mind and behavior have evolved. But I was mistaken. In the last decade, evolutionary psychology has come to refer exclusively to research on human mentality and behavior, motivated by a very specific, nativist-adaptationist interpretation of how evolution operates (e.g., Cosmides and Tooby, 1994; Buss, 1999; Daly and Wilson, 1999). This is a strange, anthropocentric usage, akin to identifying human biology with "biology" generally, or describing geography as "astronomy." This book is about evolutionary psychology more broadly and more transparently construed; about evolutionary psychology "in the round." It encompasses the behavior and mentality of nonhuman as well as human animals, and a full range of contemporary evolutionary approaches. Rather than a campaign volume by and for the like-minded, it is a debate among authoritative researchers about the ways in which evolutionary processes have shaped cognition.

The debate is presented under five broad section headings: Orientations, Categorization, Causality, Consciousness, and Culture. In the first of these, the chapters by Huber, Shettleworth, and Bitterman provide general arguments in favor of distinct conceptual and methodological approaches to investigating the evolution of cognition: phylogenetic, ecological, and psychological/comparative. In each of the remaining chapters, the author(s) adopt one or a combination of these approaches in addressing a specific issue, or set of issues, relating to the evolution of cognition.

The chapters on "Categorization" are concerned with how various animals parse their environments, how they think about, or represent, objects and events and the relations among them. Those chapters under "Causality" focus on a particular kind of relationship, that of cause and effect, asking which nonhuman animals, if any, represent this kind of relation, and how they do it. The discussions of "Consciousness" consider whether it makes sense to talk about the evolution of consciousness, and how, if at all, this phenomenon can be investigated in nonhuman animals. The final section, on "Culture," examines the cognitive requirements for nongenetic transmission of information, and the evolutionary consequences of such cultural exchange.

To help readers follow the debate, each contribution cross-references other chapters and concludes with an abstract–like summary. In addition, each section begins with a short overview identifying the main points of agreement and disagreement among the contributors to that section, and among their views and those expressed elsewhere in the volume.

The purpose of this introductory chapter is both to integrate and to propose. It addresses three elementary questions about the evolution of cognition, surveys the various answers offered by the contributors to this volume, and, at the end, combines these in a general hypothesis about the evolution of cognition. The questions are: What is cognition? What is the difference among "different" cognitive processes? What makes research on cognition "evolutionary"?

What Is Cognition?

Fortunately, a rough and ready definition is sufficient to support interesting research on the evolution of cognition, and for the present purposes I need only outline what most of the contributors to this volume assume about the nature of cognition, and to identify points of potentially confusing contention.

Most of the authors would probably agree that cognitive states and processes are (1) theoretical entities, which (2) provide a functional characterization of operations of the central nervous system, (3) may or may not be objects of conscious awareness, (4) receive inputs from other cognitive states and processes and from perception, and (5) have outputs to other cognitive states and processes and to behavior.

Regarding cognitive states and processes as theoretical entities that cause behavior distinguishes cognitive psychology from most varieties of behaviorism, and emphasises that, unlike behavior or neural tissue, they cannot be observed directly. Hypotheses about cognition can be evaluated only by testing their predictions regarding the effects of various environmental manipulations on behavior. These theoretical entities are said to provide a functional characterization of the central nervous system (CNS) to flag the fact that most of contributors to this volume assume that the same cognitive process could be implemented or instantiated in a variety of different neuroanatomical structures or neurophysiological processes. In other words, this characterization of cognition is materialist, but it does not assume a simple one-to-one mapping between cognitive and neural states and processes. Similarly, although the foregoing characterization of cognition allows that some cognitive processes may be conscious, and that their subjective status may depend on their functional role, it does not identify cognitive processes with conscious processes; consciousness plays no part in the definition of what is and is not cognitive.

Dickinson and Balleine, Bitterman, and Shettleworth are the only contributors to this book who clearly depart from the usage outlined above. Dickinson and Balleine prefer to reserve the term "cognitive" for processes that support *goal-directed* behavior, excluding, for example, associative learning from the cognitive domain. Bitterman and Shettleworth, on the other hand, favor more inclusive definitions of cognition. Bitterman equates it with " 'knowing' in the classical sense of the term, encompassing perception, learning, and understanding," whereas for Shettleworth cognition subsumes "all mechanisms that invertebrates and vertebrates have for taking in information through the senses, retaining it, and using it to adjust behavior to local conditions." These characterizations are incompatible with (4) and (5) above, which imply that cognitive processes are distinct from perceptual processes that are directly involved in dealing with sensory input and motor processes responsible for preparing effector movements. These dissenting voices highlight a truism: it matters little how we label our distinctions, but we would be unwise to let them get lost. Points 1–5 above circumscribe a set of properties of the CNS that are physically related to, but conceptually distinct from, its neurobiological and behavioral properties. Whether we label these properties "cognitive," "mental," or "intelligent" is unimportant in itself, but if we were to lose sight of their distinctiveness, there would not only be confusion, but research on the evolution of cognition/mentality/intelligence would move outside the domain of contemporary psychology. It would be reduced to an examination of the way in which evolution has affected nervous systems and motor physiology.

Similarly, it doesn't really matter whether we call associative learning or perceptual processing "cognitive" or "noncognitive information processing," but we should be alert to the possibilities that the processes on either side of these divides show different evolutionary patterns. For example, over evolutionary time, associative learning may be more conservative, and perceptual processing more labile, than (other) cognitive processes.

What Are the Differences Among "Different" Cognitive Processes?

Carving Cognition

The first question asked how we distinguish cognitive from other processes; the second examines how we distinguish one kind of cognitive process from another. The capacity to do this, the possession of conceptual knives that will carve cognition rationally and reliably into distinct pieces, is especially important in the context of an evolutionary analysis. At the most general level, evolutionary analysis uses synchronous patterns of similarity and diversity to infer historical continuity and change. Clearly, this cannot be achieved in the case of cognition unless we can work out where one kind of cognition stops and another begins.

All of the contributors to this volume carve cognition into different types, but few comment on the knives they are using, on what they consider to be the differences among different cognitive processes. If we first consider the pieces, we find that they come in a range of shapes and sizes. At one extreme, Shettleworth mentions at least 14 types of cognition: spatial memory, circadian timing, interval timing, dead reckoning, landmark use, imprinting, song learning, motor imitation, associative learning (and components thereof), social intelligence, theory of mind (and components thereof), language, reasoning about social obligations, and consciousness. At the other extreme, several authors carve the cognitive pie into conscious and unconscious processes (Clayton et al., Heinrich, Humphrey, Macphail), and/or into two or three pieces, one of which corresponds loosely with what Shettleworth calls associative learning. Thus, Bitterman, Delius, and Huber distinguish associative learning from conceptual thought (and, in the case of Huber, from language); Dickinson and Balleine, Dunbar, Macphail, Rumbaugh, and Tomasello contrast it with the representation of intentional relations (and, in the latter case, with representation of relations more generally); Mackintosh leaves out representation of intentional relations and contrasts associative learning, based on invariant feature detection, with representation of relations generally; and Bateson opposes "learning involving external reward" with recognition learning. Dichotomies that apparently have nothing to do with associative learning are mentioned by Clayton et al. (remembering facts vs. personal experiences) and Sterelny (representing mental states vs. behavior); lists of cognitive processes, similar to, but shorter than, Shettleworth's can be found in the chapters by Lefebvre (spatial memory, imprinting, song learning, [associative?] learning, and imitation, but *not* social learning) and by Richerson and Boyd (decision making, [associative?] learning, social learning, imitation, and language).

This range of methods of carving cognition is representative of contemporary research on the evolution of cognition, and some of the diversity is almost certainly due to substantive disagreements about evidence. From a scientific perspective, these are the interesting disagreements, the unresolved empirical questions, but they are difficult to isolate from the diversity due to the use of different knives, different principles of classification. For example, circadian timing, interval timing, dead reckoning, and landmark use fall within Shettleworth's inclusive definition of cognition, but others may regard them as noncognitive, perceptual processes. In this example, it is the cut between cognitive and noncognitive processes that is at issue, but some of the remaining variation may be due to the use of different knives to distinguish among processes that are agreed to be cognitive.

What/When and How Rules

Extrapolating from the shapes and sizes of their pieces of cognition, and from occasional comments about principles of classification, it seems that the contributors to this volume, and evolutionary psychologists more generally, are using two sorts of blades to carve cognition: "What/when" and "how" rules. What/when rules distinguish types of cognition according to their content (defined by inputs to or outputs from cognitive processes) and/or the time in ontogeny when they typically operate. How rules, by contrast, distinguish types of cognition in terms of the abstract principles (more or less formally specified) that characterize the way in which content information is processed.

When birdsong learning is identified as a distinct variety of cognition, it is primarily on the basis of a what/when rule something like, "Conspecific song, first season" (e.g., Catchpole and Slater, 1995). It specifies the content of what is usually learned (species-typical song) and when in ontogeny this learning usually takes place. Describing a cognitive process as "domain specific" (e.g., Shettleworth, this volume), implies that it is distinct *at least* in terms of its what/when rules. An example of a formally specified how rule is the Rescorla-Wagner equation (Bush and Mosteller, 1951; Rescorla and Wagner, 1972; Bitterman, this volume). How rules are what Sherry and Schacter (1987) describe as "rules of operation," Bitterman (this volume) as "equations," and Bateson (this volume) as "design rules."

Examples

Closer examination of two examples of behavior will, I hope, clarify the distinction between what/when and how rules. If the first, snake fear learning in rhesus monkeys (e.g., Cook and Mineka, 1990), is based on a distinctive type of cognition, then it is distinctive in terms of its what/when rules. The second, same-different categorisation by Alex the parrot (Pepperberg, 1987), seems to be based on a cognitive process with distinctive how rules.

Snake Fear Cook and Mineka (1987, 1989, 1990) have shown that rhesus monkeys acquire fear of snakes more readily than fear of flowers through exposure to a conspecific behaving fearfully in the presence of the target stimuli, that is, snakes or flowers. To check whether this effect is due to the content or identity of the stimuli (snakes vs. flowers), rather than to the differential salience of the snake and flower stimuli employed (e.g., differences in color or brightness), they did an experiment in which snake and flower stimuli were paired with food rather than fear (Cook and Mineka, 1990, experiment 3). They predicted that if the fear effect was due to differential salience, the monkeys would still learn about the snakes more readily than about the flowers, but that if it was due to the identity of the stimuli, they would, if anything, learn more slowly that the snakes signaied a positive event.

In each trial in this experiment, a monkey was shown one of four pairs of stimuli on a video screen. If it reached toward one of the stimuli (+) it was rewarded with food; reaching toward the other was not rewarded (−). Thus, the monkeys had four discrimination problems: coiled snake + / red square − (snake positive); long snake − / red square + (snake negative); chrysanthemums + / blue diamond − (flower positive); silk flowers − / blue diamond + (flower negative). The results indicated that the monkeys solved the flower problems at least as fast as the snake problems, and in some cases the flower problems were solved more quickly.

There are three things to note about this example. First, it does not show that the cognitive process underlying snake fear in monkeys differs in terms of its how rules from the kind of associative learning mediating (other) Pavlovian conditioning. Indeed, snake fear acquisition is subject to the overshadowing and latent inhibition effects (Mineka and Cook, 1986; Cook and Mineka, 1987; Heyes 1994) that are characteristic of Pavlovian conditioning more generally, and which have played a key role in the formulation of its how rules.

Second, snake fear acquisition is a distinct form of associative learning in terms of its what/when rules only if it is the content, not the salience, of the snake stimuli that is responsible for faster learning. Thus, not all variations in learning that are typically described as "quantitative" rather than "qualitative," or as being due to changes in "constants" rather than "equations" (Bitterman, this volume), provide evidence of cognition with distinctive what/when rules. More generally, the what/when vs. how distinction is *not* equivalent to the quantitative vs. qualitative distinction.

Finally, the snake fear example illustrates how difficult it can be to find out whether different rates of learning about stimuli are due to the identity, rather than the salience of the stimuli. Even the results of Cook and Mineka's (1990) subtle experiment do not show this conclusively because (1) the snake and flower stimuli in this study were not identical to those used to test observational conditioning of fear, and (2) the monkeys were required to discriminate snakes and flowers from different, arbitrary stimuli. It may have been more difficult to discriminate the red square from the snake stimuli than to discriminate the blue diamond from the flower stimuli and, if this was the case, the monkeys might have solved the snake problems more slowly even if the snake stimuli were more salient than the flower stimuli.

Alex the Parrot   Pepperberg's African Grey parrot, Alex, appears to be able to represent relations among objects in what could be described, for the want of a better word, as an "abstract" way (Pepperberg, 1987; Mackintosh, this volume). In the training phase of the relevant experiment, Alex was shown pairs of objects varying in color, material, and/or shape (e.g., a red wooden triangle and a blue wooden oval), and asked, in spoken English, "What same?" or "What different?" In the former case he was rewarded for naming a dimension on which the stimuli had a common attribute (material), and in the latter for naming a dimension on which they had different attributes (e.g., color or shape). Alex not only succeeded in learning these discriminations, but was accurate on 82 percent of transfer trials involving novel objects (e.g., a gray wooden cube and a gray woollen ball).

The process forming Alex's representations of similarity and difference (but not necessarily that linking these representations with the experimenter's questions and with reward) seems to have how rules distinct from those that characterize Pavlovian conditioning. These equations (see Dickinson, 1980 for a survey) cannot fabricate from absolute values of stimuli (e.g., redness) a representation that does not function according to its absolute values. Thus, when Alex is shown two red objects, Pavlovian processes would allow him to represent double-redness, but not in a way that he spontaneously, without further training, treats as equivalent to double-greenness. However, there is no reason to suppose that the processes mediating Alex's representation of relations are distinctive in terms of their what/when rules, no evidence that he is able to represent relations among only a subset of the stimuli he can perceive, or that he has used this capacity more during a certain phase of his ontogeny than at other times. The foregoing experiment involved arbitrary stimuli and was conducted when Alex was already mature.

In both of these examples and in many others, associative learning of the kind that mediates Pavlovian conditioning features as a kind of bench mark, as that from which potentially distinct cognitive processes are shown to differ. There are probably two sound reasons for this, as well as a third that is more contentious. The first reason is pragmatic: the how rules of associative learning are relatively well specified, and therefore in many cases the only evidence currently available that *different* how rules underlie a behavior, is that the behavior in question cannot be explained with reference to associative learning. The alternative rules have not been formulated. Second, there is evidence to suggest that the capacity for Pavlovian associative learning is present in a very broad range of vertebrate and invertebrate species (e.g., Bitterman, this volume; Mackintosh, this volume; Macphail, this volume), and therefore it is a natural contender to explain a broad range of behaviors. Third, it is sometimes claimed that it is more "parsimonious" to attribute behavior to associative learning than to an alternative cognitive process (e.g., Macphail, 1985). This reason is problematic if, going beyond the second, it assumes that associative mechanisms are necessarily simpler than nonassociative processes, or that evolution is so conservative that any behavioral adaptation that *can* be achieved by associative learning *will* be so achieved (Sober, 1998).

Inferring How from What/When

Most of the varieties of cognition discussed in this book seem, on the surface, to be circumscribed by their what/when rules. The names they are given identify a category of environmental input (e.g., spatial memory, circadian timing, interval timing, landmark use, song learning, social learning, social intelligence, reasoning about social obligations, language), of cognitive product (e.g., representations of relations, intentional relations, behavior, and mental states; remembering facts and personal experiences; decision making; recognition learning), or of behavioral product (e.g., imprinting, imitation, language). Possible exceptions are associative learning, conceptual thought, theory of mind, and consciousness, but even some of these can be construed as characterizing types of information processed rather than processing operations.

This way of labeling types of cognition may give the impression that what/when rules are considered more important than how rules, but the reverse is true. The vast majority of contributors to this volume, and to research on the evolution of cognition generally, use differences in what/when rules as markers for putative differences in how rules, and consider distinctions of the latter kind to be of primary significance in evolutionary analysis. Shettleworth makes this priority very clear: "When distinct classes of input (domains) are computed on in distinct ways as inferred from behavior, we have a distinct mental module or memory system. Computational distinctiveness is the primary criterion for cognitive modularity." Other contributors are less explicit, and do not use the language of modularity, but they seem to have a common purpose. For example, it is unlikely that Tomasello would distinguish "intentional/causal cognition" from understanding the relationship between one's own actions and their outcomes if he believed that these two differ only in terms of what is understood, and not with respect to how that understanding is achieved.

In addition to being used as markers for distinctive how rules, what/when rules are sometimes used to infer the existence of distinctive how rules. A what/when rule acts as a simple marker if, of the many slices into which cognition could be cut by characterizing its inputs or products, a researcher delineates only those types that he or she believes, on the basis of independent evidence, also to be distinctive in terms of their how rules. By contrast, a difference in what/when rules is used to infer a difference in how rules when the former is itself treated as evidence of the latter.

The chapters in this book suggest that differences in how rules can sometimes be inferred from differences in the kind of what/when rules that circumscribe cognitive products (e.g., understanding causality, representing relations, representing intentional relations), but rarely if ever from what/when rules that characterize environmental inputs (e.g., social learning) or behavioral products (e.g., imprinting). In the former case, it requires painstaking empirical work (e.g., Delius, this volume; Dickinson and Balleine, this volume; Mackintosh, this volume) to establish that the cognitive product is really of the specified kind—for example, that the animals in question are really representing causality, relations, or intentional relations—but, if this information can be secured, in conjunction with knowledge of inputs, it may provide the basis for inferring the presence of distinctive how rules. This is possible because in principle one can work out which how rules could, and which could not, generate specified outputs from specified inputs.

In contrast, at least three chapters in this volume (Bateson, Clayton et al., and Lefebvre) make it clear that, as they are currently circumscribed, how rules do not coincide with behavioral products and environmental inputs in a way that allows the former to be inferred reliably from the latter. Bateson's model of imprinting implies that this type of cognition differs from (other) recognition learning in terms of its what/when rules, but not in terms of its how rules. The experiments reported by Clayton et al. raise the intriguing possibility that spatial memory in food-storing birds, although it is distinctive in terms of what is remembered (cache locations) and when encoding takes place (during seasonal gluts), occurs via the same how rules as episodic memory in humans. Similarly, Lefebvre's demonstration that social learning ability covaries with (other) learning ability suggests that, at least in avian taxa, these two may differ in terms of whether their environmental inputs are or are not from social interactants, but not in their how rules.

Covariation between neural substrates and behavioral product or environmental input what/when rules is commonly interpreted as support for the suggestion that the former characterize important differences among cognitive processes. For example, Lefebvre (this volume) argues that the association of distinctive neural substrates with spatial memory in food-storing birds (hippocampus), parental imprinting (left intermediate medial hyperstriatum ventrale), and birdsong learning (high vocal center) contributes to making these what/when types of cognition more distinctive than social learning. This is undoubtedly true, but not because the discovery of a distinctive neural mechanism necessarily indicates that what/when rules are coincident with how rules. This would be the case only if we assumed that different neuro-anatomical structures necessarily implement different cognitive rules of operation, and that differences in what/when rules alone could not be associated with distinctive neural substrates; this assumption does not appear to be warranted. For example, food-storing birds may have larger hippocampi than related, nonstoring species (e.g., Clayton and Krebs, 1994; Clayton, 1996), not because the spatial memory of storing species operates according to distinctive how rules, but because in these birds a system using how rules common to storing and nonstoring species processes a large volume of information about the locations of food caches. Covariation between what/when rules and neural mechanisms is significant, not as a short cut to discovering diversity in how rules, but in its own right; as an indicator of the effects of evolution on what/when rules of cognition.

Addressing the question "What is different about 'different' cognitive processes?" I have suggested that the contributors to this volume use a combination of what/when and how rules to distinguish types of cognition, and that most or all of them consider distinctions based on how rules, on the way in which information is processed, to be primary, and use differences in what/when rules as markers for these distinctions, or as a basis for inferring how rule diversity. Thus, at root, the authors that postulate different ranges of cognitive processes disagree about the variety of how rules found in the animal kingdom, and it is unlikely that these disagreements can be resolved except by generating hypothetical how rules for various categories of behavior and testing them empirically against other such rules. At present, research of this kind typically examines whether behavior can or cannot be explained in terms of how rules of Pavlovian associative learning, but there is no reason in principle why other how rules should not be formulated and tested.

The current preoccupation with differentiating cognitive processes according to their how rules is understandable in historical context. It may be a healthy reaction to the many years in which the "general process" tradition denied the existence of any such diversity, and the subsequent period in which "biological boundaries" or "constraints on learning" approaches fought for the recognition of what/when variation (e.g., Johnston, 1981). However, there is a risk of over-compensation, of exaggerating the extent of how rule diversity, and of underestimating the potential contribution to behavioral adaptation of what/when variation alone.

What Makes Research on Cognition "Evolutionary"?

All of the contributors to this volume subscribe to a broadly Darwinian account of evolution. Within this, however, at least four evolutionary approaches to the study of cognition are discernable. For convenience, I will call them the ecological, phylogenetic, comparative, and selection theoretic approaches.

Ecological and Phylogenetic

The ecological and phylogenetic approaches are, to a significant degree, complementary. Each has historical roots in ethology, and proceeds from a known fact about evolution. The ecological approach focuses on the fact that evolution tends to produce adaptations, phenotypic characteristics that enable organisms to survive and reproduce in their unique environments; the phylogenetic approach emphasizes descent rather than adaptation. It concentrates on the fact that the phenotype of a given taxon depends not only on the selection pressures to which *those* animals or plants have been subjected, but also on the genetic variants that they inherited from their ancestral species.

As a consequence of this difference in emphasis, the two approaches seek evidence of different evolutionary footprints on cognition. The ecological approach anticipates that a species' cognitive capabilities will be correlated with the demands of its natural environment, and investigates the character and specificity of this correlation—which cognitive characteristics are tuned to environmental demand, and with what degree of precision. The phylogenetic approach, on the other hand, aims to chart the way in which cognitive capabilities vary with phylogenetic relatedness—to identify where in evolutionary lineages major cognitive change has occurred, and to specify the nature of these changes.

None of the contributors to this volume would deny that there are likely to be both ecological and phylogenetic trends in the evolution of cognition. Both patterns are so clearly apparent in the evolution of morphological, anatomical, and physiological characteristics, that, when we turn to cognition and behavior, the challenge is not to discover whether they are both present, but to uncover their relative contributions to particular cognitive characteristics in particular regions of the phylogenetic tree. Consequently, none of the chapters in this volume represent the ecological approach, or the phylogenetic approach, in pure form. However, Huber concentrates on the phylogenetic approach, examining its historical roots in the work of Konrad Lorenz and illuminating some of the methodological problems that make it difficult to pursue. Shettleworth, at the editors' request, makes a strong case in favor of modularity, a contemporary variant of the ecological approach.

The modularity approach is characteristic of what is currently known as "evolutionary psychology." In common with other ecological approaches, it is concerned with behavioral adaptations, but the modular approach is distinctive in that it attributes them to psychological mechanisms with specific properties. These psychological mechanisms or "modules" are thought to be "domain-specific," to have distinctive what/when rules, *and* to have distinctive how rules. Following Fodor (1983), it is often also assumed that modules are innate, have distinctive neural substrates, are automatically activated by input from the relevant domain, and are "informationally encapsulated." This means, roughly, that modules are relatively impermeable to information from central or more general cognitive processes.

The broader ecological approach is represented in the chapters by Bateson, Clayton et al., Dunbar, Heinrich, Lefebvre, Sterelny, and Tomasello. Bateson's topic, imprinting, is defined by its role in behavioral adaptation, and Clayton et al. were motivated to seek evidence of episodic memory in scrub jays by reflection on the demands of their natural ecology as food-storing birds. Dunbar, Heinrich, Sterelny, and Tomasello all express some support for the "social intelligence" or "social function of intellect" (Humphrey, 1976) hypothesis, the idea that complex social environments are a powerful stimulus for the evolution of complex cognitive capacities, and Lefebvre examines the relationship between an ecological variable, distribution of food resources, and learning and innovation in birds. However, like Dunbar's and Tomasello's chapters, Lefebvre's discussion also subsumes the phylogenetic approach, and integrates it with an ecological analysis. Dunbar and Tomasello are concerned with cognitive transitions in the primate lineage; Lefebvre examines avian taxa.

Comparative

The comparative approach to the study of cognition is represented in this volume by Bitterman, Dickinson and Balleine, Delius, Mackintosh, and Macphail. Practitioners of this approach focus intensively on the how rules of cognition (e.g., associative learning, conceptualization, goal-directedness), study them with a high level of methodological rigor in a few nonhuman taxa (including rats, pigeons, rhesus monkeys, honeybees, ravens, goldfish, and chimpanzees), and compare the results, implicitly or explicitly, with each other and with what is known about human cognition. The outcome of this comparison process, unlike those of the ecological and phylogenetic approaches, is more commonly the discovery of similarities than of differences. But, while the comparative approach emphasizes evolutionary continuity over evolutionary diversity, and the role of ontogeny rather than of phylogeny in behavioral adaptation, it is no less "evolutionary" than the other approaches.

Selection Theoretic

The selection theoretic approach, represented in this volume by Lefebvre, Richerson and Boyd, and Wilson et al., has much in common with the ecological approach. Like the latter, it is preoccupied with adaptation, with the fit between animals' behavioral and cognitive traits and the demands of their natural environments. However, the selection theoretic approach argues that this fit arises not from just one evolutionary process, natural section operating on genetic variation, but from several (e.g., Campbell, 1974; Plotkin and Odling-Smee, 1981; Campbell et al., 1997; Sober and Wilson, 1998; Wilson et al., this volume). An evolutionary selection process, a process involving variation and selective retention, operates not only on genetic variation, that is, at the phylogenetic level, but also at ontogenetic and cultural levels. In the ontogenetic case, cognitive variants—contents or processes of thought—arise from interaction between an individual animal and its environment, and are selectively lost/forgotten or retained/remembered according to the consequences of their behavioral expression for that individual. At the cultural level, the cognitive variants are contents or processes of thought characteristic of groups of individuals, and normally acquired by individuals through social interaction. They are generated within the group, or via the group's interaction with its environment, and selected according to their success in being transmitted to new individuals or groups, which may or may not be or contain biological descendants of the previous cultural generation. Thus, cultural selection may or may not constitute group selection (Sober and Wilson, 1998), and variants that are relatively successful in cultural selection may or may not enhance the reproductive fitness of the individual or group (Boyd and Richerson, 1985).

According to the selection theoretic approach, these ontogenetic and cultural processes are evolutionary in three senses: (1) Phylogenetic evolution, natural selection operating on genes, has shaped the cognitive processes that make them possible. (2) They make autonomous contributions to cognitive and behavioral adaptation. That is, phylogenetic evolution alone could not achieve the same degree of fit between cognitive systems and their environments, *and* ontogenetic and cultural processes sometimes perpetrate characteristics that are not "good for the genes," that would not be selected at the phylogenetic level. (3) The ontogenetic and cultural processes each promote adaptation through variation and selective retention, the fundamental Darwinian evolutionary algorithm.

These four approaches to studying the evolution of cognition are complementary rather than antagonistic. As figure 1.1 suggests, selection theoretic analysis can be seen as a subset of the ecological approach, the comparative perspective as a subset of the phylogenetic approach, and the combination of the ecological and phylogenetic approaches, broadly construed, as comprising the universal set of current evolutionary research on cognition. This picture is, of course, a very simple representation of complex conceptual geography. Each of the four main categories could be subdivided many times. Those adopting different perspectives often find themselves in healthy dispute, and many researchers productively combine approaches. For example, in this volume Tomasello, Dunbar, and Lefebvre combine ecological and phylogenetic perspectives, Bateson and Clayton et al. combine ecological with comparative analysis, and in their theoretical work Richerson and Boyd use the products of all four approaches. However, in spite of its simplicity, figure 1.1 provides some indication of what evolutionary psychology looks like "in the round."

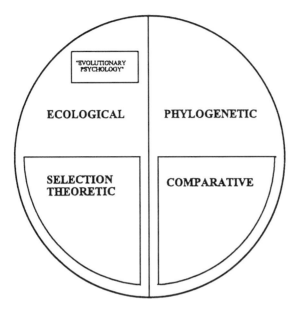

Figure 1.1
Schematic representation of relationships among components of evolutionary psychology in the round.

Evolutionary Psychology in the Round

At the beginning, I pointed out one prominent difference between the research enterprise currently known as "evolutionary psychology" (e.g., Buss, 1999), and that which is represented by this book, evolutionary psychology in the round: the former is concerned almost exclusively with human cognition and behavior; the latter investigates these phenotypic characteristics throughout the animal kingdom. Now that I have surveyed the contributors' views on the nature of cognition, on variation among cognitive processes, and on the characteristics of evolutionary analysis, further differences between the two research enterprises have become apparent. These can be summarized: (1) Evolutionary psychology in the round is concerned with the phylogenetic history, as well as the adaptive characteristics, of behavior and cognition, descent as well as selection. (2) It recognizes that behavioral adaptation can be achieved via modification of perceptual and motor processes, instead of or in addition to modification of cognitive processes. (3) It investigates the contributions to cognitive adaptation of ontogenetic and cultural processes, as well as that of natural selection operating on genes. (4) Evolutionary psychology in the round seeks independent evidence that variation in what/when rules of cognition is correlated with variation in how rules, resisting easy inferences from domain specificity to modularity. Two examples, taken from research on spatial memory in food-storing birds and motor imitation, will serve to illustrate these contrasts.

Certain birds, such as Clark's nutcrackers and Marsh tits, which experience seasonal variation in the availability of food, scatter hoard for winter survival. Cache retrieval has been demonstrated to involve memory (e.g., Clayton and Krebs, 1994), and these birds have been reported to perform better on tests of spatial memory than related species that cache less assiduously (e.g., Kamil et al., 1994; Olson et al., 1995). Furthermore, lesions of the hippocampus impair memory for cache sites (e.g., Sherry and Vaccarino, 1989), and birds that depend heavily on food storing for winter survival have larger hippocampi than related species (e.g., Krebs et al., 1989).

One interpretation of these data is as follows. Food-storing birds have an innate, spatial memory module lodged in the hippocampus. That is, natural selection operating at the genetic level has given rise to a cognitive process, based in the hippocampus, which has distinct what/when rules *and* distinct how rules; it processes spatial information, and does so in a way that differs from the processing of nonspatial information. This kind of interpretation is characteristic of "evolutionary psychology."

By its nature, evolutionary psychology in the round recognizes a range of plausible interpretations of these spatial memory data. It does not underestimate inferential complexity, even where the topic has been researched so extensively and so elegantly as spatial memory. One alternative account, which is consistent with recent evidence that the act of cache retrieval stimulates hippocampal growth (e.g., Clayton and Krebs, 1994; Lee et al., 1998), and of episodic-like memory in scrub jays (Clayton et al., this volume) is as follows. In response to selection pressure from seasonal variations in food supply, phylogenetic evolution (natural selection operating at the genetic level) has furnished certain birds with a specialized *behavior*, namely, scatter hoarding. There may be what/when distinctive perceptual and motor processes controlling this behavior, but the action of caching does not itself involve a significant cognitive component. From the point in ontogeny when hoarding behavior begins, higher than average demands are made on memory. Hoarding creates for the hoarder an environment in which food resources are scattered, and thereby exercises the memory system. This system, located in the hippocampus, grows as it deals with a higher volume of information, but neither its potential for growth, nor the how rules that it implements, have been changed by natural selection relative to those used by other species to remember spatial stimuli. Thus, according to this interpretation, the spatial memory performance of food-storing birds is a product of phylogenetic and ontogenetic specialization. Phylogenetic evolution, natural selection, has yielded a behavioral, but not a cognitive adaptation, and, provoked by this behavioral adaptation, a cognitive system with specialized what/when rules, but not distinctive how rules, emerges in the course of ontogeny.

Research on motor imitation is more diffuse, and has provided much less reliable information than that on spatial memory in food-storing birds. However, it illustrates the contrasting attitudes toward culture of evolutionary psychology and evolutionary psychology in the round.

Motor imitation, the capacity to learn a novel body movement by seeing it done, has been clearly demonstrated only among humans. Many researchers believe that it occurs in other apes (e.g., Tomasello and Call, 1997), but, like all other putative evidence of imitation in nonhuman animals, the bases of these claims have been or could be challenged (e.g., Akins and Zentall, 1996; Moore, 1996; Lefebvre et al., 1997; Campbell et al., 1999). Furthermore, it is not clear how humans, or any other animals, could imitate certain "perceptually opaque" actions (Heyes and Ray, 2000). For example, imitation of novel facial expressions, which are seen in others but felt by oneself, would seem to require some kind of cross-modal transformation of information, and it is not clear what sort of cognitive how rules could achieve this transformation. This problem not withstanding, it has been noted repeatedly that imitation learning could be the means by which many culture-specific behaviors are transmitted.

Evolutionary psychology has deduced from observations of this kind that imitation learning is a phylogenetically specialized cognitive module, which selectively processes sensory input from others' body movements according to distinctive rules of operation, is found only in humans and possibly other apes, and supports cultural transmission of information. An interpretation that is at least equally consistent with current evidence, and more in the spirit of evolutionary psychology in the round, suggests that the capacity to imitate arises from ontogenetic specialization, using cultural input, of phylogenetically general, associative learning processes (Heyes and Ray, 2000). According to this Associative Sequence Learning (ASL) hypothesis, children acquire the capacity to reproduce action units (fragments of what would normally be delineated as "an action") through contiguous experience of seeing and doing each unit, thereby forming associations between sensory and motor representations of each unit. These links establish an imitation repertoire. That is, when units in the repertoire are observed in a novel sequence, the sequence can be learned by observation alone, and the modeled movement can be reproduced. The most important sources of contiguous experience of seeing and doing action units, and therefore the most significant influences on the development of an imitation repertoire, are optical mirrors and the adult tendency to imitate infants; both, broadly speaking, are cultural phenomena. Thus, ontogenetic specialization yields a cognitive process that is distinctive in its what/when rules (it reproduces body movements) and that both supports and is supported by culture.

For both of these examples—spatial memory and imitation—more evidence is needed to establish the relative merits of the alternative interpretations I have outlined. For example, we need to know whether the hippocampi of storing and non-storing species grow at comparable rates when they are given spatial memory tasks, and, to evaluate the ASL theory of imitation, whether prior experience of seeing and doing action units facilitates subsequent imitation of sequences of these units in humans and other animals. Whatever the results of these further experiments, the spatial memory and imitation examples illustrate the nature of the biases inherent in much evolutionary psychology, and, more generally, emphasize that evolutionary psychology in the round generates and tests more complex hypotheses. Many of the contributors to this volume, myself included, would argue that such complexity is necessary to capture even the basics of the evolution of cognition, but it certainly doesn't make life easy. It is much easier to attribute all adaptive variation among cognitive processes to phylogenetically evolved modules than to investigate the nature (what/when and/or how rules) and evolutionary sources (the relative contributions of phylogenetic, ontogenetic, and/or cultural processes) of such variation.

Perhaps this difficult (but rewarding) process of enquiry can be assisted by bold hypotheses about the evolution of cognition that take account of the different types and sources of variation. In this spirit, I offer, as a parting shot, my own bold hypotheses: What/when rules of cognition are more labile, more responsive to change in ecological demand, than how rules, and adaptive specialization of cognitive processes occurs more readily at the ontogenetic than the phylogenetic level. Therefore, we will find across the animal kingdom that most evolutionary variations in cognition arise through ontogenetic specialization of what/when rules; that ontogenetic specialization of how rules and phylogenetic specialization of what/when rules occur less often; and that phylogenetic specialization of how rules is very rare indeed.

Summary

This chapter introduces the contents of this volume by addressing three fundamental questions about the evolution of cognition: What is cognition? What are the differences among "different" cognitive processes? What makes research on cognition "evolutionary"? In answer to the first of these, cognitive states and processes are loosely defined as theoretical entities providing a functional characterization of the operations of the central nervous system, which may or may not be objects of conscious awareness, and that are distinct from perceptual and motor processes. In discussing the second question, it is suggested that contemporary researchers differentiate cognitive processes using what/when rules, which specify environmental inputs and/or cognitive products, and using how rules, which specify processing operations. Inferring how rules (which are of primary concern to contemporary investigators) from what/when rules is difficult under any circumstances, and may be impossible when the latter circumscribe environmental inputs rather than cognitive products. Addressing the third question, it is argued that there are four principal evolutionary approaches to the study of cognition—ecological, phylogenetic, comparative, and selection theoretic—and that together they comprise evolutionary psychology "in the round". By contrast with what is currently known as evolutionary psychology, this research enterprise investigates phylogenetic, ontogenetic, and cultural contributions to behavioral adaptation in human and nonhuman animals. Also by contrast with the assumptions of evolutionary psychology, it is suggested in conclusion that most evolutionary variations in cognition arise through ontogenetic specialization of what/when rules; that ontogenetic specialization of how rules and phylogenetic specialization of what/when rules occur less often; and that phylogenetic specialization of how rules is exceptionally rare.

References

Akins CK, Zentall TR (1996) Imitative learning in male Japanese quail using the two-action method. Journal of Comparative Psychology, 110: 316–320.

Boyd R, Richerson PJ (1985) Culture and the evolutionary process. Chicago: Chicago University Press.

Bush RR, Mosteller F (1951) A mathematical model for simple learning. Psychological Review, 58: 313–323.

Buss DM (1999) Evolutionary psychology. Boston: Allyn and Bacon.

Campbell DT (1974) Evolutionary epistemology. In: The philosophy of Karl R Popper (Schlipp PA, ed), pp 413–463. LaSalle, IL: Open Court.

Campbell DT, Heyes CM, Frankel B (1997) From evolutionary epistemology via selection theory to a sociology of scientific validity. Evolution and Cognition, 3: 5–38.

Campbell FM, Heyes CM, Goldsmith A (1999) Stimulus learning and response learning by observation in the European starling using a two-object/two-action test. Animal Behaviour, 58: 151–158.

Catchpole CK, Slater PJB (1995) Bird song: Biological themes and variations. Cambridge: Cambridge University Press.

Clayton NS (1996) Development of food storing and the hippocampus in juvenile marsh tits. Behavioral Brain Research, 74: 153–159.

Clayton NS, Krebs JR (1994) Hippocampal growth and attrition in birds affected by experience. Proceedings of the National Academy of Sciences USA, 91: 7410–7414.

Cook M, Mineka S (1987) Second-order conditioning and overshadowing in the observational conditioning of fear in monkeys. Behavior Research and Therapy, 25: 349–364.

Cook M, Mineka S (1989) Observational conditioning of fear to fear-relevant versus fear-irrelevant stimuli in rhesus monkeys. Journal of Abnormal Psychology, 98: 448–459.

Cook M, Mineka S (1990) Selective associations in the observational conditioning of fear in rhesus monkeys. Journal of Experimental Psychology: Animal Behavior Processes, 16: 372–389.

Cosmides L, Tooby J (1994) Origins of domain specificity: The evolution of functional organization. In: Mapping the mind (Hirschfeld LA, Gelman SA, ed), pp 85–116. Cambridge: Cambridge University Press.

Daly M, Wilson MI (1999) Human evolutionary psychology and animal behaviour. Animal Behaviour, 57: 509–519.

Dickinson A (1980) Contemporary animal learning theory. Cambridge: Cambridge University Press.

Fodor JA (1983) The modularity of mind. Cambridge, MA: MIT Press.

Heyes CM (1994) Social learning in animals: Categories and mechanisms. Biological Review, 69: 207–231.

Heyes CM, Ray ED (2000) What is the significance of imitation in animals? Advances in the Study of Behavior, 29: 215–245.

Humphrey NK (1976) The social function of intellect. In: Growing points in ethology (Bateson PPG, Hinde RA, ed), pp 303–317. Cambridge: Cambridge University Press.

Johnston TD (1981) Contrasting approaches to a theory of learning. Behavioral and Brain Sciences, 4: 125–173.

Kamil AC, Balda RP, Olson DJ (1994) Performance of four seed-caching corvid species in the radial-arm maze analog. Journal of Comparative Psychology, 108: 385–393.

Krebs JR, Sherry DF, Healy SD, Perry VH, Vaccarino AL (1989) Hippocampal specialization in food-storing birds. Proceedings of the National Academy of Sciences USA, 86: 1388–1392.

Lee DW, Miyasato LE, Clayton NS (1998) Neurobiological bases of spatial learning in the natural environment: Neurogenesis and growth in the avian and mammalian hippocampus. Neuroreport, 9: 15–27.

Lefebvre L, Templeton J, Brown K, Koelle M (1997) Carib grackles imitate conspecific and zenaida dove tutors. Behaviour, 134: 1003–1017.

Macphail EM (1985) Vertebrate intelligence: The null hypothesis. Philosophical Transactions of the Royal Society B, 308: 37–51.

Mineka S, Cook M (1986) Immunization against the observational conditioning of snake fear in rhesus monkeys. Journal of Abnormal Psychology, 95: 307–318.

Moore BR (1996) The evolution of imitative learning. In: Social learning in animals: The roots of culture (Heyes CM, Galef Jr BG, ed), pp 245–265. San Diego: Academic Press.

Olson DJ, Kamil AC, Balda RP, Nims PJ (1995) Performance of four seed-caching corvid species in operant tests of nonspatial and spatial memory. Journal of Comparative Psychology, 109: 173–181.

Pepperberg IM (1987) Acquisition of the same/different concept by an African Grey parrot (Psittacus erithacus): Learning with respect to categories of color, shape, and material. Animal Learning and Behavior, 15: 423–432.

Plotkin HC, Odling-Smee FJ (1981) A multiple-level model of evolution and its implications for sociobiology. Behavioral and Brain Sciences, 4: 225–268.

Rescorla RA, Wagner AR (1972) A theory of Pavlovian conditioning: Variations in the effectiveness of reinforcement and nonreinforcement. In: Classical conditioning II: Current Research and Theory (Black AH, Prokasy WF, ed), pp 64–99. New York: Appleton-Century-Crofts.

Sherry DF, Schacter DL (1987) The evolution of multiple memory systems. Psychological Review, 94: 439–454.

Sherry D, Vaccarino AL (1989) Hippocampus and memory for food caches in black-capped chickadees. Behavioral Neurosciences, 103: 308–318.

Sober E (1998) Morgan's canon. In: The evolution of mind (Cummins DD, Allen C, ed), pp 224–242. New York, Oxford: Oxford University Press.

Sober E, Wilson DS (1998) Unto others: The evolution and psychology of unselfish behavior. Cambridge, MA: Harvard University Press.

Tomasello M, Call J (1997) Primate cognition. Oxford: Oxford University Press.

2 Psychophylogenesis: Innovations and Limitations in the Evolution of Cognition

Ludwig Huber

Mind can be understood only by showing how mind is evolved.
—Herbert Spencer, 1855

A hundred forty years after Spencer's assertion, evolutionary psychologists like Plotkin (1997) again claim that "the light of evolution" will illuminate psychology. Now at the brink of a new millennium, where does our understanding of the mind stand? Some believe that the twenty-first century could become the Century of the Mind, changing the understanding of our selves in ways that we are only beginning to imagine. Others warn against being too optimistic, because we are far from closing the gap between psychology and biology, a prerequisite for a complete understanding of cognition.

Here I want to advocate the ethological approach examined by the late Konrad Lorenz. The attraction of this endeavor stems from Lorenz's attempt to expand the basic behavior systems approach by emphasizing greater roles for learning and development, stimulus processing and integration, response organization and coordination, and the co-regulation of hierarchical and interacting motivational states. Drawing on contemporary evolutionary theory and systems theory, especially the notions of emergent macroevolutionary transitions and hierarchical levels of selection, he sought to embody cognition in biology.

If we ignore, for the moment, the artificial aspects of cognition shown by computers, we may agree that cognition is a natural ability of biological systems. It depends on—and is constrained by—a certain organization of the eucaryotic cell. Moreover, as a bio-function, it is a part of the behavioral equipment of any organism and thus subjected to the same rules as do other aspects of its phenotype. I agree with Plotkin's (1997, p. 1) formulation of Dobzhansky's famous claim that "nothing in biology makes *complete* sense except in the light of evolution."

Amazing advances have been made in our understanding of genetic principles, genetic codes have been deciphered, the complete genome of some (invertebrate) species have been encoded, and our understanding of how genetic information is transformed into proteins during the course of ontogenetic development has improved. Unfortunately, the path from DNA to cognition is often poorly understood. A one-to-one correspondence between gene and cognition does not exist. Instead, the evidence suggests a network of genetic interactions that acts on and sets up a network of neuronal circuits. These, in turn, interact to give rise to cognitive behavior. The question of how genes set up behavior affords an answer in terms of highly interactive systems acting at many levels (figure 2.1).

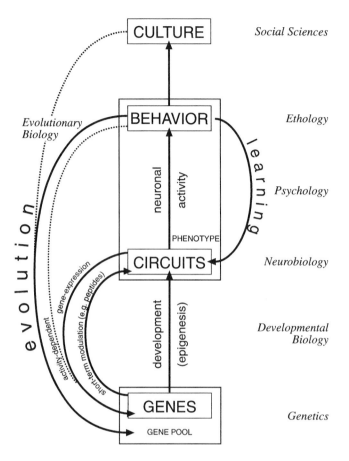

Figure 2.1
Levels and loops of cognition and the respective scientific areas. (After Plotkin and Odling-Smee, 1981;
Greenspan et al., 1994)

Behavior is an emergent property of whole organisms that result from the complex hierarchical
organization of underlying molecular, biochemical, developmental, and physiological levels ...
These levels of organization, however, do not act only in one direction: each one feeds forward
and backward onto the others through various short- and long-term mechanisms. This means
that the ultimate influence of genes on behavior is seldom direct or simple to trace. (Greenspan
et al., 1994, p. 75, 78)

If a direct reconstruction of the cognitive abilities of different species in terms of
their genetic constitution is unrealistic, why then study the evolution of cognition? Or
why is anyone interested in the phylogeny of human cognition? Although nobody

would deny that cognition has evolved, some deny that we will be able to trace its exact evolutionary path (Lewontin, 1998). Of course, the fact that evolution is historical poses problems not to the identification of evolutionary innovations, but to the identification of their sequence and consequence. Are there ways to escape the trap of mere storytelling in seeking evolutionary explanations of human cognition?

Different Approaches to the Evolution of Cognition

Despite some courageous exceptions (e.g., Rensch, 1967; Hodos, 1970; Thomas, 1980; Povinelli, 1993; Byrne, 1994; Moore, 1996), it remains a fact that the *phylogenetic* investigation of the major transitions in cognition—which I will briefly call "psychophylogenesis"—is underrepresented relative to *ecological, microevolutionary*, or *protoevolutionary* concerns (Timberlake, 1993). The Darwinian paradigm for studying how biological traits have come into existence has been used in almost all branches of biology, especially in the *comparative* disciplines. In fact, the comparative stance has also been claimed in the beginnings of modern psychology (see Bitterman, this volume). In retrospect, however, the productivity of this enterprise, measured in terms of its impact on textbooks of evolution, was quite weak. The reason might be that in the cognitive domain the focus was, at best, on evolution in their broad concern and on the assessment of (functional) similarity, rather than of how and when these abilities came into existence (Hodos and Campbell, 1969). In contrast to the research agenda devoted to the reconstruction of the concrete course of evolution, the reliance on abstract relations such as scales of intelligence and universal laws appeared to remain *protoevolutionary*, that is, does not meet the complexities of evolutionary processes.

In ethology, individual problem-solving abilities became a central object of investigation quite late in this century. At first sight, it would appear that the *ecological* approach has achieved considerable progress toward describing the evolution of cognition. For example, in order to trace the paths from specialized adaptations to environmental demands, ecological cognitivists have concentrated upon closely related species that fill divergent niches, and distant relatives that fill convergent niches (see Shettleworth, this volume). However, there is at least one reason to doubt that this approach is sufficient to reconstruct major evolutionary paths. It is commonly supposed that cognitive faculties (e.g., recovering food) are the result of selective forces exerted by specific environmental circumstances (e.g., meager periods). However, evolution is seldom as straightforward as this. The best metaphor is to view evolution as a "tinkerer," building innovations by modifying existing structures, rather than by designing them from scratch. Also, the reconstruction of the sequence of cognitive

breakthroughs lies outside the research program of traditional ecological learning theorists or behavioral ecologists.

Quite close to this research paradigm of explaining how animals solve the sorts of problems they face in their native habitats is a further, recently emerged, discipline. *Cognitive ethology* (Ristau, 1991) grew from a solid ethological background in order to understand mental-state attributions across species boundaries. The range of phenomena includes feelings and consciousness, and the sources of information involve anecdotes, as well as laboratory and field studies. However, it is worth mentioning that the idea of extending the ethological tradition to include cognitive functions and mental states is not a brand new one (Menzel, 1986). Among others, it was Lorenz who suggested that the best way to understand the human mind would be to focus on those "ratiomorphic," rather than rational, aspects that have evolved for the sake of survival. The common stance of *evolutionary epistomologists* is a "naturalized" epistemology that aims to explain "man's status as a product of biological and social evolution" (Campbell, 1974, p. 413).

Similar to the above approaches toward understanding in what respects the cognitive behavior of species differ from each other—and especially from *Homo sapiens* —is a challenge for neuroscience to improve inferences about the human brain from the comparative study of the brains of animals. This paradigm shift stands in sharp contrast to the long tradition in neuroscience to focus study on a "model" or "representative" species. As in comparative psychology, it was supposed that all mammals possess variants of the same brain, and that this justified extrapolating from one group to another. The comparative approach is guided by the fact that brains differ considerably and that our understanding of evolutionary relationships can promote fundamental insights on function (Hodos, 1970).

The Biology of Learning

Ethologists, like Lorenz, approach cognition from a behavioral point of view, emphasizing that learning is only one of several ways to cope with an unpredictable environment. If behavior functions as the means of adjusting the organism to external or internal environmental changes, in order to remain coupled with existing relevant patterns within themselves and their environments, it must be sufficiently plastic in the face of unexpected change. This renders the organism's task twofold. It must operate efficiently under known conditions, and it must maintain adaptation under new conditions with a minimum of disruption. Understanding the main classes of historical processes—constraints and innovations—and their interrelationship requires a broader framework than that used in traditional learning theory.

Stimulated by Schrödinger's famous book *What Is Life?* (1944), biological *systems theory* grew in order to discover and formulate general concepts and logical relations characteristic of living as contrasted with inorganic systems. Generally, the maintenance of coupling with the environment is the most fundamental characteristic of all self-reproducing systems. Riedl (1995) distinguishes two important principles: (1) *correspondence* with the conditions external to the system (the organism), and (2) *coherence* with the internal conditions of the system. The processes contributing to the latter task are mostly obscure to the external observer, and have been underestimated or even ignored by behaviorists focusing on the processes that lead to observable changes in behavior. Consequently, the processes involved in supporting adaptation to external circumstances are considered to be one sided, requiring the animal to "track" environmental changes. This implies that the organism is merely reacting to its environment and thus takes a rather passive role. Information is, according to the information processing paradigm, fed into the organism from outside, and thereafter stored either by genetic processes during phylogeny or by memory processes during ontogeny.

Systemic approaches have challenged this view by suggesting that external influences are only a kind of "trigger" or "selector" of internal modifications, and are severely bound by the restricted potentials of the organism. Growing from this notion, a small but quite vigorous movement, called *constructivism*, emphasizes that cognition is not the representation of a pregiven world by a pregiven mind; it is rather the construction of a world and a mind on the basis of the history of actions that a being in the world performs (Maturana and Varela, 1979).

According to Lorenz, learning is a process that occurs in accordance with those processes that operate as control mechanisms to keep the system in coherence. These conservative processes are the result of an earlier process of natural selection that has led to a high degree of structural coupling between the organism and its environment. This high degree of adaptation is responsible for the fact that only a very limited amount, or specific kind, of information is acquired during the process of ontogenetic learning, and fed into what Ernst Mayr (1974) calls *open programs*. The term "program" refers to the fact that these sets of instructions are plans for actions that appear as integrated and coordinated streams of behavior (Gass, 1985). Furthermore, it implies that the actions of the organism in the face of environmental changes have a strong conservative function, "defending" the organism against being perturbed randomly. In order to achieve this double control, that is, tracking the relevant aspects of the environment and keeping the organism in equilibrium, a considerable amount of genetic information is required. Lorenz called this predisposition for acquiring and storing relevant information the "teaching mechanism." Greenspan et al. (1994, p. 79) offer a modern formulation:

Finally, we must be mindful of the fact that [these] genetic experiments serve to promote the notion that behavior, including that of humans, is bound to be genetically determined. While it may be correct to view individual gene products as deterministic elements, continued study of the processes underlying behavior will eventually lead us to the realization that gene products are but a minute fraction of the total number of behavioral determinants. A second, small fraction will be identifiable as relatively straightforward environmental factors. Most importantly, however, the vast majority of deterministic factors will reside in the multidude of as yet unpredictable interactions between genetic and environmental factors.

It is exactly this modern view of the coalescence of causes around a highly complex and dynamic developmental process that tries to solve the "nature-nurture" debate (Plotkin, 1997). Accepting that these two processes are not mutually exclusive allows us to understand why Lorenz emphasized that "all learning ability is based on open programs which presuppose the presence, not of less, but of more information in the genome than do so-called innate behavior patterns" (1977, p. 65). The difference between closed and open behavior programs is therefore their amount of flexibility, or the degree to which the exact form of the behavior sequences they generate is contingent upon current conditions. Variation is also found in their taxonomic distribution and in their ecological appropriateness.

Instincts, reflexes, and most locomotory patterns are rigidly programmed, not only in lower animals, but also in humans. The same may also be true of communicative actions, because their interpretation by conspecifics has considerable survival value. Closed programs are observed in solitary and short-lived species, whereas in social and long-lived species, in which individuals have abundant opportunity to learn from their own and others' experience, open programs dominate (Gass, 1985). Furthermore, in early development, open programs are important for mediating the storage of specific relevant information, for example, the "object-to-be-followed" in the gosling's brain. In Mayr's scheme, another kind of brain area may then be responsible for processing and storing of all sorts of information, although its relative importance within and across species cannot be determined at the present time.

Effector systems also show variation as a function of the level of operation. A close analysis of the fine structure of behavior or action patterns suggests that inheritance is intact, whereas at the level of gross movement sequences, variability increases dramatically. Recent advances in our understanding of the development of simple movements indicates the importance of understanding learning as "a chief characteristic of living things, endowing the organism with a means to escape its limited built-in behavioral repertoire" (Kelso, 1995, p. 159). Changing behavioral repertoires in the face of a new problem is not accomplished by changing the weights of some synapses in order to strengthen or weaken certain associations, but occurs as change to the entire system. It was demonstrated that sensory stimuli trigger abrupt changes of neuroactivity patterns, which then lead to the emergence of endogenous activity patterns in the cortex (Freeman, 1995).

Looking Behind the Mirror

According to Menzel (1986), *philosophical, psychometrical, anthropocentrical,* or *technological* questions determine traditional approaches to cognition. These traditions are concerned with (1) whether animals comprehend what they are doing, (2) how the various species can be sorted according to their performance on standard intelligence tests, (3) of whether or to what degree animals do what we ourselves do, and (4) of whether or not it would be possible to "shape" intelligent performance in animals or to create artificial cognitive systems.

In contrast, in *Behind the Mirror* (1977) Lorenz started from the fundamental questions of how we as scientists come to understand nature and how we as organisms escape the prison of our brains, which are impenetrably separated from the outer reality. Only by adding the evolutionary dimension can we solve the Kantian problem that the individual has no means of checking the correspondence between the world and its self-constructed representations. Even though the single individual is still a prisoner in his constructed world, the system as such will slowly, during millions of generations, improve its constructs (Sjölander, 1993). In a nutshell, this is the *adaptionist* paradigm, holding that the result of natural selection is the generation of adaptive organic structures sustained by structural coupling with external circumstances. According to this view, not only do the genome and the brain store in-formation, but also organs themselves are a kind of in-corporated knowledge reflecting this fit.

The biological version of knowledge is based on the wider perspective of systems theory. If one accepts the existence of many different levels of integration and the notion that processes that are capable of acquiring and storing relevant information occur on many different levels and are interlinked at many points, one can speak of a hierarchy of "knowledge-gaining processes," with knowledge as a series of nested products of such a hierarchy (Plotkin and Odling-Smee, 1981). Transcending the static view of "strata of existence" by considering the nature of evolutionary change as the main concern for systemic analysis, Lorenz invented the historical dimension. The evolutionary argument is the only way to escape the "Platonic" view of natural variation, a view that is maintained even in modern cognitive science (Menzel, 1986). There is not one brain, one cognition, one problem, and one solution. Biological entities, be they structures or functions, have been generated in a dynamic way, as the result of phylogenetic and ontogenetic processes. The inescapable difficulty then becomes to track the process of innovation and to sort phenomena among which there are no clear-cut borders but all sorts of smooth transitions.

A way out of this dilemma may be found by applying fuzzy logic and chaos models. These can show that the sudden emergence of new system characteristics has nothing to do with miracles, though our scientific tools to explain the processes at the critical transition points are still insufficient. Three decades ago it would have been unreasonable to disagree with Lorenz that the historical uniqueness of phylogenetic inventions leave behind unexplainable residues. Although Lorenz rejected vitalist explanations, he believed "that no system on a higher level of integration can be deduced from a lower system, however fully one may understand this lower system" (1977, p. 35). He emphasized three crucial factors: (1) the independency and maintenance of survival capacity of the former "simpler" systems, (2) the continuity of importance and functioning of the constituent parts in the "higher" system, and (3) the impossibility of detecting any trace of those system characteristics that come into existence only at a higher level of integration.

The classic example in biology is the emergence of consciousness from the integrative activity of a large number of neurons. The single neuron fires on the basis of an "all-or-nothing" rule. It does not show the slightest sign of conscious behavior. The neuron is also a good example of the principle of simplification by specialization. The unicellular *Paramecium* is able to behave as an organism performing all the functions that serve survival, but the ganglion cell has lost most of these properties. The neuron example also demonstrates that "higher" brain functions do not emerge from the accumulation of simple elements, but from a sophisticated organization that, in turn, allows simplification at the lower levels. The mutual relationship between ascent (improved organization) and descent (simplification) may be conceived as a key characteristic of evolutionary processes.

A Hierarchy of Cognitive Capacities

The kind of progression that Lorenz touched upon in his writings was a result of his attempt to compare species according to different means of processing information about some relevant external circumstances in order to behave appropriately. The arrangement of these capacities or proclivities follows a hypothetical phylogenetic sequence of innovations that result from modifications of what has already been available at a certain point in evolution. Therefore, the proposal is based on what

Lorenz hypothesized from his enormous collection of animal behaviors and from evolutionary facts, rather than from an engineering point of view. I will explicate this point later. Lorenz remained largely reserved in superimposing the sequence of cognitive mechanisms upon the animal system.

In *Behind the Mirror* (1977), the sequence of knowledge-gaining processes is sorted into six chapters. According to Lorenz's scheme, this classification of cognitive phenomena reflects qualitative, rather than quantitative, differences. This is because each step involves the emergence of new system characteristics, though the processes involved in earlier stages remain fully functional in those species that have reached a higher stage.

Short-Term Information Gain

In addition to the genome and all processes involving individual learning, there are a number of "closed programs" that acquire and operate upon, but do not store, information about instantaneously arising conditions in the environment. The basic function of these programs is not modification or adaptation, but operation on pre-adapted structures. They occur in all species at all taxonomic levels, and represent the foundation of all experience. *Homeostasis*, or the *feedback cycle*, is the most basic means by which an organism maintains equilibrium. Together with the equally basic function of *irritability*, it allows mobile organisms to track beneficial conditions. The *amoeboid*, *kinetic*, *phobic*, and *taxis* responses are all examples of this principle. Furthermore, *innate releasing mechanisms*, *fixed motor patterns*, and *appetitive behaviors* are examples of even more complex systems that exploit short-term information.

Adaptive Modifications of Behavior (Excluding Conditioning by Reinforcement)

The fundamental difference between the mechanisms lies in their potential to modify the sensory or neuronal "machinery" of the animal, but only in a manner that improves their survival value. These open programs are the most basic means by which relevant information is acquired and stored. They can be called learning mechanisms in the sense that "all learning is an adaptive, teleonomic modification of physiological mechanisms whose operation constitutes behaviour" (Lorenz, 1977, p. 81). Only the most elementary of these mechanisms, *facilitation* of motor responses and *sensitization* of receptors, are considered to be nonassociative. The first truly associative mechanisms, distinguished on the basis of their behavioral consequences, involve *habituation*, *habit formation*, escape responses following traumatic experiences, and *imprinting*. Lorenz remained reluctant to specify the phylogenetic origin, a cautious attitude that seems justified in view of evidence for conditioning in paramecia (Hennessy et al., 1979).

Conditioning by Reinforcement

The "feedback loop through which the final success or failure of the chain of processes is able to have a modifying effect on its initiating links" (Lorenz, 1977, p. 84) represents a further "fulgurative" improvement. Lorenz assumed the higher faculty of conditioning by reinforcement developed independently in five different groups of animals: cephalopods, crustaceans, arachnids, insects, and vertebrates. He proposed three preconditions for its evolution. First, the behavior program that is adaptively modified must be open, or require a large volume of genetic information. Second, the genetic memory of the behavior program must be accompanied by an associative memory that stores the relevant context. Finally, the record of reinforcement that is fed back into the system must be sufficiently reliable, and characterized by a reduction in motivational tension. Associations are formed between a prespecified class of external information and behavioral predispositions, as exemplified by the demonstration of flavor aversion learning in rats. Pathfinding and motor learning also fit into this scheme. This behavioral conception of conditioning deviates considerably from Pavlov's physiological or "reflexological" terminology.

Lorenz distinguished several different forms of adaptive behavior modification occurring through conditioning, among which he regarded "operant conditioning" to be a special case. Only highly explorative organisms, such as the rat and some other mammals, plus a few birds, are able to associate "significant" actions (e.g., defending movements) with reinforcing signals from completely different behavior systems (e.g., food reinforcement). It is much easier to condition multipurpose responses, such as those involved in the locomotor repertoire. But it is virtually impossible, for example, to train a rat to make copulatory responses in order to gain access to food pellets (S+) or to avoid electric shock (S−).

In order to understand what role different forms of learning play in nature and why they lead to adaptive modifications of behavior, Lorenz suggested three heuristic rules. First, it is necessary to determine which subsystem of a complex, modifiable behavior pattern contains the innate information that ensures the animal learns the behavior patterns required for survival. Second, it is not possible to understand any learning process without understanding the whole system that this process modifies. Finally, the physiological nature of the reinforcement process has to be studied independently in each individual case of learning, because there is no universal reinforcement but only reinforcement dependant upon the behavior to be modified.

How does this conception fit into what is currently known about associative learning, perhaps the most general and most powerful learning mechanism in nature? And how has this mechanism evolved? Fortunately, insight into the cellular mechanism underlying classical conditioning in invertebrates, especially the marine snail *Aplysia*, has enormously improved our knowledge in this respect. A cell-biological alphabet for simple forms of learning exists and it is possible to explain certain higher forms of learning generally associated with cognition in cellular-connectionist terms by combinations of a few relatively simple types of neuronal processes (Hawkins and Kandel, 1984). Particularly, it seems as if the cellular mechanism of conditioning is an elaboration of the mechanism underlying sensitization and habituation. Even higher-order features of conditioning, including generalization, second-order conditioning, blocking, and the effect of contingency, can be accounted for by combinations of the almost simpler mechanism of sensitization.

The Roots of Conceptual Thought

Of course, the cellular model may not account for many other cognitive phenomena. Lorenz suggested eight faculties as being important for our understanding of human conceptual thought. All of these faculties are found in animals and all have their own survival value. Although it would be extremely valuable to examine the validity of Lorenz's hypotheses using the data from recent experiments, this would transcend the scope of this chapter. Instead, I point the reader's attention to the respective chapters in the present volume: (1) *abstraction* and *Gestalt perception* (Delius et al.; Mackintosh), (2) *orientation* and the *central representation of space* (Shettleworth), (3) *insightful learning* (Heinrich), (4) *voluntary movement* (Dickinson and Balleine), (5) *object and self-exploration* (Heinrich; Macphail), (6) *imitation* (Heyes; Tomasello), and (7) *tradition* (Lefebvre).

I would only add the well-studied capacities of categorization and the important cognitive breakthrough of intermodality. Ample evidence for the former capacity is available from pigeons (Huber, 1995). In the vertebrate line, *multimodal representations* have occurred above the reptilian level. A snake hunting a prey is sequentially following a "visual rabbit," an "olfactorial rabbit," and finally a "tactile rabbit" in order to swallow it (Sjölander, 1993). The dog's hunting, by contrast, is guided by a multimodal representation of a rabbit that remains active in a changing context. Also, the dog is able to dream, but the snake is not.

The Human Mind and Beyond

Lorenz regarded it paradoxical that some who refused to look at all the things that man and animals have in common underestimated the differences between them. In order to dispute Darwin's (1871) notion that the human mind differs from the mind of animals "only by degree but not of kind," one has to take two facts into account. First, with respect to most of the faculties mentioned so far, humans outperform animals. Second, the truly fundamental step forward toward the development of the human mind was only possible after a rapid accumulation of fulgurations caused by the integration of several pre-existing cognitive functions. The faculties of the human mind are characterized by new properties, such as verbal language and context-free thought, that couldn't easily be reduced to their prerequisites. However, it is of indispensable heuristic value to keep in mind all those "ratiomorphic" elements of the human mind that indicate the "survival" of older competencies. Although simple reductionism fails, it is nevertheless our only chance to understand the human mind with all its "*deficiencies of adaptation*" (Riedl, 1995) by empirically studying the cognitive components listed above.

Evolution as Innovation

Diversity is an essential feature of the living world. The general method of coping with diversity is to make comparisons. Comparisons among species have been made since Aristotle, and were also Darwin's favored scientific tool. Lorenz especially was admired for his wide-ranging and extensive experience of animal behavior, which allowed him to use an actual example for virtually any phenomenon under discussion. Many of the early ethologists, like Whitman, Heinroth, and Julian Huxley also considered species comparisons as the essence of biological science. Lorenz proposed three indispensable stages for the development of any inductive natural science, proceeding from purely observational recording and describing of fact to the orderly arrangement of these facts in a system and, finally, to the quest for the rules prevailing in the system.

The recent increase in the use of the comparative method in cognitive ethology and behavioral ecology is due to a revived interest in the function of behavioral traits. The key concept for describing and explaining behavioral or cognitive diversity is *adaptation*, which results from a dialectical relationship between an animal and its environment. In trying to uncover the reasons for evolutionary change, comparisons are made among groups of animals that share a similar way of life, inhabit a similar ecological niche, or face similar behavioral difficulties. Convergent and parallel evolutionary change can lead to phenotypic resemblance even among those members of a "guild" that are not closely related.

Adaptation and convergence were also important concepts in Lorenz's thinking. He studied animal behavior in order to elucidate the amazing facts of adaptedness, and considered "analogy as a source of knowledge" (1974, p. 229). However, comparative thinking must not stop here; the historical aspect of life needs to be included. In 1898 (p. 328; but see Atz, 1970, p. 67) Whitman wrote, "Instinct and structure are to be studied from the common standpoint of phyletic descent, and that not the less because we may seldom, if ever, be able to trace the whole development of an instinct." This sentence marks the birth of comparative ethology. Like Whitman, Lorenz was deeply convinced that a complete understanding of behavior fails if it doesn't include its origin and continuity in phylogeny. A much-cited example for the validity of evolutionary reconstruction on the basis of purely behavioral data is Lorenz's (1941) classification of 20 species of ducks by their similarities with respect to 48 behavioral traits. Nevertheless, despite support from leading evolutionists such as Simpson, Dobzhansky, and de Beer (see Atz, 1970), the phylogenetic approach to the study of behavior fell into decline.

The obvious weakness of this approach is due to: (1) the lack of a fossil record, (2) the tenuous connection between behavior and the nervous system, and (3) the difficulties associated with finding proper criteria for determining behavioral homologies (Atz, 1970). Furthermore, homology is essentially a morphological concept that enables comparative anatomists to detect phylogenetic traces far beyond the family level. The only reliable homologizing of behavior has been confined to closely related forms. In general, the continuous transmission of genetic information in phylogeny is not necessarily accompanied by the resemblance of phenotypic traits. This divergence increases with time, as does the difficulty of detecting homologous characteristics. Nevertheless, by applying indirect methods this type of evolutionary analysis remains feasible.

If the evolution of behavior proceeds in the same way as the evolution of molecular or structural characteristics, then it must at least in part have a genetic basis. Furthermore, this basis must be somewhat variable if it supplies the material on which natural selection acts. Only recently, we have witnessed a revived interest in understanding the phylogeny of behavior. This is due in part to advances in the quality of phylogenetic reconstruction (Harvey and Pagel, 1991; Martins, 1996). Modern statistical methodologies may have led to this development, and justify the notion that "we must learn to treat comparative data with the same respect as we would treat experimental results" (Maynard Smith and Holliday, 1979, p. vii). For example, comparing intraspecific and interspecific noncommunicative behaviors allows us to make plausible inferences about the nature of the behavior program (closed or open), its role in macroevolution, and the origin of major evolutionary inventions (Mayr, 1974). Such analysis reveals that noncommunicative behaviors are by far the most important factor in macroevolution. The invasion of novel habitats and the exploitation of novel food sources is facilitated by open programs and the use of cognitive and memory capacities. These cognitive strategies set up diverse selection pressures that, in turn, are themselves molded by evolution.

We must distinguish between attempts to use behavioral characteristics as a taxo-nomic tool for the study of phylogeny and systematics, and attempts to trace the evolution of particular behavioral patterns by making indirect inferences from com-parative studies. In the absence of fossil records, comparative studies of several dif-ferent species often reveal a spectrum of patterns and variation, suggesting that some species have "primitive" characteristics. Given that behavioral patterns may simplify during evolution, the assumption about what is ancestral and what is derived is not based upon the analysis of a single species, but upon the systematic comparison of many related forms. A "strong comparative inference" is possible only if a sequence of intermediate forms of the spectrum of extant species is available. Furthermore, one can make "weak inferences" on the assumption that the elements of a behavior pat-tern shared by a number of species represent ancestral traits. Using this method, Tinbergen (1959) compiled a "progress report" of the communicative behavior of gulls.

Only recently, Sober (1998) developed a strong case for the comparative method. In order to determine whether a given higher capacity is outside a species' repertoire, it is necessary to rely upon observation of the *nonoccurrence* of that behavior in the species. This, in turn, requires that many individuals be observed in appropriate, or natural, circumstances. After finding phenotypic variation among taxa, and pro-ducing several adaptive explanations for this variation, these explanations can be tested by predicting the environmental or constitutional correlates of the variation, and comparing ancestral and derived character states wherever possible (Harvey and Pagel, 1991). As a consequence, it has been repeatedly demonstrated that be-havioral characteristics have functions that differ considerably from those for which they evolved. Evolutionary, functional, and developmental constraints upon pheno-typic evolution pose fundamental problems for the validity of pure adaptionist explanations.

Therefore, adaptation does not serve as a proper guide to understanding the big trends in evolution. The synthetic view of evolution, which is based upon the prin-ciples of variation and selection, cannot explain *macroevolutionary* phenomena. Systems theory (Riedl, 1978), on the other hand, takes phylogenetic constraints into account and considers the limitations of evolution. It states that evolution cannot be reduced to genetic evolution. Any given set of phenotypes contains only a small subset of the character combinations that could be selected if they were produced. Successful adaptability at the expense of flexibility is the reason why there are so few systemic types. The only possible way in which the environment can influence popu-lation dynamics is by selection acting on the phenotype. The inherent systemic conditions of the organism restrict the number of possible transformations among population states, even in those cases where these transformations correspond to selective pressures and genetic possibilities. The crucial point here is that many genotypes fail to generate a viable and fertile phenotype independently of the environment. Therefore, even in those cases in which it is possible to describe historical environmental conditions, it is insufficient to describe the paths of phenotypic evolution.

What we need, then, is, complementary to the external factors, a closer understanding of the inner, systemic factors influencing evolution. It can be described as a feedback loop that operates at the interface between the genotype and the phenotype, and which maintains *organization*, rather than adaptation. The feedback loop leads to *coherence* within the organism, and this complements the organism's *correspondence* with its environment. As a result, structures, functions, and pathways beyond, and often in opposition to, new functional requirements became fixated or canalized. This is the reason why a cephalopod "feeds through its brain," and why a dolphin will never become a fish and a bat will never become a bird, even though selective pressures arising from the environment may act in these directions. From an adaptionist or strictly engineering point of view, it is paradoxical that our eyes are inverted (large ganglion cells sit in front of the cells that receive the incoming light), and that dolphins and giraffes have exactly seven cervical vertebra (like all other mammals) when a respective decrease and increase in number would be a functional advantage.

More generally, those aspects of morphology that vary among taxa can remain conservative within a taxon even when members of the taxon live in distinctly different environments. The above examples were selected because they illustrate that functionally "better" solutions are still possible in nature. Cephalopods have "correct" eyes; fishes are able to dispense with cervical vertebra, whereas dinosaurs possessed hundreds. The phylogenetic consequences of selection for systemic coherence are the canalization of adaptive traits, the existence of pathways in phylogeny (marked by homologies), and the establishment of higher taxonomic classes sharing the same basic characteristics ("Bauplan"). Therefore, a complete understanding of the structural or functional phenotypes present during any given phylogenetic stage cannot be achieved by mapping assumed environmental conditions onto genotypes.

We can apply these evolutionary principles, derived from morphology, to cognitive mechanisms in two ways. First, the space in which cognitive mechanisms evolve is limited and structured by constraints acting on the organism. Therefore, one can understand the evolution of cognitive mechanisms, at least in part, by understanding the constraints acting on them. This idea is clearly evident at the molecular level. Cognition is a function of the brain, which is a collection of an enormous number of cells. The brain is a combinatorial system. It not only opens a potential universe of behavioral possibilities for an organism, but also imposes significant constraints. For example, specific features of regulatory patterns cannot be altered without altering others by default.

Second, at higher levels of organization, the number of ways in which cognitive evolution can interact with the environment is limited. Consequently, there are only a few pathways along which the evolution of a cognitive faculty can proceed. These pathways are the result of the successive modification of the structures responsible for behavior. Any given cognitive invention is the result of the modification of pre-existing structures (prerequisites), which are then able to open ecological niches in which a new species can exploit the adaptive deficiencies of other species. Meta-phorically speaking, we are dealing here with the adventure of life, which takes risk and actively seeks new, unknown conditions. This process plays an important role in higher development. It does not explain higher development fully, but does play a decisive role.

Many cognitive phenomena cannot be interpreted in adaptive terms because they may not actually be adaptive. Furthermore, many cognitive mechanisms appear to be adaptive even though they evolved under fundamentally different circumstances to those in which they now operate. "Homoiology" (analogy on a homologous basis; see Riedl, 1978) is an important principle in cognitive evolution. However, constraints resulting from the preservation of functional modules can promote the evolution of adaptive complexity by enabling the establishment of complex hierarchically orga-nized systems. The fixation or conservation of brain structures or cognitive modules does not necessarily mean a halt in evolution. Extraordinary qualities may emerge from the combination of old components (as the aforementioned cell alphabet for simple forms of learning), or their gradual modification may "create" new problem spaces.

Owing to the limited amount of space available, I can only describe one example of the evolution of a cognitive faculty to illustrate this point. Moore (1996) proposed two different phylogenetic pathways leading to the evolution of imitative learning. One is found in birds, where it originates in song learning. From song learning this pathway moves to vocal mimicry, percussive mimicry, visual movement imitation, and finally cross-modal matching. The other pathway, found in primates, has its origins in skill learning, from which it moves to visual movement imitation and finally cross-modal matching. The heuristic value of this evolutionary scenario is that it can be empirically tested. For example, in our laboratory in Vienna we are currently examining whether keas (*Nestor notabilis*) are able to imitate the body movements of skilled group members. Keas are known for their extraordinary manipulative abilities and for their rich sociality. However, they have never been shown to imitate sounds, and they did not evolve from any known vocal mimics.

Conclusion

Cognition is one of the most challenging topics for the natural sciences. In humans, cognitive processes are the result of an enormously intricate brain system organized at many different levels, and consisting of approximately one million billion connections in the cortical sheet alone. The sheer intricacy and size of the brain merits more than one kind of scientific inquiry. Furthermore, given that cognition refers to the ability of living creatures to adaptively modify their behavior in order to decide what to do next, an evolutionary theory of how we came to have minds must be an essential part of the cognitive sciences. We asked, how did cognitive processes evolve? Many different kinds of behaviors can be adaptively modified by individual experience (e.g., food finding, mate choice, homeostasis). Therefore, we expect to find diversity in the information that controls behavior, regardless of whether it comes from the internal or the external environment, or from the behavior itself. In other words, there are likely to be differences in the "what/when rules" of cognition (Heyes, this volume).

According to Lorenz, not only learned behavior, but also the ability to learn (e.g., avoidance learning in paramecia, "reasoning" in bonobos) emerged in evolution. It seems completely implausible to suggest that the "how rules" (Heyes, this volume) underlying these abilities are all the same. Nevertheless, from a systemic, macro-evolutionary point of view, which takes into account what we know about the molecular and cellular basis of learning, major constraints arise at the level of single neurons. These constraints may have increased progressively for higher levels of analysis (e.g., synaptic connections, entire neuronal networks). Because processing operations are established at the level of neuronal circuitry from which complex adaptive behavior emerges, how rules should have been invented only rarely in evolution, or at least much less frequently than what/when rules.

A definitive answer to the question of how cognitive processes evolved is not currently available. To answer this question from a purely functionalist point of view would be impossible. An understanding of the evolution of cognition can only be gained by reconstructing the sequence of constraints, prerequisites, and innovations, and by taking into account the behavioral context of a broad spectrum of species, as Lorenz did. Unfortunately, such endeavors have received only scant attention in cognitive science so far.

Acknowledgments

I am grateful to Rupert Riedl, Cecilia Heyes, Sverre Sjölander, Wolfgang Schleidt, and Gerhard Medicus for their comments on earlier versions of the manuscript. I also thank Monika Kickert for allowing me to rummage in Lorenz's library.

References

Atz JW (1970) The application of the idea of homology to animal behavior. In: Development and evolution of behavior: Essays in honor of TC Schneirla (Aronson LR, Tobach E, Lehrman DS, Rosenblatt JS, ed), pp 53–74. San Francisco: Freeman.

Byrne RW (1994) The evolution of intelligence. In: Behaviour and evolution (Slater PJB, Halliday TR, ed), pp 223–264. Cambridge: Cambridge University Press.

Campbell DT (1974) Evolutionary epistemology. In: The philosophy of Karl R. Popper (Schlipp PA, ed), pp 413–463. LaSalle, IL: Open Court.

Darwin C (1871) The descent of man and selection in relation to sex. London: Murray.

Freeman WJ (1995) Societies of brains. Hillsdale, NJ: Erlbaum.

Gass CL (1985) Behavioral foundations of adaptation. In: Perspectives in ethology, vol. 6 (Bateson PPG, Klopfer PH, ed), pp 63–107. New York: Plenum Press.

Greenspan RJ, Tully R, Alvarez-Buylla A, Benjamin PR, Borst A, Fischbach K-F, Hall JC, Kupfermann I, Roth G, Sokolowski MB, Strauss R, Truman JW (1994) Group report: How do genes set up behaviors? In: Flexibility and constraint in behavioral systems (Greenspan RJ, Kyriacou CP, ed), pp 65–80. Chichester: Wiley.

Harvey PH, Pagel MD (1991) The comparative method in evolutionary biology. Oxford: Oxford University Press.

Hawkins RD, Kandel ER (1984) Is there a cell-biological alphabet for simple forms of learning? Psychological Review, 91: 375–391.

Hennessey TM, Rucker WB, McDiarmid CG (1979) Classical conditioning in paramecia. Animal Learning and Behavior, 7: 417–423.

Hodos W (1970) Evolutionary interpretation of neural and behavioral studies of living vertebrates. In: The neurosciences (Schmidt FO, ed), pp 26–39. New York: Rockefeller University Press.

Hodos W, Campbell CBG (1969) Why there is no theory in comparative psychology. Psychological Review, 76: 337–350.

Huber L (1995) On the biology of perceptual categorization. Evolution and Cognition, 1: 121–138.

Kelso JAS (1995) Dynamic patterns. Cambridge, MA: MIT Press.

Lewontin RC (1998) The evolution of cognition: Questions we will never answer. In: An invitation to cognitive science, vol. 4: Methods, models, and conceptual issues (Scarborough D, Sternberg S, ed), pp 107–132. Cambridge, MA: MIT Press.

Lorenz K (1941) Vergleichende Bewegungsstudien an Anatiden. Journal für Ornithologie, 89: 194–293.

Lorenz K (1974) Analogy as a source of knowledge. Science, 185: 229–234.

Lorenz K (1977) Behind the mirror. London: Methuen.

Martins EP, ed (1996) Phylogenies and the comparative method in animal behavior. New York: Oxford University Press.

Maturana H, Varela F (1979) Autopoiesis and cognition. Dordrecht: Reidel.

Maynard Smith J, Holliday R (1979) Preface. In: The evolution of adaptation by natural selection (Maynard Smith J, Holliday R, ed), pp v–vii. London: The Royal Society.

Mayr E (1974) Behavior programs and evolutionary strategies. American Scientist, 62: 650–659.

Menzel Jr EW (1986) How can you tell if an animal is intelligent? In: Dolphin cognition and behavior: A comparative approach (Schusterman RJ, Thomas JA, Wood FG, ed), pp 167–181. London: Erlbaum.

Moore BR (1996) The evolution of imitative learning. In: Social learning in animals (Heyes CM, Galef Jr BG, ed), pp 245–265. San Diego: Academic Press.

Plotkin H (1997) Evolution in mind. London: Penguin.

Plotkin HC, Odling-Smee FJ (1981) A multiple-level model of evolution and its implications for socio-biology. Behavioral and Brain Sciences, 4: 225–268.

Povinelli DJ (1993) Reconstructing the evolution of mind. American Psychologist, 48: 493–509.

Rensch B (1967) The evolution of brain achievments. Evolutionary Biology, 1: 26–68.

Riedl R (1978) Order in living organisms. Chichester: Wiley.

Riedl R (1995) Deficiencies of adaptation in human reason: A constructivistic extension of evolutionary epistemology. Evolution and Cognition, 1: 27–37.

Ristau CA, ed (1991) Cognitive ethology. Hillsdale, NJ: Erlbaum.

Schrödinger E (1944) What is life? Cambridge: Cambridge University Press.

Sjölander S (1993) Some cognitive breakthroughs in the evolution of cognition and consciousness, and their impact on the biology of language. Evolution and Cognition, 3: 1–10.

Sober E (1998) Morgan's canon. In: The evolution of mind (Cummins DD, Allen C, ed), pp 224–242. New York: Oxford University Press.

Spencer H (1855) Principles of psychology. London: Longman.

Thomas RK (1980) The evolution of intelligence: An approach to its assessment. Brain, Behavior and Evolution, 17: 454–472.

Timberlake W (1993) Animal behavior: A continuing synthesis. Annual Review of Psychology, 44: 675–708.

Tinbergen N (1959) Comparative studies of the behavior of gulls: A progress report. Behaviour, 15: 1–70.

Whitman CO (1898) Animal behaviour. Woods Hole, MA.

3 Modularity and the Evolution of Cognition

Sara Shettleworth

When conditions are predictable across generations but unpredictable within generations, mechanisms will evolve that allow each individual to adjust its behavior to the details of its own environment (Richerson and Boyd, this volume; Huber, this volume). For instance, a bee predictably finds food sources that are worth revisiting, but their precise appearance and location are unpredictable in advance of experience by an individual bee or colony of bees. Such predictable unpredictability makes it adaptive for individuals to be able to sense and retain information that identifies local profitable food sources and to use this information to relocate them. Similar more or less informal arguments can be made in favor of animals being able to process, store, and act on information about physical and social causation, time, rate of occurrence, and other features of the world (Dyer, 1998; Shettleworth, 1998). At the same time, however, species clearly differ enormously in the variety of sensory information available to them and the ways in which they can process and act on it. For instance, consider the one-celled organism stentor, which can react to various objects in its environment with ingestion, rejection, or escape, in a very simple yet effective way (see Staddon, 1983). To some extent, the differences among, say, stentor and a bee and a chimpanzee are the products of particular evolutionary histories and ecological niches. However, a full account of the evolution of cognition should embrace all mechanisms that invertebrates and vertebrates have for taking in information through the senses, retaining it, and using it to adjust behavior to local conditions.

In discussions of cognition in nonhumans, it is usual to try to distinguish between "cognitive" and other mind/brain processes. For instance, cognition is said to involve explicit representations of absent stimuli (Terrace, 1984), or declarative as opposed to procedural knowledge (McFarland, 1991). Reviews of the comparative psychology of learning typically place learning processes in a hierarchy: habituation, the various forms of associative learning, and "higher cognitive processes" such as concept formation, counting, and language (e.g., Thomas, 1996). A more productive approach to thinking about the evolution of cognition is to construe cognition as information processing in the broadest sense, from gathering information through the senses to making decisions and performing functionally appropriate actions, regardless of the complexity of any internal representational processes that behavior might imply (see Shettleworth, 1998). To look more narrowly risks excluding behaviors that are properly part of a complete comparative and evolutionary analysis. To see why this is so, consider behaviors that appear at first glance to involve "higher cognitive processes" such as planning and foresight but that actually may not. For instance, wild chimpanzees in some parts of Africa "fish" for termites by poking sticks or grass blades into termite mounds in such a way that the termites cling to them and can be extracted. Termite fishing is a learned behavior, perhaps evidence of chimpanzee culture (McGrew, 1992). It has been suggested that young animals learn by imitation to fish for termites, but this is debatable. Poking sticks and grasses into termite mounds and getting termites out may be an instrumentally reinforced skill that is learned by trial and error and that does not involve either specifically social learning or understanding how tools work. But if the chimps are "merely" performing a complex reinforced operant, does that mean that termite fishing is no longer part of the study of the evolution of cognition? This question is especially apposite in the light of increasing evidence that instrumental learning is mediated by subtle representational processes (see chapters in this volume by Dickinson and Mackintosh).

As another example, when a bee departs from a new food source, it turns back and faces toward the point of departure while looping around in front of it. This behavior might be described in ways that impute to the bee conscious foresight and possession of a cognitive map. However, it appears sufficient to conclude that during the "turn back and look" behavior the bee is recording a visual image that it uses to relocate a goal by moving until the visual input matches its memorized "snapshot" (Collett and Zeil, 1998). But if it turns out that the bee is matching snapshots rather than referring to a cognitive map, its behavior is no less an example of adaptive information processing. Thus, to think sensibly about the evolution of cognition we need to start with all the ways in which animals process and use information in nature to adjust individual behavior to local conditions, local on a spatial and temporal scale, from the animal's lifetime down to variations from moment to moment. In this view, learning as usually studied by comparative psychologists is not the essence of cognition; nor are explicit internal representations of the world, though preprogrammed abilities to adjust adaptively to conditions in the world are in a sense implicit representations of those conditions (Shepard, 1994). The approach sketched here differs drastically from the approach outlined by Bitterman (this volume), among other ways in being less focused on associative learning and less anthropocentric (Shettleworth, 1998). Programs like that reviewed by Bitterman illustrate important issues that have to be addressed in this area, but the comparative study of associative learning is only one piece of the much bigger picture of cognitive evolution.

If we take as "cognitive" all mechanisms that take in information through the senses and lead to behavioral adjustments to conditions that are local in time and/or space, it follows that cognition must be modular. That is, rather than being a single general purpose computer, the nonhuman or human mind consists of a collection of special purpose devices, each of which processes a distinct domain of input in a distinct and adaptively appropriate way. The variety of ways in which information must be gathered and used, even by a relatively simple animal like a bee, is too great for one general mechanism to do the job. Evolution both fine-tunes species-general modules and somehow combines the outputs of old modules in new ways or produces new modules to allow animals to solve new kinds of problems. The best illustrations of this principle come from the senses. We start here not only because the comparative study of perception is part of any broad study of the evolution of cognition, but also because it provides a powerful model of how cognition is put together and varies from species to species. After outlining some properties of sensory systems that make them a model of cognitive modules more generally, I will discuss what is meant by cognitive modularity in more detail and give examples from the processing of information about time and space. The chapter concludes with some speculations about how cognition evolves and what research could shed light on the issues raised here. Many of the ideas in this chapter have been discussed by others (e.g., Sherry and Schacter, 1987; Hirschfeld and Gelman, 1994; Shepard, 1994; Sperber, 1994; Cosmides and Tooby, 1994; Gallistel, 1995; Gigerenzer, 1997). They are developed in greater depth in a recent book (Shettleworth, 1998).

Perception as a Model of Cognitive Evolution

At the basic level of gathering information about the world, it is clear that different organs are needed for different jobs. Eyes, ears, noses, tongues, electroreceptors, and so on are all separate modules that gather information about different kinds of physical energies and process it in different, functionally appropriate, ways. The different sense organs and their associated central processing areas, as well as subprocesses within them such as color, depth, and motion perception within primate vision, are anatomically as well as functionally distinct. However, the primary criterion for modularity in most discussions of cognition is functional, with different rules of operation inferred from behavior. Nevertheless, the first reason why perception is a model of cognitive organization and evolution as a whole is that within the realm of cognition it provides an illustration of the general biological principle of separate organs for separate jobs.

A second principle is that different structures may do the same job in different lineages. Consider, for instance, the difference between the compound eyes of bees and the camera-like eyes of birds or mammals. Hypothetical computational structures obey this principle just as do different kinds of light-sensing organs. We will see examples below. As in using gas, electricity, or wood for cooking, all are equally effective ways of getting dinner, but local and historical constraints determine which a particular cook uses.

A third principle of modularity is that shared structures may be specialized in each species. This is obvious when it comes to physical organs. For example, birds all share beaks, eyes, wings, and feet, among other structures. Yet a beak may be a probe, a hammer, a nutcracker, or a flesh-tearing tool, among other possibilities. Feet may have webs, lobes, talons, or claws. Eyes and the photoreceptors within them may be placed to detect moving prey from a distance, to localize small seeds while simultaneously watching for predators, and so on (Lythgoe, 1979). The information each species takes in and the ways in which it is used are part of a package that makes sense in terms of the problems to be solved in the wild. Linked adaptive modifications of shared structures are also reflected in the relative sizes of brain areas processing different kinds of sensory information. For instance, complex relationships between lifestyle and relative sizes of visual and olfactory processing areas may be seen in primates, insectivores, and bats (Barton et al., 1995). The principles suggested by the adaptive specializations of the senses and their associated brain areas are no less applicable to more "central" information processing, as is illustrated by adaptations of hippocampus in food-storing birds and other animals that naturally face extraordinary demands on spatial memory (Sherry et al., 1992). The hippocampus is larger relative to the rest of the brain in such animals than in close relatives that do not store food or have large territories.

A fourth way in which perception is a model of cognitive organization more generally is that in addition to specializations, there are general processes, even ones that cut across modules. Within each lineage, a particular sense organ such as an eye or an ear is structured in the same general way in all species even while it is adaptively tweaked in each one. The senses share a number of functional properties, such as sensitivity to contrast, Weber's law, a tendency to adapt or habituate, and a tendency to give a bigger response to a physically bigger stimulus (Barlow, 1982). This last property seems so obvious that it is easy to forget it is not a logical necessity but a very general adaptation to the fact that something bigger or closer is likely to warrant faster and more decisive action.

Finally, the senses are a model of cognitive modularity because they exhibit prefunctional adaptive organization. An animal does not wait to somehow discover that certain wavelengths or volatile compounds are important in its life but comes ready-made with senses at least roughly tuned to the kinds of energies it is going to need to react to in its species-specific niche. This does not mean experience is unimportant, but even the capacity to be modified by that experience in a particular way is part of the package. Not only the fine-tuning of sensory systems with experience but also appropriate processing of information relevant to circadian rhythms, dead reckoning, associative learning, imprinting (Bateson, this volume), and so on, is built in.

In summary, the comparative study of perception is both part of cognition and a model for how to view cognition if we want to understand its evolution. The study of sensation and perception is more closely tied to consideration of function than is any other part of cognitive science (Marr, 1982; Shepard, 1994). Furthermore, comparative and evolutionary work in this area is probably better developed than is the study of any other aspect of cognitive evolution (e.g., Lythgoe, 1979; Dusenbery, 1992).

Cognitive Modularity in Nonhumans

What Is a Module?

The idea that cognition is modular is not new, as contemporary psychologists discussing the modularity of mind are well aware (e.g., Sperber, 1994; Gigerenzer, 1997). The paperback edition of Fodor's (1983) *The Modularity of Mind* has a phrenological head on the cover, and a recent review (Lipp and Wolfer, 1995) of specializations in rodent brains has "microphrenology" in its title, but the idea of separate psychological faculties predates the nineteenth century. The contemporary metaphor for modularity is the mind as a Swiss Army knife (Wilson, 1994; Mithen, 1996), an analogy meant to show that the most effective kind of general information processor is made from a collection of specialized parts, each of which does a particular job very well. Paradoxically, adaptive modularity and the related issue of separable memory systems (Sherry and Schacter, 1987) are debated more among students of human psychology (cf. Hirschfeld and Gelman, 1994) than among comparative psychologists. The debate about general processes as opposed to adaptive specializations in animal work has dealt mostly with species- or content-specific tweakings of associative learning mechanisms, as in taste-aversion learning (see Bitterman, this volume), rather than the overall modular organization of animal information processing, what special issues it raises, and how they might be tackled. Yet some of the clearest evidence for cognitive modularity comes from animal behavior. Moreover, only with nonhuman species is it possible to bring together comparative data from ecology, phylogeny, brain structure, and behavior to address issues about the function and evolution of modular organization.

When distinct classes of input (domains) are computed on in distinct ways as inferred from behavior, we have a distinct mental module or memory system. Computational distinctiveness is the primary criterion for cognitive modularity, although others such as anatomical separability are commonly associated with it. However, an identifiable cognitive module need not be localized in a single place in the brain. Coversely, anatomically distinct substrates for cognition need not imply interesting computational distinctions. For instance, associative learning could be subserved by circuits local to particular stimulus and response systems even though a single set of principles could describe that learning. Associative learning in honeybees and rats is hardly likely to reside in similar structures despite its functional similarity in these and other species (Bitterman, this volume). To use Heyes's (this volume) terms, in defining cognitive modules, "how" is more important than "what," even though ultimately the requirements of "what" is to be processed dictate "how."

Because modularity is seen as an evolved adaptation for efficient information processing, cognitive modules are generally thought of as innate. Indeed, evolutionary psychology is often contrasted with a psychology that sees the human mind as infinitely molded by culture (Cosmides and Tooby, 1994). However, there is no logically necessary connection between innateness and modularity. The degree to which a particular aspect of information processing is influenced by experience (i.e., how it develops), whether or not it is computationally distinctive, what information it deals with, and what its current or past adaptive value might be are all separable questions (see Shettleworth, 1998; Heyes, this volume). Experience could modify prefunctionally ("innately") organized cognitive modules in characteristic ways, presumably by rules intrinsic to each module (see Bateson, this volume, for a candidate).

Fodor's (1983) criteria for modularity include informational encapsulation: a module works by itself, disregarding information that may be provided by other modules, even when the result is stupid behavior. Visual illusions are one kind of evidence for this. Some analogs in animal behavior are described below. In humans, the degree of modular encapsulation may change during development (Hermer and Spelke, 1996; see below). One provocative view of the human mind (Mithen, 1996) suggests that cognitive modularity has been reduced during evolution, allowing more fluid communication among distinct "intelligences." Considering other possibly defining features, evidence that a candidate module can evolve independently of other modules is potentially revealing, as in the adaptive tweaking of olfaction, vision, and other senses for different niches. In animal behavior, however, some of the best illustrations of cognitive modularity involve superficially similar inputs being processed in different ways. The next two sections describe examples from temporal and spatial cognition (see also Gallistel, 1995; Shettleworth, 1998).

Modularity in Temporal Information Processing

Nearly every organism, including plants, bacteria, and human beings, has a system for adjusting its behavior and physiology to local day and night, the circadian timing system. At least in vertebrates, circadian timing can be contrasted with interval timing, which allows animals to anticipate events on a scale of seconds to a few hours. Some suggest ordinal timing, encoding events in a sequence, as a third timing system (Carr and Wilkie, 1997). Circadian timing is not usually considered part of cognition, but it is an instructive example of preprogrammed adaptive behavioral plasticity. It has some very well-described properties (Moore-Ede et al., 1982). Circadian timing allows an animal to be active at the species-appropriate phase of the 24 hour light-dark cycle. Accordingly, the primary input to the circadian system is light. Organisms in constant light or darkness typically exhibit an endogenous, free-running rhythm of slightly more or less than 24 hours. Light pushes or pulls this into what would normally be synchrony with local day and night. The effects of light or other entraining stimuli are described by a phase response curve showing how much the rhythm is delayed or advanced as a function of when a stimulus is applied in the 24-hour cycle. For example, for a nocturnal animal such as a golden hamster, a pulse of light just as the animal enters its active phase delays the onset of activity the next day (as if the animal got up too early). In contrast, a pulse of light late in the active phase advances activity the next day (as if the animal stayed active too late in the morning). The circadian rhythm has a limited range of entrainment: it will synchronize only to stimuli having a periodicity close to 24 hours. Because the circadian system cycles continuously, it provides only phase information, that is, information about how long (in terms of the phase angle of the cycle) one event is before or after another. Its output is therefore valid on an interval scale of measurement (Carr and Wilkie, 1997).

In contrast, interval timing allows behavior to anticipate arbitrary events that recur over arbitrary intervals seconds to hours long, as when animals track the times between prey captures when foraging. In the laboratory, the properties of interval timing are studied by asking animals to time the intervals between reinforcers or the durations of lights and tones (review in Shettleworth, 1998). In the best-established model of interval timing, animals acquire representations of the durations of important events to which newly experienced durations are compared (Gibbon et al., 1997). These representations are blurred, in a way described by Weber's Law. That is, short intervals are timed with smaller absolute error than longer ones, and the error is proportional to the interval being timed. Unlike circadian timing, interval timing has an aribitrary zero point (the beginning of the event being timed), and its output can be represented on a ratio scale of measurement. Because ordinal timing represents only whether one event is before or after another, in this analysis (Carr and Wilkie, 1997), interval timing is the computationally richest timing system.

To summarize, circadian and interval timing have different adaptive functions, and they differ accordingly in other respects. Effective inputs to the circadian system are light and a few other stimuli with periodicities around 24 hours, compared to stimuli from a range of modalities with arbitrary periodicities from seconds to hours for the interval timing system. The relationship between input and output is described for circadian timing by a phase response curve, whereas interval timing is mediated by a stored representation of the interval to some important event associated with a particular signal, much as in other forms of associative learning. In contrast, acquisition in the circadian system is described as entrainment of a continuously running endogenous rhythm. An entraining agent is not encoded as such but rather is represented in adjustments of the rhythm over at most a few days after its application. However, like a learning curve in the Rescorla-Wagner model of associative learning, phase response curves may reflect the discrepancy between actual and "expected" events. In the example described earlier, light in the middle of the hamster's subjective day (evidenced by its free-running activity rhythm in constant darkness) has less of an effect than light an hour or two from the beginning or end of its subjective night, when light might be thought of as more "unexpected." Circadian and interval timing are neuroanatomically and pharmacologically, as well as computationally, distinct. In mammals, the circadian clock is located in the suprachiasmatic nucleus of the hypothalamus, whereas the cerebellum, frontal cortex, and basal ganglia are thought to be involved in interval timing (review in Gibbon et al., 1997). Circadian rhythms are very ancient and phylogenetically very widespread, probably more so than interval or ordinal timing—which have, however, been tested in many fewer species.

Modularity in Spatial Information Processing

My second example of contrasting modules—those allowing animals to get back to a remembered place—is more conventionally cognitive. Spatial cognition involves different kinds of implicit computations on a number of distinct kinds of information (Gallistel, 1990; Shettleworth, 1998). Perhaps the most basic and primitive way-finding mechanism is laying down a trail and following it back to a starting place like a nest or other place of refuge. Here, information about where to go is deposited in the environment. The trail-follower need only detect the trail and determine direction relative to it. Neither of these accomplishments encodes the metric properties of space, angles and distances. Cognitively more interesting is dead reckoning, a system that is phylogenetically very widespread. In a well-studied example, a desert ant

(*Cataglyphis fortis*) leaves its nest and wanders here and there, in a twisting path, until it encounters an item of food. It picks up the food and heads straight back to the vicinity of the nest, whereupon it begins to circle around until it locates the nest entrance (Collett and Zeil, 1998). Similarly, a hamster foraging in a novel arena in total darkness takes a circuitous path, but when frightened by a sudden noise, heads back to its nest in a straight line (Etienne et al., 1998). The ability of the ant or the hamster to head straight for the nest at any moment implies that the animals are continuously recording some correlate(s) of the distance and direction traveled from home. This job is done with different organs in different kinds of animals. In small mammals like the hamster, changes in direction are sensed by the vestibular organs, whereas desert ants use the direction of the sun corrected for time of day, a sun compass. Geese derive distance from visual flow patterns, whereas some insects use distance walked.

Although dead reckoning is often referred to as path integration, most animals do not use a mechanism that literally integrates. A variety of insects and mammals have been tested by allowing them to take an outward journey along a path with two segments and then head home. When the lengths of the two segments of the outward path and the angle between them are varied, the error in homeward heading varies in a way suggesting that direction from home is computed according to a rule that weighs each direction taken during the outward journey by the distance over which it is maintained. Both mammals and insects generally turn more sharply when taking the "homeward" direction than they should, in a way that brings them across the outward path. When very different kinds of mechanisms at the neural level produce the same general pattern of error, it is reasonable to ask whether there is some function to that particular kind of error. In this case, it might be that by crossing the outward path the animal is likely to come into contact with landmarks that will guide it home (Etienne et al., 1998).

With dead reckoning, the animal's path is recorded automatically and immediately, in a single trial. Indeed, the ant or hamster that did not return to its refuge after its first trip in a new direction might not survive to make other trips. However, dead reckoning accumulates error, so it needs resetting periodically, when the animal returns to the nest. This makes it useful for repeated trips from a central place, but less useful for long journeys. Dead reckoning computes distances and directions in egocentric coordinates, as can be seen from experiments in which desert ants are picked up and placed in a new location before being allowed to start "homeward" (review in Collett and Zeil, 1998). In unfamiliar barren terrain, ants run approximately the correct distance and direction to reach home from their old location.

Landmarks tie the animal directly to the environment, but making use of them requires implicit computations on multiple perceived and remembered vectors. A classic demonstration of landmark use is Tinbergen's (1932/1972) study of the digger wasp. Tinbergen arranged objects such as a circle of pine cones around the entrance to the nest while the wasp was inside. After the wasp had made a few foraging trips, Tinbergen moved these landmarks. The wasp now searched for the nest in the middle of the pine cone circle. Different animals encode and use the information from landmarks in different ways. Bees appear to move so as to match the visual image of the world as it appears from a goal such as a source of nectar. Animals using this "snapshot matching" mechanism search farther from or closer to the goal when landmarks are made bigger or smaller, respectively. Animals with different kinds of distance perception behave differently, another example of the same function being accomplished by different mechanisms in different lineages (see Cheng and Spetch, 1998). When pigeons are trained to find grain buried in a fixed relationship to one or more landmarks, and one landmark is moved, the birds behave as if they have encoded vectors from self and goal to the landmarks. In a conflict, as when just one landmark is moved, pigeons average vectors indicated by different landmarks. They compute distance and direction components of such vectors separately, a case of modules within a module (Cheng and Spetch, 1998). Whereas dead reckoning apparently goes on automatically, all the time, features of the environment can be used as landmarks only after one learns their significance. Some attention has been given to how animals learn about landmarks and how, if at all, this learning follows associative principles (e.g., Redhead et al., 1997), but there is scope for more work on this subject (Cheng and Spetch, 1998).

Dead reckoning and landmark use qualify as distinct cognitive modules because the different kinds of input that they take (distances and directions of the self from a starting place vs. vectors involving visual or other stimuli perceived at a distance) demand different implicit computations (continuous updating of distance and direction from a starting place vs. adding, subtracting, and/or averaging multiple perceived and remembered vectors or "snapshots" involving arbitrary goals). Landmark use also typically involves some form of learning (possibly associative) about relationships of perceptible distal stimuli with the goal and perhaps also with each other. That information is stored in long-term memory, accessed when current landmarks match remembered ones (a process depending its own set of computations). Landmark use allows the animal to locate itself within a terrain that it visits repeatedly, whereas dead reckoning may be used initially in learning the locations of objects in that terrain (Gallistel and Cramer, 1996). But dead reckoning and landmark use do not exhaust the mechanisms by which animals locate themselves in space (Shettleworth, 1998). A goal may be identified by a beacon, an object that can be perceived from a distance; the animal need only learn its significance through normal mechanisms of classical conditioning. It can then approach the goal using a simple hill-climbing process involving only signals from the beacon. Another possibility well studied in psychology is response or route learning, that is, learning a stereotyped series of moves that carries one between two or more known places. Ordinal timing would have a role here in sequencing the moves. In addition, disoriented rats, small children, and some other animals respond only to the geometry of the space surrounding them and disregard landmarks or features of the surfaces defining the space that they can patently use under other circumstances (Cheng, 1986; Hermer and Spelke, 1996). This use of the geometric module parallels evidence of perceptual modularity in that apparently "stupid" behavior results from relying on just one source of information.

Other Candidates for Distinct Cognitive Modules

There are many other candidates for distinguishable information processing modules. These include some aspects of imprinting (Bateson, this volume) and song learning, which coexist in the brains of some bird species, along with more general learning abilities. They have well worked out behavioral and neural properties (Clayton and Soha, 1999; Bateson, this volume). Imitation of seen motor patterns is another ability that may appear in only a few places on the evolutionary tree (Moore, 1996). Associative learning is clearly a widely shared system, one with a number of distinct subprocesses (such as occasion setting, perceptual learning, and learning the properties of reinforcers) not necessarily shared by all species or systems capable of forming simple associations (Bitterman, this volume). Indeed, even within rats, various aspects of learning resulting from exposure to simple predictive relationships between stimuli and reinforcers are localized in different brain areas (Holland, 1997). Social intelligence, or some aspects of it, may be a distinct module or modules from physical intelligence, though exactly how these putative kinds of intelligence are related is debatable (Gigerenzer, 1997; Kummer et al., 1997). Theory of mind may be unique to a few (maybe only one) primate species, but the subprocesses that make it up, such as recognizing intentional beings via self-propelled motion, detecting the direction of another's gaze, and shared attention, may be more widespread (Baron-Cohen, 1995; Povinelli and Eddy, 1996; Emery et al., 1997). Language, reasoning about social obligations (Cosmides, 1989), and perhaps consciousness (MacPhail, this volume; Humphrey, this volume) may be unique to humans.

How Does Cognition Evolve?

Specialization of Shared Modules

If cognition is modular, it could evolve in at least three ways. Most commonly per-haps, shared modules become specialized. Examples from morphology and sensory systems were mentioned earlier in the chapter. As another example, memory has general properties that reflect the nature of the world. Old information is less likely to be useful than recent information, something that has happened more often is more likely to happen again, and so on. At the same time, species may differ adaptively in what they remember best. Given redundant visual cues to hidden food, food-storing species of birds tend to remember position much better than color and pattern, whereas nonstoring species remember spatial and other cues about equally well (Shettleworth and Hampton, 1998).

In associative learning, too, we see species-specific tweaking for specific jobs. To borrow Heyes's (this volume) terms again, *what* is learned varies adaptively across species, whereas *how* it is learned does not. For instance, monkeys' fear of snakes appears to be socially transmitted via classical conditioning (Cook and Mineka, 1990), but even though, as far as is known, its abstract properties are the same as in other cases of associative learning, the input and output are species-specific. The sight of a fearful monkey is no more likely to be of significance to a rat or a bird than the smell of rat breath is likely to be of importance to a monkey. The same can be said of flavor aversion learning, contrary to its long history of being referred to as a special kind of learning (see Bitterman, this volume). Nowadays, the generality of associative learning both within and across species is said to reflect the general properties of physical causation, a case of the adaptationist argument for specialization being turned on its head.

Different Ways of Combining Information

In Fodor's (1983) conception, modularity is primarily at the level of input systems, whereas more central processing is general across domains of information. More recent discussions of modularity in developmental and evolutionary psychology, however, see cognition as modular right through from input to decision processes (see Gigerenzer, 1995), and this is the view taken here. In this view—so-called "vertical" as opposed to Fodor's "horizontal" modularity—an important issue is how modules interact. In the simplest case, genuinely encapsulated modules are activated one at a time. Each module has a characteristic triggering algorithm (Gigerenzer, 1997), so if a creature's nervous system parses the world so that no more than one algorithm is ever triggered at once, how modules interact is a problem that never arises. In general, however, even vertical modules cannot be completely encapsulated because there needs to be a way to harmonize potentially conflicting decisions from different modules. For instance, when a disoriented rat or toddler disregards landmarks that it can patently use under other circumstances and responds only to the geometry of space, it is providing evidence for a hierarchy of information use. Ideas about how such hierarchies, or other ways of combining information, work are not very well developed (but see Gigerenzer, 1995). The problem is not unrelated to the classical ethological problem of how different drive systems interact in controlling behavior (cf. McFarland and Bösser, 1993).

Looking across different information processing systems and species, it is evident that there is a great variety of ways to combine separate sources of information, either within modules or between them. The Rescorla-Wagner model of associative learning depicts different sources of information, which might be the outputs of different sensory modules, competing for a limited amount of associative strength. Even within associative learning, however, this is not the only possibility. For instance, the temporal properties of conditioned stimuli and unconditioned stimuli may be processed in parallel with other information (Williams and LoLordo, 1995). Circadian timing is going along in parallel with other activities all the time. Perhaps the time of day when important things happen is stored automatically with their other properties (Gallistel, 1990). In occasion setting or modulation, one cue has conditional control over how other cues are used, as when a pigeon learns that in one environment red means food and green means nothing, whereas in another environment the opposite is true. Configuring is another possible mode of interaction; compound cues may be treated as separate entities with their own properties rather than as the sum of parts (Pearce, 1994).

For examples of how distinct computational modules interact during the use of information, as opposed to during its acquisition, we can turn to spatial behavior, which provides cases of parallel processing, averaging, hierarchical or conditional control, and competitive, mutually inhibitory, interactions. Several of these possibilities are illustrated by ways in which dead reckoning and landmark use interact in different species. The dead reckoning desert ant also responds to landmarks along its way. In principle, dead reckoning and landmark use could go on in parallel, with the information from landmarks interpreted in the context of rough global position information from dead reckoning. However, the ants apparently recall the local vector associated with a conspicuous landmark at different global positions. They take their direction from the landmark for a short distance and then resume the direction appropriate for their presumed dead-reckoned position (Collett et al., 1998). Dead reckoning appears to be going on continuously, but its output is inhibited in the presence of well-learned landmarks.

In hamsters, however, dead reckoning and landmarks may be averaged (Etienne et al., 1998). When a hamster has made repeated trips from its nest into a circular arena with a conspicuous landmark on one side, and the landmark is moved 90° around the edge, the hamster's homeward path shifts, but not by the full 90°. However, if the landmark is moved halfway around the arena, so landmark and dead reckoning are too discrepant, then the hamster falls back on dead reckoning and disregards the landmark. That is, there is shift to a hierarchical use of cues, with dead reckoning taking precedence. The animal may be using rough information provided by dead reckoning to recognize familiar landmarks. Perhaps the evolutionarily prior module takes priority when outputs conflict, but this is only speculation.

Evolution of New Modules

The contrasts between chimpanzee, bee, and stentor at the beginning of the chapter make clear that entire modules appear in some lineages, making possible ways of dealing with the world that are impossible or very limited otherwise. At the most basic level, species clearly differ enormously in the variety of sensory information available to them and the ways in which they can process and act on it. When cognitive skills have subcomponents, species might share one or more of the component modules without sharing the whole package. For instance, although honeybees behave like vertebrates in most tests of associative learning, they differ in paradigms that tap the ability to represent the quality of rewards (Bitterman, this volume). As another example, if theory of mind has a number of subcomponents, nonhuman primates or very young children could possess one or more but not all of them. An intentionality (i.e., self-produced motion) detector and an eye direction detector may be common to a lot of species, but their combination in a shared attention detector less common, and the interpretation of that shared attention as theory of mind confined to humans (Baron-Cohen, 1995; Hauser and Carey, 1998).

In their article on the evolution of multiple memory systems, Sherry and Schacter (1987) propose that new modules (memory systems in their terminology) arise when there is functional incompatibility between what existing modules can do and the requirements of some new adaptive problem. They also suggest that under these kinds of conditions, already existing systems might turn out to be exaptations for solving the new problems. That is, even though selected via their role in solving one adaptive problem, existing modules would have some properties that could be co-opted for other problems. A related idea is Rozin's (1976) suggestion that intelligence evolves through originally specialized mechanisms becoming accessible to new kinds of information. The social theory of intellect (see Kummer et al., 1997) might be said to assume accessibility because it implies that cognitive mechanisms evolved to deal with the complexities of social life transfered to nonsocial content. Rozin (1976) suggests that accessibility increases with development or evolution (see Mithen, 1996). A candidate example is that, like rats, disoriented toddlers rely on the geometric module and disregard landmarks, whereas young adults use available landmarks (Hermer and Spelke, 1996). Similarly, the accessibility of associative learning to a wider range of inputs and behavioral outputs might change through evolution. However, this idea should not be interpreted as suggesting associative learning or memory is localized in a single place in the brain to which new inputs get connected over the course of evolution. Moreover, to the extent that modular mechanisms are more efficient than general purpose ones (and they may not be, Wilson, 1994), an evolutionary path toward increased accessibility—i.e. reduced modularity—should not be expected (Gigerenzer, 1997; but see Mithen, 1996).

Summary and Conclusions

A broad view of cognition as information processing of all sorts, from sensation to decision making, in all species seems to require that cognitive organization be modular. Timing and spatial behavior provide relatively well-analyzed examples of adaptive differences in processing of different kinds of information. An important question for future research and theoretical development in both nonhuman and human cognition is how distinguishable modules interact in the whole behaving individual (Gigerenzer, 1995).

The modular, adaptationist view of cognitive evolution sketched in this chapter contrasts with the ideas from traditional comparative psychology reviewed by Bitterman (this volume) in a number of ways. It embraces not only associative learning, but all ways in which animals process and act on information about the world. The aim is to account for the whole panoply of evolved mechanisms that allow individuals of whatever species to adjust their behavior to features of their local environment. Specialization and adaptation are necessary parts of the story, but so is generality across species and/or situations. The expectation is not that a single hierarchical ordering of mechanisms will be found with capacities possessed only by humans at the "most complex" or "most advanced" end.

Like research on the evolution of other aspects of behavior, a systematic research program on the evolution of cognition needs to embrace species that are both closely and distantly related and examples of convergence as well as divergence. Broad comparative studies of how sensory systems and related brain areas are related to ecology can provide a model of how other aspects of cognitive evolution might be studied (an example is Barton et al., 1995; see also Lefebvre, this volume). Comparisons across widely different species, as emphasized by Bitterman and in the part of this chapter on spatial behavior, may also define the range of phenomena to be explained and may provide important tests of adaptationist hypotheses. At the same time, detailed comparisons of close relatives can reveal how differences in developmental programs result in species differences in brain and cognition (Krubitzer, 1995 provides examples) and perhaps eventually shed light on the molecular events in cognitive evolution. Finally, although my emphasis has been to draw as stark a contrast as possible with the traditional psychological approach sketched by Bitterman, careful analyses of cognitive mechanisms in the laboratory are nevertheless part of the story, along with natural history and phylogeny. "How does cognition evolve?" implies both functional and mechanistic questions about behavior. Traditionally these questions have been tackled in the separate disciplines of biology and psychology, respectively. As is evident in this book, progress can be made when people work at their interface.

References

Barlow HB (1982) General principles: The senses considered as physical instruments. In: The senses (Barlow HB, Mollon JD, ed), pp 1–33. Cambridge: Cambridge University Press.

Baron-Cohen S (1995) Mindblindness. Cambridge, MA: MIT Press.

Barton RA, Purvis A, Harvey PH (1995) Evolutionary radiation of visual and olfactory brain areas in primates, bats, and insectivores. Philosphical Transactions of the Royal Society B, 348: 381–392.

Carr JAR, Wilkie DM (1997) Ordinal, phase, and interval timing. In: Time and behaviour: Psychological and neurobehavioral analyses (Bradshaw CM, Szabadi E, ed), pp 265–327. Amsterdam: Elsevier.

Cheng K (1986) A purely geometric module in the rat's spatial representation. Cognition, 23: 149–178.

Cheng K, Spetch ML (1998) Mechanisms of landmark use in mammals and birds. In: Spatial representation in animals (Healy S, ed), pp 1–17. Oxford: Oxford University Press.

Clayton NS, Soha JA (1999) Memory in avian food caching and song learning: A general mechanism or different processes? Advances in the Study of Behavior, 28: 115–174.

Collett M, Collett TS, Bisch S, Wehner R (1998) Local and global vectors in desert ant navigation. Nature, 394: 269–272.

Collett TS, Zeil J (1998) Places and landmarks: An arthropod perspective. In: Spatial representation in animals (Healy S, ed), pp 18–53. Oxford: Oxford University Press.

Cook M, Mineka S (1990) Selective associations in the observational conditioning of fear in rhesus monkeys. Journal of Experimental Psychology: Animal Behavior Processes, 16: 372–389.

Cosmides L (1989) The logic of social exchange: Has natural selection shaped how humans reason? Studies with the Wason selection task. Cognition, 31: 187–276.

Cosmides L, Tooby J (1994) Origins of domain specificity: The evolution of functional organization. In: Mapping the mind (Hirschfeld LA, Gelman SA, ed), pp 85–116. Cambridge: Cambridge University Press.

Dusenbery DB (1992) Sensory ecology. New York: W.H. Freeman.

Dyer FC (1998) Cognitive ecology of navigation. In: Cognitive ecology (Dukas R, ed), pp 201–260. Chicago: University of Chicago Press.

Emery NJ, Lorincz EN, Perrett DI, Oram MW, Baker CI (1997) Gaze following and joint attention in rhesus monkeys (Macaca mulatta). Journal of Comparative Psychology, 111: 286–293.

Etienne A, Berlie J, Georgakopoulos J, Maurer R (1998) Role of dead reckoning in navigation. In: Spatial representations in animals (Healy S, ed), pp 54–68. Oxford: Oxford University Press.

Fodor JA (1983) The modularity of mind. Cambridge, MA: MIT Press.

Gallistel CR (1990) The organization of learning. Cambridge, MA: MIT Press.

Gallistel CR (1995) The replacement of general-purpose theories with adaptive specializations. In: The cognitive neurosciences (Gazziniga M, ed), pp 1255–1267. Cambridge, MA: MIT Press.

Gallistel CR, Cramer AE (1996) Computations on metric maps in mammals: Getting oriented and choosing a multi-destination route. Journal of Experimental Biology, 199: 211–217.

Gibbon J, Malapani C, Dale CL, Gallistel CR (1997) Toward a neurobiology of temporal cognition: Advances and challenges. Current opinion in neurobiology, 7: 170–184.

Gigerenzer G (1995) The taming of content: Some thoughts about domains and modules. Thinking and Reasoning, 1: 324–332.

Gigerenzer G (1997) The modularity of social intelligence. In: Machiavellian intelligence II: Extensions and evaluation (Whiten A, Byrne RW, ed), pp 264–288. Cambridge: Cambridge University Press.

Hauser M, Carey S (1998) Building a cognitive creature from a set of primitives: Evolutionary and developmental insights. In: The evolution of mind (Allen C, Cummins D, ed), pp 51–106. New York: Oxford University Press.

Hermer L, Spelke E (1996) Modularity and development: The case of spatial reorientation. Cognition, 61: 195–232.

Hirschfeld LA, Gelman SA, ed (1994). Mapping the mind. Cambridge: Cambridge University Press.

Holland PC (1997) Brain mechanisms for changes in processing of conditioned stimuli in Pavlovian conditioning: Implications for behavior theory. Animal Learning and Behavior, 25: 373–399.

Krubitzer L (1995) The organization of neocortex in mammals: Are species differences really so different? Trends in Neurosciences, 18: 408–417.

Kummer H, Daston L, Gigerenzer G, Silk JB (1997) The social intelligence hypothesis. In: Human by nature: Between biology and the social sciences (Weingart P, Mitchell SD, Richerson PJ, Maasen S, ed), pp 159–179. Mahwah, NJ: Lawrence Erlbaum Associates.

Lipp HP, Wolfer DP (1995) New paths towards old dreams: Microphrenology. In: Behavioral brain research in naturalistic and semi-naturalistic settings (Alleva E, Fasolo A, Lipp HP, Nadel L, Ricceri L, ed), pp 3–36. Dordrecht: Kluwer Academic.

Lythgoe JN (1979) The ecology of vision. Oxford: Clarendon Press.

Marr D (1982) Vision. New York: W. H. Freeman.

McFarland D (1991) Defining motivation and cognition in animals. International Studies in the Philosophy of Science, 5: 153–170.

McFarland D, Bösser T (1993) Intelligent behavior in animals and robots. Cambridge, MA: MIT Press.

McGrew WC (1992) Chimpanzee material culture: Implications for human evolution. Cambridge: Cambridge University Press.

Mithen S (1996) The prehistory of the mind. New York: Thames and Hudson.

Moore BR (1996) The evolution of imitative learning. In: Social learning in animals: The roots of culture (Heyes CM, Galef Jr. BG, ed), pp 245–265. San Diego: Academic Press.

Moore-Ede MC, Sulzman FM, Fuller CA (1982) The clocks that time us. Cambridge, MA: Harvard University Press.

Pearce JM (1994) Discrimination and categorization. In: Animal learning and cognition (Mackintosh NJ, ed), pp 109–134. San Diego: Academic Press.

Povinelli DJ, Eddy TJ (1996) What young chimpanzees know about seeing. Monographs of the Society for Research in Child Development, 61: 1–152.

Redhead ES, Roberts A, Good M, Pearce JM (1997) Interaction between piloting and beacon homing by rats in a swimming pool. Journal of Experimental Psychology: Animal Behavior Processes, 23: 340–350.

Rozin P (1976) The evolution of intelligence and access to the cognitive unconscious. Progress in Psychobiology and Physiological Psychology, 6: 245–280.

Shepard RN (1994) Perceptual-cognitive universals as reflections of the world. Psychonomic Bulletin and Review, 1: 2–28.

Sherry DF, Jacobs LF, Gaulin SJC (1992) Spatial memory and adaptive specialization of the hippocampus. Trends in Neurosciences, 15: 298–303.

Sherry DF, Schacter DL (1987) The evolution of multiple memory systems. Psychological Review, 94: 439–454.

Shettleworth SJ (1998) Cognition, evolution, and behavior. New York: Oxford University Press.

Shettleworth SJ, Hampton RR (1998) Adaptive specializations of spatial cognition in food-storing birds? In: Animal cognition in nature (Balda RP, Pepperberg I, Kamil AC, ed), pp 65–98. San Diego: Academic Press.

Sperber D (1994) The modularity of thought and the epidemiology of representations. In: Mapping the mind (Hirschfeld LA, Gelman SA, ed), pp 39–67. Cambridge: Cambridge University Press.

Staddon JER (1983) Adaptive Behavior and Learning. Cambridge: Cambridge University Press.

Terrace HS (1984) Animal cognition. In: Animal Cognition (Roitblat HL, Bever TG, Terrace HS, ed), pp 7–28. Hillsdale, NJ: Erlbaum.

Thomas RK (1996) Investigating cognitive abilities in animals: Unrealized potential. Cognitive Brain Research, 3: 157–166.

Tinbergen N (1932/1972) On the orientation of the digger wasp Philanthus triangulum Fabr. I. In: The animal in its world (Tinbergen N, ed), pp 103–127. Cambridge, MA: Harvard University Press.

Williams DA, LoLordo VM (1995) Time cues block the CS, but the CS does not block time cues. Quarterly Journal of Experimental Psychology, 48B: 97–116.

Wilson DS (1994) Adaptive genetic variation and human evolutionary psychology. Ethology and Sociobiology, 15: 219–235.

4 Cognitive Evolution: A Psychological Perspective

M. E. Bitterman

In this initial staking out of positions with respect to the evolution of cognition (which I interpret as "knowing" in the classical sense of the term, encompassing perception, learning, and understanding), my task is to represent the psychological tradition rooted in the work of Thorndike (1911) and Pavlov (1927)—the Thorndikian tradition. The views of Thorndike and Pavlov differed considerably, of course, and so also did the views of their various influential successors, such as Watson, Lashley, Tolman, Guthrie, Skinner, Hull, Spence, and Mowrer (Bitterman, 1967). Skinner's well-popularized views were especially deviant, although outsiders often assumed them to be typical. In fact, it would be difficult to find sharper criticisms of Skinner than those made by insiders. I remember, for example, H. L. Teuber's description of the Skinner Box as a bloodless technique of decortication, which affects both the experimenter and the animal, and is irreversible for the experimenter. Among the contemporary descendants of Thorndike and Pavlov, there is no less diversity of opinion, and yet there are some clearly discernable common assumptions. For all the publicized disagreement between psychologists and ethologists, the same assumptions are to be found in Lorenz's *Behind the Mirror* (1977).

There is general agreement that information about the world comes from sensory systems whose outputs are filtered and organized in critical ways by genetically structured perceptual mechanisms; that the mechanisms of learning, which permit adaptation to a much wider range of environments than can possibly be provided for in the genome, are themselves products of evolution; that much of learning is associative in character; that the modification of behavior by reward and punishment is of special—Lorenz (p. 84) says "epoch-making"—importance; and that understanding must depend on information supplied by learning.

The central concern of psychologists working in the Thorndikian tradition has been with learning and memory. Their earliest interest was in whether something like human understanding could be found in animals, but the results of early experiments were largely negative. Only highly experienced subjects sometimes seemed to solve problems insightfully, which suggested that, if there was something like understanding in animals, it was grounded in learning, and that was where the inquiry should begin. Questions about learning soon gave rise to questions about perception (leading to a great deal of interesting work on generalization, discrimination, and attention), as well as to questions about motivation and about the interplay of learned and unlearned behavior; for a proper appreciation of the scope of that work, see the textbook by Mackintosh (1974), a landmark in its field. Interest in the discovery of conceptual abilities did not, however, entirely disappear and in recent years has revived considerably, although still without clear outcome; see, for example, the critical analysis by Heyes (1998) of evidence for "theory of mind" in nonhuman primates.

An old criticism of Thorndikian research is that it is done in unnatural situations, although laboratory procedures for the study of learning in animals were designed from the very beginning with the behavior of the subjects in more worldly settings in mind—Thorndike's puzzleboxes for cats, Small's maze for rats, and even Skinner's key-pecking apparatus for pigeons (now commonly encountered in ecological laboratories). In *Behind the Mirror*, Lorenz does not hesitate to rely on results of maze experiments with rats and mice, and (in a discussion of Pavlov's experiments) recognizes the value of isolating specific responses "artificially" (p. 86) for purposes of quantitative analysis. In trying to understand an animal, we want to know about its behavior in as wide a range of situations as possible, and settings far removed from those in which the animal normally is found may be especially instructive. H. F. Harlow once remarked that field observations of rhesus monkeys gave little hint of the intellectual capabilities displayed in the Wisconsin General Test Apparatus.

Another criticism of Thorndikian research is that it has been concentrated on a very small number of species, and the wrong ones at that. Particularly disturbing for a time was the amount of effort devoted to rats. The answer to the objection is that, with limited resources, it is more instructive to study a small number of species intensively than a large number of species superficially; the laws of learning in any species are not given immediately in its behavior, but must be extracted painstakingly from the data of a long series of analytical experiments. In choosing a species for intensive study, we have to consider such practical questions as whether it is readily available; whether it lives well in the laboratory; and whether its sensory, motor, and motivational properties are suitable for the work. Having decided some 40 years ago that it was important to have a body of detailed information about learning in a vertebrate very different from the rat in its evolutionary history, I was led by just such practical considerations to choose the African mouthbreeding fish, *Tilapia macrocephala*, which L. R. Aronson bred in great quantity at the nearby American Museum of Natural History in New York, and which had the special advantage of a large appetite for dry food (Bitterman et al., 1958). With the development of automatic devices for feeding liquid food and small worms, the goldfish (abundant almost everywhere) proved to be even more practical. Later on, when I decided that it was important also to have a body of detailed information about learning in an invertebrate, I was led again by practical considerations to the honeybee.

And what of the early focus on learning in rats? Using data from Simpson (1945) and Walker (1964), R. B. Masterton once suggested to me that if we were starting over again and had to select a single mammalian species for intensive study, rats would be prime candidates on demographic grounds. Of the living genera of mammals, more than a third are rodents—three times the number in either of the next two largest orders. Of the rodent genera, almost two-thirds are in one or the other of two main families generally referred to as "rats"—the old-world and new-world rats and mice. *Rattus*, one of the old-world genera, has many more named forms than any other mammalian genus, and even if only 50 percent of them were true species, the number of *Rattus* species would be larger than the number in any other genus. It follows that a random sample from *Mammalia* would most probably yield a rodent, and a sample of *Rodentia* would most probably yield a rat—which, having been selected for consideration, would pass the practical tests. If we were looking for any vertebrate, the probability is somewhat greater that we would hit on a bony fish.

General-Process Theory

Of course, there has also been considerable work on learning in mammals other than rats, in vertebrates other than mammals, and in invertebrates, and nothing has so earned the skepticism of outsiders as the hypothesis, conceived early in the course of the work, that there are some quite general laws of learning. The first formulation of the so-called *general-process* view we owe to Thorndike (1911), who studied cats, dogs, chickens, monkeys, and even a species of fish (*Fundulus*), and who found only quantitative differences in their learning. The various animals learned different things, and some seemed to learn more quickly than others, but all could be understood as systems of connections governed by the Laws of Exercise and Effect. Thorndike's distinction between the content and rate of learning on the one hand, and the laws of learning on the other, is an important one. Hull (1945) puts the question about the generality of the laws of learning in a very clear way. He asks whether the equations that describe learning in various species (when we have them) will be of the same form, differing only in the values of their constants (as, in his example, the gravitational constant at Hammerfest and Madras), or whether the equations themselves will be different.

Consider the S-S contiguity principle, according to which the pairing of two stimuli—such as the pairing of a tone (the conditioned stimulus, or CS) and a bit of food (the unconditioned stimulus, or US) in Pavlovian conditioning—results in the formation of an association between them. Bush and Mosteller (1951) suggest that the growth of associative strength in the course of training can be described by a simple linear equation currently more familiar in the notation of Rescorla and Wagner (1972):

$$\Delta V = \alpha \cdot U\beta(\lambda - V) \tag{1}$$

with V representing the strength of association at the beginning of each trial; ΔV, the change in V produced by the pairing of the CS and the US on that trial; α, the salience of the CS; $U\beta$, the learning rate; and λ, the maximal strength of association that can be achieved with a given US—the asymptote of the growth function. On nonreinforced trials (that is, on trials with the CS alone), $\lambda = 0$, ΔV is negative, and V declines at a rate ($D\beta$) that may be different from $U\beta$. The constants α, $U\beta$, $D\beta$, and λ, may vary widely in value from situation to situation and from species to species, as may the conditioned response (CR) itself, and so also the relation between V and the measure of response (specified in a supplementary performance equation); but the learning equation (and the conditioning process it describes) may be the same. There is a good deal of contemporary interest in the development of quantitative theories of learning that will permit exact rather than merely ordinal predictions of experimental outcomes. Equation [1] has proved useful in deriving the results of experiments on such diverse phenomena as transitive inference in pigeons (Couvillon and Bitterman, 1992), avoidance conditioning in goldfish (Zhuikov et al., 1994), and (by Martin Shapiro in doctoral research at the University of Hawaii) risk-sensitive foraging in honeybees.

Although what many have come to think of as the ethological view is that there are no general laws of learning, we find general-process thinking by Lorenz himself in *Behind the Mirror*. There he considers at length some phenomena of learning in animals as diverse as cuttlefish, flatworms, human infants, wasps, dogs, and birds of various species. Two of the phenomena—*facilitation by practice* and *sensitization*—are interpreted as frequency or practice effects and attributed to a process like that of "'running in' an automobile" (p. 69). Thorndike's Law of Exercise comes to mind here. Four other phenomena—*habituation*, *habit*, *traumatic avoidance*, and *imprinting*—are explained in terms of association, which is defined as "the forming of a linkage between two nervous processes hitherto not causally connected" (p. 81). A seventh phenomenon is *conditioning by reinforcement* or "learning through success and failure," which Lorenz thinks of as "true conditioning" rather than "mere association." It is based, he assumes, on a feedback process found in all animals except "unicellular and lower multicellular creatures which have no centralized nervous systems" (pp. 84–87). Here, of course, Thorndike's Law of Effect comes to mind. In sum, three general processes are postulated—a frequency process and a contiguity process that are perfectly general, and a reinforcement process that operates in all but the simplest animals. Psychologists working in the Thorndikian tradition would quarrel with the substance of the theory, which is summarized in table 4.1, but would not find its form or intent at all foreign.

Table 4.1
General-process theory in *Behind the Mirror* (Lorenz, 1977)

Process	Locus of operation	Representative phenomena
Frequency	All animals	Facilitation by practice Sensitization
Association	All animals	Habituation Habit Traumatic avoidance Imprinting
Reinforcement	All animals with "centralized nervous systems"	Learning by trial and success ("true conditioning")

General-process theory is often thought to be contradicted by *adaptive specialization* —the alleged evolutionary tailoring of learning processes to the needs of particular species in particular situations—although the assumption of tailoring implies the existence of general processes to be tailored, as when Lorenz proposes that the associations involved in imprinting and traumatic avoidance may be especially persistent. One line of evidence for adaptive specialization comes from experiments in which the performance of the same species in different situations is compared. Why, asks Huber (this volume), should it be easier to train rats to avoid shock by running away from the danger signal than by making copulatory responses? The Thorndikian answer is that a response must occur before it can be rewarded, and the signal, which is paired with shock whenever the animal fails to avoid, is more likely in consequence of the pairing to elicit running than copulation. The once popular conviction that food-aversion experiments point to the operation of specialized learning processes is now widely understood to be groundless (Klosterhalfen and Klosterhalfen, 1985). The primordial finding—that rats poisoned after eating a novel food may develop an aversion to the taste of the food but not to its appearance—follows directly from the contiguity principle, given that the traces of visual stimuli fade rapidly in the relatively long interval between poisoning and illness while food remains in the gut (Bitterman, 1975). Without controls for the effects of the many variables other than learning that influence performance in such experiments, conclusions about learning are unwarranted.

Another line of evidence for adaptive specialization comes from experiments in which the performance of different species is compared in what is purported to be the same situation, and here similar difficulties are encountered. Better performance of food-storing birds as compared with nonstorers in spatial learning tasks might well be due, as Shettleworth (1993) admits, to evolutionary tailoring of their sensory or motivational properties rather than of their learning; spatial cues, she suggests, may be more salient for the black-capped chickadee than for the dark-eyed junco. Even if a difference in what she refers to as the capacity and persistence of spatial memory could somehow be demonstrated, of course, the finding would not go to the generality of whatever learning process is involved—not to the form of the learning equation, as Hull put it, but only to the values of the constants. It is often implied that certain seemingly specialized instances of learning, such as the much-advertised song learning of birds, involve processes that are entirely unique—that the tailoring is qualitative rather than merely quantitative—but little interest has been evidenced in what the unique processes might be, or how they might differ from those delineated by conventional laboratory experiments. The accommodating modular view expounded here by Shettleworth may be attractive because it suggests that we need not worry very much about such matters. The Law of Least Effort holds for mind as well as for muscle.

Scattered allegations of adaptive specialization should not be permitted to obscure the fact that there are a great many phenomena of learning that transcend particular sensory, motor, and motivational contexts, which are found in many different species, and which point to the operation of common processes—although we are still not clear as to the nature of some of those processes. The strategy of psychologists working in the Thorndikian tradition is to continue in given species to try to discover what the processes are, and in comparative experiments to examine their generality over a range of widely divergent species chosen to provide clues to their evolutionary history. Because a variety of general learning processes seem to be at work in the species that we have been studying intensively, and because it is unlikely that the whole set of them appeared together, or are inextricably linked, we should not be surprised to find animals in which certain of them are absent, or are present in a different form. It is possible, however, as Macphail (1982) suggests, that there may be no differences among existing vertebrates because the critical developments occurred at an early stage of evolution in animals now extinct.

Learning in Vertebrates and Honeybees

That there are many phenomena of learning common to our favorite vertebrate subjects, as diverse as they are, is perhaps not difficult to understand on the assumption of common processes evolved in common ancestors. That many of what appear to be the same phenomena are found also in honeybees is perhaps more difficult to understand in view of the greater remoteness of the evolutionary relationship and the presumed simplicity of even the most advanced common ancestors. Because, as Simpson (1964) notes, convergence to the point of identity or even of seriously confusing similarity is unlikely in what he refers to as elaborately polygenic behavioral

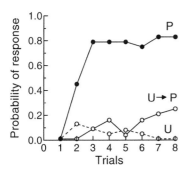

Figure 4.1
Classical conditioning in honeybees (P, paired; U, unpaired; U → P, unpaired to paired.

systems, it might be expected that resemblances in the learning of honeybees and vertebrates would be no more than superficial, but an examination of a small sample of them will show that they are quite detailed.

Consider, for example, the performance of a group of honeybee foragers (Group P) harnessed in small tubes and subjected to a series of conditioning trials with odor as the CS and a small drop of sucrose solution, applied to antennae and proboscis, as the US. As figure 4.1 shows, the odor soon comes to elicit extension of the proboscis (the CR), which at the outset is elicited only by the sucrose (Bitterman et al., 1983). The results look very much like salivary conditioning in a Pavlovian dog standing on laboratory table in Petrograd. The stimuli and responses are different, and so also is the rate of change in performance over trials (which is actually much greater in the honeybees), but the learning process may be the same—the process described by equation [1].

The possibility that the change in responding to the odor is due to experience with the stimuli apart from their pairing—say, to sensitization of the response by the experience with sucrose—is evaluated with a control procedure common in work with vertebrates. Another group of honeybees (Group U) is given the same experience with the odor and sucrose, except that the two stimuli are presented separately in random sequence (*explicitly unpaired training*). As figure 4.1 shows, these animals respond very little to the odor, which suggests that the pairing of the stimuli really is a critical factor in the performance of Group P. In vertebrates, the explicitly unpaired procedure is found not to be associatively neutral, as evidenced by the fact that a stimulus explicitly unpaired with a US is slow to condition when subsequently paired with it. Figure 4.1 shows that the same is true for honeybees; as compared with the rate of conditioning in Group P, the rate of conditioning in Group U—shown in the curve labeled U→P—is indeed slow. As to why explicitly unpaired training should retard subsequent conditioning, there is some disagreement in the vertebrate literature.

Now there is another question worth asking, which has been asked also about appetitive conditioning in vertebrates. Is the change in response to the CS a product of CS-US contiguity per se, or of the CR-US contiguity (the contiguity of response and sucrose) that the pairing of the two stimuli occasions? Although the sucrose is presented whether or not the CR occurs, the CR is always closely followed by the sucrose when it does occur, which gives us reason to suspect that what we may really have here is instrumental learning in disguise (Lorenz's "true conditioning" rather than "mere association"). We answer the question by training a new group of honeybees with two different odors. On some trials, one of the odors (S+) is paired with sucrose, but only when the CR fails to occur (*omission training*). On the remaining trials, the other odor (S−) is presented alone, serving to control for the possibility that any responding to S+ is due simply to sensitization. The results are like those for vertebrates. There is little response to S−, but a good deal of response to S+, which (because there is no CR-US contiguity) must be attributed to the contiguity of CS and US on the few trials on which the CR does not occur. It is interesting to note that Pavlov found good salivary conditioning in dogs even when the CS was paired with the US on only a small percentage of trials.

As Pavlov also found, a CS can itself act as a US in the conditioning of a novel stimulus (*second-order conditioning*), and the same is true of honeybees. After one odor has been paired with sucrose in a series of trials, a second odor that is paired with the first odor soon comes to elicit the CR. That does not happen if the two odors are explicitly unpaired in the second stage of the experiment. It does not happen either if the first odor has been explicitly unpaired with sucrose in the first stage of the experiment—the paired odors may be associated in the second stage, but the second odor will not evoke the response if the first odor does not. The vertebrate literature shows that contiguous neutral stimuli are, in fact, associated (that classical conditioning does not require a motivationally significant US), and that the same is true of honeybees has been shown by experiments on what in the vertebrate literature is called *within-compound association* (Couvillon and Bitterman, 1982).

The work on within-compound association in honeybees was done with free-flying subjects that were pretrained individually to forage for sucrose solution at a laboratory window—feeding to repletion on each visit, leaving for the hive to deposit the sucrose, and returning of their own accord a few minutes later to collect more. (The window used in such experiments is so situated as to minimize following by nestmates, a technique that Professor B. Hassenstein taught me in his laboratory at

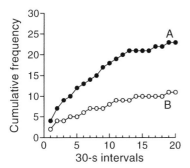

Figure 4.2
Within-compound association in honeybees. Responses in a choice test with A and B after experience with
AX and BY followed by training with X+ and Y−.

Freiburg, where I first learned to work with honeybees.) In the first stage of training,
the subjects were exposed on a series of visits to two gray targets, one (AX) labeled
with a color (A) and an odor (X), and another (BY) labeled with a different color (B)
and a different odor (Y). In the second stage of the experiment, the subjects were
trained to discriminate between two gray targets labeled with the odors, only one of
which (X) contained sucrose solution. When, in the third stage of the experiment, the
subjects were tested with two gray targets labeled only with the colors, neither containing sucrose solution, they showed a strong preference for A (the color paired
in the first stage with the odor reinforced in the second stage). In figure 4.2, some
sample results are plotted in terms of the mean cumulative frequency of responding
to each of the targets in a 10-min choice test. It seems reasonable to conclude that
color-odor associations are formed in the first stage, although not then evident in
behavior—an instance of what is called *latent learning* in the vertebrate literature.

Experiments with compound stimuli show a variety of other phenomena first discovered in vertebrates. One of them is *blocking*, which has been found both in
proboscis-extension conditioning (Smith and Cobey, 1994) and in the performance of
free-flying foragers (Couvillon et al., 1997). After reinforced training with a compound of two odors or two colors (AB), there is less response to B alone if A has
previously been paired with the same reinforcer; that is, the conditioning of B is
impaired (blocked) by the presence of the previously conditioned A. Blocking in
vertebrates is commonly explained on the assumption that the components of a
reinforced compound compete with each other for associative strength or for attention, and the same explanation may well hold for honeybees. In any case, it is
clear from the data both for vertebrates and for honeybees that CS-US contiguity,
although necessary, is not sufficient for conditioning.

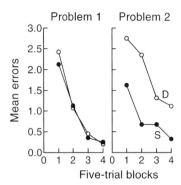

Figure 4.3
Performance of honeybees in two color-position discrimination problems with the relevant dimension the same (S) or different (D) in the two problems.

Competition for attention has been demonstrated in honeybees, again in an experiment patterned after work with vertebrates (Klosterhalfen et al., 1978). Free-flying foragers were trained with targets of two different colors in two different positions, some rewarded for choosing one of the colors independently of position (color-relevant training), and others for choosing one of the positions independently of color (position-relevant training). In a second problem, with targets of two new colors in two new positions, learning was more rapid when the relevant dimension was the same as in the first problem than when it was different. In figure 4.3, the results are plotted in terms of the mean number of errors made in each of the two problems. The results suggest that the animals learn first of all in such problems to single out the relevant stimulus dimension (see also Shapiro and Bitterman, 1998), and that dimensional selection is influenced by prior training. It is interesting to note that the results of like experiments on discriminative learning in octopuses have been interpreted in the same way (Sutherland and Mackintosh, 1971).

Another interesting phenomenon of compound conditioning found in honeybees as well as in vertebrates is *conditional discrimination* (Couvillon and Bitterman, 1988). Honeybees can learn to choose, say, a green rather than a blue target when both are scented with geraniol, but a blue rather than a green target when both are scented with peppermint. Because each of the components is equally often reinforced and nonreinforced, differential responding to the compounds cannot be understood in terms of the summed associative strengths of the components. *Spontaneous* discrimination of compounds *qua* compounds also has been demonstrated in honeybees (Couvillon and Bitterman, 1982). Subjects that have found sucrose solution on each of two targets labeled with different color-odor compounds (AX and BY) clearly prefer them to two targets labeled with the same colors and odors paired differently (AY and BX) in a subsequent choice test. The simplest interpretation in the vertebrate literature is that we are dealing in such experiments with perceptual rather than conceptual effects—that the animals learn about configural properties in the same way they learn about component properties (which also may sometimes be quite subtle)—although there is some disagreement as to how the perceptual effects are best conceived.

These detailed similarities in the results for honeybees and vertebrates represent only a very small proportion of those that have been found in a wide range of experiments (Bitterman, 1988, 1996). Differences also have turned up occasionally. The results of initial blocking experiments (Funayama et al., 1995) were negative, for example, although for reasons that now seem to be purely perceptual (Couvillon et al., 1997). A long series of recent experiments designed to look for evidence of inhibitory conditioning produced only negative results (Couvillon et al., 1999), but their meaning is uncertain because the evidence of inhibitory conditioning in vertebrates (commonly taken for granted since the time of Pavlov) is unimpressive (Papini and Bitterman, 1993). Noteworthy, too, is our failure in other recent experiments to find evidence that the control of performance by short-term memory can be modified by learning (Couvillon et al., 1998). On the whole, however, the differences are far outweighed by the similarities.

Why should it be so difficult to discover differences in the learning of animals whose most recent common ancestor lived half a billion years ago and had hardly any brain at all? At least part of the answer may be that honeybees can be studied properly only in relatively massed trials and for relatively brief periods, which rules out a search for many interesting and seemingly more complex phenomena of vertebrate learning. On these grounds alone, although for other obvious reasons as well, it seems necessary to extend the work to other invertebrates, and the trick, of course, is to find a suitable one. With a huge research budget (because to do the work well would be enormously expensive), I might be tempted to turn again to octopuses (Walker et al., 1970).

Divergence in Vertebrate Learning

When we ask whether there are differences in the learning of honeybees and vertebrates, we are referring to what we conceive to be general phenomena of vertebrate learning—phenomena that have been found, or that we assume can be found, in vertebrates of all classes. The question does not imply that there has been no divergence in vertebrate learning, although evidence of divergence is scarce indeed, and the scarcity is not due simply to the fact that psychologists have not bothered to look for it. Macphail (1982) has reviewed in considerable detail the results of a large number of comparative experiments with fishes, reptiles, birds, and mammals, including primates, which in his opinion provide no compelling evidence of qualitative differences in learning. I agree with many of his evaluations; the difficulty in establishing such differences, of course, is that performance in learning situations is influenced by variables other than learning. There are, however, several series of experiments that I think deserve further consideration, among them experiments on the so-called *paradoxical reward effects* discovered in work with rats.

One of the effects is *negative incentive contrast*, found first in a famous experiment by Elliott (1928). Two groups of rats were trained in a maze, one with bran mash as reward, and the second with (less acceptable) sunflower seeds. (Except where otherwise noted, the intertrial interval in all of the instrumental learning experiments considered here was 24 hours—a procedure that has the important advantage, among others, that the sensory antecedents of response on one trial are not contaminated by the sensory consequences of response on preceding trials.) The performance of the bran mash animals was much better than that of the sunflower seed animals until the bran mash animals were shifted to sunflower seeds. Finding sunflower seeds for the first time, they showed a good deal of disturbance, and their performance on subsequent days fell precipitously below that of the animals rewarded with sunflower seeds from the outset. In the upper portion of figure 4.4, the performance of the two groups is plotted in terms of mean errors per trial. These results, and those of like experiments with differences only in quantity of reward, suggest that instrumental behavior in rats is modulated by anticipation of its remembered consequences—energized by remembered reward and impaired by remembered frustration (Amsel, 1958)—all of which may seem perfectly commonplace until it is appreciated that quite different results are obtained in analogous experiments with other animals.

Lowes and Bitterman (1967) trained goldfish to strike a target lowered into the water at the start of each trial. The reward was a cluster of 40 (*Tubifex*) worms for one group, which then was shifted to four worms; a second group was rewarded throughout with four worms. In the lower portion of figure 4.4, the results are plotted in terms of the mean log latency of response (in seconds). Performance was better for the larger reward in the first stage, but the group shifted from the larger to the smaller reward showed no disturbance whatsoever, continuing to respond as rapidly as before the shift, and just as rapidly as a third group that continued to find the larger reward. The results suggest that instrumental learning in goldfish is different in some important way from instrumental learning in rats.

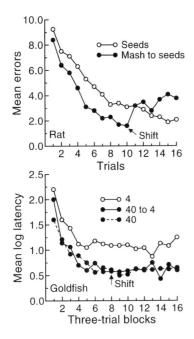

Figure 4.4
Performance of rats and goldfish shifted from preferred to less-preferred rewards compared with the performance of unshifted control groups.

It is possible, of course, that the explanation lies elsewhere. The training situations are different, the response measures are different, the rewards are different, and so also may be the differential attractiveness of the rewards. The only way to deal with such possibilities seems to be to do the same kind of experiment under systematically varied training conditions (Bitterman, 1975). It may never be possible to find conditions of whose functional equivalence for the two species we can be confident; but to the extent that the qualitative difference in their performance remains the same with variation in the training conditions, we can give less weight to the interpretation in terms of contextual variables alone. Consider an experiment in which goldfish were trained to swim in a runway rather than to strike a target, with either 40 worms or only a single worm as reward (Gonzalez et al., 1972). The 40-worm group swam more rapidly than the one-worm group, and when shifted to the smaller reward continued to swim as rapidly as before, although a group shifted from 40 worms to none soon stopped responding. With a new instrumental response and a greater discrepancy between the two reward magnitudes, the contrast effect failed again to appear.

Parallel results for the two species are obtained in experiments in which consummatory rather than instrumental responding is measured—rats licking a drinking tube, and goldfish sucking liquid food from a nipple. In each experiment, there are two groups of subjects, one fed for a brief period each day with a preferred food, and the second with a less preferred food. Both the rats and the goldfish take much more of the preferred food. Then comes a day when the animals that have been given the preferred food find the less preferred food instead. The feeding behavior of the rats is disrupted; they take much less of the less preferred food than do the rats that have known only that food (e.g., Flaherty et al., 1983)—that is, they show negative contrast. The performance of the shifted goldfish is entirely unaffected; they continue to take as much of the less preferred food as they have been taking of the preferred food (Couvillon and Bitterman, 1985).

A variation of Elliott's paradigm produces another paradoxical effect in rats—an *inverse relation* between amount of reward and resistance to extinction. One group is trained with large reward, a second with small reward, and then both groups are extinguished, which is to say that they are no longer rewarded at all. The outcome of a considerable number of such experiments with rats (e.g., Gonzalez and Bitterman, 1969) is that the large reward group performs better in training, but extinguishes more rapidly; nonreward seems to be more frustrating for rats that anticipate a large reward than for rats that anticipate only a small reward. In a runway experiment with three groups of goldfish, one trained with 40 worms, a second with four worms, and a third with a single worm, performance both in training and in extinction was directly related to amount of reward—the larger the reward, the more vigorous the performance in extinction as well as in training (Gonzalez et al., 1972).

A third paradoxical effect found repeatedly in rats is the *partial reinforcement effect* or PRE (e.g., Gonzalez and Bitterman, 1969). The procedure is to train two groups with large rewards (the effect does not occur in widely spaced trials when the reward is small)—a Consistent group rewarded on every trial, and a Partial group only on half the trials (the remaining trials unrewarded). When the reward for both groups is then discontinued, the Partial group extinguishes less rapidly than the Consistent group; that is, nonreward in extinction is less frustrating for the Partial animals, perhaps because they have already encountered it in training, where it has been followed eventually by large reward. In analogous experiments, African mouthbreeders rewarded with food pellets for striking a target (Longo and Bitterman, 1960) and goldfish rewarded with worms in a runway (Schutz and Bitterman, 1969) have failed to show the PRE.

That we are not dealing here merely with idiosyncratic properties of the species being compared is suggested by the results of analogous experiments with a variety of other animals. Negative incentive contrast has been found in consummatory experiments with opossums of two species (Papini et al., 1988), and unmistakable evidence of disturbance produced by unrealized anticipation of a preferred reward has appeared also in delayed response experiments with rhesus monkeys (Tinklepaugh, 1928) and chimpanzees (Cowles and Nissen, 1937). The PRE has been found in pigeons (Roberts et al., 1963), but neither negative contrast nor the inverse relation (Papini, 1997). The PRE also has been found in pigeons, although not in goldfish, under conditions in which the intertrial intervals were relatively short but trials with other stimuli were interpolated to control for sensory carryover (Bitterman, 1994). All three paradoxical effects have failed to appear in experiments with animals of two older vertebrate lines—turtles of two species (Papini and Ishida, 1994; Pert and Bitterman, 1970) and toads (Schmajuk et al., 1981; Muzio et al., 1992). The paradoxical effects fail also to appear in very young rats trained (necessarily) with relatively short intertrial intervals, and it is interesting in view of the dissociation evident in the pigeon data that the PRE is the earliest of the three effects to appear as the rats develop (Amsel, 1992).

This striking pattern of results, which is obscured in Macphail's (1982) treatment, suggests that instrumental learning may have undergone some important changes in common reptilian ancestors of birds and mammals, and it is regrettable that there is still so little evidence as to the nature of those changes. Funding for my own work on the problem ended rather abruptly several decades ago when peer reviewers of a new breed maligned it as a primitive Aristotelian enterprise; comparisons of rats and goldfish could not be expected to tell us anything about evolution, they advised, because rats are not descended from goldfish. In recent years, the intellectual climate has improved somewhat—nobody at least has yet felt compelled to warn the agency supporting my current work that vertebrates are not descended from honeybees— and it may be that a proposal for continuation of the vertebrate experiments would now be more favorably received, although misunderstanding lingers.

I am baffled by Shettleworth's insistence that traditional comparative psychologists, despite their "claim" to be interested in the "commonality of cognitive processes," really think of evolution as a "ladder of improvement" (1993, p. 179) and "expect that a single hierarchical ordering of mechanisms will be found with capacities possessed only by humans at the 'most complex' or 'most advanced' end" (this volume, p. 57). Whether we are judged to be disingenuous or merely confused, the implication is incorrect that the recognition both of commonality and divergence is inherently contradictory. As to improvement, it would be absurd to deny historic advance in the ability of animals to know the world, or to question the cognitive preeminence of humans. One has but to compare (at one extreme) the animals of the oldest lines that have been found in our experiments to be incapable even of simple associative learning, and (at the other) our nearest primate relatives, however impressive their perceptual and mnemonic competence, that would be hard put to design such experiments, or to evaluate the results—which is not, of course, to say that the molecular geometry of evolution is linear. Rats, as we now know, are certainly not descended from goldfish, and early Japanese horror films have prepared us well enough for the possibility that before the sun fades or the earth is destroyed by an errant comet some superordinate intelligence will appear in a crustacean. I suspect, in any case, that for the prosaic present, their confidence undiminished by an airy sermon on modularity, traditional comparative psychologists will continue to work in much the same way as before.

Summary

Comparative psychologists have been interested in perception and in the precursors of human understanding, but the main focus thus far of their work on the evolution of cognition has been on learning and memory. Conditioning experiments with a small number of widely divergent vertebrate species have yielded a lengthy list of phenomena that may reasonably be assumed on the basis of the taxonomic diversity of the subjects to be general phenomena of vertebrate learning; the results vary quantitatively with species and with training techniques, but there are common qualitative patterns that are understandable in terms of common functional principles and may well reflect the operation of homologous mechanisms of information storage and retrieval. Despite the remoteness of the evolutionary relationship, many of the vertebrate principles seem to hold also for honeybees, whose performance in conditioning experiments shows detailed similarities to that of vertebrates, although here we may suspect that the similarities are, at least in large measure, convergent. In the learning of vertebrates, there is not only extensive commonality, but evidence of broad evolutionary divergence as well; some of that evidence is provided by a set of experiments on the control of instrumental behavior by its remembered and anticipated consequences, whose results for birds and mammals are qualitatively different from those for animals of older vertebrate lines. Familiar objections to the way in which comparative psychologists have approached the problem of cognitive evolution and the conclusions to which they have been led are reviewed and evaluated.

References

Amsel A (1958) The role of frustrative nonreward in noncontinuous reward situations. Psychological Bulletin, 55: 102–119.

Amsel A (1992) Frustration theory. Cambridge: Cambridge University Press.

Bitterman ME (1967) Learning in animals. In: Contemporary approaches to psychology (Helson H, Bevan W, ed), pp 140–179. New York: D. Van Nostrand.

Bitterman ME (1975) The comparative analysis of learning. Are the laws of learning the same in all animals? Science, 188: 699–709.

Bitterman ME (1988) Vertebrate-invertebrate comparisons. In: Intelligence and evolutionary biology (Jerison HJ, Jerison IL, ed), pp 251–276. Berlin: Springer Verlag.

Bitterman ME (1994) Amsel's analysis of reward-schedule effects. Psychonomic Bulletin and Review, 1: 297–302.

Bitterman ME (1996) Comparative analysis of learning in honeybees. Animal Learning and Behavior, 24: 123–141.

Bitterman ME, Menzel R, Fietz A, Schäfer S (1983) Classical conditioning of proboscis-extension in honeybees (Apis mellifera). Journal of Comparative Psychology, 97: 107–119.

Bitterman ME, Wodinsky J, Candland DK (1958) Some comparative psychology. American Journal of Psychology, 71: 94–110.

Bush RR, Mosteller F (1951) A mathematical model for simple learning. Psychological Review, 58: 313–323.

Couvillon PA, Ablan CD, Bitterman ME (1999) Exploratory studies of inhibitory conditioning in honeybees. Journal of Experimental Psychology: Animal Behavior Processes, 25: 103–112.

Couvillon PA, Arakaki L, Bitterman ME (1997) Intramodal blocking in honeybees. Animal Learning and Behavior, 25: 277–282.

Couvillon PA, Arincorayan NM, Bitterman ME (1998) Control of performance by short-term memory in honeybees. Animal Learning and Behavior, 26: 469–474.

Couvillon PA, Bitterman ME (1982) Compound conditioning in honeybees. Journal of Comparative and Physiological Psychology, 96: 192–199.

Couvillon PA, Bitterman ME (1985) Effect of experience with a preferred food on consummatory responding for a less preferred food in goldfish. Animal Learning and Behavior, 13: 433–438.

Couvillon PA, Bitterman ME (1988) Compound-component and conditional discrimination of colors and odors by honeybees: Further tests of a continuity model. Animal Learning and Behavior, 16: 67–74.

Couvillon PA, Bitterman ME (1992) A conventional conditioning analysis of "transitive inference" in pigeons. Journal of Experimental Psychology: Animal Behavior Processes, 18: 308–310.

Cowles JT, Nissen HW (1937) Reward-expectancies in delayed-responses of chimpanzees. Journal of Comparative Psychology, 24: 345–358.

Elliott MH (1928) The effect of change of reward on the maze performance of rats. University of California Publications in Psychology, 4: 19–30.

Flaherty CF, Becker HC, Checke S (1983) Repeated successive contrast in consummatory behavior with repeated shifts in sucrose concentration. Animal Learning and Behavior, 11: 407–414.

Funayama ES, Couvillon PA, Bitterman ME (1995) Compound conditioning in honeybees: Blocking tests of the independence assumption. Animal Learning and Behavior, 23: 429–437.

Gonzalez RC, Bitterman ME (1969) Spaced-trials partial reinforcement effect as a function of contrast. Journal of Comparative and Physiological Psychology, 67: 94–103.

Gonzalez RC, Potts AK, Pitkoff K, Bitterman ME (1972) Runway performance of goldfish as a function of complete and incomplete reduction in amount of reward. Psychonomic Science, 27: 305–307.

Heyes CM (1998) Theory of mind in nonhuman primates. Behavioral and Brain Sciences, 21: 101–134.

Hull CL (1945) The place of innate individual and species differences in a natural-science theory of behavior. Psychological Review, 52: 55–60.

Klosterhalfen S, Fischer W, Bitterman ME (1978) Modification of attention in honeybees. Science, 201: 1241–1243.

Klosterhalfen S, Klosterhalfen W (1985) Conditioned taste aversion and traditional learning. Psychological Research, 47: 71–94.

Longo N, Bitterman ME (1960) The effect of partial reinforcement with spaced practice on resistance to extinction in the fish. Journal of Comparative and Physiological Psychology, 53: 169–172.

Lorenz K (1977) Behind the mirror. New York: Harcourt Brace Jovanovich.

Lowes G, Bitterman ME (1967) Reward and learning in the goldfish. Science, 157: 455–457.

Mackintosh NJ (1974) The psychology of animal learning. London: Academic Press.

Macphail EM (1982) Brain and intelligence in vertebrates. Oxford: Clarendon Press.

Muzio RN, Segura ET, Papini MR (1992) Effect of schedule and magnitude of reinforcement on instrumental learning in the toad, Bufo arenarum. Learning and Motivation, 23: 406–429.

Papini MR (1997) Role of reinforcement in spaced-trial operant learning in pigeons (Columba livia). Journal of Comparative Psychology, 111: 275–285.

Papini MR, Bitterman ME (1993) The two-test strategy in the study of inhibitory conditioning. Journal of Experimental Psychology: Animal Behavior Processes, 97: 396–403.

Papini MR, Ishida M (1994) Role of magnitude of reinforcement in spaced-trial instrumental learning in turtles (Geoclemys reevesii). Quarterly Journal of Experimental Psychology, 47B: 1–13.

Papini MR, Mustaca AE, Bitterman ME (1988) Successive negative contrast in the consummatory responding of Didelphid marsupials. Animal Learning and Behavior, 16: 53–57.

Pavlov IP (1927) Conditioned reflexes. Oxford: Oxford University Press.

Pert A, Bitterman ME (1970) Reward and learning in the turtle. Learning and Motivation, 1: 121–128.

Rescorla RA, Wagner AR (1972) A theory of Pavlovian conditioning: Variations in the effectiveness of reinforcement and nonreinforcement. In: Classical conditioning II: Current research and theory (Black AH, Prokasy WF, ed), pp 64–99. New York: Appleton-Century-Crofts.

Roberts WA, Bullock DH, Bitterman ME (1963) Resistance to extinction in the pigeon after partially reinforced instrumental training under discrete-trials conditions. American Journal of Psychology, 76: 353–365.

Schmajuk N, Segura E, Rudiaz A (1981) Reward downshift in the toad. Behavioral and Neural Biology, 28: 392–397.

Schutz SL, Bitterman ME (1969) Spaced-trials partial reinforcement effect and resistance to extinction in the goldfish. Journal of Comparative and Physiological Psychology, 68: 126–128.

Shapiro MS, Bitterman ME (1998) Intramodal competition for attention in honeybees. Psychonomic Bulletin and Review, 5: 334–338.

Shettleworth SJ (1993) Where is the comparison in comparative cognition? Alternative research programs. Psychological Science, 4: 179–184.

Simpson GG (1945) Principles of classification and a classification of mammals. Bulletin of the Museum of Natural History, 85: 1–350.

Simpson GG (1964) Organisms and molecules in evolution. Science, 146: 1535–1538.

Smith BH, Cobey S (1994) The olfactory memory of the honeybee Apis mellifera. Journal of Experimental Biology, 195: 91–108.

Sutherland NS, Mackintosh NJ (1971) Mechanisms of animal discrimination learning. New York: Academic Press.

Thorndike EL (1911) Animal intelligence: Experimental studies. New York: Macmillan.

Tinklepaugh OL (1928) An experimental study of representative factors in monkeys. Journal of Comparative Psychology, 8: 197–236.

Walker EP (1964) Mammals of the world. Baltimore, MD: Johns Hopkins University Press.

Walker JJ, Longo N, Bitterman ME (1970) The octopus in the laboratory: Handling, maintenance, training. Behavior Research Methods & Instruments, 2: 15–18.

Zhuikov AY, Couvillon PA, Bitterman ME (1994) A quantitative two-process analysis of avoidance conditioning in goldfish. Journal of Experimental Psychology: Animal Behavior Processes, 19: 342–352.

II CATEGORIZATION

The four chapters in this section discuss a fundamental issue in research on the evolution of cognition, namely, the way in which animals (including humans) categorize or represent stimuli, objects, and events in their environments. Central questions are: What are the "how rules" (Heyes, this volume) of stimulus representation? Which animals represent relations among stimuli in addition to stimulus-specific physical features? Under what conditions could animals be said to represent mental states, rather than physical features of social interactants? The first of these questions is examined most intensively in the chapters by Bateson, Mackintosh, and Delius et al. the second by Mackintosh and Delius et al. and the third by Sterelny. Tomasello's chapter, on "Causality," at the beginning of the next section, also addresses the second and third questions.

Bateson's chapter provides a commanding overview of ethological, psychological, and neurobiological research on imprinting, and makes a clear statement of what the author regards as "special" about this kind of learning. In the terms used by Heyes (this volume), he argues that imprinting has distinctive what/when rules—it typically occurs during a circumscribed period in ontogeny, is triggered by distinctive perceptual input, and has output to specialized motor systems—but the how rules through which a young bird learns the physical features of a parent are the same as those involved in other situations of perceptual learning. These how rules or "design rules" are portrayed as associative, but different from the associative mechanisms mediating Pavlovian and instrumental conditioning, learning about the causal structure of the environment. In this respect, Bateson's analysis differs from that of Mackintosh (this volume; McLaren, Kaye, and Mackintosh 1989). However, with exceptional fairness, he points out that current evidence does not decisively favor one of these associative accounts over the other.

Rather than focusing directly on the how rules of stimulus representation, Mackintosh and Delius et al. examine the question of what animals represent, stimulus-specific physical features or relations among stimuli, partly in anticipation that information about taxonomic distribution will provide hints about how rules. Delius et al. report the results of a series of his own recent experiments with pigeons, and argue robustly that they demonstrate the capacity to represent relationships of sameness and difference in these birds. Mackintosh begs to differ, finding evidence of the representation of relations in chimpanzees, corvids, and parrots, but not in pigeons. This view also contrasts with that of Tomasello, who suggests that primates alone are capable of representating relations.

This is an important debate because it has implications both for the how rules of stimulus representation, and the social function of intellect hypothesis (Dunbar, this volume; Heinrich, this volume; Sterelny, this volume; Tomasello, this volume). In simple terms, if pigeons, in addition to corvids, parrots, and primates, can represent relations, it suggests that this capacity is present in a wide range of vertebrate species, and increases the likelihood that relational representations are, or can be, formed through associative processes of some kind. Incapacity on the part of pigeons would not rule out this possibility, but it would make it more plausible that the how rules of relational representation differ from those involved in representing stimulus-specific features, something that pigeons are undoubtedly able to do. Furthermore, because corvids are not especially social creatures, and the more social species do not out-perform the others on relational learning tasks (Mackintosh, 1988, this volume), the ability to form relational representations in these birds would imply that it has not, or has not only, evolved under selection pressure from the social environment.

Sterelny's chapter may seem to be distinct from the others in this section, in both style and content, but there are strong links. He is concerned with representation, not of physical features or relations among physical features, but of mental states, and rather than discussing the how rules generating these representations, he takes a step back and specifies evidence justifying their ascription to animals. In doing so, Sterelny makes the important point that researchers (including Heyes, 1998) are often too quick to assume that representating a certain mental state, X, requires the capacity to infer, from the presence of X, other mental states that are likely to occur in the possessor of X. This requirement follows from the "inferential role" theory of meaning, but there are other coherent and respected theories of meaning in the phil-osophical literature, including one in which representations or "concepts" are iden-tified by their connections with the external world, not with one another. Pursuing this theory, Sterelny offers a general account, in terms of robustness and response breadth, of the evidential requirements for mental state represention in animals, and argues that these are met only by primates.

There are two links between Sterelny's analysis and the other chapters in this sec-tion. First, although neglected by investigators of "theory of mind," the correlational view of meaning has been applied consistently by researchers, such as Delius and Mackintosh, who want to find out how physical features of the environment are represented (Chater and Heyes, 1994). Second, their experiments, among others, raise the possibility that mental state representations, as they are defined by Sterelny, could be formed through associative processes, in the context of "acquired equivalence" experience (Delius et al., this volume). Because these processes and this kind of experience are taxonomically widespread, this, in turn, raises the possibility that mental state representations, *correlationally defined*, are formed by the members of a broad range of species.

References

Chater N, Heyes CM (1994) Animal concepts: Content and discontent. Mind and Language, 9: 209–246.

Heyes CM (1998) Theory of mind in nonhuman primates. Behavioral and Brain Sciences, 21: 101–148.

McLaren IPL, Kaye H, Mackintosh NJ (1989) An associative theory of the representation of stimuli: Applications to perceptual learning and latent inhibition. In: Parallel distributed processing: Implications of pyschology and neurobiology (Morris RGM, ed), pp 102–130. Oxford: Clarendon Press.

Mackintosh NJ (1988) Approaches to the study of animal intelligence. British Journal of Psychology, 79: 509–526.

5 What Must Be Known in Order to Understand Imprinting?

Patrick Bateson

As the result of relatively brief exposure to a particular type of object early in life, many birds and mammals will form strong and exclusive attachments to that object. This process is known as "imprinting." One particular type is known as "filial imprinting," because the object to which the young animal becomes attached is treated as a parent. Some of the characteristics of imprinting are undoubtedly due to the naïve animal searching for and responding selectively to particular stimuli. Before imprinting takes place, the young bird has clear preferences for the type of stimuli that it will subsequently learn about. It also has in place a repertoire of motor activities that facilitate the learning process and maintain proximity to the object of attachment. Learning takes place at a biologically appropriate time in the life-cycle and few would doubt that the whole process has been adapted during evolution for the kin-recognition function that it serves under natural conditions.

The image conjured up by the term imprinting is vivid and simple. At a certain stage, the wax of the young animal's brain is soft; it receives the imprint of the first conspicuous thing the animal encounters. The German term *Prägung* (translated as "imprinting") was first used by Heinroth, (1911), although Spalding (1873) had used a similar metaphor, "stamping in." Konrad Lorenz (1935), who did so much to make the phenomenon famous, liked the image because it suggests an instantaneous, irreversible process. Use of the term also led to strong claims that imprinting is quite different from associative learning (Hess, 1973). As more evidence became available, the claims were disputed and the term was held to be misleading (Bateson, 1966; Sluckin, 1972). Nevertheless, to the end of his life, Lorenz (1981) continued to treat the process as special. "Imprinting" has been retained in the literature by advocates and critics alike. (Confusingly, "imprinting" has also been used for a quite different process operating at the genomic level. The influence of one gene on another may be determined not by the dominance of the gene itself but by the sex of the parent from which it comes. See Constancia et al., 1998.)

Leaving aside the matter of whether or not the terminology is appropriate, what happens as a young animal learns the characteristics of its parent? In this chapter I shall argue that, to understand imprinting properly from a behavioral standpoint, it is not necessary to know how genes are switched on and off or any of the other intricate mechanisms of cellular machinery, interesting though such details might be. Instead, what is required is a good understanding of how the various neural subprocesses involved in learning are activated in development and how they fit together.

Early experience can also have long-lasting effects on sexual preferences, but the conditions are different from those in which the first attachments are formed. Astonishing retention of sexual preferences is found in the face of considerable sexual experience with other objects (Immelmann, 1972). However, the final hook-up between the representation of the imprinted object stored in early life and the output system controlling sexual behavior probably does not occur until much later than the original storage of the representation (Hutchison and Bateson, 1982; Bischof and Clayton, 1991; Kruijt and Meeuwissen, 1991; Oetting et al., 1995). As Bischof (1997) argues, the parallels between "sexual imprinting" and song learning in birds are striking.

Filial imprinting with a novel and conspicuous object usually occurs most readily at a particular stage of development (Bolhuis, 1991) known as the sensitive period. The range of objects that motivate and elicit social behavior is restricted by the animal's experience. When the young bird becomes familiar with one object, the likelihood of it withdrawing from dissimilar conspicuous objects increases. The first preferences formed are likely to be the ones that last, within certain constraints such as the age of the animal at its first exposure and the length of that exposure (Cherfas and Scott, 1981; Immelmann and Suomi, 1981; Bolhuis and Bateson, 1990; Cook, 1993). When a bird is well imprinted, when exposed to another object, it first withdraws, showing every sign of great alarm. By degrees this alarm habituates. Sometimes the bird starts to direct social behavior toward the new object and may become attached to it. However, if it has been well imprinted with the first object, it does not express any social behavior toward the second object—it is tame but unattached.

The sensitive period seems to be brought to an end by the formation of a social attachment (Bateson, 1987). However, even dark-reared chicks eventually are less easy to imprint than they were shortly after hatching, which may suggest that the ending of the sensitive period may not be entirely experience dependent (Parsons and Rogers, 1997).

Factors Influencing Imprinting

Many factors have relatively short-term effects on responsiveness. For example, Polt and Hess (1966) found that domestic chicks given two hours of social experience with siblings beforehand followed a moving object more strongly than did isolated birds (Lickliter and Gottlieb, 1985, 1988). Stimulation in other modalities, when presented concurrently with visual stimuli, can have a powerful motivating effect. Gottlieb

(1971) found that in domestic chicks and mallard ducklings, the sounds most effective in eliciting pursuit of a moving visual stimulus are conspecific maternal calls. Furthermore, young birds learn the characteristics of auditory stimuli played to them shortly after hatching (Gottlieb, 1988). In forming a social attachment under natural conditions, auditory signals are important in guiding the process. Ten Cate (1989) also found that in Japanese quail, the posture of a live adult female has a powerful motivating effect on the response to her by the chicks.

At one time, movement was regarded as essential in "releasing" the following response of domestic chicks and ducklings, and so in initiating the imprinting process. However, the effectiveness of the many visual stimuli used in the imprinting situation depends on such properties as their size and shape, as well as on the angle they subtend and the intensity and wavelength of light they reflect. Moreover, the rates at which these variables change are also important—hence the undoubted effectiveness of movement and flicker.

The bird clearly responds to a pattern of stimulation, and characterization of the most effective stimulus must be cast in terms of compounds. Gottlieb and his colleagues (Johnston and Gottlieb, 1981; Lickliter and Gottlieb, 1985) argue that the conditions under which imprinting is studied in the laboratory are so impoverished and artificial that the results can give a seriously misleading view of what happens in the wild. However, it does not follow that experimental analysis is, therefore, useless or that different neural systems are studied in laboratory and natural conditions. A car that is filled with low-octane fuel and runs badly does not become another car on that account. Nevertheless, the well-known sensitive period curves for chicks and ducklings, with their peaks within the first day after hatching, are probably misleading. Most processing and information storage about the mother probably takes place at least a day later under natural conditions.

The work on predispositions has increasingly focused on stimulus features found in the natural world. Strong evidence suggests that head and neck features are particularly attractive to domestic chicks (Horn and McCabe, 1984; Johnson and Horn, 1988).

The discovery of the head and neck detector was important because it suggested a dissociation of the analysis subsystem required for imprinting from the one involved in the recognition learning. Under laboratory conditions, the necessary feature detectors take longer to develop than do the ones driven by flashing lights and movement (Horn and McCabe, 1984; Bolhuis et al., 1985; Johnson et al., 1985; Bolhuis, 1989). The dissociation, which had been anticipated (Bateson, 1981), was confirmed by the analysis that led to the identification of a specific region of the brain concerned with storing a representation of imprinting objects.

Identification of a Neural Site for Imprinting

An array of different neurobiological techniques have implicated the intermediate and medial part of the hyperstriatum ventrale (IMHV) on both sides of the brain as being sites of a neural representation of the imprinting object (Horn, 1985, 1991, 1998). When evidence is open to a variety of interpretations, greater confidence in a particular explanation may be achieved by tackling the problem from a number of different angles. Each piece of evidence obtained by the different approaches may be ambiguous, but the ambiguities are different in each case. When the whole body of evidence is considered, therefore, much greater confidence may be placed on a particular meaning. An analogy is trying to locate on a map the position of a visible mountain top. One compass bearing is usually not enough. Two bearings from different angles provide a much better fix, and three bearings give the most reliable position for the top.

An important component of the triangulation procedure is to exploit the asymptotic character of learning: a phase of rapid change is followed by one of much slower change. Therefore, animals at the rapid phase will be likely to show greater activity in brain sites specifically involved in learning than those that have moved onto the slower phase, even though many other aspects of the animals' experience and activity match. Animals may be prepared in advance by under-training them or over-training them on the task in question. This technique was successfully exploited when identifying the role of IMHV as a site for the neural representation of the imprinted object in imprinted (Bateson et al., 1973; Horn et al., 1979).

Chicks that have had both left and right IMHV removed surgically are unable to imprint; if bilateral lesions are placed immediately after imprinting, the birds show no recognition of the imprinted object (see Horn, 1985). Nevertheless, these lesioned chicks will show a preference for a stimulus that has a head and neck feature over one that does not, thereby dissociating the analysis component of the imprinting process from the recognition component. The lesioning experiments also dissociated recognition learning from learning involving external reward. Chicks will learn a visual discrimination rewarded with heat after bilateral removal of IMHV (Cipolla-Net et al., 1982; Honey et al., 1995). They will also learn to press a pedal when rewarded by the view of an imprinted stimulus, even though they do not go on to learn the characteristics of that stimulus (Johnson and Horn, 1986).

Many of the detailed cellular and molecular events occurring in IMHV are beginning to be worked out and the connections between IMHV and other structures have been described (Horn, 1998). However, the links between imprinting and other learning processes occurring in parallel with it are still poorly understood.

Different Learning Rules

The use of lesions sited in IMHV is consistent with the view that imprinting might be separated from rewarded learning on functional grounds. Many of the transactions between animals and their environments involve elements of both perceptual learning, occurring without external reward, and of event-relating learning that depends on external reward (or punishment). These components of an overall change in behavior may be seen as subprocesses that are normally used in conjunction, but may depend on different rules (Bateson, 1990; Hollis et al., 1991).

When characterizing classical conditioning, Dickinson (1980) used a definition that relates to the utility of the learning process. The learning process serves to uncover the causal structure of the environment. The jobs of learning to predict and to control the environment are not the same as that of learning to categorize it. At the physiological level, similar if not identical mechanisms *may* be used to achieve these different jobs. At the behavioral level, however, different design rules would be plausible. Detecting causal structure may require classification, but establishing a classification does not involve an association of cause with effect.

In uncovering causality, detecting order is usually crucial. If the supposed cause follows an event, then the necessary contingency is likely to be missing. By contrast, when establishing a category, temporal contiguity may be important, but the order in which the features occur is not. Undoubtedly, under some experimental arrangements, a backward contingency may be extracted in classical conditioning. This raises two possibilities: the regularity of an association might allow the computation of a causal link even when the "cause" appears to follow the "effect"; alternatively, when backward conditioning does not occur, the impact of a biologically significant event might distract the subject's attention from events that follow.

The thrust of some theoretical approaches has been to explain perceptual learning and event-relating learning processes in the same terms (McLaren et al., 1989). Also, well-tried methodologies developed from the study of conditioning have been applied to imprinting itself (Abercombie and James, 1961; Zolman, 1982; Bolhuis et al., 1990; de Vos and Bolhuis, 1990; van Kampen and de Vos, 1995). Because neither the theory nor the experimental evidence has decisively suggested a unitary mechanism, I shall argue the case for learning processes that are governed by different rules.

In the real world, a complicated object often presents a substantially different set of features from one view than it does from another. In many circumstances, an animal would benefit from treating these different sets as though they were equivalent (Bateson, 1973). Consider the problem facing a bird that has to gather information about the front, side, and back views of its mother. All these views are physically distinct, and they may also take on different appearances when viewed at different distances. Information from two separate arrays of features may be combined into a single representation when the two arrays occur in the same context or within a short time of each other (Bateson and Chantrey, 1972).

Chantrey (1974) varied the time between the onset of presentation of one imprinted object and the onset of presentation of another, and subsequently required domestic chicks to discriminate between the two familiar objects in order to receive a food reward. If the objects were presented five or more minutes apart, the birds learned to discriminate between the two objects more quickly than those in the control group that had not been exposed to these two objects. However, when the two objects were presented 30 seconds or less apart, the imprinted birds took longer than the control group to learn the discrimination.

Circumstances are likely to arise when elements of a compound stimulus presented in rapid succession are processed separately. Stewart et al. (1977) were only able to obtain a classification-together effect when they replicated Chantrey's experimental conditions exactly. When they used features less salient than color, or presented the stimuli in different places, they did not get the effect—which, they argued, was fragile. Nevertheless, the point remains that when the elements of a compound are treated by an animal as part of a whole, the order of presentation does not matter. I shall return to the fragility of the effect later.

Honey et al. (1993), using a different technique than Chantrey, double-imprinted chicks and then required them to discriminate between the two imprinted stimuli. In the imprinting regime, the birds were either given alternate exposures with a mean interexposure interval of 14 seconds—the Mixed condition—or they were exposed to periodic exposures to one stimulus and then after a gap of two hours to periodic exposures to the other—the Separate condition. The pattern of imprinting was otherwise the same and the total exposure to the two stimuli was identical in the two conditions. The birds imprinted under the Mixed condition took significantly longer to learn the heat-rewarded visual discrimination than the chicks exposed under the Separate condition. The explanation is that, when stimuli are presented in alternation close together in time, they are classified together; if the birds are subsequently required to learn the discrimination, they first have to disaggregate the two representations before they are able to master the task.

A Model of Imprinting

In order to understand more fully the classification-together effect, it is helpful to have a model of what might be happening. I shall outline one developed by Gabriel

Horn and myself (Bateson and Horn, 1994). The first step in the model simulates detection of features in a stimulus presented to a young bird. Aspects of the stimulus that the bird is predisposed to find attractive are picked out at this stage. The second step involves comparison between what has already been experienced and the current input. Before imprinting takes place, no comparison is involved. Once it occurs, recognition of what is familiar and what is novel is crucial. Finally, the third stage involves control of the various motor patterns involved in executing filial behavior. The behavioral scaffolding for the imprinting process is provided by a direct link between the Analysis and Executive systems.

Figure 5.1 shows a simplified version of the architecture of the Bateson and Horn (1994) model. All modules in the Analysis System are initially linked to all modules in the Recognition System that, in turn, are linked to all modules in the Executive System, only one of which is shown here. Initial strengths of links are indicated by the thickness of the lines. All modules in the Analysis System are also linked at maximum strength directly through a By-Pass to the module in the Executive System that controls filial behavior (such as approach and following). The starting condition is shown first (figure 5.1a). The strengths of linkages between modules after the model has been exposed to a stimulus that activated Analysis module, A1, is shown next (figure 5.1b). The spontaneous excitability in the Recognition module, R2, happened to be higher than that in R1 at the time the input from A1 arrived and the activity in R1 was inhibited. The strengthening rule is that modules are conjointly active. The weakening rule is that the upstream module is inactive when the downstream module is active. The completed process is shown in figure 5.1c.

The model can readily perform a classification-together process by retaining the excitability of the Recognition modules for a finite period after they had been activated. If a second set of features are presented in alternation with the first, the level of residual excitation in the Recognition modules is critical in determining whether the two stimuli are subsequently represented in the same module. The degree of overlap in features between the two stimuli is also critical. If the overlap is high, the probability of the two stimuli sharing a Recognition module is also high, even when residual excitation from previous stimulation is zero. Conversely, when the overlap of features is low, the probability of sharing the same Recognition module is low, even with maximum levels of residual excitation.

The model also provides a ready explanation for some new empirical evidence (Bolhuis and Honey, 1994, 1998; Honey and Bolhuis, 1997). When the maternal call of the domestic hen accompanies the presentation of a visual stimulus, the domestic chick is more responsive and develops a stronger preference for the visual stimulus. However, if the auditory stimulus is played in the absence of the visual before the

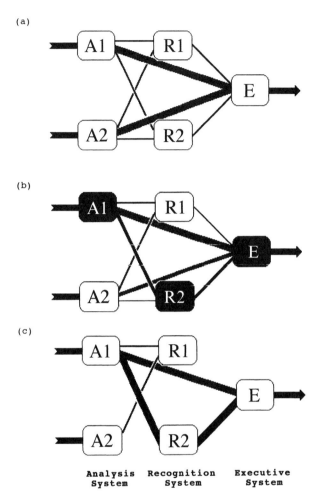

Figure 5.1
Simplified architecture of Bateson and Horn's (1994) model for imprinting. All modules in the Analysis System are initially linked to all modules in the Recognition System, which, in their turn, are linked to all modules in the Executive System, only one of which is shown here. Initial strengths of links are indicated by the thickness of the lines. All modules in the Analysis System are also linked at maximum strength directly through a By-Pass to the module in the Executive System that controls filial behaviour (such as approach and following). The starting condition is shown in panel (a). Panel (b) shows the strengths of linkages between modules after the model has been exposed to a stimulus that activated Analysis module, A1. The spontaneous excitability in the Recognition module, R2, happened to be higher than that in R1 at the time that the input from A1 arrived; activity in R1 was inhibited. The strengthening rule is that modules are conjointly active. The weakening rule is that the upstream module is inactive when the downstream module is active. The completed process is shown in panel (c).

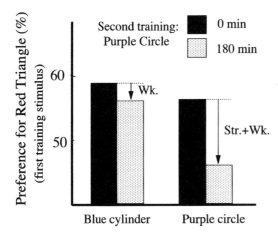

Figure 5.2
Results of an experiment by Griffiths (1998) in which domestic chicks were imprinted with a moving red triangle for 120 minutes. One group was given no further imprinting while the other was imprinted with a moving purple circle for a further 180 min. At the end of imprinting, chicks were either given a choice between the red triangle and a novel blue cylinder or between the red triangle and the purple circle. In the first test, reduction in the preference for the red triangle as the result of imprinting with the purple circle is attributed to a weakening of the control by the red triangle. In the second test, the reduction is attributed to both the weakening of control by the red cylinder and the strengthening of the control by the purple circle.

compound stimulus, the preference for the visual stimulus is weaker. From the standpoint of animal learning, an even more striking result is that if the auditory stimulus is played on its own after the compound, the preference for the visual stimulus is also weaker than when the postcompound exposure was omitted. Somewhat similar results have been obtained in other contexts (e.g., Dwyer et al., 1998) and have been referred to as "retrospective revaluation." In terms of the Bateson and Horn model, playing the auditory stimulus on its own weakens the link between the Analysis modules processing the features of the visual system and the Recognition system. This is because the downstream modules are active when the upstream modules are inactive.

The strengthening and weakening aspects of imprinting have been explored further by Daniel Griffiths in his Ph.D. dissertation (Griffiths, 1998). Chicks were exposed for 120 minutes to a moving red triangle. Half of them were then exposed for a further 180 minutes to a moving purple circle, at the end of which their preference for the red triangle was compared with the purple circle or with a novel stimulus, a moving blue cylinder. These preferences were compared with chicks that were not given a second period of exposure with the purple circle (figure 5.2). In terms of the

Bateson and Horn model, the reduction in preference for the red triangle after exposure to the purple circle is due to both a strengthening between the Analysis modules processing the purple circle and the Recognition system and a weakening between the Analysis modules processing the red triangle and the Recognition system. The extent of weakening alone may be obtained by comparing the birds given a choice between the red triangle and the blue cylinder after no further exposure or after exposure to the purple circle for 180 minutes.

Not too much should be made of the calculation of the strengthening to weakening ratio because it is difficult to allow for generalization and for the inevitable non-linearities in the underlying processes. However, throwing caution to the winds, a ratio of 4.3:1 for strengthening to weakening is obtained from the Griffiths data, which is close to the Bateson and Horn guess of 4:1. It is not for me to promote other neural net models of perceptual learning that might be able to cope well with these data (e.g., McLaren, et al., 1989; O'Reilly and Johnson, 1994). Their interest lies in showing how a model generates an experiment that allows estimating parameter values in the model.

Optimal Time Intervals

I have dwelled on some of the successes of the Bateson and Horn model. I want now to consider an interesting failure. In the Mixed/Separate design that was used to replicate the Chantrey result, a Mixed presentation of a purple circle and a red triangle during imprinting led to significantly poorer performance than a Separate presentation in the heat-rewarded visual discrimination test between the purple circle and red triangle (Honey et al., 1993). However, the result was inverted when the strong purple feature was shared by the stimuli and the stimuli were a purple circle and a purple triangle. Now the Mixed presentation showed a significantly better performance than the Separate presentation (Honey et al., 1994).

The combined results are summarized in figure 5.3. The Bateson and Horn model anticipated that two stimuli sharing a highly attractive feature would be more likely to be represented in the same Recognition module, particularly after prolonged exposure to one of the stimuli. This is because a strong link from the Analysis module responding to the high stimulus value feature, established during exposure to the first stimulus, increases the likelihood that the Recognition module responding most strongly to the first stimulus will also respond most strongly to the second stimulus. However, the effect of the Mixed condition using a purple circle and a purple triangle was not readily explained by the Bateson and Horn model.

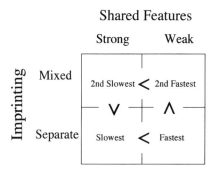

Figure 5.3
Summary of four double imprinting experiments with domestic chicks in which exposure to the two stimuli was either "mixed" or "separate" and the stimuli either shared a strongly attractive feature in common (color) or they shared relatively weak features (such as the pattern of movement). After imprinting, the chicks were required to discriminate between the stimuli with which they had been imprinted. The chicks given the separate imprinting condition in which the shared features of the stimuli were relatively weak learned the discrimination most quickly. The chicks that had been given the separate condition in which the stimuli shared a strong feature learned the discrimination most slowly.

The Honey et al. (1994) experiment was repeated with two naturalistic stimuli, a side view and a back view of a jungle fowl. This time a control was included that had not been imprinted with the two stimuli. Once again, in discrimination learning the Mixed presentation gave rise to significantly better performance than the Separate presentation, which was if anything marginally worse than not having had experience with either stimuli (Honey and Bateson, 1996).

The Bateson and Horn model can be modified to cope with these results when an additional feature is added. Supposing that some habituation occurs in the Analysis modules, then the shared features of the stimuli will habituate more than the non-shared features. As a result, in the Mixed condition, the nonshared features will stand out more relative to each other than in the Separate condition. This effect has to be superimposed on some residual activity in the Recognition system. If such residual activity was set to decay more rapidly than the dishabituation of analysis modules, the revised model simulated the empirical data. As the time between the presentations of the two imprinting stimuli was increased, the likelihood of them being classified together started high, then declined, and then rose again.

It is an empirical matter whether decay of the inferred residual activity and recovery of inferred habituation have different time courses. Therefore, a further experiment was carried out, varying the interval between presentation to a mean of 14 seconds or a mean of 28 seconds. The results of this experiment showed that doubling the time interval led to improved performance in discrimination learning (Honey and

Bateson, 1996). This supported the notion that residual activity declines more rapidly than the effects of habituation decays, leading to a lowered probability of classification together. The probability then climbs again as the powerful shared feature detector dishabituates and, when reactivated, pulls the representations of the two stimuli together.

How general are these results? If they represent a universal feature of perceptual learning, the prediction is a strong one. Perceptual learning will improve if the stimuli that are to be discriminated between are presented fairly close together in time, but the gap between them must not be too short. An optimal time interval between presentations is called for.

Links Between Imprinting and Rewarded Learning

The possibility of transfer of training after imprinting means that the neural system underlying recognition learning is connected with the one underlying rewarded learning in the intact animal. Chicks show a strong preference for the imprinting object immediately after imprinting. In contrast, when transfer of training in heat-rewarded discrimination learning is tested immediately after imprinting, the rate of learning the discrimination is unaffected by imprinting. However, if discrimination learning between a purple circle and a red triangle is delayed by six hours, then imprinting does affect the rate of learning, with those given the Mixed condition learning significantly more slowly than the ones imprinted under the Separate condition (Honey et al., 1995). Although the memory required for recognition is formed quickly, the memory sustaining transfer of training is not.

Lesion studies suggest that another representation of the imprinting stimulus (known as S') is consolidated in another region of the brain about six hours after imprinting (McCabe, 1991). The formation or the use of this representation can be prevented by placing a lesion in the right IMHV soon after imprinting. If the lesion is delayed for more than six hours, the imprinted chicks retain their preference. Moreover, the representation may be used in the heat-rewarded discrimination learning task (Honey et al., 1995). The lateralization of the processes involved in forming the second store are of great interest because of the strong evidence accumulated over many years that many processes involved in the visual control of behavior are lateralized (Andrew, 1991; Vallortigara and Andrew, 1991, 1994). The dynamics of changes taking place after imprinting have certain similarities to what happens when humans learn about faces, because the left prefrontal cortex is activated during encoding new memories for faces, whereas the right prefrontal cortex is activated during later recognition of those faces (Haxby et al., 1996). In view of the transfer of training studies with IMHV-lesioned chicks (Honey et al., 1995), the second store formed after imprinting might provide a point of contact between imprinting and rewarded learning.

Why are the two independent memory systems needed? Possibly because the associative process dependent on external reward requires different rules than the simple recognition process involved in imprinting. Why should the systems be linked? The biological advantages of using the same information in a variety of contexts can be great. In the case of the young bird, the mother's actions may prove extremely important in predicting where and when it can find crucial resources for itself. When the mother gives signals such as the food call that the chicks respond to without learning, all the chicks hear this and they are in competition with each other. So capacity for transfer of training is likely to pay the individual possessing such a mechanism.

Conclusion

Imprinting is an example of tightly constrained learning. Paradoxically, its general interest lies in its particularity. The predispositions to respond to particular features and give particular responses to the stimulus are central in the case of imprinting. Mechanisms that change as a result of experience are obviously dependent on mechanisms that developed before imprinting has taken place. Moreover, the mechanisms that existed before imprinting occurred are sometimes changed by the experience and sometimes not. In other examples of learning with different functions and involved in different motivational systems, the interdependence is less obvious, but present, nonetheless.

Perhaps the most important conclusion from the behavioral work is the need to think of a given phenomenon in terms of a series of subprocesses. Bateson and Horn (1994) referred to these subprocesses as "modules." Clearly such usage can cause confusion because "module" is a word that has come to have as many meanings as "instinct" (see the chapter by Shettleworth). As with instinct, belief in the validity of one meaning does not imply belief in the validity of other meanings. For example, many believe that the subsystems involved in imprinting have evolved as the result of a Darwinian process of evolution (which is one meaning of module). It does not follow that the subsystems are "hardwired" and do not change in the course of individual development (which is another meaning of module). Nor does it follow that the subsystems are dedicated to one function (which is yet another meaning).

Despite the ambiguities, the concept of a modular subsystem goes some way toward reconciling the alternative perspectives represented by Shettleworth in her chapter in this book and Bitterman in his. Bitterman clearly recognizes the need to explain differences in the ways in which animals learn in terms of variation in the perceptual and motivational mechanisms used in the various contexts in which learning occurs. Looked at as a whole, the properties of the entire system are different, allowing for the evolution of differences in function. Shettleworth's point is that whole learning systems may have different uses. Nonetheless, the subsystems used in one learning context may also be used in another. To paraphrase Bitterman's point in my own terms, the subsystems involved in storage of a representation of the external world may operate in the same way. However, I differ from Bitterman in supposing that representations of causality and representations of perceptual categories are achieved in different ways.

The work on imprinting has focused on the analysis of the features of the stimuli that start off the formation of the social attachment, the establishment of a representation of that combination of features, and the linking of such a representation to the system controlling social behavior. The common denominator with a great many other learning processes is creating a representation of the object to which the animal has been exposed. Representations must be formed during exploration, latent learning, and, indeed, virtually every transaction that a complicated animal has with its environment. The inference is, though, that different subprocesses have different underlying rules for plastic change. Contiguity of the various elements is likely to be important in forming a category, whereas contingency is crucial in learning dependent on external reward.

Inferences about the subprocesses involved in an animal's overall transaction with its environment are currently being examined at the neural level. The behavioral theories undoubtedly make assumptions about the nervous system, and these assumptions may prove to be false. As the neural understanding grows, the enquiry has to return to the behavioral level so that the parts may be reassembled and, if necessary, new behavioral experiments may be done. The return flow of ideas from lower to higher levels of analysis seems a much more attractive and plausible picture of collaboration among disciplines than that of relentless reductionism in which the behavioral people hand a problem to the neural people who, having done their stuff, hand it on to the molecular people.

Summary

A long debate has revolved around whether imprinting is special. The timing of the process, the features that most readily trigger learning, and the motor systems that are linked to representations stored as a result of learning are all specific to the functional context of forming a social attachment to one or both parents. The underlying neural mechanisms might be the same as those involved in other learning processes. Nevertheless, it is worth asking whether the rules involved in learning about the causal structure of the environment are different from those used in perceptual learning (of which imprinting is a special case). Time plays a different role in classical or instrumental conditioning than it does in perceptual learning. The order in which different events are experienced may matter a lot when one event causes the other. However, the order does not matter at all when the experiences are different views of the same object. Some behavioral and physiological evidence from studies of imprinting in chicks suggests that these two broad functions are served by different subprocesses but that the subprocesses are, nevertheless, in touch with each other.

Acknowledgments

I am grateful to Rob Honey, Nick Mackintosh, and the editors for their comments on earlier versions of the manuscript. I also thank Dan Griffiths for allowing me to refer to his unpublished data.

References

Abercombie B, James H (1961) The stability of the domestic chick's response to visual flicker. Animal Behavior, 9: 205–212.

Andrew RJ, ed (1991). Neural and behavioural plasticity. Oxford: Oxford University Press.

Bateson PPG (1966) The characteristics and context of imprinting. Biological Review, 4l: 177–220.

Bateson PPG (1973) Internal influences on early learning in birds. In: Constraints on learning: Limitations and predispositions (Hinde RA, Stevenson Hinde J, ed), pp 101–116. London: Academic Press.

Bateson PPG (1981) Control of sensitivity to the environment during development. In: Behavioral development (Immelmann K, Barlow GW, Petrinovich L, Main M, ed), pp 432–453. Cambridge: Cambridge University Press.

Bateson PPG (1987) Imprinting as a process of competitive exclusion. In: Imprinting and cortical plasticity (Rauschecker JP, Marler P, ed), pp 151–168. New York: Wiley.

Bateson PPG (1990) Is imprinting such a special case? Philosphical Transactions of the Royal Society B, 329: 125–131.

Bateson PPG, Chantrey DF (1972) Discrimination learning: Retardation in monkeys and chicks previously exposed to both stimuli. Nature, 237: 173–l74.

Bateson PPG, Horn G (1994) Imprinting and recognition memory—a neural-net model. Animal Behaviour, 48: 695–715.

Bateson PPG, Rose SPR, Horn G (1973) Imprinting: Lasting effects on uracil incorporation into chick brain. Science, 181: 576–578.

Bischof HJ (1997) Song learning, filial imprinting, and sexual imprinting: Three variations of a common theme? Biomedical Research Tokyo, 18: 133–146.

Bischof HJ, Clayton N (1991) Stabilization of sexual preferences by sexual experience. Behavior, 118: 144–155.

Bolhuis JJ (1989). The development and stability of filial preferences in the chick. Ph.D. dissertation, University of Groningen.

Bolhuis JJ (1991) Mechanisms of avian imprinting: A review. Biological Review, 66: 303–345.

Bolhuis JJ, Bateson P (1990) The importance of being first: A primacy effect in filial imprinting. Animal Behaviour, 40: 472–483.

Bolhuis JJ, de Vos GJ, Kruijt JP (1990) Filial imprinting and associative learning. Quarterly Journal of Experimental Psychology B Comparative Physiology and Psychology, 42: 313–329.

Bolhuis JJ, Honey RC (1994) Within-event learning during filial imprinting. Journal of Experimental Psychology: Animal Behavior Processes, 20: 240–248.

Bolhuis JJ, Honey RC (1998) Imprinting, learning and development: From behaviour to brain and back. Trends in Neurosciences, 21: 306–311.

Bolhuis JJ, Johnson MH, Horn G (1985) Effects of early experience on the development of filial preferences in the domestic chick. Developmental Psychobiology, 18: 299–308.

Chantrey DF (1974) Stimulus preexposure and discrimination learning by domestic chicks: Effect of varying interstimulus time. Journal of Comparative and Physiological Psychology, 87: 517–525.

Cherfas JJ, Scott AM (1981) Impermanent reversal of filial imprinting. Animal Behaviour, 29: 301.

Cipolla-Neto J, Horn G, McCabe BJ (1982) Hemispheric asymmetry and imprinting: The effect of sequential lesions to the hyperstriatum ventrale. Experimental Brain Research, 48: 22–27.

Constancia M, Pickard B, Kelsey G, Reik W (1998) Imprinting mechanisms. Genome Research, 8: 881–900.

Cook SE (1993) Retention of primary preferences after secondary filial imprinting. Animal Behaviour, 46: 405–407.

de Vos GJ, Bolhuis JJ (1990) An investigation into blocking of filial imprinting in the chick during exposure to a compound stimulus. Quarterly Journal of Experimental Psychology B Comparative Physiology and Psychology, 42: 289–312.

Dickinson A (1980) Contemporary animal learning theory. Cambridge: Cambridge University Press.

Dwyer DM, Mackintosh NJ, Boakes RA (1998) Simultaneous activation of the representations of absent cues results in the formation of an excitatory association between them. Journal of Experimental Psychology: Animal Behavior Processes, 24: 163–171.

Gottlieb G (1971) Development of species identification in birds. Chicago: University of Chicago Press.

Gottlieb G (1988) Development of species identification in ducklings: XV Individual auditory recognition. Developmental Psychobiology, 21: 509–522.

Griffiths DP (1998). The dynamics of stimulus representation during filial imprinting: Behavioural analysis and modelling. Ph.D. Dissertation, University of Cambridge.

Haxby JV, Ungerleider LG, Horwitz B, Maisog JM, Rapoport SI, Grady CL (1996) Face encoding and recognition in the human brain. Proceedings of the National Academy of Science USA, 93: 922–927.

Heinroth O (1911) Beiträge zur Biologie, namentlich Ethologie und Psychologie, der Anatiden. In: Verh. 5 Int. Orn. Kongr., pp 589–702.

Hess EH (1973) Imprinting. New York: Van Nostrand Reinhold.

Hollis KL, ten Cate C, Bateson P (1991) Stimulus representation: A subprocess of imprinting and conditioning. Journal of Comparative Psychology, 105: 307–317.

Honey RC, Bateson P (1996) Stimulus comparison and perceptual-learning—further evidence and evaluation from an imprinting procedure. Quarterly Journal of Experimental Psychology B Comparative Physiology and Psychology, 49: 259–269.

Honey RC, Bateson P, Horn G (1994) The role of stimulus comparison in perceptual learning: An investigation with the domestic chick. Quarterly Journal of Experimental Psychology B Comparative Physiology and Psychology, 47: 83–103.

Honey RC, Bolhuis JJ (1997) Imprinting, conditioning, and within-event learning. Quarterly Journal of Experimental Psychology B Comparative Physiology and Psychology, 50: 97–110.

Honey RC, Horn G, Bateson P (1993) Perceptual-learning during filial imprinting—evidence from transfer of training studies. Quarterly Journal of Experimental Psychology B Comparative Physiology and Psychology, 46: 253–269.

Honey RC, Horn G, Bateson P, Walpole M (1995) Functionally distinct memories for imprinting stimuli: Behavioral and neural dissociations. Behavioral Neurosciences, 109: 689–698.

Horn G (1985) Memory, imprinting, and the brain. Oxford: Clarendon Press.

Horn G (1991) Cerebral function and behaviour investigated through a study of filial imprinting. In: The development and integration of behaviour (Bateson P, ed), pp 121–148. Cambridge: Cambridge University Press.

Horn G (1998) Visual imprinting and the neural mechanisms of recognition memory. Trends in Neurosciences, 21: 300–305.

Horn G, McCabe BJ (1984) Predispositions and preferences. Effects on imprinting of lesions to the chick brain. Animal Behaviour, 32: 288–292.

Horn G, McCabe BJ, Bateson PPG (1979) An autoradiographic study of the chick brain after imprinting. Brain Research, 168: 361–373.

Hutchison RE, Bateson P (1982) Sexual imprinting in male Japanese quail: The effects of castration at hatching. Developmental Psychobiology, 15: 471–477.

Immelmann K (1972) Sexual and other long-term aspects of imprinting in birds and other species. Advances in the Study of Behavior, 4: 147–174.

Immelmann K, Suomi SJ (1981) Sensitive phases in development. In: Behavioral development (Immelmann K, Barlow GW, Petrinovich L, Main M, ed), pp 395–431. Cambridge: Cambridge University Press.

Johnson MH, Bolhuis J, Horn G (1985) Interaction between acquired preferences and developing predispositions in an imprinting situation. Animal Behaviour, 33: 1000–1006.

Johnson MH, Horn G (1986) Dissociation between recognition memory and associative learning by a restricted lesion to the chick forebrain. Neuropsychologia, 24: 329–340.

Johnson MH, Horn G (1988) Development of filial preferences in dark-reared chicks. Animal Behaviour, 36: 675–683.

Johnston TD, Gottlieb G (1981) Development of visual species identification in ducklings: What is the role of imprinting? Animal Behaviour, 29: 1082–1099.

Kruijt JP, Meeuwissen GB (1991) Sexual preferences of male zebra finches: Effects of early and adult experince. Animal Behaviour, 42: 91–102.

Lickliter R, Gottlieb G (1985) Social interaction with siblings is necessary for the visual imprinting of species-specific maternal preference in ducklings. Journal of Comparative Psychology, 99: 371–379.

Lickliter R, Gottlieb G (1988) Social specificity: Interaction with own species is necessary to foster species-specific maternal preference in ducklings. Developmental Psychobiology, 21: 311–321.

Lorenz K (1935) Der Kumpan in der Umwelt des Vogels. Journal of Ornithology, 83: 137–213, 289–413.

Lorenz KZ (1981) The foundations of ethology. New York: Springer-Verlag.

McCabe BJ (1991) Hemispheric asymmetry of learning-induced changes. In: Neural and behavioural plasticity (Andrew RJ, ed), pp 262–276. Oxford: Oxford University Press.

McLaren IPL, Kaye H, Mackintosh NJ (1989) An associative theory of the representation of stimuli: Application to perceptual learning and latent inhibition. In: Parallel distributed processing—implications for psychology and neurobiology (Morris RGM, ed), pp 102–130. Oxford: Oxford University Press.

O'Reilly RC, Johnson MH (1994) Object recognition and sensitive periods—a computational analysis of visual imprinting. Neural Computation, 6: 357–389.

Oetting S, Prove E, Bischof HJ (1995) Sexual imprinting as a 2-stage process—mechanisms of information-storage and stabilization. Animal Behaviour, 50: 393–403.

Parsons CH, Rogers LJ (1997) Pharmacological extension of the sensitive period for imprinting in Gallus domesticus. Physiology and Behavior, 62: 1303–1310.

Polt JM, Hess EH (1966) Effects of social experience on the following response in chicks. Journal of Comparative and Physiological Psychology, 61: 268–270.

Sluckin W (1972) Imprinting and early learning, 2nd edition. London: Methuen.

Spalding DA (1873) Instinct with original observations on young animals. Macmillan's Magazine, 27: 282–293.

Stewart DJ, Capretta PJ, Cooper AJ, Littlefield VM (1977) Learning in domestic chicks after exposure to both discriminanda. Journal of Comparative and Physiological Psychology, 91: 1095–1109.

ten Cate C (1989) Stimulus movement, hen behavior and filial imprinting in Japanese quail (Coturnix coturnix japonica). Ethology, 82: 287–306.

Vallortigara G, Andrew RJ (1991) Lateralization of response by chicks to change in a model partner. Animal Behaviour, 41: 187–194.

Vallortigara G, Andrew RJ (1994) Differential involvement of right and left hemisphere in individual recognition in the domestic chick. Behavioural Processes, 33: 41–57.

van Kampen HS, de Vos GJ (1995) A study of blocking and overshadowing in filial imprinting. Quarterly Journal of Experimental Psychology B Comparative Physiology and Psychology, 48: 346–356.

Zolman JF (1982) Ontogeny of learning. In: Perspectives in ethology, vol. 5: Ontogeny (Bateson PPG, Klopfer PH, ed), pp 275–323. New York: Plenum Press.

6 Stimulus Equivalencies Through Discrimination Reversals

Juan D. Delius, Masako Jitsumori, and Martina Siemann

The sensory systems of advanced animals frequently input more stimulus information into the nervous system than the motor system can possibly output as behavior patterns. This bottleneck demands a drastic information reduction. Two types of reduction can be distinguished: selective attention involving behavioral context-dependent information censoring (as when during sexual behavior food stimuli are usually not reacted to); and categorization, a pooling into fewer response outputs (as when different foods all elicit the same ingestive response). Here we are concerned with processes underlying this latter kind of information reduction, that is, how the nervous system manages to classify stimuli so that they result in a restricted number of behaviors.

In human psychology, such information pooling has been much studied under the heading of concept formation, where the responses of interest have been words, which through suitable experience, come to correspond semantically to collections of stimuli (Sloman and Rips, 1998). There are several theories about the formation of concepts but no single one has emerged as being uniquely correct (Fodor, 1998). The deviousness of the human mind at conceiving named categories exceeds any succinct hypothesis that can be put to paper. Consider the terms male and female as applied to organisms from algae to humans and to objects such as the sun and the moon. "Le soleil" and "la lune," "die Sonne" and "der Mond" are conversely male and female to franco- and germanophone people. Most theories assume that the stimuli that come to be categorized together do so on the basis of perceptual similarities, either by simply being neighbors along a physical dimension such as size or wavelength, or by sharing some physical features such as feathers or legs. The contribution of less immediate similarities of stimuli or items, such as the ability to fly or to kill, or whatever confers genders to the sun and the moon, have also been considered theoretically but have hardly been examined empirically. A stimulus categorization by these kind of functional attributes interests us here, though not so much in humans as in pigeons.

The ability of pigeons to learn to distinguish sets of stimuli that are physically similar within sets and physically different between sets (for example, slides containing humans or not containing humans) in a directly perceivable way as belonging to different categories (as being worth or not worth pecking for food returns, for example), and the competence to then spontaneously generalize this discrimination to novel but still correspondingly similar and different stimuli without additional training, was first established by Herrnstein and Loveland in 1964. Analogous results have since been replicated with a wide variety of stimuli (e.g., Lubow, 1974; Delius, 1992). Pigeons have proven not only capable of categorizing pictures of natural objects but also able to categorize artificial scenes such as impressionist and cubist paintings (Watanabe et al., 1995). Moreover, Bhatt et al. (1988) showed that they could not only classify pictures dichotomously but that they also could concurrently categorize pictures of four classes of objects. Kirpatrick-Steger and Wasserman (1996) had no particular difficulty in having pigeons categorize stimuli according to whether one of two shapes was above, below, to the left, or to the right of the other. The limits might lie in the abstractness of the properties that make the stimuli in an intended category similar. Herrnstein et al. (1989) found it difficult to train pigeons to categorize drawings of dots within closed curved lines from drawings of dots outside such lines. These limits aside, for a long time the remarkable categorization performances of pigeons were equated with an ability to conceptualize, following a definition by Keller and Schoenfeld (1950) affirming that concepts involved a generalization within classes and a discrimination between classes of stimuli.

Concepts Through Reversals

Lea (1984) argues that the term concept should be used only if the stimuli pertaining to a category are shown to be associated with each other and not only with a response or a reinforcement. He proposes that such inter-stimulus association can be demonstrated by retraining the animals with a subset of the category stimuli (or the features composing them) with reversed reinforcement allocations and then testing for whether the reversed response would spontaneously transfer to the remaining stimuli (features). If all stimuli (features) belonging to a category were bonded by associations, the response switch should transfer from the leading subset to the trailing subset.

   The procedure yielded mixed results. Lea et al. (1990) had pigeons discriminate sets of letters, and upon a single reversal they found some evidence of reversal transfer. Fersen and Lea (1990) trained pigeons to discriminate two sets of townscapes involving several features. When reversed with respect to one pair of features they showed no evidence of transfer to the other features. Bhatt and Wasserman (1989) had pigeons categorize pictures of four different types of objects, but found that reversal training did not transfer. Jitsumori (1993) got pigeons to successfully categorize artificial multifeatured stimuli according to feature addition principles but found no reversal transfer across features. Astley and Wasserman (1998) had pigeons learn to co-categorize pictures of people, flowers, cars, and chairs into two classes and similarly found only rather weak evidence of inter-stimulus associations using a response reassignment procedure. All these studies exposed the animals to only a single reversal or reassignment before testing for choice transfer. They were thus expecting that inter-stimulus associations would have arisen through the earlier categorization training rather than by the reassignment or reversal procedure itself.

Vaughan (1988) used the reversal method for both strengthening the inter-stimulus associations and testing them. Pigeons learned to discriminate slides all depicting trees but which were arbitrarily divided into a set of 20 positive and a set of 20 negative slides. The slides were projected in a random order onto a pecking key. Only pecks on the positive pictures yielded food rewards. When the pigeons had learned to discriminate, the allocation of reward and no reward was exchanged between the sets. Such reinforcement reversals were repeated until the birds became proficient at switching their choices according to the reigning allocations. Vaughan then showed that upon a reversal, experience with a few initial slides was sufficient to cause the pigeons to respond correctly to all the remaining ones. That is, when the pigeons detected that some of the slides of the sets had exchanged their functional significance, they spontaneously transferred the adequate response to the remainder.

This led Herrnstein (1990) to expand his views about conceptualization in animals. To the previously accepted levels of (a) stimulus categorization based on straightforward discrimination, (b) on brute, multiple by-rote learning, (c) on open-ended extension through generalization gradients, and (d) on common abstract relations between stimulus components, he added a new level (e) where the categorization of stimuli was not based on perceptual similarities between them but based on reinforcement contingencies that different stimuli could share. This latter level corresponded to the stimulus classification by multiple reinforcement reversals demonstrated by Vaughan (1988). Note, however, that there is nothing to prevent the processes responsible for the different levels of categorization from operating conjointly.

Equivalencies by Matching

Vaughan (1988) maintained that his pigeons had formed two equivalence sets in the sense that experience with any exemplar of each class was equally capable of eliciting a choice switch. This view conflicted with another research tradition developed by Sidman (1992) and others (Dougher and Markham, 1996). Employing the so-called symbolic matching-to-sample conditioning procedure, Sidman began by attempting to teach verbally backward humans the correspondence among pictograms of items such as a car, a bed, an ear, and so on with the written words "car," "bed," "ear," and so forth. Later he used purely arbitrary, initially meaningless stimuli. Although Sidman himself did little animal work on this (Sidman et al., 1982), his designs lend themselves to such an enterprise.

Table 6.1
Minimal equivalencies design employing a symbolic matching-to-sample procedure

1. Matching training		2. Reflexivity testing	
−L A B+	A ≡ B	oK A Ao	A ≡ A?
+B A L−	A ≡ B	oA A Ko	A ≡ A?
−M B C+	B ≡ C	oL B Bo	B ≡ B?
+C B M−	B ≡ C	oB B Lo	B ≡ B?
−B K L+	K ≡ L	oK K Ao	K ≡ K?
+L K B−	K ≡ L	etc. . . .	
−C L M+	L ≡ M		
+M L C−	L ≡ M		
3. Symmetry testing		4. Transitivity testing	
oK B Ao	B ≡ A?	oM A Co	A ≡ C?
oA B Ko	B ≡ A?	oC A Mo	A ≡ C?
oL C Bo	C ≡ B?	oC K Mo	K ≡ M?
oB C Lo	C ≡ B?	oM K Co	K ≡ M?
etc. . . .		etc. . . .	

The sample stimuli are presented on a middle pecking key and the comparison stimuli are presented on two side keys. There are six different stimuli A, B, C and K, L, M. The symbols +, −, and o stand for reward, penalty, and nonreinforcement, respectively (modified from Sidman, 1992 by the inclusion of unreinforced test trials).

Adapted for pigeons, the procedure could run as follows: On a given trial stimulus A, say pattern # might be shown on the middle key; when pecked it would switch on stimulus B, say pattern § on one side-key and stimulus K, say pattern @ on the other side-key. The comparison stimulus B is defined as matching the sample stimulus A, and if the pigeon pecks it, it is rewarded. If it pecks the comparison stimulus L, defined as not matching the sample stimulus A, it is penalized. This teaches the birds to match the sample stimulus A by choosing the stimulus B and thus to possibly learn the equivalence relation A ≡ B. Table 6.1 sketches a design attempting to teach pigeons the equivalence relations A ≡ B, B ≡ C and K ≡ L, L ≡ M, each letter standing for a different stimulus. Part 2 delineates tests for reflexivity, that is, for whether the same stimuli serving both as a sample and a comparison are recognized as equivalent. Part 3 sketches tests for symmetry, that is, whether when the stimuli that previously served as samples are now used as comparison stimuli, and conversely are still recognized as equivalent. Part 4 sketches tests for transitivity, whether pigeons can derive from the previously learned equivalencies the emergent equivalencies A ≡ C and K ≡ M. Only when pigeons pass all these tests would they command what Sidman calls the equivalence classes {A, B, C} and {K, L, M}. If the pigeons learned part 1 on the basis of a configural rather than a relational strategy, they would of course not pass them.

Language competent humans pass the tests without much difficulty, but language deficient subjects tend to fail on one or another test and only master the corresponding stages after remedial reinforced training with them. Normal children begin to fully command equivalence classes when they are linguistically competent, at the age of about six years (Sidman, 1992). Younger children tend to have difficulties with the symmetry and transitivity tests (Valero-Aguayo and Luciano-Soriano, 1996). While nonhuman primates have managed to pass some of the Sidman criteria (D'Amato et al., 1985; Yamamoto and Asano, 1995), pigeons have mostly proven incapable of passing any of them (Lipkens et al., 1988; Jitsumori, 1990; Fersen et al., 1992). Only Kuno et al. (1994), using a design bypassing the reflexivity and symmetry hurdle, got one of four pigeons to pass the transitivity test. Zentall and Urciuoli (1994) argue that pigeons variously passed the reflexivity, symmetry, and transitivity tests, but their evidence is pieced together from a methodically heterogeneous collection of experiments.

The fact that Vaughan (1988) used a different paradigm and did not test for reflexivity, symmetry, and transitivity caused Sidman to be initially critical of his equivalence class demonstration. However, when he found out that human subjects benefited from a multiple reversal pretraining with regards to passing these tests, he relaxed his views somewhat (Sidman et al., 1989; Sidman, 1992).

Reversals Continued

All studies using the reversal technique with pigeons, whether successful or not, employed many and/or complex stimuli. Because this hampers the analysis of equivalence class formation, Delius et al. (1995) ran an experiment employing only four simple stimuli. Using a simultaneous two-key conditioning procedure, pigeons were taught to concurrently discriminate the colors red/green and blue/yellow according to the scheme A+K−, B+L−, where the + and − signs mean that pecks were rewarded with food or were penalized with time-out. When the birds had learned this task, the reinforcement allocations were reversed to A−K+, B−L+, and when they had learned this they were again reversed to A+K−, B+L− (table 6.2 [1]). The reversal procedure was repeated about 35 times, until the birds became proficient in switching their stimulus choices. This was to ensure that the birds learned that the A, B and K, L stimuli were consistently yoked together. Subsequent tests for the equivalencies A ≡ B and K ≡ L involved special reversal sessions where only one of the two discrimination pairs was presented during the first ten or so trials. These leading trials gave the birds time enough to adopt an at least 85 percent correct responding. During the remainder of the session the other, trailing discrimination pair was additionally presented. The first two trials with this trailing pair went unreinforced. The pigeons

Table 6.2
Basic design of multiple reversal equivalence training and testing, typical sequences of simultaneous discrimination trials

1. Equivalencies training A/K ≡ B/L			
discrimination	*reversal*	reversal	*reversal*
A+ B+ B+ B+ A+ A+ B+ …	A+ *A− B− B− A− B−* …	*A−* B+ B+ A+ …	*B−* …
K− L− L− L− K− K− L− …	K− *K+ L+ L+ K+ L+* …	*K+* L− L− K …	*L+* …

2. Reversal test for A/K ≡ B/L? and B/L ≡ A/K?			
leading	trailing	*leading*	*trailing*
A+ A+ A+ A+ …	A+ Bo A+ Bo A+ B+ …	*A+ B− B− B−* …	*B− Ao Ao A− B−* …
K− K− K− K− …	K− Lo K− Lo K− L− …	*K− L+ L+ L+* …	*L+ Ko Ko K+ L+* …

3. Full and half reversal tests for A/K ≡ B/L?			
full reversal	*half* reversal	normalization	
B− B− A− B− A− B+ B+ A+ A+ …	A+ *B− B− B−* A+ A+ *B−* …	*B−* B+ A+ B+ …	
L+ L+ K+ L+ K+ L− L− K− K− …	K− *L+ L+ L+* K− K− *L+* …	*L+* L− K− L− …	

The stimuli forming the discriminatory pairs are shown one above the other. Reinforcement allocation reversals are marked by switches from standard to italic font and back. The symbols +, −, and o stand for reward, penalty, and nonreinforcement. For simplicity the randomized left-right position of the stimuli is not represented (after Delius et al. 1995).

showed 37 percent correct initial trials with the leading pair and 48 percent correct initial trials with the trailing pair trials. In accordance with the equivalence hypothesis, the reversal experience with the leading pair facilitated the choice switch with respect to the trailing pair. After the pigeons were additionally trained with reversals incorporating some trials with half-key red/half-key blue (A|B) and half-key green/half-key yellow (K|L) stimulus pairs meant to strengthen the associations through spatial contiguity, renewed tests yielded a more clearly significant 39 percent correct leading and 49 percent correct trailing pair difference.

However, the test results could also have arisen if the birds had adopted a nondiscriminative, 50 percent correct responding toward the initial trailing pair presentations after noticing the leading pair reversal. An additional test session series using a design by Nakagawa (1992) and not open to this option was thus run (table 6.2 [3]). Half of the sessions implemented full reversals affecting both pairs in a like manner. They alternated with sessions involving half reversals where one discrimination pair was subject to a reinforcement reversal but the other was not. Because these half reversals were at odds with the equivalencies presumably induced by the full training reversals, it was expected the birds would not adjust as well to them as to the full reversals. This happened: the pigeons showed an average 63 percent and 70 percent correct choices during the first ten trials of these two types of sessions. This

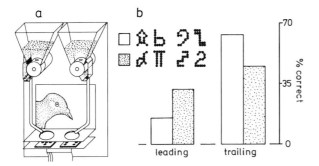

Figure 6.1
(a) conditioning platform used for the Siemann and Delius (1998a), Siemann (1998), and Jitsumori et al. (1999) studies (from Xia et al. 1996); (b) stimuli employed and average performance during the initial trials with the leading and trailing pairs during the test reversal in the Siemann and Delius (1998a; clear) and the Siemann (1998; stippled) studies.

significant difference contradicted the simpler expectancy that a relearning of two reversed pairs discrimination would be more difficult than the relearning of a single reversed pair discrimination. The result thus rather supports the notion that the color stimuli had become partly equivalent in an $A \equiv B$, $K \equiv L$ manner. Comparable results were obtained in a similar half and full reversal experiment carried out by Zentall et al. (1991).

Because red is next to yellow and green is next to blue on the wavelength spectrum, it seemed possible that stimulus generalization could have worked against the intended red $\equiv$ blue and yellow $\equiv$ green equivalencies. Siemann and Delius (1998a) therefore conducted a multiple reversal experiment using shapes. Pigeons were conditioned using platforms attached to the cages. The stimuli were light diode array patterns presented below the two transparent keys. Feeders delivered a few grains of millet onto either key (figure 6.1a). Shapes chosen to be physically dissimilar formed the pairs $A+-K-+$ and $B+-L-+$, the symbol combinations $+-$ and $-+$ indicating the repeated and synchronous reinforcement reversals they were subjected to. These came into effect whenever the pigeons had reached a criterion performance of 70 percent correct choices within a 40-trial block. Test blocks were introduced when the number of trials that the birds needed to reach this criterion roughly stabilized after some 100 reversals. There were 20 blocks of about 120 trials structured according to the leading/trailing design explained earlier. Only when the leading pair had been presented some 20 times in a row was the trailing pair presented as well.

All three pigeons yielded a better performance during the initial trials with the trailing pair than during the initial trial with the leading pair. The conditional extinction process considered earlier is unlikely to have applied because they yielded a better than 50 percent chance performance with the trailing pair. The mean scores were 63 percent and 17 percent, respectively (figure 6.1b). The large difference between the scores indicates a sizeable reversal transfer across the discrimination pairs and thus a marked A/K ≡ B/L equivalencies command. Siemann (1998) ran a repeat experiment with a similar procedure but employing different stimuli (figure 6.1b). The three new pigeons again yielded a performance advantage with the trailing pair over the leading pair, the mean scores being 45 percent and 32 percent correct (figure 6.1b). The lesser difference between the scores could be due to the fact that one of the stimulus pairs consisted of two somewhat similar shapes.

Although supporting the equivalence formation through multiple reversals, our studies could not reproduce the large reversal transfer effect obtained by Vaughan (1988). Apart from some procedural differences of doubtful relevance, there is the fact that we employed a few simple stimuli selected to be dissimilar within each of the stimulus sets, whereas Vaughan employed many complex but generally similar stimuli within each of the stimulus sets. There is evidence that similarity and the number of stimuli used for training play a role in the establishment of relational principles in pigeons (Wright et al., 1988; Delius, 1994). This is undoubtedly because the similarity factor allows the grouping process to grow upon already present stimulus generalization links and because the number factor helps to overload the nonrelational, rote learning option to which pigeons are otherwise prone (Vaughan and Greene, 1984; Fersen and Delius, 1989).

Equivalencies by Reversals

Jitsumori et al. (2000) employed more stimuli of a controlled similarity, as well as an improved multiple reversal procedure. Five pigeons made up the similarity group about which we mainly report here. Two sets of four light diode stimuli served to begin with (figure 6.2a,b). Human observers judged them to be similar within sets and to be dissimilar between sets. The allocation of the different patterns within the A, B, C, D and K, L, M, N sets of stimuli was randomized across the birds.

The pigeons were first taught the twin equivalencies A ≡ B and K ≡ L (abbreviated: A/K ≡ B/L) with the stimulus pairs A+K−, A+L−, B+L−, B+K− presented in random order (table 6.3 [1]). The training continued until the birds consistently achieved a better than 80 percent correct performance. The reinforcement allocation to the discrimination pairs was then reversed to $A-K+$, $A-L+$, $B-L+$, $B-K+$. Training continued until the above criterion was reattained. Rein-

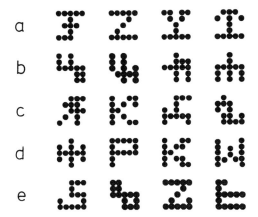

Figure 6.2
Light diode stimuli used by Jitsumori et al. (2000). The similarity group of pigeons first dealt with the patterns shown in the rows a and b and later additionally with those shown in row c. The dissimilarity group to be mentioned later dealt with the patterns shown in rows d and e.

forcements were then reversed again, and so on until the birds exhibited more than 80 percent correct within the first blocks after a reversal during three successive reversals. Then the pigeons where taught the equivalencies C/M ≡ D/N using the same procedure with the discrimination pairs C+−M−+, C+−N−+, D+−M−+, D+−N−+, where the symbols +− and −+ indicate the multiple reversals they were subjected to (table 6.3 [1]). The birds achieved the criterion on both tasks within 30–70 reversals.

To test whether the equivalencies A/K ≡ B/L, D/N ≡ C/M had been formed we examined whether a reinforcement reversal affecting the stimuli A, K and D, N would transfer to the stimuli B, L and C, M, and the converse. Test sessions began with reinforced presentations of one set of stimulus pairs, the leading pairs, until the usual criterion was reached. A test block followed. It consisted of further training trials with the leading pairs and randomly interspersed, unreinforced probe trials with the other set of pairs, the trailing pairs. A second test session proceeded identically, except that the reinforcements of the leading pairs were reversed (table 6.3b). One test session dyad involved the leading pairs A+−K−+, D+−N−+, A+−N+−, D+−K+−, and the trailing pairs BoLo, CoMo, BoMo, CoLo. The other dyad involved the leading pairs B+−L−+, C+−M−+, B+−M+−, C+−L−+ and the trailing pairs AoKo, DoNo, AoNo, DoKo. The session pairs were arranged so that when the average test score across them was over 50 percent correct this indicated a

Table 6.3
Sketch of the basic experimental design

1. Equivalencies training A/K ≡ B/L and C/M ≡ D/N

training   *reversal*

A+A+B+ A+B+ ... A+A+B+*B−A−A−B−* ... *A−B−B−*

K−L−K−K−L− ... L−K−L−*L+K+K+K+* ... *K+L+L+*

training   *reversal*

C+D +D+D+C+ ... C+ D+ *D−D−C− C−* ...

N−M−N−N−M− ... M−N−*M+M+N+M−* ...

2. Equivalencies testing A/K ≡ B/L? and C/M = D/N?

training   test   test   test

A+A+D+A+ ... A+D+Bo A+ Bo D+D+Co A+A+D+

K−K−N−N− ... N−K−Lo K− Mo N−K−Lo K−K−N−

test   *reversal*   test test   test

Co ... *B−B−C−B−* ... *C− Ao Ao B− Do* ...

Mo ... *L+M+L+L+* ... *M+ Ko NoM+ No* ...

See table 6.2 and the text for further explanations (after Jitsumori et al., 2000).

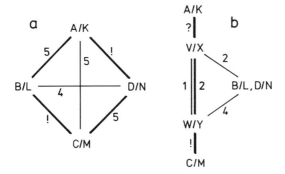

Figure 6.3
Equivalencies that were trained (thick lines) and equivalencies that could emerge by transitivity (thin lines). The equivalencies tested are flanked by the number of birds commanding them. Equivalencies inferred to have or not have been commanded by most birds are marked with ! and ? symbols; (a) before and (b) after the incorporation of dissimilar stimuli. (Modified from Jitsumori et al. 2000)

choice transfer from the leading pairs to the trailing pairs, an approximately 70 percent correct score signaling a significant transfer. The actual scores for all pairs and each bird exceeded that level by being between 78 percent and 100 percent correct, implying a command over the equivalencies A/K ≡ B/L, D/N ≡ C/M. Figure 6.3a summarizes these findings.

The pigeons were next taught the equivalencies A/K ≡ D/N, B/L ≡ C/M, using analogous procedures. Their command, however, was not directly tested. Instead, we tested whether the birds dominated the equivalencies A/K ≡ C/M, B/L ≡ D/N that had not been explicitly trained but which the pigeons could in principle derive by transitivity if they had formed the equivalence classes {A, B, C, D} and {K, L, M, N} (figure 6.3a). The test sessions were structured as before but involved the leading training/trailing test pairs A+−K−+/CoMo, C+−M−+/AoKo, B+−L−+/DoNo, and D+−N−+/BoLo. The birds achieved significant above chance level performances of between 72 percent and 100 percent correct trials with the various test pairs, except that one bird that was weak on the DoNo pair. Figure 6.3a summarizes the results. The mastery of these A/K ≡ C/M and B/L ≡ D/N equivalencies by four birds indirectly demonstrated that they also commanded the equivalencies A/K ≡ D/N and B/L ≡ C/M. They had thus integrated the equivalencies into a network so that the stimuli were associatively clustered in two separate {A, B, C, D} and {K, L, M, N} classes. Within these classes each and all member stimuli were capable of signaling a reinforcement switch causing a response switch to the remaining members.

Dissimilarities Interfere

The equivalence formation reflected by these results with similar-within and dissimilar-between stimuli is far better than that obtained during our earlier efforts using a similar procedure but with dissimilar within-class stimuli. Indeed, the results compare with those of Vaughan (1988) that also involve similar within-class stimuli. To further assess the role of stimulus similarity/dissimilarity, our pigeons were now confronted with additional equivalence tasks involving dissimilar stimuli. Four patterns that human observers judged dissimilar to one another and dissimilar to the patterns constituting the two earlier sets were constructed (figure 6.2c). The assignment of these patterns as V, W X, Y stimuli was randomized across the birds that were trained to learn the equivalencies $A/K \equiv V/X$ and $C/M \equiv W/Y$ according to the same procedure employed before. Although the birds were now experienced with the discrimination reversal routine, they took longer to learn with these stimuli than with the earlier ones. The birds were then tested in the usual manner using the leading pairs $B+-L-+$ and $D+-N-+$ and the trailing pairs VoXo and WoYo. This tested them for the mastery of the equivalencies $B/L \equiv V/X \equiv D/N$, $B/L \equiv W/Y \equiv D/N$, which they had not been explicitly taught but that they could potentially derive. The test scores with the WoYo pair were all, except in one bird, significantly above chance, but with the VoXo pair they were only significant for two birds (figure 6.3b). It seems that some birds had learned the $A/K \equiv V/X$ less well than the $C/M \equiv W/Y$ equivalencies.

We then tested whether the birds had derived the untaught equivalencies $V/X \equiv W/Y$ using the leading pairs/trailing pairs $V+-X-+$/WoYo and $W+-Y-+$/VoXo. The test scores were all close to chance except those of one bird that achieved significant scores. After a subsequent training of the $V/X \equiv W/Y$ equivalencies, a repeat of the same test revealed some asymmetry in the sense that although two birds scored significantly in both tests, two birds were successful only with the WoYo test pair, and one bird failed on both tests. The asymmetry was probably due to the fact that most pigeons had earlier learned the equivalencies $C/M \equiv W/Y$ but not learned the equivalencies $A/K \equiv V/X$ (figure 6.3b). Thus four pigeons of Jitsumori et al.'s (1999) so-called similarity group ended up incorporating dissimilar stimuli into the equivalence classes $\{A, B, C, D, W\}$, $\{K, L, M, N, Y\}$, and one forming the probably disjoint classes $\{A, B, C, D\}$, $\{K, L, M, N\}$, $\{V, W\}$, $\{X, Y\}$.

Obviously the equivalence formation through multiple reversals was evenly dissimilar within and between stimuli, although in principle within the competencies of pigeons, it is a more difficult task than when the stimuli are similar within the intended equivalence classes. This agrees with the results obtained with a separate so-called dissimilar group of four pigeons. They were trained and tested in the same way as the similar group during the first phase of the experiment, but dealt with the A, B, C, D and K, L, M, N sets composed of the dissimilar patterns shown in figure 6.2d, e. All, bar one, passed the tests for the A/K = D/N equivalencies (mean 79 percent correct), but they all except for one failed the tests for the C/M ≡ D/N equivalencies (mean 66 percent correct). When tested for command of the equivalencies A/K ≡ C/M, B/L ≡ D/N derivable by transitivity, all the birds except one passed the test for the first (mean 80 percent correct), but all birds failed the test for the second equivalencies. Overall, the dissimilar group presented a pattern of results reminiscent of that of the so-called similar group of birds when these were confronted with dissimilar stimuli: the results were characterized by individualities. As detailed by Jitsumori et al. (1999), three birds of the dissimilar group ended up commanding the equivalence classes {A, B, C}, {K, L, M}, and one bird commanding only the equivalence classes {A, B}, {K, L}.

Epilogue

Jitsumori et al.'s (2000) study provides better evidence for equivalence class formation in pigeons than that produced by several earlier reversal studies. Apart from the implementation of strict reversal criteria, the pigeons may have profited from the additional training with crossed stimulus combination (the A+−L−+, B+−K−+ pairs, in addition to the standard A+−K−+ B+−L−+ pairs) and the concurrent/successive teaching of several equivalencies (the equivalencies A/K ≡ B/L, C/M ≡ D/N, A/K ≡ B/L, D/N ≡ C/M instead of only the equivalencies A/K ≡ B/L). The reversal transfer effects revealed are comparable to those obtained by Vaughan (1988). The findings substantiate Sidman's (1992) admission that multiple reversals may powerfully promote the formation of equivalence classes. He considered reflexivity, symmetry, and transitivity to be essential properties of equivalence classes. Within the multiple reversal procedure used by Jitsumori et al. (2000), the reflexivity property is not meaningful and the symmetry property is inevitably taught. But the symmetry and the transitivity property of derived equivalencies was variously tested and verified. Because the demonstrations were mostly associated with sizeable error margins, the equivalencies commanded by the pigeons are nevertheless best viewed as conforming with fuzzy rather than formal logic sets (Yager and Zadeh, 1994).

Similarity within stimuli classes and the dissimilarity between class stimulus classes appear to foster equivalence class formation. This is not surprising, as earlier pigeon studies have shown that such relationships between category stimuli facilitates the formation of open-ended categories that can transfer to novel exemplars (e.g., Astley and Wasserman, 1992; Jitsumori and Yoshihara, 1997; see also Mackintosh, this volume). Indeed, the successful equivalence class formation with the similar patterns might well have importantly relied on intraclass stimulus generalization and interclass discriminability of the member stimuli. However, it would be short-sighted to ascribe all the effects obtained to solely these factors. Jitsumori et al. (2000) found that the patterns that had ended up belonging to one or the other of the similar stimulus equivalence classes $\{A, B, C, D\}$ and $\{K, L, M, N\}$ were still easily discriminated by the pigeons. Also, most of the similarity group pigeons learned to include the dissimilar W and Y stimuli into the equivalence classes that they finally dominated. Most of the dissimilarity group pigeons learned to form some equivalencies with exclusively dissimilar stimuli. It must also be remembered that Vaughan's (1988) excellent equivalence formation was obtained with stimuli that were just as similar within sets as between sets. It is thus still possible that a similarity between stimuli favors equivalence formation even if no dissimilarity separates the members of the stimulus sets. This may arise because the multiple reversal procedure implements a direct discrimination between class stimuli but only promotes an indirect generalization within class stimuli.

From an ethological viewpoint, the fitness utility of the ability to class diverse stimuli, items, or events as eatable, matable, threatening, shelter-spending, home-directing, and so forth for animals such as the pigeon is virtually beyond doubt. That natural stimuli sharing such functional properties will often, but not always, also share perceptual similarities is quite patent. That natural functional classes will sometimes vary over time so as to require continuous tracking by relearning is similarly plausible. Close to Vaughan's (1988) experiment, one may suspect that the recognition of classes of real trees that bear fruits and berries at given times of the year but not others might be directly important for frugivorous birds. Perhaps this is less true for the domestic pigeon, but the pigeon may have to solve related problems when searching for sites promising profitable foraging, auspicious nesting, or reassuring familiarity. Thus, perhaps the competence for forming such functional classes could be essential for their survival and reproduction. Undoubtedly a similar argument applies to other behaviorally advanced species. It seems probable that most mammals will show capable of full equivalence class formation as the experimental procedures are improved (rats: Nakagawa, 1992; Roberts, 1996; dolphins: Fersen and Delius, 2000; sea lions: Schusterman and Kastak, 1993; chimpanzees: Yamamoto and Asano, 1995).

Whether the experimental procedures that have been hitherto used in the attempts to demonstrate such class formation are ecologically well adjusted is not certain. The evolutionary circumstance that the behavioral competencies of an animal species must be tuned to the demands that the socioecological niche made on its recent ancestors suggests that it may be a worthwhile effort to adapt the laboratory procedures closer to the natural conditions. The abilities of pigeons regarding the formation of equivalence classes might be context specific and we may not yet have struck the optimal cognitive module (Shettleworth, this volume). It might be worth trying other procedures that employ more varied response requirements, more varied reinforcement consequences, and more temporally persistent schedules of reinforcement reversals than those used in the studies reviewed here. Indeed, if it was possible to devise more efficient procedures, it may be possible to extend the reversal paradigm to analogical equivalence problems encapsulated by the statement "a key is to a lock as an opener is to a can" (Premack, 1988). Suppose one would train pigeons separately on the equivalencies $A/K \equiv B/L$ using food/no-food reinforcement reversals and the equivalencies $C/M \equiv D/N$ using water/no-water reinforcement reversals. Would they then reveal reversal transfer across these pairs of equivalencies? Such a transfer in turn would argue against a narrow modular specialization of this cognitive competence.

With the possible increases in task sophistication, it will be necessary at some point to take into consideration that the avian brain size is more constrained in its progressive, anagenetic evolution than is the brain of mammals. This is because the flight capability generally imposes a limit on the body/weight independent, allometric growth of brain weight, the secondary flightlessness of some avian families notwithstanding (Jerison, 1973). If in humans variations in individual intelligence only emerge when this species is challenged with the harder items of intelligence tests, one can expect that individual pigeons may reach the limits of their intellect as they are faced with ever more difficult tasks. Moreover, pigeons are almost certainly not the cleverest avian species; the study of equivalence formation in parrots and corvids may well turn out to be more revealing (Delius et al., 2000). Indeed, some of the vocal labeling competencies exhibited by an African grey parrot may already constitute informal evidence of a remarkable capacity for equivalence formation in at least one such species (Pepperberg, 1996; see also Manabe et al., 1995, budgerigars).

These evolutionary and comparative considerations also oblige us to consider the neural mechanisms that must have evolved to enable the neurally more advanced animals, including pigeons, to learn equivalence classes. This ability must be based on secondary networks of neurons following the primary layers of the visual system engaged in extracting the basal features of visual stimuli. In mammals one would obviously consider the participation of secondary projection areas of the visual cortex. In birds, with their rather different brain make-up, the issue is less certain. But for what it is worth, neuroanatomists now consider larger parts of the avian forebrain (especially the structures known as ektostriatum and neostriatum) as equivalent to the mammalian neocortex, in that they probably fulfill similar information processing on the basis of an analogous, even if with a histologically less distinct structuring (Veenman, 1997). A small part of this cortical mass may even be equivalent to the prefrontal cortex of mammals (Aldavert-Vera et al., 1999), which is in turn reckoned to be the main substrate of the supramodular general intelligence in humans. Artificial neural networks, which to some extent are conceived to mimic the connectivities of cortical structures, have already shown to be amply capable of categorization and conceptualization-like feats comparable to those produced by pigeons and indeed, humans (Gluck, 1991; Roitblat and Fersen, 1992). The synaptic weights of the inputs of intermediate (or hidden) layer units or clusters of units will, with suitable simulated categorization training, come to adjust themselves so that these units or clusters will more or less indiscriminately respond to any stimulus belonging to the category they happen to represent when these stimuli are applied to the input layer. The network model may prove helpful in explaining why the equivalence effects obtained in the various reversal and matching studies have been relatively variable. All the factors that we have tentatively identified as contributing to that variability—stimulus similarities, stimulus complexities, number of stimuli, and number of reversals—are of the kind already suspected to affect concept formation in such networks.

Networks composed of at least three layers of neuronlike units are necessary to account for the formation of perceptual concepts, where the units of the intermediate, hidden layer are those principally mediating the connectivity coding of concepts (Watanabe et al., 1993). However, preliminary exploration suggests that four-layer networks might be more effective in implementing equivalencies through reversals, the additional layer enabling the formation of a distinct response/reinforcement switch circuitry. Pigeons would in any case not be short of neural layers as the first stage of their visual system alone, the tectum opticum, already contains some 15 layers (Güntürkün, 1991). Hidden units are, in any case, only effectively recruited into nodes or clusters if the training stimulus sets bear predisposing similarities/dissimilarities, are complex enough (many stimuli, many features), and if reversals occur often enough for an concept-conform activation of these units to yield a processing advantage. Otherwise, such neural networks have a tendency to settle on a by-rote categorization, two-layer networklike manner of processing that lacks the element of concept-defining inter-stimulus associations. Networks that operate on definite instrumental conditioning principles (Siemann and Delius, 1998b) would appear to be the most promising substrates for exploring the mechanisms of equivalence class formation inasmuch as they can readily incorporate the effects of reinforcement switches so central to the multiple synchronous reversal procedure that has been the main subject of this chapter.

Summary

This chapter argues that, contrary to widespread opinion, pigeons are capable of forming equivalence classes of visual stimuli. The multiple reinforcement reversal procedure originally introduced by Vaughan (1988) and recently developed by Jitsumori et al. (2000) might be more advantageous in this respect than the more popular symbolic matching-to-sample procedure advocated by Sidman (1992). This may be mainly so because the former method obviates a symmetry stage that is essential to the latter method. Although we show that physical stimulus similarities facilitate the formation of equivalence networks, it has also been demonstrated that functional similarities alone can be sufficient to yield equivalence associations. It is suggested that equivalence formation by reinforcement reversal may be within the capabilities of simple multilayer neural networks and that avians possess nervous systems that are complex enough to incorporate the requisite neuronal circuitry. From an evolutionary perspective there can be little doubt that equivalence formation capacities must be in high demand in avian natural habitats.

Acknowledgments

We thank the Deutsche Forchungsgemeinschaft and the Japanese Ministry of Education for support, Prof. I. Morgado-Bernal (Barcelona) for hospitality, and J. Grante (Exeter) for corrections.

References

Aldavert-Vera L, Costa-Miserachs D, Divac I, Delius JD (1999) Presumed "prefrontal cortex" lesions in pigeons: Effects on visual discrimination performance. Behavioral Brain Research, 102: 165–170.

Astley SL, Wasserman EA (1992) Categorical discrimination and generalization in pigeons: All negative stimuli are not created equal. Journal of Experimental Psychology: Animal Behavior Processes, 18: 193–207.

Astley SL, Wasserman EA (1998) Novelty and functional equivalence in superordinate categorization by pigeons. Animal Learning and Behavior, 26: 125–138.

Bhatt RS, Wasserman EA (1989) Secondary generalization and categorization in pigeons. Journal of the Experimental Analysis of Behavior, 52: 213–224.

Bhatt RS, Wasserman EA, Reynolds WF, Knauss KS (1988) Conceptual behavior in pigeons: Categorization of both familiar and novel examples from four classes of natural and artificial stimuli. Journal of Experimental Psychology: Animal Behavior Processes, 14: 219–234.

D'Amato MR, Salmon DP, Loukas E, Tomie A (1985) Symmetry and transitivity of conditional relations in monkeys (*Cebus apella*) and pigeons (*Columba livia*). Journal of the Experimental Analysis of Behavior, 44: 35–47.

Delius JD (1992) Categorical discrimination of objects and pictures by pigeons. Animal Learning and Behavior, 20: 301–311.

Delius JD (1994) Comparative cognition of identity. In: International perspectives on psychological science: Leading themes (Bertelson P, Eelen P, d'Ydewalle G, ed), pp 25–40. Hillsdale, NJ, Hove, UK: Erlbaum.

Delius JD, Ameling M, Lea SEG, Staddon JER (1995) Reinforcement concordance induces and maintains stimulus associations in pigeons. Psychological Record, 45: 283–297.

Delius JD, Siemann M, Emmerton J, Xia L (2000, in press) Cognitions of birds as products of evolved brains. In: Brain, evolution and cognition (Roth G, Wullimann MF, ed), New York, Wiley.

Dougher MJ, Markham MR (1996) Stimulus classes and the untrained acquisition of stimulus functions. In: Stimulus class formation in humans and animals (Zentall TR, Smeets PM, ed), pp 137–152. Amsterdam: Elsevier.

Fersen Lv, Delius JD (1989) Long-term retention of many visual patterns by pigeons. Ethology, 82: 141–155.

Fersen Lv, Delius JD (2000) Transfer of discriminative response reassignments in dolphins (*Tursiops truncatus*): Evidence for concept formation with auditory stimuli. Animal Cognition, in press.

Fersen Lv, Emmerton J, Delius JD (1992) Unexpected discrimination strategy used by pigeons. Behavioural Processes, 27: 139–150.

Fersen Lv, Lea SEG (1990) Category discrimination by pigeons using five polymorphous features. Journal of the Experimental Analysis of Behavior, 54: 69–84.

Fodor J (1998) When is a dog a dog? Nature, 396: 325–327.

Gluck MA (1991) Stimulus generalization and representation in adaptive network models of category learning. Psychological Science, 2: 50–55.

Güntürkün O (1991) The functional organization of the avian visual system. In: Neural and behavioural plasticity: The use of the domestic chick as a model (Andrew RJ, ed), pp 92–105. Oxford: Oxford University Press.

Herrnstein RJ (1990) Levels of stimulus control: A functional approach. Cognition, 37: 133–166.

Herrnstein RJ, Loveland DH (1964) Complex visual concept in the pigeon. Science, 146: 549–551.

Herrnstein RJ, Vaughan W, Mumford DB, Kosslyn SM (1989) Teaching pigeons an abstract relational rule: Insideness. Perception and Psychophysics, 46: 56–64.

Jerison HJ (1973) Evolution of the brain and intelligence. New York: Academic Press.

Jitsumori M (1990) No equivalences through symbolic matching in pigeons (unpublished experiment).

Jitsumori M (1993) Category discrimination of artificial polymorphous stimuli based on feature learning. Journal of Experimental Psychology: Animal Behavior Processes, 19: 244–254.

Jitsumori M, Siemann M, Lehr M, Delius JD (2000, subm.) The formation and expansion of equivalence classes in pigeons: Emergent stimulus relations through discrimination reversals.

Jitsumori M, Yoshihara M (1997) Categorical discrimination of human facial expressions by pigeons: A test of the linear feature model. Quarterly Journal of Experimental Psychology, 50B: 253–268.

Keller FS, Schoenfeld WN (1950) Principles of psychology. New York: Appleton-Century-Crofts.

Kirpatrick-Steger K, Wasserman EA (1996) The what and the where of the pigeon's processing of complex visual stimuli. Journal of Experimental Psychology: Animal Behavior Processes, 22: 60–67.

Kuno H, Kitadate T, Iwamoto T (1994) Formation of transitivity in conditional matching to sample by pigeons. Journal of the Experimental Analysis of Behavior, 62: 399–408.

Lea SEG (1984) In what sense do pigeons learn concepts? In: Animal cognition (Roitblat HL, Bever T, Terrace HS, ed), pp 263–277. Hillsdale: Erlbaum.

Lea SEG, Ryan CME, Kirby RM (1990) Instance to category generalization following pigeon's learning of an artificial concept discrimination (unpublished manuscript).

Lipkens R, Kop PFM, Matthijs W (1988) A test of symmetry and transitivity in the conditional discrimination performances of pigeons. Journal of the Experimental Analysis of Behavior, 49: 395–409.

Lubow RE (1974) Higher-order concept formation in the pigeon. Journal of the Experimental Analysis of Behavior, 21: 475–483.

Manabe K, Kawashima T, Staddon JER (1995) Differential vocalization in budgerigars: Towards an experimental analysis of naming. Journal of the Experimental Analysis of Behavior, 63: 111–126.

Nakagawa E (1992) Effects of overtraining on reversal learning by rats in concurrent and single discriminations. Quarterly Journal of Experimental Psychology, 44B: 37–56.

Pepperberg IM (1996) Categorical class formation by an African grey parrot (Psittacus erithacus). In: Stimulus class formation in humans and animals (Zentall TR, Smeets PM, ed), pp 71–90. Amsterdam: Elsevier.

Premack D (1988) Minds with and without language. In: Thought without language (Weiskrantz L, ed), pp 46–65. Oxford: Clarendon.

Roberts WA (1996) Stimulus generalization and hierarchical structure in categorization by animals. In: Stimulus class formation in humans and animals (Zental TR, Smeets PM, ed), pp 35–54. Amsterdam: Elsevier.

Roitblat HL, Fersen LV (1992) Comparative cognition: Representation and processes in learning and memory. Annual Review of Psychology, 43: 671–710.

Schusterman RJ, Kastak D (1993) A California sea lion (Zalophus californianus) is capable of forming equivalence relations. Psychological Record, 43: 823–839.

Sidman M (1992) Equivalence relations and behavior: A research story. Boston: Authors Cooperative.

Sidman M, Rauzin R, Lazar R, Cunningham S, Tailby W, Carrigan P (1982) A search for symmetry in the conditional discrimination of rhesus monkeys, baboons and children. Journal of the Experimental Analysis of Behavior, 37: 23–34.

Sidman M, Wynne CK, Macguire RW, Barnes T (1989) Functional classes and equivalence relations. Journal of the Experimental Analysis of Behavior, 52: 261–274.

Siemann M (1998) Equivalencies by reversals in pigeons (unpublished experiment).

Siemann M, Delius JD (1998a) Induction of stimulus associations by reinforcement concordances in pigeons. In: Göttingen neurobiology report 1998 (Elsner N, Wehner R, ed), pp 447. Stuttgart: Thieme.

Siemann M, Delius JD (1998b) Algebraic learning and neural network models for transitive and non-transitive responding in humans and animals. European Journal of Cognitive Psychology, 10: 307–334.

Sloman SA, Rips LJ, ed (1998). Similarity and symbols in human thinking. Cambridge: MIT Press.

Valero-Aguayo L, Luciano-Soriano MC (1996) Relaciones de equivalencia: Un estudio de replicación del efecto de la relación simétrica sobre la transitiva. Apuntes de Psicología, 37: 25–39.

Vaughan W (1988) Formation of equivalence sets in pigeons. Journal of Experimental Psychology: Animal Behavior Processes, 14: 36–42.

Vaughan W, Greene SL (1984) Pigeons' visual memory capacity. Journal of Experimental Psychology: Animal Behavior Processes, 10: 256–271.

Veenman CL (1997) Pigeon basal ganglia: Insights into the neuroanatomy underlying telencephalic sensorimotor processes in birds. European Journal of Morphology, 35: 220–233.

Watanabe S, Lea SEG, Dittrich WH (1993) What can we learn from experiments on pigeon concept discrimination? In: Vision, brain and behavior in birds (Zeigler HP, Bishof H-J, ed), pp 351–376. Cambridge: MIT Press.

Watanabe S, Sakamoto J, Wakita M (1995) Pigeons' discrimination of paintings by Monet and Picasso. Journal of the Experimental Analysis of Behavior, 63: 165–174.

Wright AA, Cook RG, Rivera JJ, Sands SF, Delius JD (1988) Concept learning by pigeons: Matching-to-sample with trial-unique video picture stimuli. Animal Learning and Behavior, 16: 436–444.

Xia L, Delius JD, Siemann M (1996) A multistimulus intelligence platform for pigeon conditioning. Behavior Research Methods, Instruments, and Computers, 28: 49–54.

Yager RR, Zadeh LA, ed (1994). Fuzzy sets, neural networks and soft computing. New York: Van Nostrand Reinhold.

Yamamoto J, Asano T (1995) Stimulus equivalence in a chimpanzee. Psychological Record, 45: 3–21.

Zentall TR, Steirn JN, Sherbourne LM, Urciuoli PJ (1991) Common coding in pigeons assessed through partial versus total reversals of many to one conditional and simple discriminations. Journal of Experimental Psychology: Animal Behavior Processes, 17: 194–201.

Zentall TR, Urciuoli PJ (1994) Emergent relations in the formation of stimulus classes by pigeons. Psychological Record, 43: 795–810.

7 Abstraction and Discrimination

Nicholas J. Mackintosh

The use of words then being to stand as outward marks of our internal ideas, and those ideas being taken from particular things, if every particular idea that we take in should have a distinct name, names must be endless. To prevent this, the mind makes the particular ideas, received from particular objects, to become general. . . . This is called abstraction, *whereby ideas taken from particular beings become general representatives of all of the same kind; and their names general names, applicable to whatever exists conformable to such abstract ideas. . . . Thus the same colour being observed in chalk or snow, which the mind yesterday received from milk, it considers that appearance alone, makes it a representative of all of that kind; and having given it the name whiteness, it by that sound signifies the same quality wheresoever to be imagined or met with; and thus universals, whether ideas or terms, are made.*
—John Locke (1690; bk II, ch. 11, 9)

In the next paragraph of his essay, Locke famously went on to assert that "brutes abstract not." But it seems clear enough that, in Locke's definition, many animals behave *as if* they abstracted general ideas from particular instances (even if only a few have learned to associate general names with them). Thus if I rewarded a pigeon for pecking at a screen whenever a white object was shown on it but withheld reward whenever a black object was displayed, it is quite certain that having been trained with a variety of different stimuli (milk bottles, pieces of chalk, a field covered in snow, a white triangle, versus a lump of coal, a raven, a black cat, a black triangle), the pigeon would generalize appropriately to novel white and black pictures. Although Locke would attribute such generalization to the abstraction of general ideas, there is a simpler explanation: the pigeon has detected an invariant feature common to a number of different pictures, and associated that feature with reward.

In what follows, I argue that this ability to detect invariant features in a variable set of stimuli provides a sufficient account both of discrimination learning and so-called categorization learning. The representational process involves nothing more than decomposing complex stimuli into sets of elements or features. Other levels of representation are indeed possible, and available to at least some animals: the best evidence for this comes from the demonstration of response to *relationships* between two or more stimuli. That this is indeed a different level of representation is suggested by the observation that not all animals provide evidence of response to relationships.

Discrimination and Categorization

We know, from ethological observation and experiment, that an animal's discriminative behavior is often controlled by only one or two features of an otherwise complex stimulus. The newly hatched herring gull chick that pecks as enthusiastically at a red knitting needle with a white band near its tip as it does at a lifelike model of a herring gull's head, is showing that the main (only?) feature of the adult that controls this begging response is the red spot at the top of the beak contrasting with the white head. The fact that the chick's behavior is so tightly controlled by such a simple feature of a complex stimulus seems a limitation (albeit, of course, a normally perfectly viable one), rather than evidence of abstraction or human intelligence. Similarly, the pigeon's discriminative behavior and generalization in my hypothetical experiment is well captured by an elementary, single-layered connectionist network, which decomposes objects presented to it into constituent features or elements. If the network is trained on this discrimination it will learn it, and generalize to novel stimuli, because the set of units activated whenever white stimuli are shown to it will end up with stronger connections to the reward unit than will those activated by black stimuli.

Comparative psychologists have often gone along with Locke in describing the discriminative behavior and generalization of their subjects as evidence of possession of general ideas or concepts. Thus Fields (1932) trained rats to discriminate an equilateral triangle from a circle, and found good transfer (or generalization) to different sized triangles, as well as to isosceles and right-angle triangles. He described his research as a study in concept formation—"the development of the concept of triangularity by the white rat." It was left to Karl Lashley, with characteristic acumen, to note the simpler explanation:

The fundamental process, the identification of common properties in two or more constellations of elements, seems to be almost universal among animals, appearing whenever a differential reaction is established. (Lashley, 1938, p. 163)

Lashley's argument amounted to saying that there is no difference of principle between the case where an animal is trained on a discrimination between a single stimulus associated with reward (S+) and another associated with its absence (S−), and shows transfer to new stimuli that are variants on these two; and the case where animals are required to discriminate between two or more large sets of stimuli, several dozen pictures of trees, people, and patches of water serving as the S+ set, and equal numbers of other pictures containing no trees, or people, or water as the S− set, and again show good transfer to new stimuli (Herrnstein, 1984). Some experimenters, it is true, have described such research as the study of concept learning or categorical concept formation (e.g., Wasserman et al., 1988). But Herrnstein himself was reasonably clear that categorization learning involves little that is new:

To categorize, which is to detect recurrences in the environment despite variations in local stimulus energies, must be so enormous an evolutionary advantage that it may well be universal among living organisms.... Categorization is just object constancy. (Herrnstein, 1984, p. 257)

It may well be difficult to specify the nature of the common features or elements that pigeons use to solve such categorization problems. It is surely the case that natural categories are only rarely defined by a single necessary or sufficient attribute, but more commonly by conjunctions or disjunctions of correlated features (Herrnstein, 1984). But these are not sufficient reasons for supposing that pigeons are doing anything more complex than associating a large number of pictures and/or the features they contain with a reward, and then showing transfer to new pictures to the extent that they contain features previously associated with a reward. Several lines of evidence strongly suggest that such an analysis is sufficient.

For example, pigeons are remarkably adept at learning visual discriminations between several hundred pictures arbitrarily designated by the experimenter as the S+ set and several hundred others designated as S− (von Fersen and Delius, 1989). Because there is no categorical basis for the distinction between the S+ and S− set, there is no basis for generalization to novel stimuli. But given this remarkable ability to memorize the wholly arbitrary reward assignments of hundreds of pictures, it seems reasonable to suppose that, if trained to associate 40 pictures of trees with a reward, they will have associated a large number of "tree features" with a reward, and that most novel pictures of trees will be more likely to contain one or more of these features than pictures containing no trees. It is also the case that some categorizations are very much easier for the pigeon than others, and some of these differences seem explicable in terms of the salience of their identifying features. Thus Roberts and Mazmanian (1988) found that pigeons, unlike people, learned to discriminate pictures of kingfishers from other birds much more rapidly than pictures of birds from other animals, or pictures of animals from nonanimals. Only in the first case did they initially show any evidence of successful transfer to new pictures. A clue to the reason for the relative ease of the kingfisher-other bird discrimination is that when the other birds were selected to be brightly colored, the discrimination was significantly disrupted.

Moreoever, experiments in which pigeons have been trained to discriminate between more carefully specified sets of stimuli (Brunswik faces, Huber and Lenz, 1993; segments of circles, Mackintosh, 1995) suggest that discriminative performance and transfer are an orderly function of the number and value of features associated with reward. Finally, there is little doubt that the most powerful and widely accepted account of the behavior of people trained to categorize artificial sets of stimuli is a simple associative one, where exemplars, or their features, are associated with category membership, and transfer is based on generalization from stored exemplars or weight changes in an elementary associative network (Nosofsky and Kruschke, 1992).

In spite of their frequently rather glib talk of conceptualization or concept formation, I suspect that few of those who have experimented on pigeons' categorical discrimination learning would seriously dispute this analysis. Even Wasserman, for example, allows that "stimulus similarity might effectively mediate transfer from training to testing stimuli" in these experiments (Wasserman, 1997, p. 127). Moreover, there is reason to believe that a similar analysis applies equally well not only where people are asked to categorize artificially constructed stimuli, but also to the case of nonhuman primates categorizing more natural stimuli (Roberts and Mazmanian, 1988). Tomasello and Call, who are not generally slow to draw a sharp distinction between the cognitive capacities of primates and nonprimates, acknowledge that

The ability to make sense of the perceptual world by discriminating features and categorizing phenomena is a basic cognitive capacity of many animal species. (Tomasello and Call, 1997, p. 133)

Superordinate Concepts?

Animals can, however, do not categorize only on the basis of perceptual similarity. Suggestive evidence of categorization on the basis of use or function comes from a study by Savage-Rumbaugh et al. (1980), where two chimpanzees, Sherman and Austin, sorted various types of food and tools into these two categories, and were equally adept at sorting the labels (lexigrams) associated with previously uncategorized items. Although they might have been partly relying on the difference in perceptual characteristics between the two classes of object—for example, the materials of which foods and tools are composed, rather than their use or function (see Tomasello and Call, 1997)—there is no doubt that many animals, including pigeons, are capable of categorizing together pictures that are not instances of any natural category, and surely have no features in common that differentiate them from a second set of pictures that they place into a different category. For example, Astley and Wasserman (1998) showed pigeons four sets of pictures—cars, chairs, flowers, and people. Although there is ample evidence that pigeons discriminate among all four classes of stimuli (Wasserman et al., 1988), in this study they were initially required to sort them into only two classes, that is, to make one response to pictures of cars and flowers, and a second response to pictures of chairs and people. They were then trained to make two new responses to cars and to chairs, and finally tested to see if they would also respond in this new way to flowers and people. They did (albeit not at a very high level of accuracy).

Wasserman (1997) argues that this procedure established two superordinate categories (one of cars and flowers, the other of chairs and people) which, because they could not be based on perceptual similarity, provide a clear case of conceptualization (see also Lea, 1984, where much the same hypothetical experiment is described as potential proof of an animal's possession of a concept). But the mechanisms underlying such categorization are as readily understood in associative as in conceptual terms. Consider the following experiment by Vaughan (1988), where the stimuli were 40 pictures, quite arbitrarily divided into two sets, 1 and 2, and the birds were originally rewarded for responding to Set 1 and not for responding to Set 2. After they had learned this discrimination, the reward assignments were reversed and then, every few sessions, repeatedly reversed, for a total of over 100 reversals. At the beginning of each new reversal, the birds showed they remembered the previous reward assignment of the stimuli by responding below chance. After 20 or more reversals, however, they learned each new reversal within a single session, and toward the end of this first session were responding above chance to pictures whose newly reversed reward assignment they had not yet experienced. In other words, experience of the reversed assignment of some of the pictures in Set 1 was sufficient to enable them to respond above chance to the remaining pictures in that set.

All that the pictures in Set 1 shared in common, to distinguish them from the pictures in Set 2, was their earlier common history of reinforcement. But this common history was sufficient to establish, in Vaughan's terminology, an equivalence class. Although there have been several failures to find evidence of such equivalence classes in pigeon categorization experiments (see Delius's chapter in this volume), success does not seem too surprising (e.g., Zentall et al., 1993), and the mechanism underlying such success is readily documented in rather simpler experiments (Nakagawa, 1992; Zentall et al., 1993). Nakagawa (1992) trained rats concurrently on two quite independent visual discrimination problems, and then required them to learn the reversal either of both discriminations or of only one (with continued retraining on the other). If (but only if) they had received extensive overtraining on the original discriminations, they found it much easier to reverse both rather than only one. The result is very similar to Vaughan's in implying that a sufficiently long common history of reinforcement (overtraining in Nakagawa's experiments, repeated reversal in Vaughan's) shared by two or more stimuli establishes a functional equivalence between them, such that the reinforcement of a new response to one will generalize to the other(s). The mechanism underlying this effect is one long familiar to associative learning theory, namely, the process of "acquired equivalence" or Hull's mediated generalization (see Honey and Hall, 1989).

Relational Concepts

Perceptual similarity based on common features, and mediated generalization based on a common history of association, may be sufficient to account for many instances of transfer of discrimination or categorization. I do not believe that in either case it helps to talk of conceptualization or abstraction. Are there other instances of discrimination or categorization that are more usefully characterized in these terms?

For some years now, comparative psychologists' most popular example of a supposedly abstract concept has been identity, or sameness or difference. This certainly raises a new issue, for we are now talking about a *relationship* holding between two or more stimuli, rather than any feature or attribute of a single stimulus or stimulus array. Do animals (and if so which animals) show evidence of sensitivity to the relationships holding between two or more stimuli (and if so, which relationships)? According to Köhler (1918), the phenomenon of transposition was evidence that even the humble chicken responded to relationships such as brighter or darker, larger or smaller. If trained to choose the larger of two stimuli, and then given a choice between their original S+ and an even larger stimulus, the chickens chose the hitherto unseen larger stimulus in preference to their familiar S+. But Spence's (1937) classic analysis demonstrates how transposition can arise from the interaction of gradients of excitation and inhibition conditioned independently to S+ and S−. Given an appropriate choice of the shapes of these excitatory and inhibitory gradients, Spence argues, it is easy to show that the net excitatory value of the large S+ might be less than that of the even larger stimulus in Köhler's experiment. Spence's analysis was vindicated by the demonstration that the empirical postdiscrimination gradients obtained from pigeons trained on a successive wavelength discrimination between an S+ of 550 nm and an S− of 560 nm, did not peak at S+, but rather at stimuli of 530 or 540 nm (Hanson, 1959; this is the so-called "peak shift"). More recently, Wills and Mackintosh (1998) provided empirical evidence for Blough's (1975) re-interpretation of Spence's interacting gradients in terms of common elements. Pigeons (and people) will show a peak shift along a wholly artificial "dimension," where neighboring stimuli are constructed of overlapping sets of arbitrary icons.

Nevertheless, there is evidence that transposition may not be entirely accounted for in terms of Spence's or Blough's nonrelational theories (see Gonzalez et al., 1954). Riley and his colleagues (see Riley, 1968) have shown that the opportunity for simultaneous comparison of two stimuli differing in, say, brightness, both makes it easier for rats to learn the discrimination between them, and increases the incidence of transposition on subsequent test. The obvious interpretation seemed to be that simultaneous comparison of two stimuli differing in brightness made the relationship between them (one is brighter/darker than the other) more salient. But here, at least, as Riley notes, there is an even more obvious explanation of such effects in terms of a fairly low-level sensory process—that of contrast. By and large, the perceived brightness of any part of the visual field is a direct function of the amount of light reflected from that part of the field, and an inverse function of the amount of light reflected from neighboring parts of the field. If S+ and S− differ in luminance and are shown side by side, the presence of the objectively lighter S+ will decrease the perceived brightness of S−, just as the presence of the objectively darker S− will increase the perceived brightness of S+. Contrast increases the perceived difference between them, thus making discrimination between them easier to learn and, even in Spence's analysis, could increase the incidence of transposition. Wills and Mackintosh (1999) show that this may be the *only* sense in which pigeons show evidence of relational learning in such experiments. As Fetterman (1996) notes, what may be loosely described as evidence of sensitivity to abstract relationships may often be more appropriately analyzed as a hard-wired consequence of the structure of particular sensory systems.

Several other attempts to find evidence of relational learning in pigeons have been equally unsuccessful. Pearce (1991) trained pigeons to make one response to two vertical bars of the same height and another to two bars differing in height, and found no sign of learning until the two bars were actually touching one another—at which point a rather simple solution becomes available: make one response to a single wide bar (with a straight edge at the top) and another to a bar with a step in its top edge. Both Aydin (1991) and Wills (1996) failed to replicate in pigeons the results of a study of relational learning in rats by Lawrence and DeRivera (1954), where subjects were required to make one response to a vertical rectangle whose top half was lighter than the lower half, and another response when the top half was darker than the lower.

Sameness and Difference

I do not know whether the relationship of sameness or difference is any more abstract than the relationship of darker/brighter. It is certainly no easier to establish the nature of the processes involved in an animal's solution of a same-different discrimination.

A common procedure for studying same-different discrimination learning is to train animals on matching to sample or oddity discriminations, where they must choose between two alternative stimuli, A and B, one of which is the same as, the other different from, the sample stimulus (A on some trials, B on others) shown at the beginning of each trial. In an alternative procedure, only two stimuli are shown on each trial. One response is required when the two stimuli are the same (AA or BB) and a second response is required when the two are different (AB). Animals ranging from pigeons, crows, parrots, rats, and racoons, to monkeys and apes have all solved such problems (see Roitblatt and Fersen, 1992; Tomasello and Call, 1997, for reviews). The question is how they do it. The solution of a single problem, it seems obvious enough, could be based on specific conditional or configural learning, without any need to appeal to the animal's detection of the relationship between the stimuli: perform one response to the AA and BB configurations, another to the AB and BA configurations; or learn that if the sample is A, choose A not B, if it is B, choose B not A. Just as in categorization experiments, elucidation of what animals have learned depends on their performance on transfer tests.

There is now ample evidence that some birds (crows, rooks, jays, Wilson et al., 1985; an African grey parrot, Pepperberg, 1987), as well as monkeys and apes (see Tomasello and Call, 1997), show excellent transfer to wholly novel stimuli after training on matching or oddity discriminations with no more than one or two pairs of stimuli. Is this sufficient to establish that they learned to use the relationship (same or different) between sample and choice stimuli as the basis for their solution? It seems a reasonable interpretation, but there is an alternative, first noted by Premack (1983). In the typical matching or oddity problem, a trial starts with the presentation of the sample alone, to which the animal is required to respond before the choice stimuli are presented. It follows that if the sample was A, the choice stimulus, A, will be relatively more familiar (recently encountered) than the alternative B. Perhaps the problem is solved as a relative novelty-familiarity discrimination. Such a solution would, of course, transfer perfectly well to new stimuli, C and D, and so on. Novelty-familiarity seems a particularly plausible basis for the results of an experiment by Young et al. (1997). On some trials the birds were required to peck at each of 16 different pictures or icons shown one after the other, and then to make a "different" response. On others, the same icon (which could be any one of the 16) was presented 16 times in succession, with the birds required to peck at each presentation, before finally making a "same" response. The birds learned the discrimination and transferred moderately well to new icons.

A novelty-familiarity solution seems rather harder to imagine for the two-stimulus same-different discrimination (AA or BB versus AB or BA), and corvids, parrots, and primates have all solved and transferred such discriminations. It is most clearly ruled out by two variants of such problems. Pepperberg (1987) trained her parrot, Alex, with objects varying in color, material, and shape. His task was to specify the attribute(s) that differed between two otherwise similar objects—for example a red, wooden triangle versus a green, wooden triangle—or an attribute that was the same in two otherwise dissimilar objects—for example, a red, wooden triangle versus a red, leather circle. His performance on transfer tests to novel objects was impressively accurate. Equally convincing is the evidence of second-order relational learning in some primates. Premack's chimpanzee, Sarah, learned and transferred to novel stimuli the following matching problem: if the sample was two identical objects (AA), the correct choice stimulus was the one with two other identical objects (XX) rather than the one with two different objects (YZ). If the sample contained two dissimilar objects (BC), then YZ was correct rather than XX. Premack found that not all chimpanzees would transfer this solution to novel stimuli, and suggested that "language" training, of the kind experienced by Sarah, was necessary to enable them to do so. Subsequent studies have shown that this is clearly not true (e.g., Thompson et al., 1997). The fact remains that only chimpanzees have solved and transferred this problem, and not all chimpanzees have done so. Nevertheless, as Gillan et al. (1981) show, it is only a small step from this to generalized analogical reasoning, where Sarah has shown that she can detect whether a wide range of relationships (not just same or different) between two objects, A and A′, is or is not the same as the relationship between B and B′.

Can Pigeons Learn a Same-Different Discrimination?

Rather than analyze further the basis for such relational learning by primates and some birds, many comparative psychologists have devoted more energy to the rather less interesting question—whether pigeons are capable of relational learning at all. In spite of confident earlier claims to the contrary, it now seems reasonably clear (e.g., Wilson, et al., 1985; Wright et al., 1988) that after training on a single matching or oddity discrimination with only one pair of stimuli (A and B), pigeons show *no* reliable evidence of transfer to novel stimuli. But is that sufficient to prove that they are incapable of transferring a same-different rule? Not at all. According to Delius (1994), such experiments have proved little or nothing: "most of the evidence denying the identity-oddity concept to pigeons must be dismissed in retrospect as being due to the employment of patently inadequate methods" (p. 37).

These patently inadequate methods, it should be stressed, have been quite sufficient to yield decisive evidence of transfer in other birds and primates, and have shown good transfer in corvids and squirrel monkeys, but none in pigeons, when the various species have been trained under essentially the same conditions (Wilson et al., 1985; D'Amato et al., 1986). The minimal conclusion, therefore, must be that it is harder to obtain evidence of generalized same-different discrimination in pigeons than in many other animals. Given the paucity of other evidence for relational learning in pigeons, this should not come as a surprise.

But the pigeon's obstinacy is no match for some comparative psychologists' faith in its intellectual prowess. Two types of experiment have apparently yielded evidence of successful transfer of matching oddity or same-different discriminations in pigeons. The first (e.g., Lombardi et al., 1984; Wright et al., 1988) has simply given even more extensive training on an even larger number of different pairs of stimuli. The second (e.g., Cook et al., 1995; Wasserman et al., 1995) greatly increases the number of stimuli in the arrays between which birds are asked to discriminate. In the standard same-different discrimination, animals learn to make one response to AA or BB and another to AB or BA. In Wasserman et al.'s experiment, the stimulus arrays consisted of 16 icons in a 4×4 grid. If these are labelled A to P, there were 16 "same" stimuli consisting of 16 repetitions of A, or of B, and so on. The "different" stimuli were similar 4×4 arrays, but with each of the 16 icons appearing once. By the end of training, pigeons were about 85 percent correct, and when tested with a novel set of icons responded correctly on 70 percent of trials.

The problem with these newer procedures is that, at the same time as they provide better evidence of transfer, they also introduce the possibility of new bases for such transfer. Where birds are trained on a very large number of different matching or oddity discriminations, it becomes difficult to rule out the possibility that transfer will be based on the physical similarity between supposedly novel test stimuli and some of the stimuli used in training. The type of stimuli used by Cook and Wasserman and their colleagues suggests a different possibility. An obvious difference between a 4×4 array of As and a 4×4 array consisting of the 16 letters A to P each occurring once, is that the former has a regular texture and the latter does not. This would apply to the type of stimuli used by Cook, where the same displays consisted of the regular repetition of a particular type of item (let us say, As) and the different displays consisted of a large number of As, plus a single odd item, a B, or a small block of odd items. Both Cook and Wasserman argue against any such interpretation of their data on the rather strange grounds that their birds did not show perfect transfer to novel stimulus arrays, and therefore must have learned something about the actual physical properties of their training stimuli. So they must have, but it does not seem difficult to accept that they could have learned both something about the textural difference between same and different stimuli, and something about the specific individual items they contained.

Young et al. (1997) attempted to rule out such an interpretation by spreading the 16 icons in their same and different arrays over a random subset of 25 possible locations in a 5×5 grid, reasoning that the "decidedly disorderly" and "notably untidy" arrays thus generated would mean that the "same" stimuli no longer had a more regular texture than the "different" stimuli. They still observed good transfer (about 75 percent correct) to arrays of novel icons. But the fact remains that although less regular than the 4×4 "same" arrays used by Wasserman et al. (1995), the "same" arrays in this experiment must always have contained clumps, or long rows or columns, of regular texture. The obvious test of this analysis is to reduce the absolute number of icons in the same and different displays: an array of 16 or 12 identical icons, even if spread over a 5×5 grid, will inevitably produce areas of uniform texture, but an array of only two or four icons may not. And indeed, when Young and Wasserman trained pigeons concurrently on same-different discriminations with either 2, 4, 8, 12, or 16 icons in each display, their birds showed no sign of even learning (let alone transferring) the solution to the two- or four-icon displays. It is worth recalling that a two-item array (AA versus AB) is the standard same-different discrimination solved and transferred by rooks, parrots, and primates.

Enough, for the moment, of pigeons. For what it is worth, my own reading of the evidence is that no convincing case has yet been made that pigeons respond to the relationship between two or more stimuli. Others will, no doubt, dispute that conclusion. They may be right. But to prolong the discussion further would be to invest it with more importance than it deserves. For one thing, all I am suggesting is that the evidence presently available does not provide a particularly convincing case for relational learning in pigeons (as it does, say, for chimpanzees). It would be merely foolish to assert that pigeons are *incapable* of relational learning.

My argument has been designed to establish a single point. It is possible to distinguish among three rather distinct ways in which animals represent a set of stimuli. First, they can represent them as arrays or configurations of features or elements defined in terms of their own absolute values (allowing for known mechanisms of sensory interaction). Second, they can represent them in terms of the relations holding between two or more arrays—one is brighter or darker than another, two others are the same, and so on. Finally, they can compare the relations holding between two or more arrays with those holding between others: the relationship between A and A′ can be compared to that between B and B′. At a first approximation, pigeons (and no doubt many other animals) trained on a single discrimination problem (whether describable as a relational discrimination or not) provide an example of the first type of representation; some other birds and most primates an example of the second; and chimpanzees given appropriate prior experience (although we do not know what is or is not appropriate) an example of the third.

People

It is, of course, tempting to describe these different modes of representation as more or less abstract, complex, advanced, or intelligent. In part as a way of resisting that temptation, I shall conclude by presenting evidence for all three levels of representation in people. No one seriously doubts that adult humans understand the notion of both first-order and second-order relationships between events. It is, perhaps, harder to accept that elementary associative analyses also apply to the behavior of people. But the success of such analyses in the realm of categorization learning should not be forgotten. In many categorization experiments, however, there is often no abstract or rule-governed structure in the stimulus set to allow an alternative mode of solution, and where there is, people may indeed show sensitivity to it (e.g., Regehr and Brooks, 1993).

Thus a fairly natural preconception of many cognitive psychologists has been that where abstract structure or relationships between stimuli are available to guide choice, people will normally use such information to reduce the burden on memory imposed by learning the solution to a problem by rote (i.e., by simple associative learning). The preconception is often justified. When people and pigeons are trained on either a simple discrimination between two stimuli differing in brightness, or on a categorization task between a series of wedge-shaped stimuli, where long, thin wedges belong to one category and short fat wedges to the other, they behave differently to test stimuli that fall beyond the range of values they saw during training (Aitken, 1996; see also Mackintosh, 1997; Wills and Mackintosh, 1998). The pigeons show a peak shift: that is, they respond more rapidly to stimuli beyond S+ (or the S+ set) in the direction away from S−; but as the test stimuli move yet further away from S+, they stop responding. This is the behavior predicted by interacting gradients of generalization or by an elementary associative analysis. But people show true relational transposition: they continue to treat stimuli as belonging to the S+ category even when they are far removed from S+. It seems that they have learned that short fat wedges belong to one category and long thin ones to the other; the shorter and fatter (or the longer and thinner) the wedge seen on a test trial, the more securely it can be assigned to its correct category. They have labeled, and responded to, the *relationship* between the stimuli encountered in training.

But people do behave exactly like pigeons, and show nothing but a peak shift, if trained under certain circumstances. In Wills and Mackintosh's study, when the stimulus "dimension" was created by constructing stimuli of overlapping sets of arbitrary icons, both people and pigeons displayed similar peak shifts, responding more positively to a novel stimulus lying closer to S+ on the artificial dimension than to S+ itself, but less positively to a stimulus even further removed from S+.

Aitken was able to demonstrate a peak shift in people trained on the categorization task between long, thin and short, fat wedges. Here the secret was to move in the direction of an implicit learning task by presenting the wedge-shaped stimuli embedded in a great deal of other, irrelevant information, scheduling trials in rapid succession so that subjects had no time to stop and analyze the situation, and turning their task into a reaction time task, where they had to respond as rapidly and accurately as possible to a target stimulus appearing on the left or right of the screen. The location in which the target would appear was, in fact, sometimes predicted by the shape of the wedge that, along with other irrelevant stimuli, appeared at the beginning of some trials. Few subjects ever realized this—although their reaction times were faster on trials when a predictive wedge appeared than on trials when one did not. In other words, they could be described as learning implicitly. And then, when tested with a range of long, thin and short, fat wedges, they showed a classic peak shift.

I take this last experiment as evidence that, even where a relationship between two or more stimuli is available to control people's behavior, they may not always detect that relationship. But the preconception that people must detect and use relationships between events, or abstract structure, or rules to guide their decision making, is so strong that it is often accepted by cognitive psychologists as the explanation of their subjects' behavior, even when those subjects disclaim all knowledge of the relationships, rules, or structure. Their abstraction of the rules or structure is then said to be unconscious or implicit. Thus after exposure to strings of letters generated by an artificial grammar, subjects typically perform well above chance when asked to categorize as grammatical or ungrammatical new letter strings they have not seen before (e.g., Reber, 1989). Even though subjects are typically unable to articulate the rules underlying the problems they have apparently solved, Reber credits them with implicit knowledge of those rules.

But why is a simple associative analysis not just as capable of explaining categorization learning here as it is in other cases? The exposure phase of the experiment teaches subjects that certain letter strings are "grammatical," and their task on the test is to categorize new letter strings as grammatical or nongrammatical, on the basis of their similarity to this initial set (Perruchet and Pacteau, 1990). Here, as in the case of animal experiments, it has seemed that one way of distinguishing between a simple associative and a rule-based account, would be to test subjects not only with novel strings constructed from the same set of letters used in training, but also with strings constructed according to the same rules but from an entirely different set of letters.

The answer suggested by a whole series of such experiments is that people do show some transfer when tested with entirely new sets of letters, but their performance is significantly worse than when they are tested on novel strings constructed from the familiar set (see Whittlesea and Dorken, 1993). Depending on one's point of view, it is possible to point to above-chance performance as clear evidence of some rule learning, or to the significant decrement as evidence of rather little rule learning. A rather more fruitful approach is illustrated in one of Whittlesea and Dorken's experiments. Here, they exposed subjects to letter strings under three different conditions: in the standard condition, they were asked to memorize the strings; in a second condition, they were told that the letter strings were a distractor from their primary task; in a third, they were asked to count the number of repetitions of a particular item in each string. The three types of instruction had only a small effect on test performance to novel strings constructed from the original letter set. But significant differences appeared when subjects were tested on a new set of letters. The standard, memorizing condition produced the standard result: performance significantly above chance, but significantly worse than on the familiar set of letters. When the original task had been presented as a distractor, subjects were at chance on the test with the novel set. But when asked to count repetitions, they performed as well on the novel set as on the familiar set. Whittlesea and Dorken's reasonable interpretation was that under distractor conditions subjects encoded only the surface features of the letter strings without noting the relationships (repetitions) between items; in the repetition condition, they did encode these relationships, which became more important than the surface features; and in the standard condition they did a bit of both.

It is thus surely misleading to imply that participants in artificial grammar experiments learn the abstract rules that generate legal strings, whether unconsciously or consciously, let alone that they do so automatically. What they learn depends, as ever, on their reading of the task set them. Variations in what they learn under different instructions are better described as variations in how they encode the strings. When Whittlesea and Dorken's subjects were asked to note repetitions, they did not suddenly start learning the rules of the artificial grammar; they learned about the relations among items. What psychologists often describe as the abstraction of rules (whether by people or other animals) can very often be understood as learning about the relationships between events. In the present case, of course, appropriate performance on a transfer test to novel sets of letters depends on more than noting the relationship between two items in a string, it requires responding to relationships between relationships. Seeing that the string MQVVVAM is in one important sense the same as the string XBEEEHX requires noting the position of repeated and non-repeated items in each string, as well as the number of repetitions.

There is thus ample evidence that, under different circumstances, people will respond simply to the surface features (absolute properties) of items in an array, to the relation holding between two or more items in an array, and to the second-order relation holding between the relations between items in different arrays. The ability to detect and respond to such relationships, I should argue, often provides a better account of problem solving and transfer than does appeal to the notion of abstract rules.

The Evolution of Cognition

What implications does the analysis sketched here hold for the question of the evolution of cognition? One pervasive theme common to several chapters in this book has been to see how far a "general process" approach to the study of learning and cognition remains valid, or whether cognition must be characterized as modular. The answer given to this question depends partly on the type of behavior studied, and partly on the range of processes counted as cognitive. Cognition is modular if it is defined to include specialized systems for, say, dead reckoning or circadian timing; but even Shettleworth acknowledges that associative learning is widespread and has certain general properties that allow animals to learn about the causal relationships among a very wide variety of events. The research I have discussed has been concerned with associative learning, and to that extent it is about some rather general processes. But my argument has attempted to show that the power of associative learning to solve different kinds of problems varies dramatically with the nature of the stimulus representations that serve as input to the associative system. That is a conclusion that should be entirely congenial to the modular theorist who sees perceptual systems as the archetypal modules.

As Thorndike (1911) argued some years ago, the basic laws of associative learning are common to animals ranging from crab to monkey to human baby (although we now know that these laws are rather different from those Thorndike envisaged). Differences between crabs and monkeys were to be found in what stimuli they associated with what consequences—in my terminology, in what levels of representation are available to them. This analysis implies both continuity and discontinuity. The discontinuity is between the representation of stimuli simply in terms of their individual physical characteristics and the representation of the relationships between stimuli. The perception of relationships permits the generalization of the solution learned to one problem to other problems that share no physical features in common with the first. In the end, it permits analogical reasoning.

According to Tomasello (see chapter 9), "it is the understanding of relational categories in general that is the major skill differentiating the cognition of primates from that of other mammals." But he goes on to argue that such relational understanding has its origins in the need to understand third-party social relationships. While Tomasello and I agree on the key importance of relational understanding, I remain sceptical of his claim that only primates are capable of such understanding (the evidence from corvids and parrots cited above seems reasonably convincing to me), and also of his argument that the origins of such understanding are social. Not all corvids, for example, are particularly social, and in our own work we found no evidence of differences between those species that were social and those that were not (Mackintosh, 1988).

My analysis, however is also an argument for mental continuity, and not only in the sense envisaged by Thorndike. There is also evidence of continuity in the basic level of stimulus representation. Although people are obviously capable of perceiving and understanding relationships among events and relationships between relationships, experimental paradigms can be devised that reveal the operation of the simpler representational level. Cambridge students, who normally show relational transposition, will behave like pigeons and show only a peak shift if trained in certain ways with certain kinds of stimulus. When stimuli are presented as incidental distractors to the subject's main task, people will not detect the relationships between them that they would otherwise use to relieve the burden of rote memorization.

Although Charles Darwin (1871) proposed that comparative psychology should seek evidence of mental continuity between humans and other animals, I argue that he placed too much emphasis on finding evidence of precursors to, or elements of, human conceptual thought, reasoning, or even language in the behavior of other animals. But there is equal, perhaps even greater, value in finding evidence of the operation of basic, general processes in people. That, of course, was one of the goals of an earlier generation of behaviorists. But it is none the worse for that. I believe that it will prove just as fruitful, and command more respect, then the strategy that seeks, rather breathlessly and with more enthusiasm than caution, to find evidence of abstract concepts in pigeons. Cognitive psychologists find it rather easy to pour withering scorn on that particular endeavor (Chater and Heyes, 1994).

References

Aitken MRF (1996) Peak shift in pigeons and human categorisation. Ph.D. thesis, University of Cambridge.

Astley SL, Wasserman EA (1998) Novelty and functional equivalence in superordinate categorization by pigeons. Animal Learning and Behavior, 26: 125–138.

Aydin A (1991) Relation learning in pigeons. Master's thesis, University of Wales.

Blough DS (1975) Steady state data and a quantitative model of operant generalization and discrimination. Journal of Experimental Psychology: Animal Behavior Processes, 1: 3–21.

Chater N, Heyes C (1994) Animal concepts: Content and discontent. Mind and Language, 9: 209–246.

Cook RG, Cavoto KK, Cavoto BR (1995) Same-different texture discrimination and concept learning by pigeons. Journal of Experimental Psychology: Animal Behavior Processes, 21: 253–260.

D'Amato MR, Salmon DP, Loukas E, Tomie A (1986) Processing of identity and conditional relations in monkeys (Cebus apella) and pigeons (Columba livia). Animal Learning and Behavior, 14: 365–373.

Darwin C (1871) The descent of man and selection in relation to sex. London: John Murray.

Delius JD (1994) Comparative cognition of identity. In: International perspectives on psychological science: Leading themes (Bertelson P, Eelen P, d'Ydewalle G, ed), pp 25–40. Hillsdale, NJ, Hove, UK: Erlbaum.

Fetterman JG (1996) Dimensions of stimulus complexity. Journal of Experimental Psychology: Animal Behavior Processes, 22: 3–18.

Fields PE (1932) Studies in concept formation I: The development of the concept of triangularity by the white rat. Comparative Psychology Monographs, 9: 1–70.

Gillan DJ, Premack D, Woodruff G (1981) Reasoning in the chimpanzee: I. Analogical reasoning. Journal of Experimental Psychology: Animal Behavior Processes, 7: 1–17.

Gonzalez RC, Gentry GV, Bitterman ME (1954) Relational discrimination of intermediate size in the chimpanzee. Journal of Comparative and Physiological Psychology, 47: 385–388.

Hanson HM (1959) Effect of discrimination training on stimulus generalization. Journal of Experimental Psychology, 58: 321–334.

Herrnstein RJ (1984) Objects, categories, and discriminative stimuli. In: Animal cognition (Roitblat HT, Bever TG, Terrace HS, ed), pp 233–262. Hillsdale, NJ: Erlbaum.

Honey RC, Hall G (1989) Acquired equivalence and distinctiveness of cues. Journal of Experimental Psychology: Animal Behavior Processes, 15: 338–346.

Huber L, Lenz R (1993) A test of the linear feature model of polymorphous concept discrimination with pigeons. Quarterly Journal of Experimental Psychology, 46B: 1–18.

Köhler W (1918) Nachweis einfacher Structurfunktionen beim Schimpansen und beim Haushuhn. Abhandlungen der Königlich Preussischen Akademie der Wissenschaften, Phys. Math. Klasse, 2: 1–100. Translated and condensed as "Simple structural functions in the chimpanzee and in the chicken." In: A source book of gestalt psychology (Ellis WD, ed) pp. 217–227. London: Routledge and Kegan Paul.

Lashley KS (1938) The mechanism of vision. XV. Preliminary studies of the rat's capacity for detail vision. Journal of General Psychology, 18: 123–193.

Lawrence DH, DeRivera J (1954) Evidence for relational transposition. Journal of Comparative and Physiological Psychology, 47: 465–471.

Lea SEG (1984) In what sense do pigeons learn concepts? In: Animal Cognition (Roitblat HL, Bever T, Terrace HS, ed), pp 263–277. Hillsdale, NJ: Erlbaum.

Locke J (1690) An essay concerning human understanding. 1st ed. (abridged and edited by A.S. Pringle-Pattison) 1924. Oxford: Oxford University Press.

Lombardi CM, Fachinelli CC, Delius JD (1984) Oddity of visual patterns conceptualized by pigeons. Animal Learning and Behavior, 12: 2–6.

Mackintosh NJ (1988) Approaches to the study of animal intelligence. British Journal of Psychology, 79: 509–526.

Mackintosh NJ (1995) Categorization by people and pigeons. Quarterly Journal of Experimental Psychology, 48B: 193–214.

Mackintosh NJ (1997) Has the wheel turned full circle? Fifty years of learning theory, 1946–1996. Quarterly Journal of Experimental Psychology, 50A: 879–898.

Nakagawa E (1992) Effects of overtraining on reversal learning by rats in concurrent and single discriminations. Quarterly Journal of Experimental Psychology, 44B: 37–56.

Nosofsky R, Kruschke JK (1992) Investigations of an exemplar-based connectionist model of category learning. In: The psychology of learning and motivation (Medin DL, ed), pp 207–250. San Diego: Academic Press.

Pearce JM (1991) The acquisition of abstract and concrete categories by pigeons. In: Current topics in animal learning: Brain, emotion, and cognition (Dachowski L, Flaherty C, ed), pp 141–164. Hillsdale, NJ: Erlbaum.

Pepperberg IM (1987) Acquisition of the same/different concept by an African Grey parrot (Psittacus erithacus): Learning with respect to categories of color, shape, and material. Animal Learning and Behavior, 15: 423–432.

Perruchet P, Pacteau C (1990) Synthetic grammar learning: Implicit rule abstraction or explicit fragmentary knowledge. Journal of Experimental Psychology: General, 119: 264–275.

Premack D (1983) The codes of beast and man. Behavioral and Brain Sciences, 6: 125–167.

Reber AS (1989) Implicit learning and tacit knowledge. Journal of Experimental Psychology: General, 118: 219–235.

Regehr G, Brooks LR (1993) Perceptual manifestations of an analytic structure: The priority of holistic individuation. Journal of Experimental Psychology: General, 122: 92–114.

Riley DA (1968) Discrimination learning. Boston, MA: Allyn and Bacon.

Roberts WA, Mazmanian DS (1988) Concept learning at different levels of abstraction by pigeons, monkeys, and people. Journal of Experimental Psychology: Animal Behavior Processes, 14: 247–260.

Roitblatt HL, von Fersen L (1992) Comparative cognition: Representation and processes in learning and memory. Annual Review of Psychology, 43: 671–710.

Savage-Rumbaugh ES, Rumbaugh DM, Smith ST, Lawson J (1980) Reference—the linguistic essential. Science, 210: 922–925.

Spence KW (1937) The differential response to stimuli varying within a single dimension. Psychological Review, 44: 430–444.

Thompson RKR, Oden DL, Boysen ST (1997) Language-naive chimpanzees (Pan troglodytes) judge relations between relations in a conceptual matching-to-sample task. Journal of Experimental Psychology: Animal Behavior Processes, 23: 31–43.

Thorndike EL (1911) Animal Intelligence: Experimental Studies. New York: Macmillan.

Tomasello M, Call J (1997) Primate cognition. Oxford: Oxford University Press.

Vaughan W (1988) Formation of equivalence sets in pigeons. Journal of Experimental Psychology: Animal Behavior Processes, 14: 36–42.

von Fersen L, Delius JD (1989) Long-term retention of many visual patterns by pigeons. Ethology, 82: 141–155.

Wasserman EA (1997) The science of animal cognition: Past, present, and future. Journal of Experimental Psychology: Animal Behavior Processes, 23: 123–135.

Wasserman EA, Hugart JA, Kirkpatrick-Steger K (1995) Pigeons show same-different conceptualization after training with complex visual stimuli. Journal of Experimental Psychology: Animal Behavior Processes, 21: 248–252.

Wasserman EA, Kiedinger RE, Bhatt RS (1988) Conceptual behavior in pigeons: Categories, subcategories, and pseudocategories. Journal of Experimental Psychology: Animal Behavior Processes, 14: 235–246.

Whittlesea BWA, Dorken MD (1993) Incidentally, things in general are particularly determined: An episodic processing account of implicit learning. Journal of Experimental Psychology: General, 122: 227–248.

Wills SJ (1996) Relational Learning in Pigeons? Ph.D. thesis, University of Cambridge.

Wills SJ, Mackintosh NJ (1998) Peak Shift on an artificial dimension. Quarterly Journal of Experimental Psychology, 51B: 1–31.

Wills SJ, Mackintosh NJ (1999) Relational learning in pigeons? Quarterly Journal of Experimental Psychology, 52B: 31–52.

Wilson B, Mackintosh NJ, Boakes RA (1985) Transfer of relational rules in matching and oddity learning by pigeons and corvids. Quarterly Journal of Experimental Psychology, 37B: 313–332.

Wright AA, Cook RG, Rivera JJ, Sands SF, Delius JD (1988) Concept learning by pigeons: Matching-to-sample with trial-unique video picture stimuli. Animal Learning and Behavior, 16: 436–444.

Young ME, Wasserman EA, Dalrymple RM (1997) Memory-based same-different conceptualization by pigeons. Psychonomic Bulletin and Review, 4: 552–558.

Zentall TR, Hogan DE (1974) Pigeons can learn identity or difference, or both. Science, 191: 408–409.

Zentall TR, Sherburne LM, Steirn JN (1993) Common coding and stimulus class formation in pigeons. In: Animal cognition: A tribute to Donald A Riley (Zentall TR, ed), pp 217–236. Hillsdale, NJ: Erlbaum.

8 Primate Worlds

Kim Sterelny

Primate Mind Readers

Do nonhuman primates understand anything about other's minds? What would show such understanding? What is the simplest mind capable of representing other minds? When, why, and how did primates become "mind readers," aware not just of the likely future behaviors of their social partners, but of the mental causes of those behaviors as well? This paper seeks to answer some of these questions in the context of the "social intelligence hypothesis." This currently popular theory suggests that cognitive evolution in the primate lineage has been driven by selection for social skills. At some point in time, primate society became complex. This increase in complexity drove selection for increased individual intelligence, and with that increase in intelligence, primate society became yet more complex. Primate fitness became increasingly dependent on the skills of social navigation. The result was a feedback loop for ever higher intelligence adapted to solving the problems of a complex social life. In turn, selection for social intelligence became selection for mind reading capacities, for the actions of others are tracked best though representing the mental states that generate those actions.[1] In the jargon of the literature, such animals are known as "mind readers," in contrast to lowly behavior readers, capable only of representing others' actual and potential behaviors. Mind readers do not just represent but metarepresent.

Perhaps through the influence of the social intelligence hypothesis, there is a widespread expectation that the transition from behavior reading to mind reading took place somewhere in the evolution of the great ape clade. The main weight of experimental and field studies has been to probe for evidence of mind reading in this group. These investigations will be my focus, too, but in considering them it is important not to slide into seeing mind reading as a surrogate for cognitive sophistication in general. We should resist the temptation to suppose that any signs of cognitive sophistication signal the shift to mind reading. Behavior readers need not be restricted to simple reinforcement learning. Thus Dickinson and Balleine (this volume) argue that rats understand the causal relations between acts and outcomes. Imitation, too, is cognitively sophisticated, but despite claims to the contrary (see, for example, Tomasello, this volume) it does not show mind-reading capacities—or so I argue (Sterelny, 1998). It is possible to be (relatively) smart and be unable to metarepresent. It is a heterodox claim of this paper that it is also possible to metarepresent despite being (relatively) simple.

In considering the shift from behavior reading to mind reading, I shall depend on an idea about the adaptive advantages of representation. So it's important to develop an account of the presumed benefits of metarepresentational capacities. The most obvious is an enhanced capacity to anticipate others' actions in both cooperative and competitive interactions. In their famous paper on the evolution of communication, Krebs and Dawkins assume that this is the critical advantage of mind reading (Krebs and Dawkins, 1984). It's often thought that mind reading is useful to anticipate behavior in novel circumstances. For example, Tomasello (this volume) argues:

this kind of cognition enables organisms to solve problems in especially creative, flexible, and foresightful ways. Thus, in many cases intentional/causal understanding enables an individual to predict and control events even when their usual antecedent is not present—if there is some other event that may serve to instigate the mediating force. For example, an individual might create a novel way to distract a competitor. (p. 173)

In this picture, behavior readers learn specific environment/response rules. If you meet Fred at the banana feeder, stay well clear for otherwise he will bite you. These rules, the idea goes, will leave the behavior reader with no basis for predicting an agent's behavior in novel circumstances. What will Fred be like at the mango feeder? On this view, as primate environments become more unpredictable, a metarepresenting primate has skills of social navigation that a behavior reading primate lacks. One empirical challenge is to provide independent evidence of increasing environmental heterogeneity. That is not easy, for heterogeneity depends in part on how animals categorize their world. If a baboon characterizes its world in concrete, sensory terms, it will often find itself in a seemingly novel environment. If it is equipped with more abstract categories, it will much less often be in novel environments. There are other problems as well. The advantage accrues only to very sophisticated mind readers. Thus Tomasello's example turns on novelty leaving an agent's goals unchanged but changing the potential means to those goals. New environments will often have that impact on an agent's belief and preference structure. But not always: novelty can change an agent's preferences. So in predicting how another agent will act in a novel environment, the mind reading animal will need to know whether the novelty causes a re-ordering of preferences or just of instrumental beliefs. This is very fancy mind reading.

There is a second possibility. Readers may benefit by an ability to use others as instruments that tell them about the world. They exploit mind-world and behavior-world relations to find out about the world as it is now rather than agents' future behaviors. Dennett coined the term "an information gradient" to describe groups in which individuals vary a good deal in what they know (Dennett, 1983). An information gradient selects for the capacity to use others as sources of information about the world. The idea of using others as information sources has been discussed mostly in the context of imitation, but use of others need not be as cognitively sophisticated as imitation. Others can be sources of information about what in the environment is important. Reading others' motivations is a plausible takeoff point for the use of others as information stores. Hence the phenomenon in social learning known as stimulus enhancement: a heightened attention to others' interests.

If there has been selection for mind reading, mind readers must behave differently from behavior readers, and the fitness benefits of mind reading must be in the behavior of mind readers. Moreover, a behavioral difference that is only very subtly different, or one that is very rarely manifested, would probably not produce enough benefits to pay its way. Mind reading capacities are probably quite costly, at least if they require neocortical expansion (see Dunbar, this volume), so these behavioral differences should be striking. There has been a good deal of observational and experimental work in the primatological community trying to (a) isolate the behavioral signature of mind reading, and (b) verify or falsify the existence of that signature in nonhuman primates. There may be no behavioral magic bullet that establishes the existence of mind reading. As Whiten and Dennett emphasize, the difference between behavior reading and mind reading may be in a overall pattern of competence rather than in a specific skill, accessible to mind readers but not behavior readers. We cannot assume there are unambiguous signs of mind reading.

In the next section, I sketch a general account of representation and its function, and apply it to a view of primate metarepresentation. In the following sections, I exploit that general theory with two case studies, before concluding with a general moral. The first case concerns a relatively basic feature of another's mind: its focus of visual attention. The second concerns a more sophisticated and less behaviorally overt feature: another agent's knowledge.

Representing Mental States

Our capacity to understand and predict the behavior of others is usually taken to depend on a grip of "folk psychology," an implicit theory that links an agent's beliefs, preferences, emotions, and the like to his behaviors, though this view is now more controversial than it once was (Sterelny, 1997). This account of our ability to understand other agents has generated a tendency to identify the question "Do non-human primates represent the mental states of other animals?" with "Do nonhuman primates have a theory of mind?" On this line of thought, mind readers have a grip on something like folk psychology. In her recent sceptical review of "the primate theory of mind" literature, Heyes embraces this suggestion. She writes:

an animal with a theory of mind believes that mental states play a causal role in generating behaviour, and infers the presence of mental states in others by observation of their appearance and behaviour under various circumstances. (Heyes, 1998; p. 102)

To those who interpret the debate this way, an animal possesses concepts of mental states only if that animal has appropriate expectations about the connections among beliefs, preferences, and behavior. This is the natural view to take if concept possession is tied to inferential connections between concepts. This is known as the "inferential role" theory of meaning. Defenders of this view hold that the meaning of a concept derives in part or whole from the web of inferential connections among the beliefs in which that concept figures. Thus, for example, what makes my tiger-concept a tiger-concept are the inferential connections from tiger-beliefs to beliefs about animals, predators, prey, large striped cats, and so on. My tiger concept is defined by my implicit theory of tigers—my tiger lore—as revealed by this web of inference. For those who accept an inferential role to a theory of meaning, it is very natural to identify the possession of the concepts of belief, preference, and the like with the acquisition of something like folk psychology, a set of beliefs about the connections among beliefs, preferences, intentions, and behavior. In this view of concepts, to have a concept of belief is to have mastered a belief theory.

However, this view of concept possession is not mandatory. There are alternative views in which concepts are identified not by their connections in the internal economy of the mind but by their relations to the external world. So let's briefly back off to the more general problem: what is it for an animal to represent something? I have argued that an organism represents a feature of its world, as distinct from merely responding to it, if it can track that environmental feature via more than one kind of proximal stimulus. An animal that represents X is an animal with several independent channels of information about the X-ish features of its environment. It multi-tracks X (Sterelny, 1995, 1999). Consider a contrasting case. Arthropods often have beautifully ingenious ways of detecting relevant features of their environment, but they are often dependent on a single proximal cue. Thus the hygienic behaviour of ants and bees—their disposal of dead nestmates—depends on a single cue, the oleic acid decay produces. They have nothing equivalent to perceptual constancy mechanisms, mechanisms that would enable them to track the liveliness of their nestmates in different ways. Communication among ants in their nests typically depends on very specific chemical signals.

As successful coordination in a nest or a hive shows, cue-bound behavior can be very efficient. But control systems based on specific cues are fragile in important ways. An organism that can track its environment only through a single, specific cue is very limited in its ability to use feedback to control and modulate its behavior, for it relies on change in that single cue. Moreover, organisms whose behavior is cue-bound are unlikely to have capacities that are robust over a range of different environments, for environmental shifts will often disrupt their cues. The capacity to track functionally relevant features of the environment in more than one way is required for behavioral capacities to be robust.

In distinguishing between cue-bound organisms and those that track a given feature of their world through multiple clues, we need to distinguish between the use of multiple cues and variation in, and generalization of, a single stimulus. This is straightforward where organisms multitrack their world through distinct sense modalities. But the zebra that tracks the degree of threat posed by a hyena from both its posture and its gaze direction is using two cues, not one, even though using vision for both. The distinction between the use of two cues and stimulus generalization from a single cue is probably hard to define precisely. After all, no two hyena approaches will project onto the eyes of a zebra exactly the same retinal stimulus. But many particular cases are clear. For instance, consider the much discussed phenomenon of mirror self-recognition, the ability of chimps and perhaps other great apes to recognize their own image in a mirror. Heyes rightly argues that mirror self-recognition does not demonstrate possession of a concept of the self (Heyes, 1994, 1995). She points out that animals that find their way through physically cluttered environments have to adjust their behavior to the position of their body in space, so they must have a "body concept" of some kind. Information about their body is used to control their behavior. Mirror self-recognition is just a less usual example of the same phenomenon, and no more shows self-consciousness than does the behavior of a nimble bull in a china shop. But although self-recognition does not demonstrate self-consciousness, it does show an ability to track bodily features using unusual perceptual inputs. So animals capable of mirror self-recognition do not have a cue-bound body concept. Their body concept is a real representation of their body, for they can use unusual information channels to update it.

So let's deploy this representation/detection distinction to get a fix on representational capacities of primates. Primates in general adapt their behavior to the psychological states of other primates. Chimps, for example, respond differentially to chimps that are motivated to attack them. That is, they often recognize the clues, the threats that signal the imminence of attack. Their own behavior is adapted to behaviors caused by a distinctive psychological state. They recognize and respond to sets of behaviors that are cues to, because consequences of, particular psychological states. So in this very minimal sense primates *track* the psychological states of other primates just as ants track the property of being a nestmate. They respond, often appropriately, to the threat of attack through a flow of information about the motivational states of the potential aggressor to the mind of the responding primate. Further, they act according to behavior rules that specify their appropriate action, given that state of the other agent. However, tracking mental states is one thing; representing rather than detecting them, another. We need to know how bonobos, for instance, categorize the behavior of other bonobos. So suppose:

1. one bonobo always reads actions a, b, c, d, e . . . as actions of the same type;

2. actions a, b, c, d, e are in fact always generated by a distinctive mental state Q; let's suppose Q is anger.

At this point, the bonobo is at least detecting the mental states of an other, for its response covaries with anger. Its behavior is adapted to that feature of the environment. Our bonobo is representing rather than merely detecting the mental states of others if:

3. a, b, c, d, e do not have any single simple sensory cue in common.

There is recent work suggesting that chimps track visual attention by a simple cue, "face visible." Bonobos, let's suppose, do not track anger like this. Body posture, facial expression, and vocalizations can all independently feed into the "placate threat" behavior rule.

If the anger behaviors that the bonobo categorizes together share no *single* distinctive sensory cue, the bonobo is not stimulus bound with respect to anger, but can track it via a variety of its manifestations. This conclusion is strengthened as the bonobo's capacity to track anger approaches completeness:

4. Not only are a, b, c, d, e produced by anger. The bonobo responds in the same way to all or most of the behaviors anger typically produces.

Putting this together, then, a primate responds to the mental state of another if it can track—that is, it responds distinctively with some reliability—to some suite of behaviors that are actually caused by some specific mental state; anger or fear, for example. If, as de Waal suggests, a bonobo appeases angry behavior by trading sex for peace (de Waal, 1989) it is *tracking anger*. We investigate whether this is anger detection or anger representation through experimentally probing the robustness of the tracking. In particular, it is detection rather than representation if this capacity is cue-bound. At the same time, we can experimentally investigate the sophistication of this tracking by probing the *breadth* of the responses to anger. Does the anger-reader adapt to angry behavior differently in environments that cause that behavior to be expressed differently? Does it respond differently if the physical or social environment is different in important ways? Does it respond to anger differently depending on its recognition of other mental states of the animal? Or is the "anger behavior" rule simple: run! So this picture defines two separate experimental investigations. We investigate a primate's capacity to represent a mental state by investigating *the robustness of its ability to track that mental state*. Robustness is the variety of observational cues it uses in tracking. We can also investigate *the breadth of its response to tracking*. Breadth is the extent to which the tracker's expectations about, and responses to, the agent's behavior are appropriately modified by what else the tracker notices.

We can then think of an animal's social intelligence developing via two sorts of behavior rules. *Recognition rules* link a reader to tracked mental states. We search for the animal's recognition rules by fixing as far as we can the reader's environment, but varying behavioral cues of a single underlying cognitive state, to see whether the reader gives the same response to these different cues. I have been arguing that an animal is mind reading only if it has, for some mental states, a battery of recognition rules. *Output rules* govern responses to the states a reader can track. We probe an animal's output rules by fixing the reader's cue, varying the environment, and testing for different responses.

In a forthcoming paper, I argue that the capacity to represent evolves from the capacity to detect when organisms live in *informationally translucent environments.* Environments are translucent to an organism to the extent that ecologically relevant features of their environment map in complex, one-many ways onto their transducible world. If food, shelter, predators, mates, friends, and foe map in complex ways onto detectable physical signals, cue-driven organisms' behavior will often misfire. I need to factor translucence into the distinction between multiple and cue-bound tracking of the environment. In a very minimal sense, an animal capable of forming a conditioned association is capable of multiply tracking a feature of its environment. Pavlov's notorious dog learned to track the arrival of food not just through the sight of it on its way but through the sound of a bell as well. But this is not a form of multiple tracking in the sense I have been describing, for the dog, as its response shows, has no ability to use the flow of information down one channel to check the reliability of the other at that same time. Multiple tracking, which it adapts organisms to the translucence problem, must involve some form of integration or cross-channel checking. It is also important to distinguish between the use of multiple cues and change in a single cue over time. The fact that an animal exhibits plasticity over time in its responsiveness to a feature of its world does not show that it tracks that feature multiply at a time. So there is a difference between: (1) adding extra triggers of a given action;[2] (2) developing through learning a new and more complex trigger consisting of a gestalt whose elements are not individually salient; and (3) being able to use a number of independent, but cross-checked, information channels. Only (3) adapts an animal to the problem of translucence.

The importance of cross-talk between channels is implicit in Whiten's discussion of deception and its unmasking, for example. Deception may be unmasked by a combination of cues and hence by readers' attempts to track motivation through several cues (Whiten, 1996). For example, the agent's known history might cue the fact that its actual behavior will be at variance with its advertized behavior. Vervets can learn to discount unreliable conspecific's alarm calls. A clearer example of the advantage of cross-talk depends on the fact that advertising might "leak"—tell-tale cues might undercut an animal's advertising. De Waal has some nice, though anecdotal, evidence of chimps trying to suppress leakage; for example, trying to suppress signs of anxiety in confrontations. The environment might "leak" as well. That is, the agent might be acting in a way that the observer knows is inappropriate for the actual environment. For instance, it may be acting as if it can see something the agent knows is not there.[3]

So in my view, representation is tied to this strong sense of multitracking, and multiple tracking is an adaptation to the problem posed by translucent environments. Many versions of the social intelligence hypothesis are best seen as arguments that the social environments of primates—or particular primates—are informationally translucent. These hypotheses imply that often the relationship between behavioral cue and inner state will be complex. No single cue in isolation from others is to be relied on. For example, great apes need to track some inner states, and they can track them only by representing them. They need to exploit a *multiplicity of signs* of inner states, rather than a single proximal surrogate. As Povinelli and Cant point out in their discussion of orangutans, the sheer size of great apes is important, for it leads to physically less stereotyped behavior (Povinelli and Cant, 1995). That in itself means that the inner causes of those behaviors are harder to read off behavioral cues. If an animal moves through its environment in a highly stereotyped way, a particular postural position might well be an adequate single cue for flight/attack. If motion is unstereotyped, and functionally defined behavior patterns cross-classify behaviors defined by motor patterns, behavioral cues to motivational states will be less straightforward.

The social and cognitive complexity of primates exacerbates the problems of the observer. For example, if Tomasello (this volume) is right in thinking only primates track the relations between third parties and adjust their behavior accordingly, primate social behavior will be less predictable on the basis of single cues than the social behavior of other animals. The greater the number of factors that jointly determine an agent's behavior, the more an observer needs to notice if he or she is to predict that agent's action. Shifting-balance social organizations—organizations that are unstable mixes of cooperative and competitive interactions—may similarly exacerbate the prediction problem. In some monkey societies rank is inherited through the mother. Gibbon populations may be composed of highly cooperative families based on a monogamous pair. In such societies, it is perhaps in the interests of all parties to make behavior reading as easy as possible. But the more dynamic the mixture of cooperation and competition, and the more important concealment and deception becomes, then the less transparent the environment becomes. In this view, sheer group size would not be in itself significant. For though size might impose memory demands, it is a transparent, not translucent, feature of the environment.

The main point is not whether these plausibility considerations are correct. Rather it is that this picture of representation leads to a more empirically tractable account of the distinction between behavior reading and mind reading. My suggestion here converges with those of Whiten (1996) and Sober (1998). They both treat mind reading as positing a hidden variable connecting an animal's current and future behavior, though their views are not based on this account of the detection/representation distinction. They argue that the advantage of routing prediction through a hidden variable is coding efficiency. There is no behavior that only an agent employing a hidden variable analysis can predict. But as the predictive demands on a agent rises, it becomes ever more efficient to predict on the basis of assignments of belief and motivation to other agents. This is where their suggestions and mine come together. The coding efficiency derives from the fact that there are distinct overt signs of the inner mental state, and in distinct environments that inner state will generate different behaviors. If you can track the inner state, you need not track separately each way stimulus and behavior are linked.

A Case Study: Visual Attention and Implicit Knowledge of Other Minds

Experimental work testing for a fully fledged great ape theory of mind has generated results that are at best equivocal. One response has been to develop and test less ambitious ideas about what apes know about others' minds. An important example of this has been the investigation of the extent to which chimps understand visual attention. This is important because representing attention does not seem to be a particularly demanding problem—attention has an overt behavioral signature. Yet experimental results suggest that chimps' grip on visual attention is surprisingly limited. Insofar as chimps understanding hiding, stalking, and the like they must have at least a capacity to track the visual attention of others. They can follow the direction of gaze to its target (Whiten, 1997 p. 164). But Povinelli and Eddy ran a series of experiments that seem to show both that their capacity to track visual attention may be cue-bound, and their grip on the impact of attention on behavior might be equally impoverished. In these experiments, chimps were first trained to use their natural begging gesture to beg food from a trainer, moving either to the right or left side of an enclosure (depending on the trainer's location), and begging through a hole in a clear wall. The experiments tested for general attention by having tests in which one trainer offered food, the other a valueless object. Chimps had no trouble asking for food. Probe trials were alternated with standard trials to confirm a continuing motivation to ask for food. There seems no reason to suppose that the experimental set up posed any special problem to the chimps. In the probe trials, the chimps were offered the choice between seeking food from a trainer that was attending to them, and ones that were not. A number of different "attention-defeaters" were tested. Inattentive trainers variously had buckets over their head, were blindfolded, sat facing away, or sat with their hands over their eyes. In those cases in which distraction might have been a problem, the attentive trainers had matched "distracters." They sat with buckets on their shoulder, with a blindfold around their mouth, and with hands over their ears, respectively (Povinelli and Eddy, 1996).

The striking result is that the chimps performed at chance on all tasks except those involving the pairing of trainers facing away or facing forward. Even this seemed to depend on a very crude cue. Results dropped back down to chance when the experiment was redone with both sitting facing away, but one looking back over the shoulder. Povinelli and Eddy did test the idea that there were too many distracters, simply overwhelming the chimps, though really this only looks plausible with bucketed and blindfolded trainers. They redesigned the experiments so the chimps were first familiarized with trainers with odd accoutrements, but this redesign did not change the essential results. The chimps did eventually learn to beg from attending trainers, but this seems to be because they extracted the rule of attending to the trainer whose face was visible. Thus they returned to chance performance if they had to discriminate between trainers with eyes open and ones with their eyes shut. The experimental upshot read at face value is that either chimps can detect but not represent visual attention, or they have very limited means of using their representation of visual attention to track behavior, or both. Povinelli himself seems to interpret his experiments as showing a limited chimp grasp of the attention-to-behavior link. That is, they have impoverished output rules. But it's equally possible that their problem lies with the appearance-to-attention link. They rely on crude signals of attention, rather than failing to understand the behavioral import of attention.

In my view, these results are input/output ambiguous. In reading about the experiment, I wanted to know if the chimps made noises, gestures, or other attention-gaining activities. These rigid directions of gaze would certainly be very anomalous in the chimps' natural life. However, that might explain why chimps can survive being cue-bound with respect to visual attention. The cue "I see an agent's face" does track attention just because direction of gaze is not rigid. Sooner or later, mostly sooner, you will be spotted. Attention may be a transparent feature of their world, and hence not one that they need to track using many cues. Even if that is so, they may be well equipped to manipulate and use visual attention.

I think there are experimental results that lend some support to the idea that chimps track attention fragilely, by a simple cue, but their response breadth is not impoverished. Once they track attention they know what to do with it. In particular, they know how to maintain (and gain) it. Gomez reports a series of experiments along these lines (Gomez, 1996). Povinelli's chimps were asked to choose between attentive and inattentive trainers. Gomez's chimps were asked to make the trainers attentive, to attract attention. Gomez's trainers variously had their back to chimp, had their eyes closed, had their head peering into a corner of the enclosure, and had their eyes looking over the top of the chimp. While finding the "eyes closed" task tough, Gomez's chimps performed much better than Povinelli's.

Gomez himself interprets these issues via a distinction between implicit and explicit knowledge. The intuitive idea is that implicit information is more context bound, and perhaps more like knowing-how than knowing-that, than is explicit information. Knowledge becomes more explicit the more it can be exported from very particular contexts and activities. He interprets his work as showing that though chimps and gorillas might not have explicit knowledge about other primate's mental lives, they do have implicit know-how about them. In particular, they have know-how about behaviorally overt mental states like seeing.

However, the distinction between implicit and explicit representation is more a placeholder for a theory of representation than a theory in itself. These issues are more empirically tractable if we disaggregate the implicit/explicit distinction into tracking robustness and response breadth. Consider, for example, response breadth. I doubt whether any behavior is absolutely unconditional, for the motivational state of the reader will normally matter. But there may be some that are independent of what else the agent represents about his/her environment. So the breadth of the reader's response will depend on (1) the range of other features of the agent the reader tracks, and (2) the extent to which response depends not just on the other agent but the rest of the environment. The effect of the presence of supporters of one party or the other; the physical geography of the interaction; the value of a resource (in situations of conflict) and the like are all relevant to output breadth. (3) As the example of visual attention shows, response breadth can also depend on the capacity to manage inter-action. Can a reader direct attention in a wide range of situations and rather subtly (as some of the "tactical deception" anecdotes suggest) or only crudely, by touching and screaming?

To the extent that an animal's response depends on variation in its (nonsocial) environment, we need to consider the ways animal's categorize their environment. Are these categories concrete and sensory, or are they sometimes functional and ab-stract (see Macintosh, this volume; Bateson, this volume)? One important instance of this debate about how animals see their world centers on causation, on the causal connection between events. Rumbaugh and Hillix (this volume) argue that some primates understand some causal chains. Dickinson and allies argue that even rats can get it (Dickinson and Shanks, 1995; Dickinson and Balleine, this volume), whereas Tomasello (this volume) argues that true understanding of causal relations is unique to human cognition.

The distinction between robust tracking and response breadth is helpful in trying to discern the real disagreements here. Dickinson and Balleine argue that rats under-stand causality. Rats, they argue, are intentional agents because their behavior is governed through an interaction of their preferences and their instrumental beliefs. These instrumental beliefs are causal beliefs. Dickinson and Balleine argue that rats understand the causal relation between their acts and the outcomes they experience. Tomasello, in contrast, argues that nonhuman primates do not understand the causal relations between events in their environments. Unless rats are smarter than monkeys, it seems they cannot both be right. On analysis it turns out that Dickinson and Balleine are concerned with recognition rules, whereas Tomasello focuses on response breadth. Dickinson and Balleine are concerned with tracking, with what relationship in their environment rats track. Their experimental strategy is to present rats with a range of environments in which the relationship between A and B is sometimes causal, some-times probabilistic, sometimes merely contiguous (so B follows A often, but it follows not-A as well). They then use a simple behavior (the willingness of the rat to press a lever) to test whether rats are tracking a causal relationship between A and B, or whether they are tracking some other relation (perhaps temporal continuity) that overlaps the causal one. They are not primarily concerned with the cues through which rats track causal connection; still less are they concerned with showing that rats can use this knowledge flexibly, over a range of tasks. Tomasello, by contrast, is concerned with response breadth. He knows that primates keep track of relations among different events in their world, but he doubts that they understand causal relations because they cannot do much with their knowledge. Thus he cites the experiments of Visalberghi, experiments that show that neither monkeys nor apes can select an appropriate tool for a simple physical manipulation without extensive trial and error learning.

In sum, the distinction between tracking robustness and response breadth is a useful analytic tool in probing the debates about visual attention and many associated issues. In particular, it helps us to disaggregate these debates. It is important to see that there is no a priori reason to expect these features of mind reading to be linked. Detection can be severed from breadth: an agent may track willingness-to-play through a single cue, the play face, yet might have a rich set of behavior rules about the consequences of this state. Equally, as far as I can see, the different aspects of breadth might vary independently of one another. It would then be an interesting empirical discovery to show that they were in fact linked. Equally, an evolutionary or developmental hypothesis that predicted linkage, too, would be important.

Detecting a "Theory of Mind": What the Experiments Show

I have urged that the capacity to represent others' minds is not tied to the possession of a theory of the connections among belief, preference, and behavior. I further argued that there are plausibility considerations that suggest that primates do represent, and not merely detect, others' mental states. But the stronger claim—that primates have something like a theory of other minds—is interesting and important in its own right.

What would show that an animal had something like a theory of mind? Both Whiten (1996) and Heyes (1998) have flirted with the idea that role reversal, perspective taking, and similar experiments might be a diagnostic test for a theory of mind. In a simple form of role reversal experiments, chimps are trained in one of two roles. They must either indicate a bin with food to an ignorant human who then shares it, or to accept advice from a knowledgeable human. Povinelli reported that three of four chimps showed role reversal: having been trained in one role, they performed in the other. Whiten agrees that there are problems with the original experiment—perhaps learning the new role was merely accelerated—but he is inclined to the view that *if* chimps grasp "role reversal," it shows mind reading. The chimp does not merely copy the behavior of the agent whose role has been occupied. Role reversal is not just delayed imitation, at least not if imitation is just motor-pattern imitation (Whiten, 1996).

Heyes is sceptical about all actual experiments alleged to show a primate theory of mind. But she is inclined to be concessive on the "role taking" experiments of the original Premack and Woodruff paper (Premack and Woodruff, 1978). In that paper, Premack and Woodruff reported a chimp, Sarah, who chose photographs that represented solutions to a series of problems other agents faced. The idea is that to solve this task, Sarah had to have the concept of a plan and to attribute plans to other agents; she had to identify the intended final goal of a series of actions. Heyes points out that Sarah's successes are not decisive, for each individual case may be explained away. But she concedes there is no unitary killjoy hypothesis explaining away Sarah's performances.

I do not think these experiments, even if redone to avoid possible artifacts of the kind Heyes discusses, show anything like a folk psychology. Instead, I think they can be explained through Byrne's idea of a behavioral program. In discussing gorilla imitation, he argues that there was evidence that great apes have the ability to learn from others not by mimicking each chunk of motor behavior, but by understanding a behavioral program. The program is the overall organization and sequencing of the acts that jointly compose a skill (Byrne, 1995, 1997). Gorillas, for example, frequently eat thistles and other rather awkward plants, so they often need to do a good deal of manual processing of their food before they can eat it. This processing is quite complex, and involves a division of labor between the hands that changes through different stages of the processing. If some skills depend on behavioral programs, imitation can involve copying that program rather than a specific motor pattern. Though there is plenty of anecdotal evidence of great ape imitation, experimental evidence for imitation is surprisingly thin (Byrne, 1995; Russon, 1997). But if great apes are capable of imitation, it is impressive because it enables the observer to extract the program from the motor behavior.

Heyes (personal communication) is very dubious about the adequacy of this re-analysis, because she doubts that the notion of a behavioral program has been specified in ways that make it testable. In her view, Byrne has no criteria for distinguishing imitation of a behavioral program from an inaccurate or partial impersonation of it. He cannot distinguish between program level imitation and imitation of the detailed sequence of behavior that is not error-free. Heyes' challenge is well taken, but at least in principle there is an empirical distinction between program level imitation and mere inaccurate imitation.

First, if social learning consisted of the inaccurate imitation of a full behavioral routine, we would not expect errors to have the same pattern across different subjects. They ought to be distributed at random. Not so if social learning is program level imitation. Different subjects should be invariant with respect to the components of a skill identified in the behavioral program. If, say, gorillas have the capacity for program level learning and show this capacity in, say, learning from a model how to eat artichokes, we would expect, on the same task, different subjects—because they segment the task in the same way—to resemble the model in the same respects. Not so if the errors are just noise.

Second, imitation is experimentally distinguished from other forms of social learning through an experimental design in which a given outcome can be achieved in more than one way. Then, if the audience accomplishes the task *using the model's technique*, we have reason to think that they are learning about means, not just ends, from the model. This is known as the "two action" test. If we nest one two-action test inside another, we can distinguish program level imitation from merely inaccurate imitation. We need a task that (1) permits solution through more than one behavioral program; that is, the task can be decomposed into subtasks in different ways. (2) There are different but equally adequate ways of performing the subtasks. Each subtask is a two-action test itself. For example, I gather that chimps sometimes use their feet rather than their hands for a task. So suppose the mimic shares with the model a segmentation of the overall task, but uses its feet rather than its hands. Because variations in the component activities would not be errors or mistakes, that would be program imitation rather than error-ridden impersonation. There is no error here. The chimp has learned from the model a decomposition of the task into components. We have overall similarity in their choice of means but not similarity of detailed physical motions; there is no imitation at the subtask level.

I have no idea whether experimental evidence would support the claim that the great apes have the capacity to represent behavioral programs. But I think this idea is well defined enough to be an alternative hypothesis to theory of mind explanations of their fancier behavioral capacities. If, for example, chimps show role reversal, it is an impressive cognitive achievement. It shows an ability to abstract away from the motor details to an overall program of action. It is like learning social roles, or learning game roles. Chimps may be able to learn the rules of the Giving/Sharing/Pointing game. It's another behavioral program. They recognize what the game is, and what their role is in it, through the training experience. If chimp social behavior is structured in various ways without being stereotyped, it would not be surprising if they could do this. Collective hunting, and chimp war-making, if that turns out to be part of their standard repertoire, may be natural examples of coordinated unstereotyped acts in which different players play different roles, but not always the same role.

Heyes certainly does not think any experiment so far performed is strong enough to establish that a primate is mind reading. For example, she agrees that the killjoy results of the Povinelli and Eddy attention monitoring experiments are bad news for the idea that chimps understand the role of visual attention in behavior. But her crucial claim is that the experiment is not strong enough to deliver a positive result. It cannot confirm that chimps *understand* the importance of what an agent sees for what it can do. She argues that

simple discrimination techniques ... can tell us which observable cues chimpanzees use when deciding who to approach for food, but they cannot tell us why the chimpanzees used those cues. (Heyes, 1998; p 108)

Imagine that the data were as cleanly positive as they could have been. We still would have been left with two hypotheses. One is according to which chimpanzees know that one should beg from those with visible eyes, because only those whose eyes you can see can see you; the other hypothesis suggests that chimps only have a

tendency to beg from people with visible eyes, and while the chimpanzee may even know that begging from people with visible eyes is more likely to lead to reward, they do not explain this contingency to themselves in mental terms, or in any other way. (p 108)

This is right. But there is an analogous problem for the experimental design she proposes. She adds bells and whistles to the design of the "knower/guesser" experiments of Povinelli. In these "perspective taking" experiments, chimps were tested for their grip on the connection between knowing and seeing. In the first stage of the experiment, the chimp is in a room with two experimenters. One baits a bin (the knower) after the other has left the room. The absent trainer (the guesser) returns and both trainers point at a container. In Povinelli's experiment half the chimps learned to follow the knower's advice. But the critical, second stage of this experiment tested for the robustness of this effect by seeing whether the chimps continue to ask for the right advice when the guesser's advice is rendered obviously useless by another means—in particular, by having a bag over the head while the bin was being baited (Povinelli et al., 1990).

Heyes points out that the original experimental design is not quite sensitive enough to test whether taking the knower's advice really depends on getting the connection between seeing and knowing. But she thinks this is the right kind of experiment because it enables us to zero in on exactly what the chimps notice in a situation. In the training regime—stage one of the experiment—a *causal cue* and a *sensory cue* covary. Leaving the room is the sensory cue that covaries with the causal cue of being unable to see which of the bins is baited. The sensory cue of staying in the room covaries with the causal cue of being able to see the baited bin. In the probe trials, both stay in the room, and the guesser has a bag over her head. In Heyes' view, this experimental design fails to exclude the possibility of transfer on the basis of merely sensory rules of thumb. Perhaps chimps were just tracking "visible head." In that case they will still succeed in the probe trials, but not by understanding the knowing/ seeing connection. She thus suggests an experimental design involving the use of transparent and opaque glasses to minimize the chances of chimps using a sensory rule of thumb to track seeing.

Heyes' experimental design will help us tell whether chimps are representing rather than detecting seeing. Her design would tell us whether chimps can use multiple cues for tracking the properties of ignorance and knowledge. But this appears not to be her worry. She does not want to probe the recognition rules for seeing. Rather, she is interested in the chimps' understanding of the causal importance of seeing. But this is an issue of breadth, of the output rules. For this, I do not see how her experimental design is any advance on that of Povinelli. No experimental design in this family probes for breadth of tracking, for a broad band of capacities *to act on seeing*. Once chimps track seeing, to succeed in these experiments they need only to master fairly simple, unconditional output rules. They represent seeing, but perhaps without great breadth. For example, in one of Premack's experiments, one chimp removed the blindfold that prevented a trainer following her to a bin she wanted opened. But she need only understand that there is a connection between unobstructed line of sight and the capacity to follow her. She need not understand that connection is mediated through a covert inner state, or that it is important for a whole swag of other potential interactions. Similarly, a chimp could succeed in these experiments by following the rule "beg for food from those who saw it" without having any theory of the inner causes of behavior or appreciation of the role of seeing in numerous other contexts. They only need to track and respond to visual contact. So although Heyes's experimental design can help us triangulate on seeing as the critical cue that chimps represent and use, I do not see how it could play a critical role in helping us identify a recognizable though rudimentary folk psychology in chimp minds.

Nothing in this argument downplays the value of experimentally probing chimp worlds. Rather, the point is that *no single experiment* by itself reveals broad behavioral competence on the primates' part. Moreover, there is no privileged breadth, the attainment of which we could reasonably regard as criteria for having folk psychology. Our evidence here will be of the sort Whiten and Dennett recommend. The more circumstances in which chimps can exploit and use the relevance of line of sight, the more they count as understanding that line of site is mediated through the mind. I take this point to be methodological rather than metaphysical. If Fodor is right, there is some unique piece of cognitive architecture that constitutes having folk psychology. Even so, its experimental signature will be fuzzy. So I think this is the best we can do: a chimpanzee has more of a theory of mind (1) the more mental states of others it can track; (2) the more of these it can represent rather than detect; (3) the broader its behavioral competences are, with respect to those tracked states. But this is good enough to go on with.

Summary

In my view, an organism *represents a feature* of its world, as distinct from merely *responding* to it, if it can track that environmental feature via more than one kind of proximal stimulus. Arthropods often respond to the world in adaptively complex ways but via a single information channel. They are (often) cue-bound with respect to the features of the world that matter to them, and only detect and respond to their world. In contrast, animals capable of mirror self-recognition show an ability to track bodily features using unusual perceptual inputs.

I use this representation/detection distinction to get a fix on representational capacities of primates. A primate responds to the mental state of another if it can track—that is, respond distinctively with some reliability—to some suite of behaviors that are actually caused by some specific mental state. If, for example, a bonobo appeases angry behavior by trading sex for peace, it's tracking anger. We investigate whether this is anger detection or anger representation through experimentally probing the *robustness* of the tracking. At the same time, we can experimentally investigate the sophistication of this tracking by probing the *breadth* of the responses to anger. Does the anger-reader adapt to angry behavior differently in environments that cause that behavior to be expressed differently? So this picture defines two separate experimental investigations. We investigate a primate's capacity to represent a mental state by investigating the robustness of its ability to track that mental state. Robustness is the variety of observational cues it uses in tracking. We can also investigate the breadth of its response to tracking. Breadth is the extent to which the tracker's expectations about the agent's behavior or its appropriate response are appropriately modified by the agent's environment and the other mental states the mind reader tracks.

An animal's social intelligence develops via two sorts of behavior rules. Recognition rules link a reader to tracked mental states. An animal is mind reading only if it has, for some mental states, a battery of recognition rules. Output rules govern responses to the states a reader can track. We probe an animal's output rules by fixing the reader's cue, varying the environment, and testing for different responses.

Notes

1. The central idea of the social intelligence hypothesis is due to Humphrey (Humphrey, 1976) and Jolly (Jolly, 1966), both reprinted in Byrne and Whiten, 1988. Since their early formulations, it has been developed in somewhat different ways by Dunbar, Tomasello, Byrne, Whiten, and others.

2. Extra triggers may well have a functional salience of their own. Adding redundancy into behavioral control may well be important if false negatives are to be avoided.

3. There is a nifty discussion of this possibility in Hauser's discussion of food calling in domestic chickens. Males produce false calls a good deal less often when females are close and in a position to see whether the male has food (Hauser, 1997). This is probably a case both of environmental and behavioral leaking. If I remember my days as a chickenherd correctly, calling is accompanied by excited pecking. So unless the males are smart enough to peck at nothing (which I doubt), their behavior, not just their circumstances, will give them away. Hens are able, if Hauser is right, to cross-check a social signal of food (male calling) against physical evidence.

References

Byrne RW (1995) The thinking ape: Evolutionary origins of intelligence. Oxford: Oxford University Press.

Byrne RW (1997) The technical intelligence hypothesis: An additional evolutionary stimulus to intelligence? In: Machiavellian intelligence II: Extensions and evaluations (Byrne R, Whiten A, ed), pp 289–311. Cambridge: Cambridge University Press.

Byrne RW, Whiten A (1988) Machiavellian intelligence. Social expertise and the evolution of intellect in monkeys, apes, and humans. New York: Oxford University Press.

de Waal F (1989) Peacemaking among primates. Harvard: Harvard University Press.

Dennett D (1983) Intentional systems in cognitive ethology: The "panglossian paradigm" defended. Behavioral and Brain Sciences, 6: 343–390.

Dickinson A, Shanks D (1995) Instrumental action and causal representation. In: Causal cognition: A multidisciplinary debate (Sperber D, Premack D, Premack AJ, ed), pp 5–24. Oxford: Clarendon Press.

Gomez J-C (1996) Non-human primate theories of (non-human primate) minds: Some issues concerning the origins of mind-reading. In: Theories of theories of mind (Carruthers P, Smith P, ed), pp 330–343. Cambridge: Cambridge University Press.

Hauser M (1997) Minding the behavior of deception. In: Machiavellian intelligence II: Extensions and evaluations (Byrne R, Whiten A, ed), pp 112–143. Cambridge: Cambridge University Press.

Heyes CM (1994) Reflections on self-recognition in primates. Animal Behaviour, 47: 909–919.

Heyes CM (1995) Self-recognition in primates: Further reflections create a hall of mirrors. Animal Behaviour, 51: 1533–1541.

Heyes CM (1998) Theory of mind in nonhuman primates. Behavioral and Brain Sciences, 21: 101–134.

Humphrey NK (1976) The social function of intellect. In: Growing points in ethology (Bateson PPG, Hinde RA, ed), pp 303–317. Cambridge: Cambridge University Press.

Jolly A (1966) Lemur social behaviour and primate intelligence. Science, 153: 501–506.

Krebs J, Dawkins R (1984) Animal signals, mind-reading and manipulation. In: Behavioural ecology: An evolutionary approach (Krebs JR, Davies NB, ed), pp 380–402. Oxford: Blackwell Scientific.

Povinelli D, Cant JGH (1995) Arboreal clambering and the evolution of self-conception. Quarterly Review of Biology, 70: 393–421.

Povinelli DJ, Eddy TJ (1996) What young chimpanzees know about seeing. Monographs of the Society for Research in Child Development, 61: 1–152.

Povinelli DJ, Nelson KE, Boysen ST (1990) Inferences about guessing and knowing by chimpanzees (Pan troglodytes). Journal of Comparative Psychology, 104: 203–210.

Premack D, Woodruff G (1978) Does the chimpanzee have a theory of mind? Behavioral and Brain Sciences, 1: 515–526.

Russon AE (1997) Exploiting the expertise of others. In: Machiavellian intelligence II: Extensions and evaluations (Byrne R, Whiten A, ed), pp 174–206. Oxford: Oxford University Press.

Sober E (1998) Black box inference—when should intervening variables be postulated? British Journal for the Philosophy of Science, 49: 469–498.

Sterelny K (1995) Basic minds. Philosophical Perspectives, 9: 251–270.

Sterelny K (1997) Navigating the social world: Simulation versus theory. Philosophical Books, 37: 11–29.

Sterelny K (1998) Intentional agency and the metarepresentational hypothesis. Mind and Language, 13: 11–28.

Sterelny K (1999) Situated agents: The descent of desire. In: Biology meets psychology: Constraints, conjectures, connections (Hardcastle V, ed), pp 203–219. Cambridge: MIT Press.

Whiten A (1996) When does smart behaviour-reading become mind reading? In: Theories of theories of mind (Carruthers P, Smith P, ed), pp 277–292. Cambridge: Cambridge University Press.

Whiten A (1997) The Machiavellian mindreader. In: Machiavellian intelligence II: Extensions and evaluations (Whiten A, Byrne RW, ed), pp 144–172. Oxford: Oxford University Press.

III CAUSALITY

The authors in this section debate the issue of which nonhuman animals, if any, understand causality, and the related question of whether understanding action-outcome relationships is achieved via different how rules (Heyes, this volume) than understanding causal relationships among action-independent events, and/or understanding social interactions among conspecifics.

Tomasello begins the section with a very clear claim. Nonhuman primates can learn the relations between their own actions and the outcomes of those actions, and they can represent some relations between objects and between the actions of third parties, but humans alone can understand the latter in a "causal/intentional" way. In other words, only humans attribute observed interactions among animate and inanimate objects to mediating forces; physical forces in the case of inanimate objects and intentional or mental states in the case of other animals.

Tomasello's view contrasts with those of Dunbar, Rumbaugh et al., and, most markedly, with that of Dickinson and Balleine. Using information about neocortical volume, as well as behavioral data, Dunbar argues that causal/intentional understanding is present in other great apes, not just humans. Similarly, Rumbaugh et al. find evidence of this kind of understanding in language trained chimpanzees and in other nonhuman apes that have not had experience in the use of symbols for communication. However, like Tomasello, both Dunbar and Rumbaugh et al., assume that understanding of the relationship between one's own actions and their outcomes is taxonomically widespread and cognitively unimpressive; perhaps it occurs through associative mechanisms, and certainly it does not involve intentional processes. By contrast, Dickinson and Balleine report the results of a series of carefully designed experiments which, they argue, indicate that rats learn some action-outcome relationships in an intentional way.

This contrast is not wholly attributable to the fact that Dickinson and Balleine regard processing as intentional when it involves first order mental states, such as beliefs and desires, whereas Tomasello describes processing as intentional only when it seems to involve second order mental states, such as the ascription of beliefs and desires to others. The residual point of contention is whether causal understanding necessarily invokes some content-specific force to explain the observed connection between cause and effect, as Tomasello implies, or whether human and nonhuman animals can understand that action X causes outcome Y in a "content-free" or "Humean" way (Dickinson and Balleine), without the cognizer having any "theory" about mediating forces or mechanisms. In the terms used by Heyes (this volume), the two parties disagree about the specificity of the what/when rules of causal understanding.

Although contrasting, Tomasello's and Dickinson and Balleine's analyses are not irreconcilable. For example, "content-free" or "Humean" causal understanding might be widespread among mammals (or vertebrates more generally; see Heinrich, this volume), having evolved as the basis of goal-directed action. It warrants the label "causal understanding" because, from the human perspective, it tracks causal relationships between actions and outcomes, and, crucially, it is based on how rules distinct from those of associative learning. This kind of causal understanding continues to be used by humans in assessing the outcomes of their own actions (Mackintosh, this volume; Macphail, this volume), but humans can also use culturally evolved theories to postulate forces mediating action-outcome relationships, whether the "agent" in these relationships is the cognizer, another person, or an inanimate object.

9 Two Hypotheses About Primate Cognition

Michael Tomasello

I would like to propose two hypotheses about primate cognition. The first has to do with the cognition of primates as an order, and how it may be different from that of other mammals; the second has to do with the cognition of human beings as a species, and how it may be different from that of other primates. Both of the proposed distinctions represent novel biological adaptations that primarily concern processes of social cognition. The uniquely primate social-cognitive adaptation makes possible a more complex social life; the uniquely human social-cognitive adaptation makes possible a cultural life.

Uniquely Primate Cognition

There is excellent evidence that the individuals of most species of primate recognize other individuals in their own groups. In interacting with these individuals, they form social relationships with them. In particular situations they are quite good at predicting what other individuals will do, based upon both general contextual information and on their past experience with particular individuals' behavioral tendencies. They form complex coalitions and alliances with groupmates, and cooperate and compete with them in many other kinds of important activities. Most primate individuals follow the gaze of conspecifics, and learn from them socially in a number of different situations. The large amount of evidence supporting the existence of these primate cognitive skills is extensively reviewed in Tomasello and Call (1994, 1997).

The problem for the question of primate uniqueness is that many other mammalian species recognize individuals in their groups, form relationships with them, and "read" their behavior in various ways (Green and Marler, 1979). In addition, a number of nonprimate mammals also form coalitions and alliances—the best-studied being lions, hyenas, and dolphins (see papers in Harcourt and de Waal, 1992)—and also cooperate with one another in other ways as well (Packer and Ruttan, 1988). But one difference in the coalitions and alliances of primates, pointed out by Harcourt (1992), is that primates seem to select their partners based on their appropriateness, given the opponent and circumstance. Thus, when female baboons engage in a protected threat, they do not very often solicit a low-ranking male in order to threaten a high-ranking male, but rather the opposite. This selectivity with regard to the relative rank of ally and foe suggests the possibility that primates do not just understand their own social relationships, but they also understand something of the relationships that third parties have with one another.

Protected Threat — X chooses as an ally Y, who outranks opponent Z

Grooming Competition — X chooses to groom the highest ranking

    among several available individuals

Recruitment Screams — X understands the recruitment scream of Y as

    indicating Y's subordinance to Z

Redirected Aggression — X (or X's kin) is attacked by Y, and so X

    retaliates by attacking Y's kin

Separating Interventions — X perceives Y and Z in a friendly interaction

    and, anticipating an undesired alliance, intervenes to break it up

Mediating Reconciliations — X observes that Y and Z have fought and

    so intervenes to try to encourage their reconciliation

Respect for "Ownership" — X observes that Y "controls" Z (e.g.,

    sexually) and so respects that control relation

Figure 9.1
Naturalistic evidence of primate understanding of third-party social relationships involving dominance, kinship, and "friendship." (Note that some of these behaviors have other interpretations; see Tomasello and Call, 1997.)

There is strong evidence for this understanding of third-party social relationships in a number of different primate species (Tomasello and Call, 1994). Observational evidence involves at least seven different common behaviors. For example, redirected aggression, in which you attack me but I retaliate by attacking your relative—indicating my knowledge of the kinship relation between the two of you. The other six behaviors are listed and briefly described in figure 9.1. In addition, there are at least two pieces of experimental evidence. First, Cheney and Seyfarth (1980) played a previously recorded vocalization of one of three juvenile vervet monkeys to its mother and two other adult females who also had absent offspring. Each female responded to her own juvenile's call by looking toward the call's source. But when the call of one of the other females' offspring was played, they looked to the appropriate mother—often before she had made any overt movement or sign of recognition. This anticipatory behavior would seem to indicate that individuals recognize the third party relationship holding between particular mothers and their offspring. Second, and perhaps most importantly, Dasser (1988a) found evidence for the understanding of *categories* of social relationships. She rewarded longtail macaques for choosing various pictures of one mother-offspring pair over pictures of pairs of unrelated groupmates. Subjects were then asked to choose between pictures of other mother-offspring pairs and other unrelated pairs. Subjects consistently chose the mother-offspring pairs, demonstrating their ability to see a categorical relationship among a number of different pairs of this type (Dasser, 1988b, also obtained similar results in a study of the sibling relationship).

Because they were concerned with cognitive skills that distinguish primates from other animals, Tomasello and Call (1997) searched the literature on the social mammals that have been most studied—especially, lions (e.g., Packer, 1994), elephants (e.g., Moss, 1988), hyenas (e.g, Zabel et al., 1992), and dolphins (e.g., Connor et al., 1992)—and found none of the seven pieces of observational evidence for the understanding of third party social relationships depicted in table 9.1; and there are no experiments, either. One problem, of course, is that these researchers may not have been looking for these behaviors. In general, primatologists are more interested in cognitive skills than are behavioral biologists studying social mammals. And so, although future research may tell a different story, for now I think the absence of evidence from social mammals is significant. My hypothesis is thus that although many animals recognize individuals and form relationships with them, only primates understand and form categories of third party social relationships. Obviously, keeping track not only of one's own direct relationships, but also the relationships that hold among others in the group, makes for special cognitive complexities in the social domain.

Very different, but nevertheless converging, evidence for the validity of this conclusion comes from the domain of physical cognition. As compared with other mammals, there is some evidence that primates are especially skillful in dealing with relational categories as manifest, for example, in discrimination learning problems involving oddity, transitivity, and relation matching (Thomas, 1980). Understanding these categories is clearly similar to understanding third-party social relationships in that they both involve the understanding of how two external entities relate to one another. In the experimental studies with objects, however, it takes many hundreds of trials, sometimes thousands of trials, for individuals to begin making the appropriate discriminations. This is in contrast to the understanding of categories of third-party social relationships that seem to come to them so naturally. Following Humphrey's (1976) general line of reasoning, therefore, one hypothesis is that primates evolved the ability to understand categories of third-party social relationships, and in the laboratory we may sometimes tap into this skill using physical rather than social objects if we train individuals long enough. Indeed, it is difficult to think of specific problems in the physical world with which the understanding of relational categories would be of direct help, whereas in the social world there are all kinds of situations in which the understanding of third-party social relationships would immediately make for more effective social action.

Overall, then, it is the understanding of relational categories in general that is the major skill differentiating the cognition of primates from that of other mammals (cf. Mackintosh, this volume). The hypothesis, however, is that the original evolutionary adaptation was for understanding the third-party social relationships of conspecifics, and this may be extended to physical objects only with special efforts in special circumstances. A further hypothesis is that the understanding of relational categories is an evolutionary precursor—a kind of halfway house—for the uniquely human cognitive ability to understand the intentional relations that conspecifics have to the external world and the causal relations that inanimate objects and events have with one another.

Uniquely Human Cognition

It is widely believed that nonhuman primates have an understanding of the intentionality of conspecifics and the causality of inanimate objects and events. I do not believe that they do, and I have argued and reviewed evidence extensively for this negative conclusion (Tomasello, 1990, 1994, 1996; Tomasello et al., 1993; Tomasello and Call, 1994, 1997). However, it should be made very clear that this negative conclusion about the understanding of intentionality and causality is quite specific and delimited. I believe that nonhuman primates do have an understanding of all kinds of complex physical and social concepts, they possess and use all kinds of cognitive representations, they clearly differentiate between animate and inanimate objects, and they employ in their interactions with their environments all kinds of complex and insightful problem-solving strategies (as reviewed above). It is just that they do not view the world in terms of the kinds of intermediate and often hidden "forces"—underlying causes, reasons, intentions, and explanations—that are so important to human thinking.

In the social realm, the evidence for nonhuman primate understanding of the intentionality of other animate beings is of two sorts. First, there are two experimental studies that purport to show that chimpanzees understand others as intentional beings. Premack and Woodruff (1978) had the chimpanzee Sarah choose pictures to complete video sequences of intentional human actions (e.g., she had to choose a picture of a key when the human in the video was trying to exit a locked door). Her success in the task led to the inference that she knew the human's goal in the depicted actions. However, Savage-Rumbaugh et al. (1978) produced similar results using as stimuli simple associates; for example, their apes also chose a picture of a key when shown a picture of a lock with no human action occurring at all. This raises the possibility that what Sarah was doing was simple associative learning. (Premack [1986] reported that in a subsequent study he could not train Sarah to discriminate videos of humans engaged in intentional vs. nonintentional actions, and Povinelli et al. [1998] were also not able to find this discrimination in their six chimpanzee subjects. The results of Call and Tomasello [1998] are mixed.)

The other study is that of Povinelli et al. (1990), who found that chimpanzees preferred to ask for food from a person who had witnessed its hiding over someone who had not witnessed its hiding—the inference being that they could discriminate a "knowledgeable" from an "ignorant" human. The problem in this case is that the apes in this study only learned to do this over many scores of trials with feedback on their accuracy after every trial (Heyes, 1994; Povinelli, 1994), and this is also a problem for the study of Woodruff and Premack (1979), in which chimpanzees learned after many trials with feedback to direct humans to the box without food so they could obtain the one with food (what some call "deception"). The problem is thus that the chimpanzees in these studies did not bring a knowledge of others' intentionality to the experiment, but rather they learned how to behave to get what they wanted as the experiment unfolded. In a study in which learning during the experiment was all but ruled out, Call and Tomasello (in press) found that chimpanzees showed no understanding of the false beliefs of others.

But because all of these experiments are artificial in various ways, other investigators have turned to the natural behavior of chimpanzees and other nonhuman primates for positive evidence of the understanding of intentionality. The problem in this case is that almost all of the reported observations are anecdotes that lack the appropriate control observations to rule out competing explanations (Byrne and Whiten, 1988). But even in reliable (replicable) cases it is not clear what is going on cognitively. For example, de Waal (1986) observed a female chimpanzee on repeated occasions hold out her hand to another in an apparent appeasement gesture, but when the other approached she attacked him. This might be a case of humanlike deception: the perpetrator wanted the other to believe that she had friendly intentions when in fact she did not. It is just as likely, however, that the perpetrator wanted the other individual to approach her (so she could attack), and so performed a behavior that had in the past led conspecifics to approach in other contexts. This use of an established social behavior in a novel context is clearly a very intelligent and perhaps insightful strategy for manipulating the behavior of others, but it is not clear that it involves the understanding and manipulation of the intentional states of others.

I should also point out some things that nonhuman primates in their natural habitats do not do (apes raised in something resembling a human cultural environment do some of them—see discussion below). In their natural habitats, nonhuman primates:

• do not point or gesture to outside objects for others;
• do not hold objects up to show them to others;
• do not try to bring others to locations so that they can observe things there;
• do not actively offer objects to other individuals by holding them out;
• do not intentionally teach things to others.

They do not do these things, in my view, because they do not understand that the conspecific has intentional and mental states that can potentially be affected.

So the most plausible hypothesis is that nonhuman primates understand conspecifics as animate beings capable of spontaneous self-movement—indeed, this is the basis for their social understanding in general and their understanding of third-party social relationships in particular—but they do not understand others as intentional agents in the process of pursuing goals. Nonhuman primates see a conspecific moving toward food and may infer, based on past experience, what is likely to happen next, and they may even use intelligent and insightful social strategies to affect what happens next. But human beings see something different. They see a conspecific as trying to obtain the food as a goal, and they can attempt to affect this and other intentional states, not just behavior. This somewhat subtle difference of social perception and understanding will be explicated more fully below, as will some of the profound consequences it has for all aspects of social life and cognition.

In the physical realm—and with specific reference to primate understanding of causality—Visalberghi has recently observed some limitations in primates' skills at adapting to novel foraging tasks in which some understanding of causality is required (Visalberghi and Limongelli, 1996). The basic task involves the subject using a stick to push food out of a clear tube. In one set of tasks, the tools are varied, with some being too short, or too fat, or not rigid enough to work properly. The basic idea is that if an individual understands the physical causality involved in how the stick works to extract the food from the tube—physical force transferred from self to stick to food—it should be able to predict just from perceptual inspection of a tool, without extensive trial and error, whether or not it will effect the required causal sequence. Although apes are a bit more skillful than capuchin monkeys at this task, both succeed with the novel tools only after much trial and error. In a recent task variation, these same species were given a clear tube with a small trap under one part. If subjects appreciate the causal force of gravity and the physics of holes and sticks moving objects, they should learn to avoid this trap as they attempt to push the food through the tube (i.e., they should always push the food out the end away from the trap). But neither capuchins nor chimpanzees learned to do this quickly; for example, all four chimpanzee subjects behaved at chance levels for 70 or more trials. In a final twist, after the animals had learned through trial and error to avoid the trap, the tube was flipped over—so that the trap was on top of the tube and posing no danger. Subjects of both species (the chimpanzees in a study by Reaux, 1995) still pushed the food away from the trap, not understanding its new harmless status. Two- to three-year-old children behave much more flexibly and adaptively on these tube problems— seeming to understand something of the causal principles at work—from the very earliest trials (Visalberghi and Limongelli, 1996). The conclusion is thus that non-human primates have many cognitive skills involving physical objects and events; they just do not perceive or understand underlying causes as mediating the dynamic relations among these objects and events.

By way of summary, I would like to be fully explicit about what differentiates intentional/causal cognition from other types of cognition. First, this form of thinking concerns the relations among external events. Thus, many animals understand that their own actions produce results in the world, and they repeat the actions needed to produce desired results; this is the sine qua non of behavioral and cognitive adaptations. But only primates also understand and categorize something of the relations among external entities, even in the absence of their own behavioral involvement. But, in addition, the understanding of intentionality and causality concern the understanding of mediating forces in these external events that explain "why" a particular antecedent-consequent sequence occurs as it does (typically not readily observable), and this understanding is unique to humans. Thus, for humans, the weight of the falling rock "forces" the log to splinter; the goal of obtaining food "forces" the organism to look under the log. Obviously, the way these forces work are very different in the causality of inanimate objects and the intentionality of animate beings, but the overall structure of the reasoning processes involved is of the same general nature. This can be clearly seen in figure 9.2, which depicts one physical causal situation—different physical events that create a force that causes a fruit to drop—and one social causal situation—different social events that create a psychological state that causes an individual to flee.

In terms of evolution, then, the hypothesis is that human beings built directly on the uniquely primate cognitive adaptation for understanding external relations; they

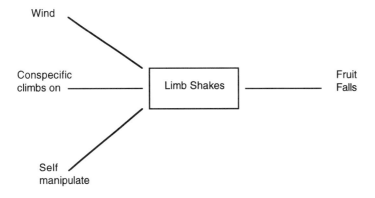

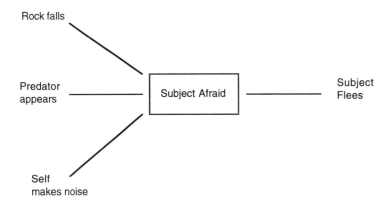

Figure 9.2
Graphic depiction of one physical causal event (top) and one social causal event (bottom). In both cases many different antecedent events may create the force that causes the consequent event.

just added a small but important twist in terms of mediating forces such as causes and intentions. This scenario gains some of its plausibility from the fact that it provides for continuity between uniquely primate and uniquely human cognitive adaptations. Moreover, my hypothesis is that, just as primate understanding of relational categories evolved first in the social domain to comprehend third-party social relationships, human causal understanding also evolved first in the social domain to comprehend others as intentional agents. There is currently no way of knowing if this is true, of course, but for many of the people of the world, when they are in doubt as to the physical cause of an event, they quite often invoke various types of animistic or deistic forces to explain it; perhaps this is the default approach. My hypothesis is that the uniquely human ability to understand external events in terms of mediating intentional/causal forces emerged first in human evolution to allow individuals to predict and explain the behavior of conspecifics and has since been transported to deal with the behavior of inert objects.

We have no idea when this might have occurred, but one possibility is that it was characteristic of modern humans as they first evolved somewhere in Africa some 150–200,000 years ago—indeed it defines modern humans cognitively—and this may even explain why they outcompeted other hominids as they migrated all over the globe. The competitive advantages of intentional/causal thinking are mainly two. First, this kind of cognition enables organisms to solve problems in especially creative, flexible, and foresightful ways. Thus, in many cases intentional/causal understanding enables an individual to predict and control events even when their usual antecedent is not present—if there is some other event that may serve to instigate the mediating force. For example, an individual might create a novel way to distract a competitor away from something over which they are competing (e.g., by placing food in the opposite direction), or a novel tool for generating the force needed to move an obstacle. Conversely, if an event occurs in a circumstance in which the mediating force is somehow blocked, it could be predicted that its usual consequent will not follow. For example, an individual could block the visual access of a competitor to the object of their competition, or could prevent a stone from rolling down a hill by placing another stone under it. Causal and intentional understanding thus have immediate consequences for effective action, as they open up the possibility of finding novel ways to either manipulate or suppress mediating forces. The second advantage of intentional/causal understanding derives from its powerful transforming role in processes of social learning. That is, understanding the behavior of other people as intentional directly enables certain very powerful forms of cultural learning and sociogenesis, and these forms of social learning are directly responsible for the special forms of cultural inheritance characteristic of human beings.

Cultural Inheritance

In the most general biological sense of the term, cultural inheritance is a widespread phenomenon in the animal kingdom (see Heyes and Galef, 1996, for a recent survey). Its evolutionary significance is immense as, essentially, it allows for another channel of inheritance, and one that operates on a much quicker time scale, with much more flexibility, than biological inheritance (Boesch and Tomasello, 1998). There are many different forms of cultural inheritance and transmission, however. For example, individuals of a species may be exposed to new learning experiences because they stay physically close to conspecifics but still not learn anything from the behavior of the conspecifics directly—as when the youngster stumbles upon, and so learns, the location of water while following its mother. Also important are processes of stimulus enhancement, in which one animal is attracted to the object with which another is interacting, and then learns things on its own about that object—as when a chimpanzee youngster is attracted to a stick its mother has discarded, which then sets in motion certain individual learning experiences. In some cases, such as some bird species, there are also adaptive specializations for learning about the actual behavior of conspecifics through such things as the mimicking of species-typical vocalizations. This kind of learning is truly social in the sense that something is being learned from the actual behavior of conspecifics, but it is generally very narrowly specialized with no repercussions beyond the single behavior.

In the human case, however, it seems that something more profoundly social is at work. Developing human beings do not just follow their mothers, become attracted to objects their mothers are touching, or mimic conspecific behavior in one narrow domain. Human youngsters acquire from their elders and other conspecifics all kinds of cultural behaviors, skills, artifacts, symbols, conventions, values, attitudes, and beliefs. They are able to do this because the species' unique cognitive adaptation that enables humans to understand conspecifics as intentional agents, like themselves, potentiates some especially powerful forms of social learning known as cultural learning (Tomasello et al., 1993).

Chimpanzee Culture

Although the "spread" of potato washing as a novel behavior in one group of human provisioned Japanese macaques is well known, it turns out that the most likely explanation for that behavior is socially influenced individual learning. One individual invented the behavior by walking into the water with the potatoes thrown to her by humans, and her relatives and friends followed her into the water with their potatoes and invented the behavior for themselves—with perhaps some processes of stimulus enhancement operative as well (Galef, 1992). A much better species for investigating possible cultural processes in nonhuman primates is chimpanzees (McGrew, 1992; Wrangham et al., 1994).

The best known example is chimpanzee tool use. For example, chimpanzees in the Gombe National Park (as well as several other groups elsewhere) fish for termites by probing termite mounds with small, thin sticks. In other parts of Africa, chimpanzees simply destroy termite mounds with large sticks and attempt to scoop up the insects by the handful. Field researchers such as Boesch (1993) and McGrew (1992) claim that specific tool use practices such as these are "culturally transmitted" among the individuals of the various communities. The problem is that it is possible that chimpanzees in some localities destroy termite mounds with large sticks because the mounds are soft from rain, whereas in other localities there is less rain, so the mounds are harder, and thus the chimpanzees there cannot use this strategy. In such a case there would be group differences of behavior—superficially resembling human cultural differences—but with no type of social learning involved at all. In such cases the "culture" is simply a result of individual learning driven by the different local ecologies of the different populations (and so it is sometimes called "environmental shaping").

Although environmental shaping is likely a part of the explanations for group differences of behavior for all species, experimental studies have demonstrated that more than this is going on in chimpanzee culture. Tomasello (1996) reviewed all of the experimental evidence on chimpanzee imitative learning of tool use (a total of five studies) and concluded that chimpanzees are very good at learning about the dynamic affordances of objects that they discover through watching others manipulate them, but they are not skillful at learning from others a new behavioral strategy per se. For example, if a mother rolls over a log and eats the insects underneath, her child will very likely follow suit. This is simply because the child learned from the mother's act that there are insects under the log—a fact she did not know and very likely would not have discovered on her own. But she did not learn how to roll over a log or to eat insects; these are things she already knew how to do or could learn how to do on her own. (Thus, the youngster would have learned the same thing if the wind, rather than its mother, had caused the log to roll over and expose the ants.) This is what I have called emulation learning, because it is learning that focuses on the environmental events involved—the changes of state in the environment that the other produced—not on a conspecific's behavior or behavioral strategy (see also Nagell et al., 1993).

Chimpanzees are thus very intelligent and creative in using tools and understanding changes in the environment brought about by the tool use of others, but they do not seem to understand the instrumental behavior of conspecifics in the same way as do humans. For humans, the goal or intention of the demonstrator is a central part of what they perceive, and indeed the goal is understood as something separate from the various behavioral means that may be used to accomplish the goal. Observers' ability to separate goal and means serves to highlight for them the demonstrator's method or strategy of tool use as an independent entity—the behavior used in an attempt to accomplish the goal, given the possibility of other means of accomplishing it. In the absence of this ability to understand goal and behavioral means as separable in the actions of others, chimpanzee observers focus on the changes of state (including changes of spatial position) of the objects involved during the demonstration, with the motions of the demonstrator being, in effect, just other motions. The intentional states of the demonstrator, and thus her behavioral methods as distinct behavioral entities, are simply not a part of their experience.

The other well-known case is the gestural communication of chimpanzees (Goodall, 1986; Tomasello, 1990). In ongoing studies of the gestural signalling of a captive colony of chimpanzees, Tomasello and colleagues have asked whether youngsters acquire their gestural signals by imitative learning or by a process of ontogenetic ritualization (Tomasello et al., 1985, 1989, 1994, 1997). In ontogenetic ritualization a communicatory signal is created by two organisms shaping each others' behavior in repeated instances of a social interaction. For example, an infant may initiate nursing by going directly for the mother's nipple, perhaps grabbing and moving her arm in the process. In some future encounter the mother might anticipate the infant's impending behavioral efforts at the first touch of her arm, and so become receptive at that point—leading the infant on some future occasion still to abbreviate its behavior to a touch on the arm while waiting for a reponse ("arm-touch" as a so-called intention movement). Note that there is no hint here that one individual is seeking to reproduce the behavior of another; there is only reciprocal social interaction over repeated encounters that results eventually in a communicative signal. This is presumably the way that most human infants learn the "arms-over-head" gesture to request that adults pick them up (Locke, 1978).

All of the available evidence suggests that ontogenetic ritualization, not imitative learning, is responsible for chimpanzees' acquisition of communicative gestures. First, there are a number of idiosyncratic signals that are used by only one individual (see also Goodall, 1986). These signals could not have been learned by imitative processes and so must have been individually invented and ritualized. Second, longitudinal analyses have revealed quite clearly, by both qualitative and quantitative comparisons, that there is much individuality in the use of gestures with much individual variability both within and across generations—suggesting something other than imitative learning. It is also important that the gestures that are shared by many youngsters are gestures that are also used quite frequently by captive youngsters raised in peer groups with no opportunity to observe older conspecifics. Finally, in an experimental study, Tomasello et al. (1997) removed an individual from the group and taught her two different arbitrary signals by means of which she obtained desired food from a human. When she was then returned to the group and used these same gestures to obtain food from a human in full view of other group members, there was not one instance of another individual reproducing either of the new gestures.

My conclusion is thus that chimpanzee youngsters acquire the majority, if not the totality, of their gestures by individually ritualizing them with one another. The explanation for this learning process is analogous to the explanation for emulation learning in the case of tool use. Like emulation learning, ontogenetic ritualization does not require individuals to understand the behavior of others as separable into means and goals in the same way as does imitative learning. Imitatively learning an arm-touch as a solicitation for nursing would require that an infant observe another infant using an arm-touch and know what goal it was pursuing (viz., nursing)—so that when it had the same goal it could use the same behavioral means (viz., arm-touch). Ritualizing an arm-touch, on the other hand, only requires the infant to anticipate the future behavior of a conspecific in a context in which it (the infant) already has the goal of nursing. Once again I must emphasize that ontogenetic ritualization is a very intelligent and creative social learning process that is very important in all social species, including humans. But it is not a learning process by means of which individuals attempt to reproduce the behavioral strategies of others.

These two domains thus provide us with two very different sources of evidence about nonhuman primate social learning. In the case of tool use, it is very likely that chimpanzees acquire the tool use skills they are exposed to by a process of emulation learning. In the case of gestural signals, it is very likely that they acquire their communicative gestures through a process of ontogenetic ritualization. Both emulation learning and ontogenetic ritualization require skills of cognition and social learning, each in its own way, but neither requires skills of imitative learning in which the learner comprehends both the demonstrator's goal and the strategy she is using to pursue that goal—and then in some way aligns this goal and strategy with her own. Indeed, emulation learning and ontogenetic ritualization are precisely the kinds of social learning one would expect of organisms that are very intelligent and quick to learn, but that do not understand others as intentional agents with whom they can align themselves. It should also be noted that with respect to the other main process involved in cultural transmission, teaching, only the study of Boesch (1991) reports evidence of chimpanzee teaching, and this for only two clear instances (over many years of observation). This is as compared with much intentional teaching in all human societies (Kruger and Tomasello, 1996). This difference again is plausibly attributed to differences of social cognition, as teaching requires some understanding of what others do and do not know (Cheney and Seyfarth, 1990).

Human Cultural Evolution and the Ratchet Effect

We may conclude, then, that whereas chimpanzees clearly create and maintain cultural traditions very broadly defined, these rest on different processes of social cognition and social learning than the cultural traditions of human beings. In some cases this difference of process may not lead to any concrete differences of outcome in social organization, information transmission, or cognition. But in other cases a crucial difference emerges. This manifests itself in processes of cultural evolution, that is, processes by which a cultural tradition changes over time within a population. One possible change is that a particular cultural tradition could simply die out, for example, if the environmental function disappeared or the social structure of the group changed, or for any of many other reasons. It might also happen that a cultural tradition stays the same over a long period of time, as it serves its function adequately and environmental conditions remain constant.

But beyond dying out and staying the same, some cultural traditions change over time in ways that seem to be adaptive and, moreover, in ways that seem to accumulate modifications made by different individuals over time in the direction of greater complexity such that a wider range of functions is encompassed—what may be called cumulative cultural evolution or the "ratchet effect." For example, the way that human beings have used objects as hammers has evolved significantly over human history. This is shown in the artifactual record by various hammerlike tools that gradually widened their functional sphere as they were modified again and again to meet novel exigencies, going from simple stones, to composite tools composed of a stone tied to a stick, to various types of modern metal hammers, and even mechanical hammers (some with nail-removing functions as well; Basalla, 1988). Although we do not have such a detailed artifactual record, it is presumably the case that some cultural conventions and rituals (e.g., human languages and religious rituals) have become more complex over time as well, as they were modified to meet novel communicative and social needs. This process may be more characteristic of some human cultures than others, or some types of activities than others, but all cultures would seem to have at least some artificats produced by the ratchet effect. However, there do not seem to be any behaviors of other animal species, including chimpanzees, that show cumulative cultural evolution (Boesch and Tomasello, 1998).

Tomasello et al. (1993) argue that cumulative cultural evolution depends on imitative learning, and perhaps active instruction on the part of adults, and cannot be brought about by means of "weaker" forms of social learning such as local enhancement, emulation learning, ontogenetic ritualization, or any form of individual learning. The argument is that cumulative cultural evolution depends on two processes, innovation and imitation (possibly supplemented by instruction), that must take place in a dialectical process over time so that one step in the process enables the next. Thus, if one individual chimpanzee invented a more efficient way of fishing for termites by using a stick in a novel way that induced more termites to crawl onto it, youngsters who learned to fish via emulation of this individual would not reproduce this precise variant because they would not be focused on the innovator's behavioral techniques. They would use their own method of fishing to induce more termites onto the stick, and any other individuals watching them would use their own methods as well, and so the novel strategy would simply die out with the inventor. (This is precisely the hypothesis of Kummer and Goodall, [1985], who believe that many acts of creative intelligence on the part of nonhuman primates go unobserved by humans because they are not faithfully preserved in the group.) On the other hand, if observers were capable of imitative learning, they might adopt the innovator's new strategic variant for termite fishing more or less faithfully. This would put them into a new cognitive space, so to speak, in which they could think about the task and how to solve it in something like the manner of the innovator. All of the individuals who have done this are then in a position, possibly, to invent other variants that build on the intitial one—which others then might adopt faithfully, or even build on, as well. The metaphor of the ratchet in this context is meant to capture the fact that imitative learning (with or without active instruction) provides the kind of faithful transmission that is necessary to hold the novel variant in place in the group so as to provide a platform for further innovations, with the innovations themselves varying in the degree to which they are individual or social/cooperative.

And so the overall conclusion is that human cultural traditions may be most readily distinguished from chimpanzee cultural traditions—as well as the few other instances of culture observed in other primate species—by means of their trajectories over time. Human cultural traditions accumulate modifications over time; that is, they have "histories." They do this because the cultural learning processes that support them are of an especially powerful sort. Their power derives from the fact that they are supported by the uniquely human cognitive adaptation for understanding others as intentional beings like the self—which creates forms of social learning that act as a ratchet by faithfully preserving newly innovated strategies in a social group until there is another innovation that replaces it. As previously noted, these innovations may vary in the degree to which they are individual or social/cooperative, and indeed cultural innovations in the case of humans comprise a complex mix of individual and social processes.

Conclusion

Evolutionary fairy tales about the evolution of human cognition are currently extremely popular. All of them, including this one, are highly speculative (cf., Bitterman, this volume; Shettleworth, this volume). But most of these evolutionary fairy tales do not take explicit account of the fact that human beings and chimpanzees have been reproductively isolated for only 6 million years or so—about the same time that mice and rats have been reproductively isolated. And so we cannot just multiply cognitive differences between humans and other primates at will and posit a genetic basis for each one. There has not been enough time for that. My proposal is that there is just one major cognitive difference between humans and their nearest primate relatives— the understanding of others as intentional beings like the self—and that this then enables a radically new form of cultural inheritance, which changes the *process* of cognitive evolution. The fact that this one uniquely human cognitive adaptation may be seen as an extension of the one uniquely primate cognitive adaptation—the understanding of relational categories in general—is a further advantage of the hypothesis.

And so my evolutionary fairy tale, like all evolutionary fairy tales, is massively underspecified by the data. We have virtually no direct evidence of the lives led by many of our important primate ancestors, including both the common ancestor to chimpanzees and humans some 6 million years ago and the first modern humans some 200,000 years ago. But the study of primate behavior and cognition is gradually building up to a point where we may ask a sharper set of questions than was heretofore possible of the minimal fossil and artifactual evidence that we do have. The goal is to integrate information gained from the observational and experimental study of living primates with that gained from the study of fossil and artifactual remains to make forever more constrained and accurate theories on the evolution of primate, including human, cognition.

Summary

Two hypotheses about primate cognition are proposed. First, it is proposed that primates, but not other mammals, understand categories of relations among external entities. In the physical domain, primates have special skills in tasks such as oddity, transitivity, and relation matching that require facility with relational categories; in the social domain, primates have special skills in understanding the third-party social relationships that hold among other individuals in their groups. Second, it is proposed that humans, but not other primates, understand the causal and intentional relations that hold among external entities. In the physical domain only humans understand causal forces as mediating the connection between sequentially ordered events; in the social domain only humans understand the behavior of others as intentionally directed and controlled by desired outcomes. Intentional/causal understanding of this type opens the way for cumulative cultural evolution (the ratchet effect), which is responsible for many of humans' most distinctive cognitive skills and products. Both these uniquely primate and these uniquely human cognitive skills are hypothesized to have their origins in adaptations for negotiating complex social interactions.

References

Basalla G (1988) The evolution of technology. Cambridge: Cambridge University Press.

Boesch C (1991) Teaching among wild chimpanzees. Animal Behaviour, 41: 530–532.

Boesch C (1993) Towards a new image of culture in wild chimpanzees? Behavioral and Brain Sciences, 16: 514–515.

Boesch C, Tomasello M (1998) Chimpanzee and human culture. Current Anthropology, 39: 591–604.

Byrne RW, Whiten A (1988) Machiavellian intelligence. Social expertise and the evolution of intellect in monkeys, apes, and humans. New York: Oxford University Press.

Call J, Tomasello M (1998) Distinguishing intentional from accidental actions in orangutans, chimpanzees, and human children. Journal of Comparative Psychology, 112: 192–206.

Call J, Tomasello M (1999) A nonverbal false belief task: The performance of children and great apes. Child Development, 70: 381–395.

Cheney DL, Seyfarth RM (1980) Vocal recognition in free-ranging vervet monkeys. Animal Behaviour, 28: 362–367.

Cheney DL, Seyfarth RM (1990) How monkeys see the world. Chicago: University of Chicago Press.

Connor RC, Smolker RA, Richards AF (1992) Dolphin alliances and coalitions. In: Coalitions and alliances in human and nonhuman animals (Harcourt AH, de Waal FBM, ed), pp 415–443. New York: Oxford University Press.

Dasser V (1988a) A social concept in Java monkeys. Animal Behaviour, 36: 225–230.

Dasser V (1988b) Mapping social concepts in monkeys. In: Machiavellian intelligence. Social expertise and the evolution of intellect in monkeys, apes, and humans (Byrne RW, Whiten A, ed), pp 85–93. New York: Oxford University Press.

de Waal F (1986) Deception in the natural communication of chimpanzees. In: Deception: Perspectives on human and nonhuman deceit (Mitchell R, Thompson N, ed), pp 221–244. Albany, NY: SUNY press.

Galef Jr, B.G. (1992) The question of animal culture. Human Nature, 3: 157–178.

Goodall J (1986) The chimpanzees of Gombe. Patterns of behavior. Cambridge, MA: Harvard University Press.

Green S, Marler P (1979) The analysis of animal communication. In: Handbook of behavioral neurobiology (Marler P, Vandenberg J, ed), pp 73–158. New York: Plenum.

Harcourt AH (1992) Coalitions and alliances: Are primates more complex than non-primates? In: Coalitions and alliances in human and nonhuman animals (Harcourt AH, de Waal FBM, ed), pp 445–471. New York: John Wiley and Sons.

Harcourt AH, de Waal FBM (1992) Coalitions and alliances in humans and other animals. New York: Oxford University Press.

Heyes CM (1994) Cues, convergence and a curmudgeon: A reply to Povinelli. Animal Behaviour, 48: 242–244.

Heyes CM, Galef Jr, B.G., ed (1996). Social learning in animals. The roots of culture. New York: Academic Press.

Humphrey NK (1976) The social function of intellect. In: Growing points in ethology (Bateson PPG, Hinde RA, ed), pp 303–317. Cambridge: Cambridge University Press.

Kruger A, Tomasello M (1996) Cultural learning and learning culture. In: Handbook of education and human development: New models of teaching, learning, and schooling (Olson D, ed), pp 169–187. Oxford: Blackwell.

Kummer H, Goodall J (1985) Conditions of innovative behavior in primates. Philosphical Transactions of the Royal Society B, 308: 203–214.

Locke A (1978) The emergence of language. In: Action, gesture, and symbol: The emergence of language (Locke A, ed), pp 1–18. New York: Academic Press.

McGrew WC (1992) Chimpanzee material culture: Implications for human evolution. Cambridge: Cambridge University Press.

Moss CJ (1988) Elephant memories. Boston: Houghton Mifflin.

Nagell K, Olguin K, Tomasello M (1993) Processes of social learning in the tool use of chimpanzees (Pan troglodytes) and human children (Homo sapiens). Journal of Comparative Psychology, 107: 174–186.

Packer C (1994) Into Africa. Chicago: University of Chicago Press.

Packer C, Ruttan L (1988) The evolution of cooperative hunting. American Naturalist, 132: 159–198.

Povinelli DJ (1994) Comparative studies of animal mental state attribution: A reply to Heyes. Animal Behaviour, 48: 239–241.

Povinelli DJ, Nelson KE, Boysen ST (1990) Inferences about guessing and knowing by chimpanzees (Pan troglodytes). Journal of Comparative Psychology, 104: 203–210.

Povinelli D, Perilloux H, Reaux J, Bierschwale D (1998) Young chimpanzees' reactions to intentional versus accidental and inadvertent actions. Behavioural Processes, 42: 205–218.

Premack D (1986) Gavagai! Cambridge, MA: MIT Press.

Premack D, Woodruff G (1978) Does the chimpanzee have a theory of mind? Behavioral and Brain Sciences, 1: 515–526.

Reaux J (1995). Explorations of young chimpanzees' (Pan troglodytes) comprehension of cause-effect relationships in tool use. Masters thesis, University of Southwestern Louisiana.

Savage-Rumbaugh ES, Rumbaugh DM, Boysen ST (1978) Sarah's problems in comprehension. Behavioral and Brain Sciences, 1: 555–557.

Thomas RK (1980) Evolution of intelligence: An approach to its assessment. Brain, Behavior and Evolution, 17: 454–472.

Tomasello M (1990) Cultural transmission in the tool use and communicatory signaling of chimpanzees? In: "Language" and intelligence in primates: Developmental perspectives (Parker S, Gibson K, ed), pp 274–311. New York: Cambridge University Press.

Tomasello M (1994) The question of chimpanzee culture. In: Chimpanzee cultures (Wrangham RW, McGrew WC, de Waal FBM, Heltne PG, ed), pp 301–317. Cambridge, Massachusetts: Harvard University Press.

Tomasello M (1996) Do apes ape? In: Social learning in animals: The roots of culture (Heyes CM, Galef Jr. BG, ed), pp 319–346. New York: Academic Press.

Tomasello M, Call J (1994) Social cognition of monkeys and apes. Yearbook of Physical Anthropology, 37: 273–305.

Tomasello M, Call J (1997) Primate cognition. Oxford: Oxford University Press.

Tomasello M, Call J, Nagell K, Olguin K, Carpenter M (1994) The learning and use of gestural signals by young chimpanzees: A trans-generational study. Primates, 35: 137–154.

Tomasello M, Call J, Warren J, Frost T, Carpenter M, Nagell K (1997) The ontogeny of chimpanzee gestural signals: A comparison across groups and generations. Evolution of Communication, 1: 223–253.

Tomasello M, George B, Kruger A, Farrar J, Evans E (1985) The development of gestural communication in young chimpanzees. Journal of Human Evolution, 14: 175–186.

Tomasello M, Gust D, Frost GT (1989) The development of gestural communication in young chimpanzees: A follow up. Primates, 30: 35–50.

Tomasello M, Kruger AC, Ratner HH (1993) Cultural learning. Behavioral and Brain Sciences, 16: 495–552.

Visalberghi E, Limongelli L (1996) Acting and understanding: Tool use revisited through the minds of capuchin monkeys. In: Reaching into thought (Russon AE, Bard KA, Parker ST, ed), pp 57–79. Cambridge: Cambridge University Press.

Woodruff G, Premack D (1979) Intentional communication in the chimpanzee: The development of deception. Cognition, 7: 333–362.

Wrangham RW, McGrew WC, de Waal FBM, Heltne PG (1994) Chimpanzee cultures. Cambridge, Massachusetts: Harvard University Press.

Zabel CJ, Glickman SE, Frank LG, Woodmansee KB, Keppel G (1992) Coalition formation in a colony of prepubertal spotted hyenas. In: Coalitions and alliances in human and nonhuman animals (Harcourt AH, de Waal FBM, ed), pp 113–135. New York: Oxford University Press.

10 Causal Cognition and Goal-Directed Action

Anthony Dickinson and Bernard W. Balleine

For students of the real evolution of natural cognition, the virtual evolution of synthetic cognition is instructive. In his video game, *Creatures*, Grand (Grand et al., 1996) has created synthetic creatures, Norns, that respect real biological processes. Each Norn has a genome in the form of a single, haploid chromosome, consisting of 320 interacting genes that are crossed and spliced at gene boundaries during reproduction. These genes code not for superficial characteristics but rather for underlying physiological and biochemical structures and processes, such as the reactions of metabolism, hormonal systems, immune responses to environmental antigens, and ageing. Moreover, their survival in the population of Norns is determined by their contribution to reproductive fitness.

Norns are also endowed with synthetic cognition in that they learn about their demanding, if virtual environment. They learn to exploit resources to assuage their nutritional deficits and stave off death by starvation, to avoid predation and infection, to court mates, and to reproduce. And it requires only passing familiarity with these creatures to experience the irresistible demand to adopt an "intentional stance" (Dennett, 1987) to their more florid emergent behaviors—"cooperation in playing with a ball, or 'chase' scenes resulting from 'unrequited love'" (Grand et al., 1996)—let alone their impressive competence in controlling their environment in face of the vicissitudes of life. But this manifest intentionality is entirely illusory: there are no representations of goals in the brains of Norns nor any knowledge of the consequences of their actions.

The Norn's genome also codes for the basic structure of its brain, which consists of two lobes. The "concept" lobe contains 640 neurons that receive 128 sensory inputs from external stimuli, as well as from internal ones generated by the Norn's drives. This network of neurons serves to create "object" and "event" configural neurons for inputs that co-occur before supplying an output to the "decision" lobe containing the units controlling the Norn's behavior. It is the plasticity of these connections between the "concept" and "decision" lobes that enables a Norn to learn and thereby to adapt its behavior to environmental contingencies. Importantly, this plasticity is controlled by the classic stimulus-response (S-R)/reinforcement process: whenever an output from the "concept" lobe that activates a "decision" neuron is followed by the detection of a reward state, the respective connection is strengthened. Correspondingly, the detection of punishment weakens the connection.

These reinforcement and punishment processes implement Thorndike's (1911) positive and negative "Laws of Effect." The specification of a rewarding event has a precedent in Hull's (1943) drive-reduction theory of reinforcement. Each Norn is endowed with 13 different drives, ranging from hunger and pain to loneliness and boredom, that are continuously monitored and adjusted in response to environmental and physiological inputs. For a Norn, a reward is simply an event that reduces a currently active drive, whereas punishment arises from a drive increase.

Although the S-R/reinforcement process embodied in a Norn is a sophisticated implementation of the standard learning algorithm of neobehaviorist psychology, what *Creatures* illustrates so clearly is the capacity of such a simple mechanism of docility to endow Norns with the appearance of being purposive and goal-directed agents when, in fact, they are just habit machines performing whatever response has been previously reinforced in the presence of the current stimulus input. Their behavior is not governed by knowledge of the pleasure, pain, boredom, or loneliness produced by different actions, whatever the labels are attached to their drive states. All that is necessary is that fluctuations of these internal states provide both a stimulus input to elicit the appropriate response and a reward or punishment signal to change the strength of S-R connections.

Many overtrained, well-practiced responses, including much of human behavior, are probably simple habits maintained by the S-R/reinforcement mechanism (e.g., Dickinson et al., 1995), and, indeed, there may well be many animals that are no more than habit machines like Norns. We also know, however, that some real creatures are capable of true goal-directed actions, actions that are, at the time of their execution, controlled by two representations: (1) a representation of the causal nature of the instrumental relationship between an action and its consequence or outcome; and (2) a representation of the current value of the outcome. Mediation by an action-outcome representation with causal content is required if we are to regard the action as *directed* toward the outcome in any sense beyond the purely descriptive. Furthermore, the action must be controlled at the time of its execution by a representation of the value of the outcome for the agent if we are to regard the behavior as directed to a *goal*. Thus, under our psychological definition, actions must be mediated by intentional representations to be truly goal-directed and purposive.

In this chapter, we argue that the human capacity for goal-directed action is shared with other animals, specifically the humble laboratory rat. Two main sources of converging evidence are offered in support of this thesis. The first comes from studies of the sensitivity of the instrumental behavior of rats to both the current value of the goal and the causal relationship between action and outcome; the second arises from the compelling concordance between human causal judgments and the rat's goal-directed actions.

Goal Revaluation

The functional advantage conferred by goal-directed action can be illustrated by considering the hypothetical case of foraging by an omnivorous animal, such as a rat. To simplify the scenario, we assume that there are only two available food sources, each of which is deficient in some essential nutrients but which provide a balanced diet when intermixed: one is rich in carbohydrates and another in proteins. Access to each source requires a different, learned action: for example, hunting in the case of proteins and gathering in the case of carbohydrates. Consider now a foraging episode in which the rat comes across an unexpected and abundant source of starch on which it gorges to a novel state of carbohydrate satiety. Following this episodes, the forging decision faced by the rat is whether now to hunt or to gather.

In a state of carbohydrate satiety, a simple, functional evaluation obviously favors hunting over gathering, and yet this decision would defeat a habit-bound Norn. Let us assume that during previous foraging episodes both actions have been equally reinforced by their appropriate food rewards in the presence of an input from the hunger drive produced by a deficit in both resources. As a consequence, the hunger-hunt and hunger-gather connections have equal strength. Now, for the first time, the Norn experiences a novel state of carbohydrate satiety, a state that has no pretrained connections with either action, with the result that the creature finds itself with very little inclination to perform either activity and, at best, vacillating between hunting and gathering. In the absence of knowledge of the causal relationship between each action and the associated food, the Norn cannot choose to hunt rather than gather on the basis of the fact that protein should now have a higher goal value than further carbohydrate intake.

By contrast with the Norns, we know that rats do make the appropriate choice in this foraging scenario. For example, we (Balleine and Dickinson, 1998a) made rats hungry by restricting access to their general maintenance diet and then trained them to press a lever and pull a chain—the laboratory analogs of hunting and gathering—with one action reinforced by protein-rich food pellets and the other by a starch solution. The two actions were trained in separate sessions and the action-food assignments counterbalanced across animals. Although every response was reinforced initially, the reinforcement schedule was gradually changed so that at the end of instrumental training each response was reinforced with a probability of 0.05. In other words, on average, only every twentieth response was rewarded with the appropriate food, but the specific number of responses required for each reward varied randomly. This intermittent schedule of reinforcement simulates the fact that not every attempt at hunting or gathering is successful. We then simply prefed the animals one of the foods to satiety for one hour before giving them the choice between performing the two actions.

During this choice test, all eight rats preferred the action trained with the non-prefed food from the outset of the choice test. It should be noted that no rewards were given in this test. If the actions are rewarded during such a test, any difference in performance can reflect a selective reduction of the reinforcement produced by the prefed food. In the absence of rewards, however, the choice of one action over the other must reflect knowledge about the relationships between the actions and their associated foods acquired during the initial instrumental training and the deployment of this knowledge in response to the devaluation of one of these outcomes by prefeeding.

Instrumental Contingency

For a Norn, the critical feature of an instrumental contingency is the temporal contiguity between the response and the outcome, for all that is required to strengthen the response is that it be followed by an effective reinforcer. A simple contingent schedule (figure 10.1A), such as that employed in our specific satiety experiment, confounds the causal relationship with a contiguous one; not only does the action cause the outcome, but the two are also paired in time. The classic demonstration that instrumental action is sensitive to causality unconfounded by contiguity comes from studies varying the instrumental contingency when the probability that an action is paired with the outcome is held constant (Hammond, 1980). Following the specific satiety test, we (Balleine and Dickinson, 1998a) retrained our rats to lever press and chain pull in separate sessions on the schedule in which the action delivers the appropriate food with a probability of 0.05 (figure 10.1A). Thus, as previously, one action was paired with the food pellets and the other action with the starch solution. The instrumental contingency was then degraded by presenting one of the foods with the same probability without a response, so that these outcomes were unpaired with both responses. Thus, for each animal the unpaired outcome was either the food pellets or the starch solution, and the effect of these unpaired outcomes on performance could be compared when the outcome paired with the action was either the same as (figure 10.1B) or different from the unpaired outcome (figure 10.1C).

The effect of degrading the instrumental contingency depended upon whether the paired and unpaired outcomes were the same or different. When the paired and unpaired foods were of the same type (figure 10.1B), that is, both were pellets or

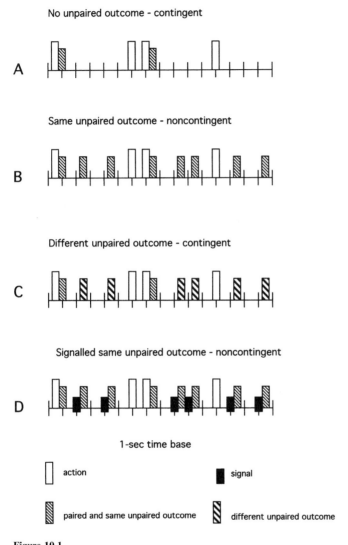

Figure 10.1
Schematic representations of different action-outcome contingencies. (A) A contingent schedule with no unpaired outcomes; (B) a noncontingent schedule in which the unpaired outcomes are the same as the paired outcomes; (C) a noncontingent schedule in which the unpaired outcomes are different from the paired outcomes; (D) a noncontingent schedule in which the unpaired outcomes are the same as the paired outcome but preceded by a signal. In the figure the probability of the paired and unpaired outcomes are 0.5 per sec, whereas in the instrumental conditioning experiments with rats the probabilities were 0.05 per sec.

both were the starch solution, the performance rates declined. This decline is to be expected if the rats are sensitive to not just to the contiguous relationship between the action and outcome but also to the causal effect of the action on the likelihood of the outcome. Under this noncontingent schedule, the action has no effect on the likelihood of an outcome as the probabilities of paired and unpaired outcomes are identical. Whether or not the rat presses the lever or pulls the chain, an outcome occurs on average once every 20 seconds.

In contrast to the action trained with the same paired and unpaired outcomes, performance was sustained when the paired and unpaired foods were different (figure 10.1C; see also Colwill and Rescorla, 1986). All eight rats performed the action trained with the paired food that differed from the unpaired one more than the action trained with the same paired food. The sustained performance with different paired and unpaired outcomes provides further evidence that the rats are sensitive to the causal relationship between action and outcome. When the two outcomes are the same, neither the frequency of food nor its type can be controlled by the rats and performance declines. By contrast, the composition of the diet can be altered by responding when the paired and unpaired foods differ. Although the overall frequency of the food is unaffected by responding, higher rates of performance increase the proportion of the paired food in the diet. The fact that our animals sought variety by continuing to perform the action trained with the different outcome indicates that they are sensitive to the causal relationship between action and an outcome and not just to their contiguity.

In summary, the specific satiety test demonstrates that the instrumental actions of the rat are controlled by a representation of the current value of the outcome and mediated by a representation of the action-outcome relationship. Moreover, the fact that rats perform an instrumental action more vigorously when they can control either the absolute or relative frequencies of a particular outcome shows that they are sensitive to the causal property of an instrumental contingency. Taken together, these findings suggest that their instrumental behavior should be regarded as a good candidate for goal-directed status under a psychological definition that appeals to intentional representations. But whether such behavior is more than a candidate is impossible to determine with certainty.

Although the sensitivity to goal-devaluation and the instrumental contingency lies beyond the scope of the S-R/reinforcement mechanism of Norns, there are other equally mechanistic systems that might explain the goal-directed character of instrumental action without appealing to intentional representations (Dickinson, 1994). The problem is, of course, that, other than speech acts, behavior never carries its intentionality on its sleeve, and, faced with this problem, we have adopted the strategy of seeking converging evidence to bolster the attribution of causal content to the rat's representation of an instrumental contingency.

Causal Judgment and Instrumental Action

One tactic in the strategy of bringing converging evidence to bear on the representational content mediating instrumental action compares the acquisition of such actions by rats with that of causal judgments in humans. Dickinson and Shanks (1995) document the concordance between these two forms of learning. Just as the acquisition and terminal levels of lever pressing by rats is reduced by imposing a delay between this action and the delivery of a food reward (e.g., Dickinson et al., 1992), so are judgments of the causal effectiveness of a similar action in producing an outcome by human subjects. When people are asked to rate the causal effectiveness of pressing the space bar on a computer keyboard in producing a visual display on the monitor, their judgments decline systematically with the length of the delay between the action and this outcome (e.g., Shanks and Dickinson, 1991).

Animal action and human causal judgments also exhibit comparable sensitivity to the degradation of the instrumental contingency by the delivery of unpaired outcomes. Recall that an instrumental action can be rendered causally ineffective by delivering unpaired outcomes with the same probability as paired ones (figure 10.1B) and that the rate of lever pressing by rats declines systematically as the difference in the probability of the paired and unpaired outcomes is reduced. The same is true of human performance when the outcomes are given a nominal value (Shanks and Dickinson, 1991) and, more importantly, of causal judgments of the effectiveness of their actions (e.g., Wasserman et al., 1983; Shanks and Dickinson, 1991).

Although the concordance between animal action and human causal judgment suggests a common acquisition process, it is equally explicable in terms of independent but convergent processes. With the exception of the action-outcome delay, the other concordances arise from behavioral and cognitive patterns that approximate to the normative adaptation. An agent really does exercise greater control over the outcome when the probability of the paired one is higher than that of the unpaired one. Consequently, even if animal action and human judgments are mediated by different psychological processes, adaptive selection should ensure that these processes converge on the same output profile.

A convergence account warrants less credence, however, if it can be shown that animal behavior and human cognition are subject to similar causal illusions. There is no reason why natural selection should produce convergent misrepresentation.

Dickinson and Shanks (1995) note that such an illusion can be generated on a noncontingent schedule. Dickinson and Charnock (1985; see also Hammond and Weinberg, 1984) initially trained rats to lever press on the standard contingent schedule (figure 10.1A) and then switched to the noncontingent schedule in which the same outcome was equally probable in any second with and without a response (figure 10.1B). We have already noted that lever pressing has no effect on the likelihood of an outcome on a noncontingent schedule and leads to a loss of responding. In the Charnock and Dickinson study, however, each presentation of an unpaired outcome was preceded by a brief visual signal (figure 10.1C) for one group of rats. The presence of this signal produced a more sustained level of responding compared to that of animals in another group for which the visual stimulus was presented with the same probability but randomly related to the delivery of unpaired outcomes.

Although this signaling effect is anticipated by certain theories of learning (see Dickinson and Shanks, 1995), the intuitive explanation is that the signal marks the presence of a potential cause of the unpaired outcomes, thereby discounting these outcomes in the evaluation of the control exerted by the instrumental action. This control is illusory, however; an animal has no more control over the occurrence of outcomes under the signal condition than under the random one. Importantly, causal judgments show exactly the same signaling illusion. Shanks (1989) asked for ratings of the causal effectiveness of pressing the space bar in producing the visual outcome under a noncontingent schedule. A condition in which the unpaired outcome were signaled consistently yielded higher causal ratings than one in which the signal stimulus occurred randomly.

This brief survey reveals a concordance between the instrumental performance of rats and judgments of the causal effectiveness of an action by humans. This concordance is observed not only across manipulations that affect the objective relationship between action and outcome, but also under conditions that induce an illusion of causal control. We take this to be at least presumptive evidence that goal-directed actions by rats and causal beliefs by humans are acquired by a common process.

The Representation of Goals

Our psychological definition of goal-directed action requires not only that the action be mediated by a representation of the causal relationship between action and outcome or, in other words, by a causal belief, but also by a representation of the value of the outcome. This definition is, of course, no more than the claim that goal-directed actions as those mediated by the interaction of the beliefs and desires of folk

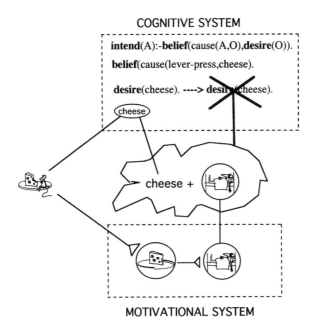

COGNITIVE SYSTEM

MOTIVATIONAL SYSTEM

Figure 10.2
Schematic representation of the interaction between the cognitive and motivational systems during the devaluation of a food reward by incentive learning. The contents of the cognitive system illustrate in PROLOG the causal belief and desire for the outcome acquired during instrumental training and the rule of practical inference to generate an intention for the action (see Heyes and Dickinson, 1990), whereas the motivation system contains an associative connection between units activated by the food and gastric illness acquired during aversive conditioning. Presentation of the food outcome during re-exposure leads to the cognizance of the food at the same as feeling ill, an experience that removes of the desire for the outcome from the cognitive system.

psychology through the process of practical inference (Heyes and Dickinson, 1990). Cognitive theories of this type (e.g., Tolman, 1959; Bolles, 1972) have a legacy in comparative psychology that is almost as venerable and enduring as that of the S-R/ reinforcement theories of neobehaviorism. Following Heyes and Dickinson (1990), the content of an instrumental belief and a desire for food (in this case cheese), and their interaction through a rule of practical inference to derive an intention to perform the instrumental action, is illustrated in the Cognitive System of figure 10.2 in the form of a little PROLOG program. We have already attempted to establish grounds for arguing that lever pressing by rats can be mediated by a causal belief. What the PROLOG program makes clear, however, is that this intentional account of goal-directed action also depends upon demonstrating a role for a motivational representation in the form of a desire.

The motivational processes of Norns are simple and mechanistic in nature. Nutritional deficits give rise to a drive state of hunger that then provides an input to the neural units of the "conceptual" lobe and thereby a stimulus for triggering responses that have been previously reinforced when the creature was hungry. Some theorists have attributed a general invigorating and activating property to such drive states (e.g., Hull, 1943). But whatever the details of a drive theory, it is clear that the processes invoked by such a theory can be directly realized by physiological and neural systems that detect the nutritional state of the body; in principle at least, the stimulus input to the "conceptual" lobe can simply be the output of a chemoreceptor detecting, for example, the sugar concentration of the blood.

By contrast, the origin of a desire is obscure, at least a desire with the requisite representational properties to rationalize an intentional action through a process of practical inference. In the case of human social and cultural goals—prestige, justice, honor, and even culturally determined food preferences—there is no problem, at least in principle, for these desires can be acquired through the representational channels of language. But in case of animals, the explanatory gulf between a desire for a goal and a signal of its biological utility is alarmingly wide. In the absence of an interface between these apparently incommensurate states and processes—one intentional in character and the other mechanistic—the grounding of desires in physiologically relevant processes founders and with it a cognitive explanation of goal-directed action.

Our answer to this problem is that all desires and therefore goals have to be learned, even those grounded in the most basic biological needs. To acquire a desire for cheese, we have to experience our own reactions to a mature cheddar and learn through experience how these reactions are enhanced by good appetite (and a pint of beer) at lunch time or by the mild specific satiety state induced by a delicious pudding (and smooth claret) at dinner. We refer to this process as *incentive* learning (Dickinson and Balleine, 1994, 1995). According to incentive learning theory, the physiological state induced by food deprivation does not automatically and directly give rise to a desire for a specific food, or to any desire for that matter; rather, the desire is acquired by experience with food in this state.

Evidence for incentive learning comes from studies of shifts in motivational state. Consider the case of a nondeprived rat that is trained to lever press for a particular, mildly attractive food and then tested for the first time when it is deprived of its maintenance diet, and is hungry. If the nutritional deficits induced by the food deprivation automatically enhance the desire for the food, the rat should press more vigorously when hungry than when nondeprived. Surprisingly, no such enhancement is observed unless the animal has had experience with the food when hungry (Balleine,

1992), and therefore the opportunity to learn that the food is more desirable when hungry than when nondeprived. We have demonstrated that incentive learning plays a role in the control of the instrumental behavior of rats across a variety of shifts in motivational state (see Dickinson and Balleine, 1994, for a review). Even the devaluation of a food reward by specific satiety involves incentive learning. Prefeeding a specific food to satiety does not directly reduce the desirability of that food but rather allows the animal to learn that the food is less attractive when in the particular satiety state induced by prolonged feeding on that very food (Balleine and Dickinson, 1998b).

These incentive learning studies demonstrate that desires, even for commodities of primary biological utility, are disconnected from the physiological mechanisms that confer this utility. The cognitive processes controlling goal-directed action have to be interfaced with these mechanisms through incentive learning for desires to reflect the basic needs of the animal. Moreover, this disconnection applies not only to states induced by nutritional deficits, but also to noncognitive forms of learning. For example, if a rat becomes sick after ingesting a novel food or drink, it will subsequently avoid consuming that commodity, a form of aversion learning that Garcia (1989) argues is noncognitive or implicit in nature in the sense that it does not depend upon an intentional representation of the causal or predictive relationship between the food and illness. Rather than showing learning that the food predicts illness, Garcia (1989) maintains that the aversion reflects a direct change in the animal's reactions to the food itself from ingestive ones to reactions reflecting disgust, and in agreement with this account we have found that devaluation of a food reward by conditioning an aversion often requires incentive learning.

It is worth considering goal devaluation by aversion conditioning in more detail because it provides a model for analyzing the modulation of desires by incentive learning. We (Balleine and Dickinson, 1991) trained rats to press a lever for a novel food in a single session and then immediately induced gastric illness by an injection of lithium chloride. This treatment is known to condition an aversion to the food so that the rats will no longer eat it. The question at issue, however, was whether the aversion treatment also devalues the food as a goal of lever pressing. If the aversion conditioning is a noncognitive form of learning, it should have no direct impact on the desire for the food and consequently upon the subsequent propensity to lever press. This is exactly what we found: when tested in the absence of the food, these rats pressed just as much as animals that had not received the aversion treatment. To produce a devaluation effect, we had to re-expose the animals to the food between aversion conditioning and testing.

Figure 10.2 illustrates the processes that we assume takes place during this re-exposure. As a result of the instrumental training, the rats acquire a belief about the causal effectiveness of lever pressing in producing the food reward, in this case a lump of cheese. Moreover, by experiencing the pleasure of cheese during training they acquire a desire for it. The result of the aversion conditioning, however, is not represented intentionally, but rather brings about a change in the motivational system. This is illustrated in figure 10.2 by the formation of an associative connection between a unit activated by the food and one that generates the gastric illness reactions. In the absence of any further experience, however, the cognitive and motivational systems continue to function in isolation and the aversion latent in the motivational system has no impact on the animal's cognitive evaluation of the food and therefore on the control of lever pressing.

Re-exposure to the cheese provides an interface for these two systems. The rat perceives the cheese in the form of an intentional representation while at the same time detection of this stimulus activates the illness reactions through the associative connection in the motivational system. Thus, during re-exposure the rat cognizes the cheese at the same time as feeling ill with the consequence that the desire for cheese in removed from the corpus of its intentional representations.

We acknowledge, of course, that this account is far too baroque and elaborate an edifice to stand on the foundations of incentive learning alone. The interesting feature of the aversion procedure, however, is that it provides the opportunity test further predictions of the dissociation between the cognitive and motivational systems. For example, if we could reduce the severity of the gastric malaise during re-exposure we should attenuate the devaluation effect. This we did by using an anti-emetic. The design of the study is illustrated in table 10.1 (Balleine et al., 1995). As in the previous experiment, we gave the rats a single session of instrumental training, but in this case we trained them to perform two actions, lever pressing and chain pulling, for different novel rewards. The animals were thirsty during training, so the rewards were a sugar water and a salt solution. Immediately following this training session, all animals were injected with lithium chloride to condition aversions to both the sugar and the saline.

Table 10.1
Design of Balleine, Garner, and Dickinson (1995)

Instrumental Training (operant chambers)	Re-exposure (drinking cages)	Choice Test (operant chambers)
$(A_1 \rightarrow O_1; A_2 \rightarrow O_2)$ LiCl	Ond: O_1; Veh: O_2	Veh: A_1 vs A_2 Ond: A_1 vs A_2

A, lever pressing or chain pulling; O, sucrose solution or saline outcome; Ond, ondansetron injection; Veh, vehicle injection. LiCl, lithium chloride injection.

During re-exposure, the rats were given access to both solutions in drinking cages on separate days. Importantly, prior to the re-exposure to one solution, we injected the rats with the anti-emetic ondansetron, which acts by blocking the serotonergic receptors in the brain. Under this regime, the solution re-exposed without the anti-emetic is experienced in conjunction with nausea, which, according to our incentive learning account, produces a loss of desire for this commodity. By contrast, the nausea should be attenuated for the solution experienced under ondansetron, with the result that the animals retains a greater desire for this reward.

This prediction was fulfilled in a subsequent test of instrumental performance in the absence of the outcomes: the rats performed the action trained with the reward re-exposed under ondansetron more than the action trained with the outcome re-experienced without the anti-emetic. So it does appear to be the affective reactions experienced in conjunction with a reward that determine its desirability. This basic design also allowed us to test one further and perhaps stronger prediction of the incentive learning account. To recap, an essential feature of this account is the claim that desires are intentional representations that have no direct channels of communication with basic motivational mechanisms except through the interface of the affective reactions produced by these mechanisms when activated by the goal object. Consequently, at the time when an action is performed in the service of a desire, the state of the motivational system should have no impact upon performance of that action, even though it was this system that determined the desire at the time of incentive learning. To express this claim in a more concrete form: to avoid performing an action trained with a reward that the rat has previously experienced in conjunction with gastric malaise, it does not need to feel nauseous at that time of instrumental performance; the animal just knows that this particular outcome is no longer desirable.

We tested this prediction simply by attenuating any nausea at the time of instrumental testing with ondansetron. If such reactions directly control instrumental performance, the administration of the anti-emetic should reduce the difference between the performance of the actions trained with the two outcomes, one re-exposed under the ondansetron and the other without the drug. By contrast, if the assignment of the relative values of the outcomes is fixed cognitively at the time of re-exposure to the outcomes, whether or not the illness reactions are blocked during the instrumental test should have no influence on performance. Our test results favored this latter alternative. The relative performance of the two actions was unaffected by whether or not the rats were given the anti-emetic prior to the instrumental test. Thus, goal-directed actions are controlled by desires for outcomes that are not directly modulated by the revelant states of the motivational system.

In summary, we argue that incentive learning provides the required interface between the intentional processes controlling goal-directed action and the motivational mechanisms that ground the value of primary goals in biologically relevant variables. Just as causal knowledge about the effectiveness of instrumental actions has to be learned, so have desires for the outcomes of those actions. The origin of both instrumental beliefs and desires in experience accords with their representational status.

A Just So Story of Goal-Directed Action

Every psychologist—but perhaps not every biologist who should know better—can be allowed just one Just So story about the evolution of their favored behavioral competence. As our credit has not yet been squandered, in print at least, we take this opportunity to squander it now. Our story for intentional cognition in general and goal-directed action in particular is as follows. When neural plasticity first evolved to support learning, it endowed animals with just those behavioral capacities that we observed in Norns. In addition to innate responses and their modulation by habituation and sensitization, these animals could also learn to control their environment to gain access to necessary resources to sustain life and reproduction and to avoid predation and damage by the simple S-R/reinforcement mechanisms. A model of such a creature is the marine snail, *Aplysia californica*, whose conditioned defensive responses are thought to be reinforced by the presynaptic facilitation of sensory-motor synapses by an input from a facilitating neuron activated by the reinforcer (Hawkins et al., 1983). And indeed, this basic mechanism, or one that is functionally very similar, has been conserved in more complex nervous systems to provide a basis for simple habit learning. For example, the gain of the spinal sensory-motor synapses mediating the stretch reflex in primates can be modulated by instrumental reinforcement (Carp and Wolpaw, 1994).

As we have repeatedly pointed out, the main limitation of the S-R/reinforcement mechanism is its inability to respond to changes in the utility of reinforcers without further experience of the instrumental contingency. As a consequence, such creatures are incapable of exploiting the benefits endowed by goal-directed action. Although attempts have been made to confer at least the illusion of purposiveness by elaborating the basic S-R/reinforcement mechanisms within the framework of both the classic neobehaviorist theory (e.g., Hull, 1952) and contemporary neural connectionism (e.g., Donahoe et al., 1993), our strong claim is that the capacity for true goal-directedness cannot be founded upon this basic habit mechanism. Purposive action required the evolution of an entirely new way of computing behavioral control upon neural processing and plasticity, one that supports intentional representations of the instrumental contingency and goal value and their interaction through a practical inference process.

In accord with this evolutionary trajectory, Balleine and Dickinson (1998a) reported that sensitivity to the instrumental contingency and goal value depends upon an intact prelimbic area of the rat's prefrontal cortex. Following lesions of this area, rats are insensitive to whether unpaired outcomes are the same as or different from the paired ones; prefeeding does not have a selective impact of the response trained with the prefed outcome. In fact, prelimbic lesions appear to convert a goal-directed rat into an S-R Norn-like creature and, significantly, lesions of the corresponding area of the human cortex produces profound deficits in the planning and execution of goal-directed actions (e.g., Shallice and Burgess, 1991).

We characterize this instrumental representation as encoding the causal relationship between action and outcome; this is necessary if the resulting action is to be not only generated by the process of practical inference, but also a rational consequence of this inference. Some may object, however, to this characterization on the grounds that any causal representation worth its name should encode the specific generative process, be it mechanical or social, by which an action causes its outcome and should support inferences and insights based on an understanding of the generative process. Claims have certainly been made for content-specific causal understanding by both chimpanzees (see chapters by Dunbar and by Rumbaugh and Hillix, but also by Tomasello) and ravens (see chapter by Heinrich). Although not denying a role for content-specific models in the causal reasoning, at least in the case of humans and perhaps even great apes and corvids, our claim is that we and other animals, including the rat, can represent basic content-free causal power. Although this claim raises philosophical and psychological issues that lie well beyond the scope of the present discussion, never have any of the numerous human subjects studied in our laboratory queried the request to rate the causal effectiveness of their actions, even in the most impoverished, content-free operant task, and in the absence of any knowledge of the underlying causal process. What we refer to as a causal representation is simply the knowledge that informed their judgments.

Our claim then is that an animal endowed with the appropriate cognitive resources can represent a simple contingency between events as causal, a claim that lies firmly within the Humean tradition. Moreover, just as Piaget suggested that ontogony of causal cognition is founded on the experience of the consequences of action, so we argue that this form of cognition evolved in the service of goal-directed action. However, the burden that we place on our just so story of the evolution of purposive action is not solely that of reconfiguring neural processing to support causal cognition, but also that of generating an interface between intentional representations and the neural signals of motivationally relevant physiological states. In the case of Nornlike creatures, motivation provides no problem, at least in principle: the output of a chemoreceptor supplies a direct input to the S-R and reinforcement mechanisms. But how such an output gives rise to a desire is far from clear. Our answer is that it cannot directly. What it can do, however, is to generate a hedonic or affective experience—pleasure, pain, disgust, and such like—which when experienced in conjunction with the intentional representation of the object of these affective reactions creates an appropriate desire. In other words, desires are grounded in our affective reactions to potential goal objects.

A model of the process we have in mind can be illustrated by the orofacial reactions of rats to novel tasting solutions (Grill and Berridge, 1985). When rats, like humans, are given sweet solutions to drink for the first time, they make a number of ingestive consummatory responses, such as rhythmic mouth movements and tongue protrusions. By contrast, bitter solutions elicit aversive or rejection reactions: head shakes, chin rubs, and face washing. Importantly, these ingestive reactions are directly responsive to motivational manipulations: they are enhanced by food deprivation (Berridge, 1991) and transformed to aversive responses by taste aversion conditioning (Berridge et al., 1981). Although these responses are direct indices of the hedonic evaluation of the tastes for Grill and Berridge (1985), we interpret them as no more than precursors of affect that should still occur in animals incapable of hedonic and affective experience. Therefore, Norn-like creatures should exhibit a full complement of the appropriate consummatory reactions, but in the absence of any accompanying hedonic or affective experience. As Macphail (this volume) points out when discussing the "function of feeling," there is no good reason why a Norn should experience or feel at all; pleasure, pain, elation, and fear have no functional role within the mechanism controlling its adaptive behavior. Its S-R habits ensure that it presses the right "levers" and avoids the right "stimuli" without the need to feel any emotional, affective, or hedonic response to the reinforcers that strengthen these habits.

It is only with the evolution of the intentional control of goal-directed action that there is a function for the feelings and affective reactions elicited by motivationally significant events, that of grounding the assignment of value to the outcomes of action in biologically relevant processes. Thus, the evolution of the cognitive resources for goal-directed action had to be accompanied by the co-evolution of capacity of consummatory reactions, or more strictly neural processes controlling them, to support the appropriate affective and hedonic experiences. We can now no longer postpone labeling the interface at which cognition meets affect: it is simple, non-reflexive consciousness. Under our account (Balleine and Dickinson, 1998c), the primary function of this form of consciousness is to provide an interface between motivational and cognitive processes that allows for the conjoint cognizance of an intentional goal representation and the affective experience produced by the goal object or state and thereby ensures that desires are grounded on biologically important states and events.

Our account for the evolution, mechanisms, and function of affective experience is clearly akin to that suggested by Humphrey (this volume) in his analysis of sensation and its relation to perception. Humphrey argues that sensation arises from the internalization of responses to stimuli in complex nervous systems that were originally directed to the sensorium in simple animals, and that this "privatization" of sensory responses supports both conscious sensory experience and an interaction with cognitively mediated perception. The orofacial responses of the rat to gustatory stimuli provide a good model of such privatization in that these response are controlled by low levels of sensory processing in the brain stem (Grill and Berridge, 1985). By contrast, changes in the desire for foods brought about by specific satiety and incentive learning appear to be encoded at the highest level of gustatory processing in the insular cortex (Balleine and Dickinson, 1998b), where they are well placed to interact with causal beliefs about the instrumental contingency encoded in the adjacent prefrontal cortex.

Our account of the origins and function of primary consciousness, we hope, goes some way to answering the first of Macphail's (this volume) two problems by identifying a function for feeling and affect. Our response to the second, "Which animals are conscious?" is grotesquely simple. In our psychological classification of the fauna of our biosphere there are just two kinds of animals: S-R robots and cognitive creatures that are also endowed with intentional representations, affective experience, and the ability to integrate the two in consciousness (this is one better than synthetic biospheres where, to the best of our knowledge, there are only robots, at least as realized in semicomplete creatures). The tests by which we assign membership to the two classes is also simple. To be a member of the cognitive class, the animal simply has to be capable of true goal-directed action as assayed by sensitivity to goal revaluation, the causal relationship between action and outcome, and incentive learning. As assayed by these criteria, the present membership of this class is one: the laboratory rat. We are, of course, ready to admit the primates by proxy, and a good case can also be made for corvids (Clayton et al., this volume; Heinrich, this volume). Other than these, to the best of our knowledge, the election is wide open.

Summary

We have argued that the goal-directed actions of the rat are mediated by intentional representations of the causal relationship between action and outcome and of the value assigned to the outcome. Although this thesis yields no critical test, converging evidence was offered in support of the claim. First, we demonstrated that the instrumental actions of the rat are sensitive both to the current value of the outcome and to the causal relationship between the action and outcome in a way that cannot be explained by S-R/reinforcement processes. Secondly, the concordance between these actions and human causal judgments suggests that instrumental peformance is based upon a causal representation of the action-outcome relationship.

Having argued that at least one animal represents the causal nature of action-outcome relationship, we speculated that the capacity for such intentional control of behavior evolved primarily to support goal-directed action. The evolution of intentional control brings in its wake a number of problems, however, most notably that of grounding representations of the value of potential goals in biologically relevant states and variables, that is, in the biological equivalent of the drive states of Norns. Our answer to this problem is that the capacity for goal-directed action requires not only the evolution of intentional representations, but also the co-evolution of an interface between these representations and the animal's biological responses to the goal objects, events, or states. This interface, we suggest, is simple, nonreflexive consciousness in which the biological evaluation of a potential goal is manifested as an affective or hedonic response conjointly with an intentional representation of the goal. The assignment intentional value is based upon this concurrent experience of the goal representation and the associated affect.

References

Balleine B (1992) Instrumental performance following a shift in primary motivation depends upon incentive learning. Journal of Experimental Psychology: Animal Behavior Processes, 18: 236–250.

Balleine B, Dickinson A (1991) Instrumental performance following reinforcer devaluation depends upon incentive learning. Quarterly Journal of Experimental Psychology, 43: 279–296.

Balleine B, Dickinson A (1998a) Goal-directed instrumental action: Contingency and incentive learning and their cortical substrates. Neuropharmacology, 37: 407–419.

Balleine B, Dickinson A (1998b) The role of incentive learning in instrumental outcome revaluation by sensory-specific satiety. Animal Learning and Behavior, 2: 46–59.

Balleine B, Dickinson A (1998c) Consciousness: The interface between affect and cognition. In: Consciousness and human identity (Cornwell J, ed), pp 57–85. Oxford: Oxford University Press.

Balleine B, Garner C, Dickinson A (1995) Instrumental outcome devaluation is attenuated by the anti-emetic ondansetron. Quarterly Journal of Experimental Psychology, 48B: 235–251.

Berridge KC (1991) Modulation of taste affect by hunger, caloric satiety, and sensory-specific satiety in the rat. Appetite, 6: 103–120.

Berridge KC, Grill HJ, Norgren R (1981) Relation of consummatory responses and preabsorptive insulin release to palatability and learned taste aversions. Journal of Comparative and Physiological Psychology, 95: 363–382.

Bolles RC (1972) Reinforcement, expectancy, and learning. Psychological Review, 79: 394–409.

Carp JS, Wolpaw JR (1994) Motoneuron plasticity underlying operantly conditioned decrease in primate H-reflex. Journal of Neurophysiology, 72: 431–442.

Colwill RM, Rescorla RA (1986) Associative structures in instrumental learning. In: The psychology of learning and motivation (Bower GH, ed), pp 55–104. Orlando, FL: Academic Press.

Dennett D (1987) The intentional stance. Cambridge, MA: MIT Press.

Dickinson A (1994) Instrumental conditioning. In: Animal cognition and learning (Mackintosh NJ, ed), pp 45–79. London: Academic Press.

Dickinson A, Balleine B (1994) Motivational control of goal-directed action. Animal Learning and Behavior, 22: 1–18.

Dickinson A, Balleine B (1995) Motivational control of instrumental action. Current Directions in Psychological Science, 4: 162–167.

Dickinson A, Balleine B, Watt A, Gonzalez F, Boakes RA (1995) Motivational control after extended instrumental training. Animal Learning and Behavior, 23: 197–206.

Dickinson A, Charnock DJ (1985) Contingency effects with maintained instrumental reinforcement. Quarterly Journal of Experimental Psychology, 37B: 397–416.

Dickinson A, Shanks D (1995) Instrumental action and causal representation. In: Causal cognition: A multidisciplinary debate (Sperber D, Premack D, Premack AJ, ed), pp 5–24. Oxford: Clarendon Press.

Dickinson A, Watt A, Griffiths WJH (1992) Free-operant acquisition with delayed reinforcement. Quarterly Journal of Experimental Psychology, 45B: 241–258.

Donahoe JW, Burgos JE, Palmer DC (1993) A selectionist approach to reinforcement. Journal of the Experimental Analysis of Behavior, 60: 17–40.

Garcia J (1989) Food for Tolman: Cognition and cathexis in concert. In: Aversion, avoidance and anxiety (Archer T, Nilsson L-G, ed), pp 45–85. Hillsdale, NJ: Erlbaum.

Grand S, Cliff D, Malhotra A (1996). Creatures: Artificial life autonomous software agents for home entertainment. Technical Report, University of Sussex.

Grill HJ, Berridge KC (1985) Taste reactivity as a measure of the neural control of palatability. In: Progress in psychobiology and physiological psychology (Sprague JM, Epstein AN, ed), pp 1–61. San Diego: Academic Press.

Hammond LJ (1980) The effects of contingencies upon appetitive conditioning of free-operant behavior. Journal of the Experimental Analysis of Behavior, 34: 297–304.

Hammond LJ, Weinberg M (1984) Signaling unearned reinforcers removes suppression produced by a zero correlation in an operant paradigm. Animal Learning and Behavior, 12: 371–374.

Hawkins RD, Abrams TW, Carew TJ, Kandel ER (1983) A cellular mechanism of classical conditioning in Aplysia: Activity-dependent amplification of presynaptic facilitation. Science, 219: 400–405.

Heyes C, Dickinson A (1990) The intentionality of animal action. Mind and Language, 5: 87–104.

Hull CL (1943) Principles of behavior. New York: Appleton-Century-Crofts.

Hull CL (1952) A behavior system. New Haven, CT: Yale University Press.

Shallice T, Burgess W (1991) Deficits in strategy application following frontal lobe damage in man. Brain, 114: 727–741.

Shanks DR (1989) Selectional processes in causality judgment. Memory and Cognition, 17: 27–34.

Shanks DR, Dickinson A (1991) Instrumental judgment and performance under variations in action-outcome contingency and contiguity. Memory and Cognition, 19: 353–360.

Thorndike EL (1911) Animal intelligence: Experimental studies. New York: Macmillan.

Tolman EC (1959) Principles of purposive behavior. In: Psychology: A study of a science (Koch S, ed), pp 92–157. New York: McGraw-Hill.

Wasserman EA, Chatlosh DL, Neunaber DJ (1983) Perception of causal relations in humans: Factors affecting judgments of response-outcome contingencies under free-operant procedures. Learning and Motivation, 14: 406–432.

11 Causal Reasoning, Mental Rehearsal, and the Evolution of Primate Cognition

Robin I. M. Dunbar

During the last decade, much has been made of the Machiavellian intelligence (or social brain) hypothesis, which claims that primates have cognitive abilities that outstrip those of nonprimates in one particular respect, the ability to handle a complex social world (Byrne and Whiten, 1988; Whiten and Byrne, 1997; Brothers, 1990). We do not have any real understanding of the cognitive mechanisms that are involved in this; indeed, we do not even know for sure whether the differences between primates and nonprimates are qualitative or simply quantitative. However, considerable interest has focused on the role of abilities like theory of mind (ToM) as a key feature of social cognition (see for example Byrne, 1995; Tomasello and Call, 1997), at least in so far as it seems to demarcate hominoids (humans and great apes) from other species (Dunbar, 1998).

In this paper, I first review the evidence for the social brain hypothesis and then consider two other respects in which the cognitive abilities of primates might differ from those of nonprimates (and more particularly those in which hominoids might differ from other primates). These are the ability to reason causally and the ability to engage in mental rehearsal.

Causal reasoning must be one of the fundamental bases on which all cognitive processes operate. Dickinson (1980; Dickinson and Balleine, this volume) argues that inferential reasoning can be shown experimentally in rats, probably because declarative coding forms the very basis on which an animal's knowledge about the world is organized (see also Rumbaugh and Hillix, this volume). Beyond this, mental rehearsal (the ability to practice or think through a problem in the mind) provides a cognitive mechanism by which the impact and success of alternative strategies can be evaluated so that the behavioral tactics used to implement the chosen strategy can be executed most effectively. These two components can be seen as being especially important in the way that humans go about their everyday business, especially (but not exclusively) in the social world. They underlie the processes of everyday social interaction, our reflections on the nature of the world in which we live, and our attempts to produce culture. How do other species of primates compare with us in these terms?

The Social Brain Hypothesis

The growing concensus of the past decade has been that primate brain evolution has been driven principally by the demands of the social world rather than the demands of the physical/environmental world (Brothers, 1990; Byrne, 1995; Barton

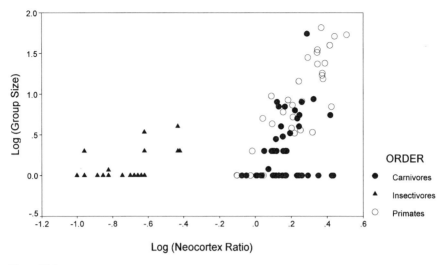

Figure 11.1
Regression lines for mean social group size plotted against mean neocortex ratio (volume of neocortex divided by volume of the rest of the brain), for various mammalian orders. Each point is the mean for a single genus. The axes are $\log_{10}$-transformed. The carnivores with large neocortices and groups of size one are mainly bears.

and Dunbar, 1997; Dunbar, 1998). This is not to suggest that remodeling of brain parts to cope with specific physical world problems has not happened, but rather to point out that primate brain size has increased across species largely because of changes in the size of the neocortex, and that changes in the size of the neocortex correlate with changes in social variables such as group size rather than with any ecological variables (Dunbar, 1992, 1998). In addition, a number of other studies have demonstrated that neocortex size in primates correlates with at least measures of social skills: mating behavior (Pawlowski et al., 1998), grooming clique size (Kudo and Dunbar, in prep.), and social play (Lewis, subm.).

Two other important observations arise out of this work. One is that some (but not all) other mammals lie on the same gradient as primates in terms of the relationship between social group size and neocortex size (figure 11.1). This is especially true of carnivores (Dunbar and Bever, 1998), but may also be true of the cetaceans (Marino, 1996; Tschudin, 1998). Carnivores differ from primates only in so far as they do not extend so far along this gradient: primates simply have bigger brains (neocortices) and bigger groups than those characteristic of carnivores. At the same time, it is worth emphasizing here that both prosimian primates and insectivores seem to lie on a more "primitive" gradient compared to anthropoid primates and

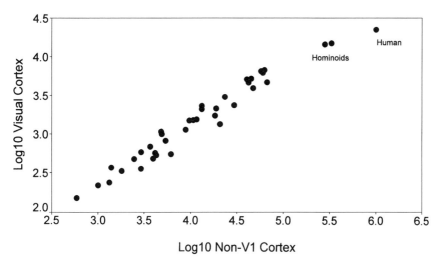

Figure 11.2
Volume of the primary visual area (area V1) plotted against the volume of the rest of the neocortex (non-V1), for individual anthropoid primate species. Axes plot $\log_{10}$-transformed values. (Redrawn from Joffe and Dunbar 1997)

carnivores, in the sense that their distributions lie to the left of these two orders. In this respect, prosimians seem to share with insectivores some primitive traits reflecting a reduced level of sociality.

The second point concerns the amount of neocortex volume devoted to visual processing. Vision is clearly very important to the daily lives of primates; indeed, as a group, their lives may be said to be dominated by vision. This raises an important question: is the increase in brain size simply due to the need to have more accurate and refined visual processing, or does it reflect the amount of what we might refer to as tertiary processing (thinking about the output of the visual system's analyses of primary visual input)? Unfortunately, the databases currently available (principally Stephan et al., 1981) do not distinguish the sectors of the primate neocortex in any great detail. However, they do provide data on the size of the primary (V1) visual area for a sample of species. This has allowed us to examine the relationship between V1 and the rest of the neocortex (Joffe and Dunbar, 1997).

Figure 11.2 shows that the size of V1 and the rest of the neocortex are correlated. Visual and non-V1 neocortex volume increases with increasing brain size. In part this reflects the fact that brain size increases with increasing body size, probably because only large-bodied animals are able to spare sufficient energy to support larger brains. However, the relationship between the two components is not linear: V1 appears to reach an asymptotic size with the largest bodied primates (great apes and humans), whereas the rest of the neocortex continues to increase in size. This is significant in view of the fact that it is precisely these areas in the prefrontal cortex that have recently been shown by PET scan studies to be active during the processing of ToM tasks in human subjects (Frith, 1996).

Joffe and Dunbar (1997) interpret this result as implying that, after a certain point, further increases in visual acuity are not gained by continued increases in the amount of cortical processing area devoted to primary visual analysis. Thereafter, it pays species to devote whatever additional gains they may have in total brain capacity (as a result of increasing body size) to the nonvisual areas of the cortex. Of course, it is impossible to be sure that none of these areas play a role in visual processing (we are unable to exclude the V2 visual area, for example), but we can at least say that, whatever role visual processing plays at this level, it is not concerned with primary visual analysis. It may involve interpretation of visual patterns, but not the basic processes of pattern recognition per se.

It is, I think, significant that the point at which the distribution in figure 11.2 starts to level off is precisely that which corresponds in terms of body size to the great apes. Apes thus seem to mark a point at which a significant change occurs in the amount of cortical processing capacity available for higher order processes. This is significant for two reasons. First, if we carefully examine the data on social group size versus neocortex size, we discover that there are further grades to be identified even within the primates: the apes seem to lie on the same gradient as the monkeys (and the carnivores) but are moved further to the right (Dunbar, 1993). Humans appear to lie on the ape line rather than the monkey line (Dunbar, 1993). In other words, apes seem to need more computing power to support a group of a given size than monkeys do. One reason for this might be that apes engage in some kinds of (social?) cognition that are not found in monkeys, and that these processes are computationally much more costly than the standard mechanisms used by monkeys and other mammals.

The second reason why this finding is significant concerns precisely this mechanism. Apes appear to be the only species, aside from humans, for which there is even circumstantial evidence to suggest that they can pass a false belief task (Povinelli et al., 1990; Povinelli, 1994; O'Connell, 1995).

A false belief task requires the subject to understand that another individual holds a belief that the subject knows (or at least believes) to be false. A classic test of this used on children is the so-called Smartie Test. (Smarties are candies similar to M&Ms and sold in small tubes approximately five inches long.) A child is shown a Smartie tube and asked what it contains; every child will naturally respond that it contains Smarties. The cap is then removed from the tube and the child shown that it actually contains pencils. The child is then asked: if your best friend comes in now, what will he/she think is in the tube? Children who can differentiate their knowledge of the world (the tube contains pencils) from the knowledge of another (naïve) individual (the tube contains Smarties) are deemed to be demonstrating that he or she is aware that others may have contradictory beliefs about the world. At this stage, the child is said to have a theory of mind (ToM).

Children are not born with ToM, but develop it more or less spontaneously at about four years of age. More importantly, perhaps, children continue to develop more sophisticated versions of this ability with time, such that human adults can aspire to at least four (exceptionally perhaps six) levels of belief-state reflexivity (Kinderman et al., 1998). In other words, where a child of five can figure out that *I believe that you think something's the case* (two orders of reflexivity), adults can aspire to four (*I believe that you think that I want you to understand that something's the case*), and occasionally more. These are now commonly referred to as levels of intentionality, following Dennett (1983).

Although the evidence is still equivocal (see Heyes, 1993, 1998), there is at least prima facie evidence to suggest that great apes (but probably not monkeys) can solve false belief tasks (i.e., aspire to second order intentionality). Povinelli (Povinelli et al., 1990, 1991) has shown that great apes (but not monkeys) appear to be able to distinguish between knowledge and ignorance in human trainers. In a more direct attempt to test false belief, O'Connell (1995) used a mechanical analog of a false belief task and found that chimpanzees performed about as well as four-and-a-half year old children (i.e., those that have just acquired ToM) and significantly better than autistic adults (who conventionally fail false belief tasks, even though of normal IQ) (figure 11.3).

Theory of mind may thus provide a kind of Rubicon that separates the apes (and humans) off from other primates. However, we are a long way from conclusively proving that even apes have ToM (Heyes, 1998; Tomasello and Call, 1997).

Causal Reasoning

Given the preceding results, the question arises as to whether the apes exhibit any evidence for other kinds of special cognitive abilities not found in other species. Over and above the arguments deployed by Dickinson (1980; Dickinson and Balleine, this volume) and others (e.g., Rumbaugh and Hillix, this volume) for the species-generality of inferential reasoning, causal reasoning would seem to be an important

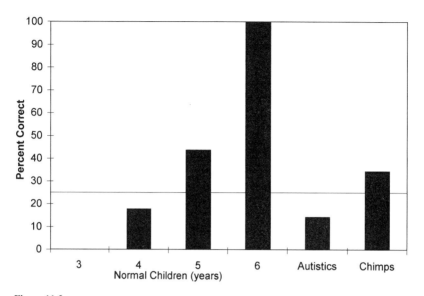

Figure 11.3
Percent correct responses on the mechanical analogue to a false belief task by normal children, autistic adults and chimpanzees. The horizontal line indicates the level of random responses (25 percent correct). (redrawn from O'Connell 1995)

process underpinning the mental world of any cognitively advanced species. Hence, we might reasonably expect to find evidence for these abilities to be widespread, at least among the higher vertebrates. Nonetheless, Visalberghi and Limongelli (1994) have shown that capuchin monkeys, at least, are poor performers on tasks that require causal reasoning, whereas apes perform quite competently (Limongelli et al., 1995). On the basis of these results, they conclude that monkeys probably do not, in general, exhibit competences in this domain, whereas apes do.

This apparent conflict of views may reflect differences in the kinds of tasks investigated. Visalberghi and Limongelli (1994) tested monkeys on a task that required them to reason about physical relationships (inferring that the use of a rod to reach a reward item from one end of a tube might result in the reward falling into a trap, whereas inserted into the other end it would result in the reward becoming accessible). Köhler's (1925) classic experiments, of course, suggested that chimpanzees could solve problems of this general kind, so the Visalberghi-Limongelli findings might suggest an important dichotomy between apes and monkeys.

In contrast, Dickinson (1980) considers problems more directly biological in nature—the ability to infer that if an action makes one ill, then a stimulus predicting an event for which the action would be appropriate should lead to a reduction in the frequency with which that action occurs. If A implies action B and B implies C (becoming ill), then don't do B when A occurs. Rats were apparently able to solve problems of this kind. Dickinson's intrepretation of classical conditioning experiments, combined with the results obtained by Domjam and Wilson (1972) that imply that rats have a kind of *theory of biology*, might lend credence to some kind of domain-specific reasoning ability. In other words, certain kinds of biologically valent phenomena make intuitive causal sense, even to mammals as humble as the rat, whereas other kinds of (less familiar?) physical phenomena do not. One implication of these results is clearly that presenting animals with purely physical problems (as Visalberghi and Limongelli did) will lead to negative results, whereas presenting them with logically similar problems in a biologically more meaningful domain will result in positive results. Cheney et al. (1995) carried out tests of baboons' ability to make causal inferences in the social domain (inferring who was threatening whom on the basis of vocalizations played back from a hidden speaker). Their finding that baboons do well on this kind of task supports the suggestion that there may be domain-specific reasoning abilities. We might infer from these findings that causal reasoning in the biological domain is universally characteristic of mammals (and perhaps birds), whereas causal reasoning in the social domain might be characteristic of primates (or perhaps only apes), but not other mammals.

This might thus prompt us to ask: (1) whether apes differ from monkeys in this respect, and (2) whether primates in general (and apes in particular) are any better at causal reasoning tasks when these are in the social domain as opposed to the physical domain.

In an attempt to explore these questions, O'Connell (1995) developed a series of experimental tests based on Leslie's (1982; Leslie and Keeble, 1987) now classic study of causality in young infants. Leslie was concerned with the question of whether causality is a natural category inherently present in young infants before they have had an opportunity to learn about such things either through language or by trial-and-error experience.

Leslie's test involved an habituation-dishabituation format in which film of two circles moving into and out of contact was played to infants as young as 27 weeks of age. In the training trials, one circle moves across to touch the other circle, which then moves away as though pushed. In the subsequent test trial, the film is the same except that the circles do not actually meet. An understanding of causality was inferred if, having habituated to the training film, the infants once more attended to the test film, as though surprised by an "unnatural" event. It is, of course, possible to quibble with Leslie's conception of causality here, as well as with his experimental design. However, given the difficulty of doing experiments to test such concepts, our aim should perhaps be a less ambitious one: if we accept Leslie's criterion as a test of something in humans, we can at least ask whether monkeys and apes are able to perform to the same standard. If this tests any kind of causal understanding in children, then we have to ascribe the same cognitive abilities to any primates that can pass the test. We can worry about just what Leslie was actually testing later.

To test primates on this task, three separate sets of video clips were prepared. Series I was identical to Leslie's original film. Series II involved a social interaction between humans: person A is sitting on a chair eating a banana; person B sits down next to person A and pushes person A off the chair, then takes the banana. In the test sequence, person A falls off the seat without being touched by person B and the banana moves across to person B without being touched. Series III involved the hunting sequence from the BBC film *Too Close for Comfort*, in which a group of the Taï chimpanzees chase, capture, and dismember a red colobus monkey; in the test sequence, the film was played backwards so that the monkey was reassembled and escaped backwards from its pursuers. Each of the film clips was 20 seconds long (30 seconds in the case of Series III), and was repeated over and over again throughout a 5-minute test period.

Subjects were tested individually on their own. Half the animals were shown the normal (contact) sequence first, and half the unnatural (no contact) sequence first. Where possible, those animals that were shown the natural (contact) sequence of Series I first were shown the unnatural (no contact) sequence of Series II first, and vice versa. Each trial began when the subject was looking at the video screen in its cage. The subject's behavior was recorded on video. In each series, animals were allowed to view the training sequence in sets of three repetitions. A mean time of looking at the screen was determined for the first three repetitions, and then the sequence replayed in sets of three until the subject had produced a set of three looking times that were lower than the mean of the first three. This was taken to indicate habituation. The second tape in the same series was then played three times and the amount of time spent looking at the screen during each was measured.

Series I and II were tested on 11 common chimpanzees, two bonobos (pygmy chimpanzees), and five spider monkeys housed at Twycross Zoo, East Midlands (England). Series III was shown only to the chimpanzees because neither bonobos nor spider monkeys are known to hunt in the wild.

For the chimpanzees and bonobos, there was no significant difference between the duration of looking on the first or last habituation trials for those that saw the film sequences in the order contact/no-contact compared to the reverse on all three series (ANOVAs, $P > 0.05$). However, for both sequences, the duration of looking was

Table 11.1
Duration of gaze fixation on screen in the habituation-dishabituation experiment on causality

Film	Order[a]	Trial[b]	Mean Duration of Looking (sec)		
			Chimpanzees	Bonobos	Spider monkeys
1	C-NC	Hab	7.0	6.0	9.3
		Dishab	23.3	35.5	14.5
		N	3	2	4
1	NC-C	Hab	5.8	–	2
		Dishab	8.3	–	1
		N	6	–	1
2	C-NC	Hab	10.0	5.0	–
		Dishab	35.7	26.0	–
		N	3	1	–
2	NC-C	Hab	4.6	6.0	5.3
		Dishab	6.4	58.8	8.3
		N	5	1	4
3	C-NC	Hab	17.5	–	–
		Dishab	56.0	–	–
		N	4	–	–
3	NC-C	Hab	11.6	–	–
		Dishab	43.4	–	–
		N	5	–	–

Listed values are the duration of the last habituation trial and the first dishabituation trial (see text for details).
[a] C, contact; NC, no contact
[b] Hab, last habituation trial; Dishab, first dishabituation trial; N, number of subjects

significantly lower on the last habituation trial than on the first one, demonstrating habituation (Series I: $F_{1,16} = 27.03$, $P < 0.001$; Series II: $F_{1,12} = 30.25$, $P < 0.001$; Series III: $F_{1,12} = 6.71$, $P < 0.025$). Thus, the subjects can be considered to have habituated to the training sequences.

Following Leslie (1982), the crucial comparison is the first dishabituation trial in the test series with the last habituation trial in the training series. The results are summarized in table 11.1. Again, with the exception of Series I, there were no differences among subjects shown the films in different orders. But for two of the three series, the duration of looking during the first dishabituation trial was significantly longer than that for the last habituation trial (matched-pairs t-tests: Series I, $t_{11} = 2.74$, $P = 0.021$; Series II, $t_9 = 2.07$, $P = 0.068$; Series III, $t_8 = 5.17$, $P = 0.001$; Fisher's procedure for combining probabilities from independent tests: $\chi^2 = 26.92$, df $= 6$, $P < 0.001$). The marginally significant result for Series II was due entirely to the poor rate of response on the no-contact/contact sequence; three of the four animals shown the contact film first had longer looking durations during the dishabituation than during the habituation period. Thus, overall, the chimpanzees showed convincing evidence of an understanding of causality, at least in so far as Leslie's test can be considered evidence for that in humans.

In contrast, the spider monkeys showed very poor response rates. Only three of the five monkeys had longer looking times in the first dishabituation trial on Series I ($t_7 = 1.40$, $P = 0.204$), and only two of the three monkeys shown Series II had longer looking times on the dishabituation trial ($t_2 = 1.44$, $P = 0.286$). These results do not show any evidence of an understanding of the underlying causality in these sequences (Fisher's procedure for combining probabilities from independent tests: $\chi^2 = 5.68$, df $= 4$, $P > 0.1$).

In summary, we seem to have some evidence for an intuitive appreciation of causality in the chimpanzees, but not in the monkeys (at least in so far as New World spider monkeys are representative of the monkeys as a whole), just as Visalberghi and colleagues claimed. Note once again that Series I is a physical problem, as with the Visalberghi-Limongelli tests. Note, however, that the chimpanzees seemed to respond significantly more strongly to Series III (chimpanzee social events) than to Series I (physical events). Although Series II is notionally social, in retrospect the use of human subjects makes it difficult to interpret its significance from the monkeys' point of view: did they see this as a social problem or a physical problem? The fact that the chimpanzees themselves responded only weakly to this series (their results were barely significant) lends support to this. Perhaps this particular experiment needs repeating using footage of monkeys if we are to have a fair test of monkeys' abilities in the social domain.

Mental Rehearsal

I deem mental rehearsal to be important because it seems to underlie so much of what humans do. Humans seem to spend a great deal of time mulling over possible future actions, practicing them mentally or evaluating the possible outcomes of alternative options. We have therefore attempted to determine whether the ability to rehearse something mentally has any influence on its performance. This test was based on a series of four puzzle boxes of varying complexity that were presented to two chimpanzees at Twycross by O'Connell (1995) and to two chimpanzees at the Welsh Mountain Zoo, six orangutans at Chester Zoo, and 61 primary school children aged three to seven years by McAdam (1996).

The four puzzle boxes were graded in complexity by the number of operations that had to be executed to obtain the food reward inside (table 11.2). In each case, two

Table 11.2
Number of operations required to open the puzzle boxes used to test mental rehearsal

Box	Number of operations	Operations
A	2	Undo catch, open hatch
B	3	Identify larger hatch, open catch, open hatch
C	4	Recognize that hatch is behind perspex partition, lift partition, open catch, open hatch
D	5	Recognize that partition blocks access to reward, lift partition, tip box with partition lifted so reward slides to far end, undo catch, open door

boxes were presented to each subject without prior sight; the other two were left outside the animal's cage for 24–48 hours before being given to the animal, during which time it could observe but not touch the box. In the case of the children, the constraints imposed by class time meant that the process of mental rehearsal had to be speeded up. Rather than being allowed to see the boxes for 24 hours, the children were allowed to study the boxes from a distance for 20 minutes before being given them. To ensure that they engaged in mental rehearsal during this period, the children were asked to draw the boxes.

The time each subject took to open the box from the moment it was handed the box was recorded. The order of presentation of boxes and their appearance in the prior-view/no-view conditions was counterbalanced as far as possible. However, for each subject, the two prior view conditions were always presented last.

Unfortunately, the two chimps at the Welsh Mountain Zoo declined to take part in the experiment, so the chimpanzee sample is reduced to two animals. Because of the experimental design, both of these animals received the boxes in the same order and under the same conditions.

We first used the children to provide a complexity ranking for the boxes based on the time taken to solve the puzzles for the first (no prior view) box they were presented with. According to this criterion, the boxes were ranked in the order A < B < C < D (figure 11.4), though the difference between boxes A and B is not significant. This ranking agreed with our intuitive view (table 11.1). Hence in analyzing the data, we need to take box identity into account.

Table 11.3 gives the mean time to open the box for the three species on each of the four puzzle boxes under the prior-view and no-view conditions. Table 11.4 gives the results of the ANOVA analyses of these data.

When age (in years) and box are held constant as covariates (both have significant effects), the time taken to solve the puzzles is significantly affected by whether or not

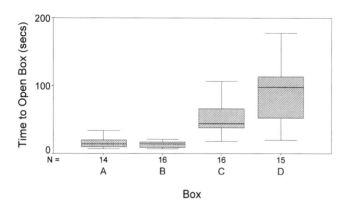

Figure 11.4
Relative difficulty of the four puzzle boxes listed in table 11.1, measured as the time to solve the puzzle by naive children (based on first time naive exposures only).

Table 11.3
Mean solution times for subjects on individual puzzle boxes in the tests of mental rehearsal

| | Mean time to solution (sec) with and without mental rehearsal | | | | | |
| | Children | | Orangutans | | Chimpanzees | |
Box	with	without	with	without	with	without
A	8.4 ± 3.2	17.1 ± 10.1	90.5 ± 83.1	656.0 ± 644.9	—	107.5 ± 38.9
B	11.1 ± 4.5	21.6 ± 27.5	190.3 ± 89.0	476.0 ± 345.7	60.0 ± 7.1	—
C	16.4 ± 8.5	40.4 ± 19.9	396.0 ± 8.5	218.8 ± 130.8	—	182.5 ± 53.0
D	36.1 ± 15.9	65.7 ± 21.3	802.0	780.4 ± 476.3	55.0 ± 7.1	—

Table 11.4
ANOVA analysis of time to solve puzzle boxes with and without mental rehearsal for 61 children, 2 chimpanzees, and 6 orangutans (for data given in table 11.3)

| | Children | | Chimpanzees | | Orangutans | |
Source of Variation	F	P	F	P	F	P
Covariates						
Age (years)	19.671	<0.001	*	*	*	*
Individual subject	*	*	1.53	0.283	40.95	0.024
Box	81.441	<0.001	1.78	0.253	18.06	0.051
Main Effects						
Prior view	32.023	<0.001	7.20	0.055	64.94	0.015

* Not tested.

the children had a chance to view and think about the boxes before tackling them. That this is not simply a practice effect due to the fact that unviewed boxes are always given first can be shown by restricting the comparison to the last two boxes shown. Both of these are prior view conditions and both have at least two no-view exposures beforehand, but the last box presented has an additional practice opportunity compared to the third box. If the results are solely due to a practice effect, there should be a significant difference between boxes 3 and 4. In fact, there is no difference due to order of presentation ($F_{1,118} = 0.00$, $P = 0.986$), although there are significant covariate effects due to age ($P = 0.004$) and box type ($P < 0.001$).

Although only two chimpanzees were tested and both received the same order of presentation, their results suggest that an opportunity for mental rehearsal has a just significant effect on performance. Because of the small sample, however, we cannot distinguish between order of presentation and viewing condition.

The results for the orangutans suggest that there were significant differences both among individual orangs and among boxes in terms of the animals' ability to solve the puzzles. More importantly, when these are held constant as covariates, there is also a significant difference between the prior-view and no-view conditions. Once again, the small sample makes it difficult to distinguish clearly between order of presentation and viewing condition. However, we can check on possible order (or learning) effects by seeing whether being presented as the third or fourth box has any effect on time to solve the puzzle (i.e., when viewing condition is held constant). With box and orang identity controlled for as covariates, presentation order in the prior viewing condition has no effect on performance ($F_{1,8} = 0.329$, $P = 0.582$).

In summary, this study suggests that the opportunity to think about a puzzle before having to solve it does reduce significantly the time taken to solve the puzzle in at least three species of great apes. To the extent that this allows animals to test out or rehearse particular solution strategies, such a mechanism can be expected to be an important factor in how animals cope with the situations they encounter. Comparable tests have not yet been carried out on monkeys, so we do not know whether primates vary in their abilities in this respect.

Summary

It has been known for more than two decades that primates have larger brains for body size than all other vertebrates. This appears to be a consequence of the fact that primate social groups are both larger and more intensely structured than those of other taxa, and that it is the computations requied to maintain the coherence of these groups through time that is so demanding of computing power. Within the primates, there appear to be some important grades in respect of this relationship: apes seem to need more computing power to handle groups of a given size than monkeys, who in turn need more computing power than prosimians. I have shown that there are important differences in volumes of certain brain parts (notably parts of the neocortex) between the great apes and other primates that suggest a likely reason why these animals may have greater intellectual powers than monkeys. This is simply a consequence of scaling effects that allow animals above a certain body size to devote a higher proportion of their cortical capacity to nonvisual processing.

In addition, I have been able to demonstrate that great apes (but perhaps not monkeys) possess at least one key cognitive ability (theory of mind) that is crucial to the kinds of higher cerebral activities so characteristic of humans. This may or may not prove to be a distinctive feature of the cognitive capacities of the hominoids that mark them off from other primates. But for the moment, we can at least claim that this capacity is not unique to humans. There are, however, at least some neuranatomical hints as to why this capacity might be limited to the great ape clade.

Animals' abilities to manage the information they use in this context is likely to be dependent on some fundamental cognitive abilities. I explored two of these here, the understanding of causality and the role of mental rehearsal. Although it is likely that both of these are domain-specific in their effectiveness (primates seem to be more competent at social tasks than nonsocial tasks), the studies we have carried out at least suggest that great apes possess both these cognitive abilities. In contrast, monkeys show no evidence of an innate understanding of causality (tests of mental rehearsal have yet to be carried out). These results confirm the earlier findings of Visalberghi and co-workers suggesting that apes, but not monkeys, are able to understand causality.

References

Barton RA, Dunbar RIM (1997) The evolution of the social brain. In: Machiavellian Intelligence (Whiten A, Byrne R, ed), pp 240–263. Cambridge: Cambridge University Press.

Brothers L (1990) The social brain: A project for integrating primate behaviour and neurophysiology in a new domain. Concepts in Neurosciences, 1: 227–251.

Byrne R (1995) The thinking ape: Evolutionary origins of intelligence. Oxford: Oxford University Press.

Byrne RW, Whiten A (1988) Machiavellian intelligence. Social expertise and the evolution of intellect in monkeys, apes, and humans. New York: Oxford University Press.

Cheney DL, Seyfarth RM, Silk J (1995) The responses of female baboons (*Papio cynocephalus ursinus*) to anomalous social interactions: Evidence for causal reasoning? Journal of Comparative Psychology, 109: 134-141.

Dennett D (1983) Intentional systems in cognitive ethology: The "Panglossian Paradigm" defended. Behavioral and Brain Sciences, 6: 343–390.

Dickinson A (1980) Contemporary animal learning theory. Cambridge: Cambridge University Press.

Domjam M, Wilson NE (1972) Specificity of cue to consequences in aversion learning in the rat. Psychonomic Science, 26: 143–145.

Dunbar RIM (1992) Neocortex size as a constraint on group size in primates. Journal of Human Evolution, 20: 469–493.

Dunbar RIM (1993) Co-evolution of neocortical size, group size and language in humans. Behavioral and Brain Sciences, 16: 681–735.

Dunbar RIM (1998) The social brain hypothesis. Evolutionary Anthropology, 6: 178–190.

Dunbar RIM, Bever J (1998) Neocortex size predicts group size in carnivores and some insectivores. Ethology, 104: 695–708.

Frith C (1996) Brain mechanisms for having a "theory of mind." Journal of Psychopharmacology, 10: 9–16.

Heyes CM (1993) Anecdotes, training, trapping and triangulating: Do animals attribute mental states? Animal Behaviour, 46: 999–1010.

Heyes CM (1998) Theory of mind in nonhuman primates. Behavioral and Brain Sciences, 21: 101–134.

Joffe T, Dunbar RIM (1997) Visual and socio-cognitive information processing in primate brain evolution. Proceedings of the Royal Society, London, B, 264: 1303–1307.

Kinderman P, Dunbar RIM, Bentall R (1998) Theory-of-mind deficits and causal attributions. British Journal of Psychology, 89: 191–204.

Köhler W (1925) The mentality of apes. New York: Kegan, Paul, Trench, Trubner.

Leslie A (1982) The perception of causality in infants. Perception, 11: 173–186.

Leslie A, Keeble S (1987) Do six-month-old infants perceive causality? Cognition, 25: 265–288.

Lewis KP (submitted) A comparative study of primate play behaviour: Its implications for the study of cognition.

Limongelli L, Boysen ST, Visalberghi E (1995) Comprehension of cause-effect relations in a tool-using task by chimpanzees (Pan troglodytes). Journal of Comparative Psychology, 109: 18–26.

Marino L (1996) What can dolphins tell us about primate evolution? Evolutionary Anthropology, 5: 81–86.

McAdam MR (1996). Mental rehearsal. M.Sc. thesis, University of Liverpool.

O'Connell S (1995). Theory of mind in chimpanzees. Ph.D. thesis, University of Liverpool.

Pawlowski B, Lowen CB, Dunbar RIM (1998) Neocortex size, social skills and mating success in primates. Behavior, 135: 357–368.

Povinelli DJ (1994) What chimpanzees (might) know about the mind. In: Chimpanzee cultures (Wrangham RW, de Waal FBM, Heltne PG, ed), pp 285–300. Cambridge, MA: Harvard University Press.

Povinelli DJ, Nelson KE, Boysen ST (1990) Inferences about guessing and knowing by chimpanzees (Pan troglodytes). Journal of Comparative Psychology, 104: 203–210.

Povinelli DJ, Parks K, Novak MA (1991) Do rhesus monkeys (Macaca mulatta) attribute knowledge and ignorance to others? Journal of Comparative Psychology, 105: 318–325.

Stephan H, Frahm H, Baron G (1981) New and revised data on volumes of brain structures in insectivores and primates. Folia Primatologica, 35: 1–29.

Tomasello M, Call J (1997) Primate cognition. Oxford: Oxford University Press.

Tschudin A (1998). The use of neuroimaging in the assessment of brain size and structure in odontocetes. Ph.D. thesis, University of Natal.

Visalberghi E, Limongelli L (1994) Lack of comprehension of cause-effect relations in tool using capuchin monkeys (Cebus apella). American Psychological Association, 108: 15–22.

Whiten A, Byrne R, ed (1997). Machiavellian intelligence. Cambridge: Cambridge University Press.

12 Cause-Effect Reasoning in Humans and Animals

Duane M. Rumbaugh, Michael J. Beran, and William A. Hillix

Causality

David Hume set the stage for discussions of causality by giving it an operational definition that held that in a causal relationship, an effect had to follow the cause invariably and be contiguous with the cause. Whether an event is a cause or an effect depends on which occurs first. Animals, like humans, seemingly enforce the requirement that "cause precedes effect." Responses are readily conditioned when the conditioned stimulus precedes the unconditioned stimulus, but difficult or impossible to condition when the unconditioned stimulus precedes the conditioned stimulus.

John Stuart Mill (cited in White, 1995) contributed to the analysis of causality by suggesting methods that could be used to infer causal relationships. Much later, Jean Piaget (1930, 1974) concluded that children's understanding of causality passes through various stages (cf. White, 1995), just as other aspects of their development progress through stages. In the first two stages, the child learns that he or she has efficacy, that certain results (like nursing) can be brought about, but the child has no understanding of how this is achieved. In stage 3, the child learns to distinguish cause and effect, for example by visual observation of the position of the hands after experiencing attempts to move them. Later, the child comes to believe he or she has lasting powers of his or her own and finally comes to infer causes after observing effects. This last stage of causal understanding might be very helpful in linguistic interactions, when it is necessary to connect actions of listeners with the language generated by speakers. The behavior of apes in language-rich environments, discussed later, indicates that they have probably reached Piaget's final stage of causal understanding.

Probabilistic Causality

Animals, it appears, share with humans the need to make causal inferences in an uncertain universe. Brunswik (1943, 1952), in contrast to Hume, recognized that there are no "sure things" in the real world, and that organisms are reduced to making best guesses about the validity of cues. These best guesses are used to select behaviors that are likely to be adaptive. B. F. Skinner (1948) brought a related perspective to the same problem when he called many behaviors "superstitious." To call a behavior superstitious implies that the organism has attributed causal power to an action that had only a fortuitous relationship to an effect. Thus, the idea of causality may arise in such circumstances, with some attributions of causality being nothing more than superstitious. Skinner's pigeons and rats suggest that they may be over-eager to attribute effectiveness to their actions; the analysis of contingencies of reinforcement (Ferster and Skinner, 1957) can be viewed as an analysis of organisms' tendencies to attribute causality to actions. The slow extinction of learned responses demonstrates an unwillingness to give up that attribution.

In almost all cases, there are hidden mechanisms that connect "causes" to "effects." In the case of the rat, its internal timing system energizes the rat's bar pressing response for the delivery of the pellet shortly after the operant system's circuit completes a "time out" interval. Only through the course of trials does the rat's behavior become synchronized with the mechanics of the operant conditioning system that controls the effectiveness of the bar.

Types of Causal Relationships

Here it is useful to divide causal relationships into four classes. First are the purely naturalistic relationships that occur in the physical (including biological) environment. Rocks fall and crush plants and animals, the moon and sun pull earth's water and cause tides, and so on. Second are relationships between the behavior of organisms and their physical consequences: the ape eats fruit and feels fuller, the carpenter misses the nail and smashes a finger. Third are relationships between events in the environment and the behavior of organisms: the ape sees the red fruit and climbs the tree, Pavlov's dogs salivate to the conditioned stimulus. Fourth are relationships between the behaviors of two organisms: the proper interaction between two bonobos leads to copulation. The fourth class is of particular interest because it includes communicative relationships; for example, communication by apes using a language designed by humans. The later parts of this paper describe this fourth class of causal relationships.

Ideal and Real Causality Detectors

What should the ideal causality detector be like? First, it should be able to sort through any environment and discover precisely what situations are likely to follow what earlier situations, no matter how complex either the cause or the effect might be (see Shettleworth, this volume, for a discussion of how organisms acquire information). Second, the cause-effect association should be detected no matter how great the distance between cause and effect, in either time or number of intervening steps.

Going beyond detection, an ideal organism should be able to intervene in causal chains and thereby bring about desired effects. Humans have gone very far toward molding the world to their own desires, creating new artificial causal fields that do not exist in the natural world. The evolution of organisms as causality detectors can be seen as an evolution toward the ideal causality detector. That evolution involves an increase in length of memory, an ability to analyze a multiplicity of probabilistic relationships and identify those that indicate causal relationships, and an ability to mold the relationships discovered.

Simple and Emergent Abilities

We believe that psychology, in its overly enthusiastic attempt to apply Lloyd Morgan's canon, has made a mistake by trying to explain complex behaviors in terms of processes that are "simply too simple." Both Pavlovian and Skinnerian conditioning protocols encouraged the belief that the unconditional stimulus (for Pavlov) or reinforcer (for Skinner) simply established specific responses to specific stimuli or contexts. The behavioral effects of reinforcement are so powerful that they have led to the mistaken belief that learning is simply behavioral change. Our alternative view is that learning should be thought of as a change of state in the central nervous system that can play a role in computing novel and creative solutions to unrehearsed, novel, problems. Although the classical and respondent conditioning paradigms provide a basis for good science, their simplicity can be misleading when we are seeking to understand what is learned and how that learning can influence the emergence of creative methods of solving problems (see Bitterman, this volume, for an excellent review of the Thorndikian tradition). Therefore, we have proposed a new class of behaviors, called *emergents*, that are appropriately applied by organisms to novel situations for which there is neither a specific reinforcement history nor specific training/learning context (Rumbaugh et al., 1996b). These creative emergent behaviors might be afforded through causal understanding by the organism. To apply creative, appropriate solutions to new problems using both new and old responses requires an understanding of the possible outcome of a given response prior to ever testing that response in the new situation.

Animals as Causal Analysts

One possible indication of an organism's ability to detect causal relationships is the ability to delay response to a stimulus. The longer an animal can wait after observing the placement of food, and still go to the location of the food, the better its memory for the association between cause and effect. Rats under laboratory conditions cannot remember an association for 30 seconds if they are not allowed to maintain an orientation toward the location, but animals with larger brains generally do better—particularly in more natural test situations.

Great apes can remember some episodic associations for days, if not longer. The language-competent chimpanzee, Panzee (Menzel, 1999) has recently displayed a remarkable ability to remember and communicate the location of a hidden food or object to a blind observer. She is allowed to observe one experimenter hiding a food item outside her cage. Then, after several hours or even days, she will solicit the attention of an unknowing caregiver. Panzee very reliably selects the relevant lexigrams and gestures to communicate the name of the item and where it is hidden outdoors. By pointing with a finger and directing her gaze she specifies the location and then asks that the item be given to her. Out of 34 trials with different foods or objects hidden in different sites among the trees adjoining her cage area, she was remarkably precise on both naming the item hidden and directing the caregiver to its location.

Clayton et al. (this volume) provide compelling data indicating that birds can remember what type of food was cached, where it was cached, and when it was cached. The birds are also able to update their memory for foods already recovered. However, the authors note that there is no evidence that birds use autonoetic consciousness in their recall of past events, meaning there is no evidence that they remember the event ("I placed food in that location in the past") rather than know a fact about the environment ("There is food located in that place"). According to Tulving and Markowitsch (1998, as cited by Clayton et al., this volume), autonoetic consciousness is only present in language-competent individuals. Therefore, we propose that Panzee here demonstrates episodic memory as defined by Tulving and Markowitsch, because she used linguistic behavior to provide information about occurrences she recalled from her personal past. Episodic memory appears not to be a uniquely human phenomenon.

There are also dramatic exceptions to memory limitation in smaller-brained animals. One is the ability of animals to remember an association between the smell and taste of a new food and a subsequent illness (Garcia and Koelling, 1966; Revusky and Garcia, 1970). When Garcia first reported that animals could form an association between taste and nausea over a period of an hour, or even several hours, the result was so unexpected that he had difficulty publishing his work. Animals are also prepared to form some kinds of associations more quickly and over longer time delays than they are other types of associations (Garcia et al., 1968). Put in terms of causality, animals can form some kinds of causal connections much more easily than other kinds; it is easy for them to determine that food with a particular taste causes nausea, but difficult for them to determine that a bright light or a sound causes nausea. On the flip side, it is easy for them to determine that a bright light means that a shock is forthcoming, but difficult for them to associate the taste of a food with shock. Species' brains are uniquely prepared to detect causal relationships that are critical for survival.

This suggests a clear sequence of abilities to detect and affect causal relationships. First, virtually all animals respond to connections between stimuli, as in the classical conditioning experiment. Subjects remember the connection between a bell and food by making a new response to the conditioned stimulus. However, even in the classical conditioning experiment we find several indications of cognitive operations (Rescorla, 1988). For example, once a conditional stimulus becomes effective in eliciting the conditioned response, a second stimulus, though temporally coupled with the established conditioned stimulus, rarely accrues any effectiveness as a conditional stimulus. This suggests that the subject perceives the second stimulus as superfluous, and disregards it. Once the organism completes a sufficient causal analysis, it appears to search no further.

A second ability is that animals affect causal chains by responding to signals (i.e., a discriminative stimulus) indicating that a particular chain is available; in the operant experiment the subject responds to the discriminative stimulus and is reinforced as a consequence.

Third, animals show that they recognize relationships between causal situations by generalizing learned responses to similar situations.

Fourth, animals transfer responses to situations that differ on more than a single stimulus dimension, thus making available a host of previously learned responses. Responses may be used in new contexts because of one or more principles that relate them. This kind of transferring of responses (or, alternatively, their new uses of learning) can produce disproportionately greater learning and problem-solving effectiveness than is available for simple transfer along a stimulus dimension from one situation to another.

A fifth ability is the ability to learn or construct, through trial and error or cognition, a chain of responses that lead to a goal. This ability is often combined with an ability to respond to relationships between stimuli—for example, choosing the most efficient route to a goal in a multiple-choice, video-formatted task.

A sixth, somewhat distinct, ability is the ability to recognize that the behavior of other organisms can be controlled, for example by threat displays or, in the case of language-trained animals, through the strategic use of symbols on keyboards, or hand signs, or other "symbolic" communication so as to engage in preferred activities.

There was a long and sometimes rather acrimonious controversy about whether animals "really" respond to relationships, or whether their choices are determined by overlapping stimulus generalization gradients, but the exact mechanism of response is irrelevant for the present purpose. Animals do respond to relationships and to complex qualities of stimuli, and this opens up a new dimension of possible causal relationships, compared to responses to absolute values of simple stimuli.

Harry F. Harlow's (1949) research on "learning to learn" showed that monkeys learned to respond to complex stimuli and task characteristics. The monkeys progressed from an initial stage in which they required hundreds of trials to solve a problem (for example, choosing from a given pair of objects the one that always concealed a reward) to a final stage in which they solved each new problem in a single trial. In this final stage, if by chance they chose correctly on the first trial with a new pair of objects, they then continued to choose that object on subsequent trials; if they chose incorrectly, they immediately switched their choice on all subsequent trials. Their initial trial and error learning progressed to a final stage of seeming insight in which performance on each new problem suggested a rule, to wit, "If rewarded for choosing a particular object of a given pair, continue to choose it; if not rewarded, shift immediately to the other object on all subsequent trials." The ability to follow such rules in Harlow's tests and even in computerized learning-set testing (Washburn et al., 1989) reveals a potential to recognize that the causal structure of a situation can change from trial to trial.

Finally, there is the ability to adduce cause-effect relationships through observation, an ability emphasized in Bandura's (1971) studies related to his social learning theory. If causal relationships can be adduced via observation alone, that provides a great addition to an organism's adaptive armament. We now turn our attention to the evidence that animals adduce cause-effect relationships through observation.

Observational Learning, Causality, and Language Acquisition in Animals

Rumbaugh's (1977) group succeeded in training the chimpanzee, Lana, to use "stock sentences of request" in order to obtain food and other privileges. Lana indicated her wishes via a keyboard with lexigrams inscribed on the keys (figure 12.1). From the view of causality, a given sequence or stock sentence (i.e., Please machine give piece of apple—or bread, chow, orange, etc.) always produced a predictable consequence. Thus, Lana could learn that her key presses were efficacious; her behavior

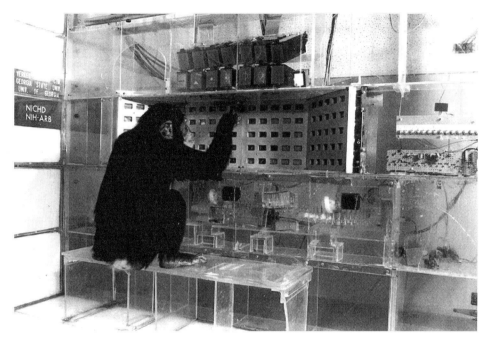

Figure 12.1
Lana at her computerized keyboard in the early 1970s. Each key was embossed with a word-lexigram. As each key was used, it gained additional brilliance and a facsimile of the lexigram on its surface was produced in an array of small projectors above her keyboard. The projectors allowed her to check her accuracy, to make statements of request to us, and allowed us to ask her questions.

was the cause, and the delivery of food or other reinforcers was the effect that reliably followed her correct key presses.

The chimpanzees Sherman and Austin also learned to use lexigrams in order to make requests (Savage-Rumbaugh, 1986) for specific items. Savage-Rumbaugh initially just assumed that the apes "knew" that their lexigrams represented the things/foods that they had used for making their requests known; however, later their "knowing" was tested by asking the animals to give the name of each specific item requested earlier (Savage-Rumbaugh, 1986; Savage-Rumbaugh et al., 1983). Sherman and Austin initially failed! Specific training ensued. Sherman and Austin were next presented with the items that they had successfully requested, and they were reinforced if they responded by pressing the correct name-lexigram for each one, in turn. A single reinforcer (a highly preferred food) was used on all correct trials. Initially they appeared to be confused by always getting the same consequence (i.e., reinforcer). It was as though they expected to get each item named, just as they had in the request task. Because they failed miserably in this naming training, the procedures were modified. Now instead of giving only the same reinforcer for correct naming, Sherman and Austin first received a small portion of the item correctly named before receiving the larger reward used from the beginning of this training. Sherman and Austin learned naming in this context rather quickly and soon it was no longer necessary to give them even a taste of the item named. They learned that naming an item was quite a different task than requesting it.

Analyzing these observations from the point of view of causal relationships is instructive. In the requesting paradigm, the behavior of the animal is the cause, and obtaining each of the various items requested (i.e., food or an object) is the effect. By contrast, in the naming paradigm, the behavior of the animal (i.e., selection of the lexigram that serves as the item's name) is the consequence, with the presentation of the named items the cause.

Subsequently, two independent programs of research on animal language drastically changed beliefs about the abilities of some animals and the best ways to have them master rudiments of human language. The results were scientifically superior to those based on operant conditioning. First, Sue Savage-Rumbaugh and her colleagues (Savage-Rumbaugh et al., 1993; Savage-Rumbaugh and Lewin, 1994) tried to teach Matata, a female bonobo (*Pan paniscus*), to use lexigrams by using traditional operant techniques. They had almost no success. But Matata's adopted son, Kanzi, who only observed the training situation in the course of his early development, spontaneously learned without formal training all that they had been trying to teach Matata. He also spontaneously extended the use of his knowledge to make novel requests, to announce intended actions, and to propose games that were not even part of Matata's sessions. By age four years, he showed that he understood the meanings of several dozen spoken words. During this process, most of his learning was "silent," in that there was nothing in his overt behavior that indicated he was mastering such complex relationships and language skills. Indeed, it was only when Matata was separated from him, when he was $2\frac{1}{2}$ years old, that his learning became manifest; but it manifested on the very first day's work with him. Thus, his early rearing, which included daily observations of his mother's language training, served to structure his development so as to include complex language skills. Primates' general social and cognitive competence, including their ability to discern and affect cause-effect relationships, is very dependent on their early environment. If their rearing environment is severely impoverished, even for only the first two years of their infant development, they never recover and remain cognitively as well as socially compromised (e.g., poor at breeding, parenting, and social commerce), as revealed in tests when tested as young adults, age 14 years (Davenport et al., 1973).

In sum, Kanzi's manifest linguistic competency was acquired silently through the course of being reared in a language-structured environment. Only much later did he manifest his competent understanding and use of the lexigrams and comprehension of much of his caregivers' spoken English. Kanzi's language acquisition can be viewed through the causal lens as an opportunity to learn about causal connections of language use by others around him and how he could affect those connections through his use of lexigrams.

At nearly the same time as Savage-Rumbaugh's work, Pepperberg (1985, 1990a, 1990b) was training an African grey parrot, Alex, using the "model-rival" approach. This involved having Alex observe linguistic interactions between two people, who served alternatively as "models" and "rivals" for Alex. The model/rivals talked about and exchanged objects that they hoped would interest Alex. Alex could observe and enter the conversation at will. He eventually attained the ability to ask for, choose, and describe the color, shape, and materials of the objects with which he was familiar.

The success of these two animal language projects and the continued success of the ape language project with successful replications of the above findings (Brakke and Savage-Rumbaugh, 1995, 1996; Savage-Rumbaugh et al., 1992, 1998) has significantly affected our view of animals' abilities to detect and affect causal chains. Clearly, animals have an emergent ability (Rumbaugh et al., 1996a, 1996b) to learn highly complex skills through observation, and what they learn in such situations further affects their ability to learn about causal chains, predict consequences, and affect their worlds with symbols.

The Assumption of Causal Understanding in Language Acquisition

The experimenters at the Language Research Center interacted with Kanzi as though all of his uses of the lexigram keyboard were intentional and "correct" requests, even if they thought that they were not (Savage-Rumbaugh, 1986; Savage-Rumbaugh and Lewin, 1994). Note that this strategy is absolutely correct if we assume that the organism is a causality detector; it can see that the matching consequence always follows the same lexigram choice, whether the animal intended to produce that consequence or not. The animal does not experience a lack of consequence, nor does it experience confusing after effects in the form of attempts to correct its "errors."

As stated above, Pepperberg (1985, 1990a, 1990b) taught the African Grey parrot, Alex, to use vocalizations to make requests and answer questions by using the similar "model/rival" approach, with model and rival talking about objects and behaving in accordance with what they said. When Alex entered the conversation, he was rewarded by being given the object requested. As with the animals at the Language Research Center, it was assumed that Alex really did want whatever item he requested. Further, Alex had the opportunity to observe all the "causal" relationships between his human model/rivals. This is an ideal situation in which to learn relationships, and it resembles the contextual way in which human infants learn human language both by interacting with parents and by observing parents and others interacting with each other. Note also that these contexts are designed so that the subject is allowed to respond spontaneously, and that these responses are efficacious. Further, a broad range of different responses is available, rather than the single responses that have for so long been the standard in the typical classical or operant conditioning experiment.

Beyond Observational Learning

The story of Kanzi (Savage-Rumbaugh and Lewin, 1994; Savage-Rumbaugh et al., 1998) goes well beyond the simple fact of observational learning. Despite (or perhaps because of) his lack of formal training, Kanzi not only learned to use lexigrams, but also eventually to understand several hundred spoken English words (Savage-Rumbaugh and Lewin, 1994). No ape trained in language via discrete trial presentations has ever been shown to comprehend such a large vocabulary in tightly controlled test situations. Both Kanzi, age seven years, and Alia, a $2\frac{1}{2}$-year-old child, were presented with 660 novel sentences (i.e., not familiar, trained, or modeled by others) requesting that they do a variety of actions in reference to places, people, and materials (Savage-Rumbaugh et al., 1993). For example, Kanzi and Alia were asked to take an object to a stated person or location ("Take the gorilla [doll] to the bedroom," "Give Karen a carrot," "Take the vacuum cleaner outdoors"), to do something to an object ("Hammer the snake"), or to go somewhere and retrieve an object ("Get the lettuce that's in the microwave oven"). Sentence types also included several types of reversals—such as, "Make the doggie bite the snake," vs. "Make the snake bite the doggie." Alia and Kanzi correctly carried out the requests on about 70 percent of the sentences. Kanzi was correct on 81 percent of the sentences in which the key words were presented in both orders; Alia was correct on only 64 percent of the same questions.

Kanzi also learned to create and use stone tools to gain access to baited food sites. After observing the anthropologist Nick Toth create stone flakes by striking two

Figure 12.2
Kanzi learned to knap flint so as to produce sharp-edged chips with which to cut ropes and nylon cables as necessary to obtain prized incentives. He learned this skill by observation and by experience. He now turns the cobble so as to be able to strike an edge that is more likely than others to flake a sharp chip.

rocks together, Kanzi demonstrated a similar effort (Savage-Rumbaugh and Lewin, 1994; Toth et al., 1993). Kanzi became able to create stone flakes, evaluate their probable effectiveness in cutting ropes of varying thickness, and create additional, more effective flakes, if necessary (figure 12.2). Kanzi was never trained to create the flakes in any specific manner. He was simply provided with a model. Kanzi's causal understanding was demonstrated in three very impressive ways. First, Kanzi came to develop his own method of creating flakes through throwing one rock into another on the ground. This suggested Kanzi's understanding that it was the force of one rock striking another, and not the way in which the rocks were held, that created the flakes. Although it is true that the way in which the rocks were held greatly facilitated the creation of good flakes, Kanzi recognized that force itself was the key to creating flakes. Kanzi also demonstrated knowledge of the likelihood that a given flake would be sufficient to cut a rope of some thickness prior to beginning the cutting. He would discard flakes that were not sharp enough and create new flakes better suited for the thickness of a particular rope. Third, Kanzi came to hold the cobble so as to hit it where it had a less than 90 degree edge, thereby enhancing the production of large and very sharp chips of flint.

Language Learning Improves Other Areas of Causal Understanding

The evidence from the animal language studies discussed above indicates that the opportunity to observe linguistic interactions among language-using models enhances the ability to understand other types of causal relationships. After his exposure to a language-rich environment and consequent ability to understand several hundred unique English utterances, Kanzi learned after a very short period of observation, as had Sherman and Austin earlier (Savage-Rumbaugh, 1986; Savage-Rumbaugh and Lewin, 1994), that a joystick could be used to control the movement of an icon in the game of PacMan (a video game). It was as if Kanzi had understood through his experiences with symbols that very "unnatural" relationships between causes and effects were possible; it was not difficult for him to discern the relationship between pressure on a joystick and the movement of the PacMan symbol. Other language-competent apes also learned how to use the joystick just by observation; however, those without substantial language skills learn to manipulate a joystick only through protracted operant training.

Causality, Control, and Prediction

Other research at our laboratory (Rumbaugh et al., 1989; Washburn and Rumbaugh, 1991) demonstrated that rhesus monkeys can be trained via operant conditioning procedures to use a joystick with extraordinary competence in a wide variety of video-formatted tasks. From this research came a series of very interesting findings. It was discovered that these monkeys would rather work at their computers for food (i.e., continue to "cause" its delivery) than simply to obtain it "for free." Rhesus also prefer to control which task they work on; the accuracy and rate of their performance on tasks that they choose (cause to occur) is higher than when they work on the same tasks assigned by computer software. Both apes and rhesus monkeys respond predictively in pursuing erratically moving targets with their joysticks. They don't head for or shoot at the spot where the target is, but for where it will be, making appropriate allowance both for the speed with which they can move their cursor and for the speed and trajectory of the target. This behavior suggests an awareness that the conditions of tasks can change across time.

Causal Chaining and Communication

One aspect of intelligence is the ability to construct covertly, rather than to be taught explicitly, a sequence of actions in order to bring about an effect. Humans are, of course, the preeminent creators of causal chains, from those that enabled them to produce the pyramids of ancient Egypt to those that enable us to create the giant passenger jets of today. The coordination of work by throngs of people is made possible through the use of language, and only humans have produced these extremely complex constructions. But do animals ever exhibit even a rudimentary ability to create causal chains that require true communication?

Even animals that would usually be considered rather unintelligent, like wasps, are capable of executing long sequences. They prepare nests and then attack, kill, transport, and arrange several spiders in position in a nest, after which they lay eggs on their victims and close the nest. However, they carry out only one such complex and extended causal sequence, and it is almost certainly genetically programmed.

The situation is probably different with great apes. Köhler's best chimpanzee student, Sultan (Köhler, 1925), was able to construct the following sequence of goal-directed actions for himself, in a chain that was neither instinctive nor explicitly trained. The steps were to (1) pick up the very short stick that was immediately available, (2) use it to drag within reach a second longer stick, (3) join the two sticks by inserting the end of one into the hollowed end of the other, (4) use this longer stick to drag within reach a third stick, (5) join it to the first two to make a still longer stick, and (6) use the three joined sticks to drag in food that was otherwise beyond his reach!

The beginnings of the emergent ability to construct cooperative causal chains might be inferred from the observation of cooperative hunting, engaged in by several species, including lions, chimpanzees, and wolves. However, cooperative hunting is coordinated through each individual's direct observation of the behavior of other hunters in the group, not (at least not demonstrably) through the exchange of symbolic information.

The two chimpanzees, Sherman and Austin, did, however, bring about desired effects through symbolic communication (Savage-Rumbaugh, 1986). One of the chimpanzees, let us say Sherman, observed food being placed in a container where it was not accessible except through the use of a tool. The second chimpanzee, in this case Austin, could not observe the placement of the food, and so did not know what tool was needed. Sherman could see what tool was needed, and he communicated this information to Austin using a word-lexigram board that displayed more than 100 symbols. Austin had access to the tools; Sherman didn't. Austin retrieved the requested tool and passed it to Sherman through a small window. Sherman used the tool to obtain the food, and then carried it to the window and shared it with Austin. If Austin by mistake gave Sherman a tool not requested, Sherman rejected it and brought Austin's attention via the lexigram keyboard to the item requested.

Social communication through the use of learned symbols was essential to this coordinated construction of a causal sequence leading to food. Savage-Rumbaugh (1986; also Savage-Rumbaugh et al., 1998) reports many other such instances of true goal-directed communication, for example when Sherman and Austin spontaneously used labels from food cans and boxes to communicate when their keyboard was denied them, or when Kanzi helped novice research assistants find word-lexigrams that they were having difficulty finding on the keyboard.

These examples represent genuine social construction of causal chains, and if the symbols had not been meaningful to the apes, they would have lacked the "causal power" to influence the behavior of the listener (Savage-Rumbaugh, 1990). Although these social causal chains are orders of magnitude short of what was needed to build a pyramid, they document chimpanzees' ability to acquire the basic capacity to cooperate through the formation of causal chains and thereby achieve effects that they could not otherwise manage. Contrasting the causal chains of the wasp and the social chain constructed by Sherman and Austin defines the extremes of the continuum between the "biological smartness" of the wasp and the "psychological intelligence" of the chimpanzee. The elaboration of such social causal chains underlies human culture and technology. And there is good reason to believe that the evolution of the primate brain has, in particular, served to enhance intelligence and the probabilities of detecting causal chains and the ability to construct them for creative applications. Figure 12.3 presents data supporting this view. As a positive function of primate brain size and complexity, as well as body size, the capacity to transfer a small increment of learning accrued in object-quality discrimination learning-set tasks, is profoundly enhanced and altered (Rumbaugh, 1997). The consequence is a systematic *qualitative* shift from negative to positive transfer of learning. This shift, both in direction (negative to positive) and amount of transfer as the primate brain evolved, might well be the fundamental parameter of our own remarkable intelligence, as well as of language.

Summary and Conclusions

The concept of causality is much more complex than one might think after reading David Hume's account. "Causes" may be probabilistic, and effects may be delayed. Both causes and effects may be extremely complex. Causes always occur in a total context, so that a "cause" that is sufficient in one context may be ineffectual in another. There are several types of causal relationship; for example, an environmental event may bring about an action, or an action may bring about an environmental event.

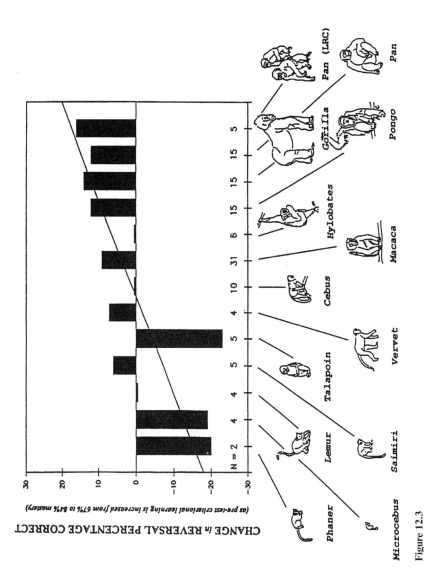

Figure 12.3
The effects of a slight increase in learning (i.e., from 67 percent to 84 percent correct in a series of two-choice discrimination problems) upon the transfer-of-training skills of primate taxa, ranging from prosimians to New and Old World Monkeys and apes. Requiring that the subjects learn "just a bit more," resulted in a marked decrement of the transfer-of-learning efficiency for most of the small-brained, small-bodied primate taxa. By contrast, it resulted in an extraordinary gain in transfer efficiency for the great apes. The group at the extreme right is for language-competent apes of the Language Research Center. (Number of subjects per taxa given along the baseline.)

The larger-brained organisms, at least, develop an increasing ability to understand and manipulate causes with increasing experience, starting with the recognition of their own ability to bring about consequences through their actions. Humans' ability to understand and affect causal changes passes through developmental stages; Piaget suggested that there were six. The great apes appear to reach the same ultimate stage, at least in a primitive form, as humans. Thus the adaptive ability to understand and manipulate causal relationships appears to increase both with experience and with brain size. Language learning, both in humans and in apes, dramatically increases the capacity to respond flexibly and persistently to environmental events, and makes possible increased social cooperation in producing causal chains through mutual behavior management via the use of symbols. However, language training is not a prerequisite for the understanding of basic causality.

Others have also proposed candidates for the understanding of causality. Dunbar (this volume) presents more convincing data that non-language-trained apes demonstrate a clear understanding of causality and, also, evidence that the opportunity for apes to rehearse mentally prior to engaging a task improves their performance. We propose that mental rehearsal is only beneficial to an organism that can understand/anticipate the range of outcomes of actions that it has yet to make. It can do so based solely on its past opportunities to observe the behaviors of others and from its own relevant experiences. And this would require, in turn, an understanding of the causality of its actions in the past. Dickinson and Balleine (this volume) also propose adding at least the rat to the list of organisms capable of goal-directed action as assayed, in part, by a sensitivity to the causal relationship between actions and outcomes. Others believe in the causal understanding of animals, but state that only humans have an understanding of both the causality and the intentionality of organisms engaging in external events (Tomasello, this volume). Humans, according to this view, know not only why something happens, but also why the organisms that caused it to happen wanted it to happen. Whether other animals demonstrate this intentional/causal cognition is undecided.

Organisms eschew noisy and unreliable information, perhaps because it is difficult or impossible to extract causal relationships from such information. They prefer structured information, particularly that which allows them to perceive and manipulate social relationships and communication; such exposure in some species allows them to comprehend symbolic interchanges and to acquire basic competence in language. Particularly during early development there is a clear benefit of being reared in an environment that is logically structured and, within bounds, predictable.

In keeping with Darwin's postulate of psychological as well as biological continuity between humans and other animals, we conclude that the differences between animal and human causal understanding have been produced by quantitative changes that, from time to time, lead to the emergence of qualitatively new capacities.

Acknowledgments

The authors acknowledge grant support from NICHD (06016 and 38051) and the College of Arts and Sciences, Georgia State University.

References

Bandura A (1971) Social learning theory. New York: General Learning Press.

Brakke KE, Savage-Rumbaugh ES (1995) The development of language skills in bonobo and chimpanzee —I. Comprehension. Language and Communication, 15: 121–148.

Brakke KE, Savage-Rumbaugh ES (1996) The development of language skills in Pan—II. Production. Language and Communication, 16: 361–380.

Brunswik E (1943) Organismic achievement and environmental probability. Psychological Review, 50: 255–272.

Brunswik E (1952) The conceptual framework of psychology. International Encyclopedia of Unified Science, 1: 1–102.

Davenport RK, Rogers CM, Rumbaugh DM (1973) Long-term cognitive deficits in chimpanzees associated with early impoverished rearing. Developmental Psychology, 9: 343–347.

Ferster CB, Skinner BF (1957) Schedules of reinforcement. New York: Appleton-Century-Crofts.

Garcia J, Koelling R (1966) Relation of cue to consequence in avoidance learning. Psychonomic Science, 4: 123–124.

Garcia J, McGowan BK, Ervin FR, Koelling R (1968) Cues—their relative effectiveness as a function of the reinforcer. Science, 160: 794–795.

Harlow HF (1949) The formation of learning sets. Psychological Review, 56: 51–65.

Köhler W (1925) The mentality of apes. New York: Kegan, Paul, Trench, Trubner.

Menzel C (1999) Unprompted recall and reporting of hidden objects by a chimpanzee (*Pan troglodytes*) after extended delays. Journal of Comparative Psychology, 113: 426–434.

Pepperberg IM (1985) Social modeling theory: A possible framework for understanding avian vocal learning. Auk, 102: 854–864.

Pepperberg IM (1990a) Cognition in an African Gray parrot (Psittacus erithacus): Further evidence for comprehension of categories and labels. Journal of Comparative Psychology, 104: 41–52.

Pepperberg IM (1990b) Conceptual abilities of some nonprimate species, with an emphasis on the African Grey parrot. In: "Language" and intelligence in monkeys and apes: Comparative developmental perspectives (Parker ST, Gibson KR, ed), pp 469–507. Cambridge: Cambridge University Press.

Piaget J (1930) The child's conception of physical causality. London: Routledge & Kegan Paul.

Piaget J (1974) Understanding causality. New York: Norton.

Rescorla RA (1988) Pavlovian conditioning: It's not what you think it is. American Psychologist, 43: 151–160.

Revusky S, Garcia J (1970) Learned associations over long delays. In: The psychology of learning and motivation: Advances in theory and research (Bower GH, ed), pp 1–83. New York: Academic Press.

Rumbaugh DM, ed (1977). Language learning by a chimpanzee: The Lana project. New York: Academic Press.

Rumbaugh DM (1997) Competence, cortex and animal models: A comparative primate perspective. In: Development of the prefrontal cortex—evolution, neurobiology and behavior (Krasnegor NA, Lyon R, Goldman-Rakic PS, ed), pp 117–139. Baltimore, MD: Paul H. Brookes.

Rumbaugh DM, Richardson WK, Washburn DA, Savage-Rumbaugh ES, Hopkins WD (1989) Rhesus monkeys (Macaca mulatta), video tasks, and implications for stimulus response spatial contiguity. Journal of Comparative Psychology, 103: 32–38.

Rumbaugh DM, Savage-Rumbaugh ES, Washburn DA (1996a) Toward a new outlook on primate learning and behavior: Complex learning and emergent processes in comparative perspective. Japanese Psychological Research, 38: 113–125.

Rumbaugh DM, Washburn DA, Hillix WA (1996b) Respondents, operants, and emergents: Toward an integrated perspective on behavior. In: Learning as a self-organizing process (Pribram K, King J, ed), pp 57–73. Hillsdale, NJ: Erlbaum.

Savage-Rumbaugh ES (1986) Ape language: From conditioned response to symbol. New York: Columbia University Press.

Savage-Rumbaugh ES (1990) Language as a cause-effect communication system. Philosophical Psychology, 3: 55–76.

Savage-Rumbaugh ES, Brakke K, Hutchins S (1992) Linguistic development: Contrasts between co-reared Pan troglodytes and Pan paniscus. In: Proceedings of the 13th International Congress of Primatology (Nishida T, ed), pp 293–304. Tokyo: University of Tokyo Press.

Savage-Rumbaugh ES, Lewin R (1994) Kanzi. New York: Wiley.

Savage-Rumbaugh ES, Murphy J, Sevcik RA, Brakke KE, Williams SL, Rumbaugh DM (1993) Issue 2 & 3. In: Language comprehension in ape and child. Monographs of the Society for Research in Child Development, pp 13–33.

Savage-Rumbaugh ES, Pate JL, Lawson J, Smith RT, Rosenbaum S (1983) Can a chimpanzee make a statement? Journal of Experimental Psychology: General, 112: 457–492.

Savage-Rumbaugh ES, Shanker S, Taylor TJ (1998) Apes, language, and the human mind. New York: Oxford University Press.

Skinner BF (1948) "Superstition" in the pigeon. Journal of Experimental Psychology, 38: 168–172.

Toth N, Schick KD, Savage-Rumbaugh ES, Sevcik RA, Rumbaugh DM (1993) Pan the tool-maker: Investigations into the stone tool-making and tool-using capabilities of a bonobo (Pan paniscus). Journal of Archaeological Science, 20: 81–91.

Washburn DA, Hopkins WD, Rumbaugh DM (1989) Automation of learning-set testing: The video-task paradigm. Behavior Research Methods, Instruments, and Computers, 21: 281–284.

Washburn DA, Rumbaugh DM (1991) Rhesus monkey (Macaca mulatta) complex learning skills reassessed. International Journal of Primatology, 12: 377–388.

White PA (1995) The understanding of causation and the production of action. From infancy to adulthood. East Sussex, UK: Lawrence Erlbaum Associates.

IV CONSCIOUSNESS

The first two chapters in this section, by Humphrey and Macphail, each advance a general thesis about the evolutionary origins of consciousness; in a complementary way, the chapters by Clayton et al. and Heinrich each focus on a consciousness-related capability in a single species. Clayton et al. report experiments on episodic memory in scrub jays, and Heinrich surveys his research on insight in ravens.

Like Dickinson and Balleine (this volume), Humphrey and Macphail are primarily concerned with conscious sensations, rather than, for example, consciousness of cognitive operations. Humphrey concentrates on sensory qualia, such as "redness," Macphail on sensations of pain and pleasure, and Dickinson and Balleine on feelings of attraction and aversion, but they are all interested in relatively simple conscious reactions to external objects and events, and they all agree that these reactions are private in the sense of being directly accessible only to the subject.

Using an elegant clock analogy, Humphrey argues that the conscious reactions that are sensory qualia were once overt reactions, and that they have been "privatized." Early in evolutionary history, behaving reflexively in distinct ways to objects with different physical properties enhanced reproductive fitness. Over time, increasing perceptual and cognitive sophistication rendered these overt reactions unnecessary or maladaptive, but, instead of disappearing, they were internalized in the form of sensory qualia. Thus, according to Humphrey, by virtue of their privacy, sensory qualia cannot and do not have an adaptive function, but their behavioral precursors were favored by natural selection.

Dickinson and Balleine propose that consciousness is an interface between the motivational systems regulating animals' biological needs and the cognitive system governing their goal-directed action. This account is akin to Humphrey's in that both hypotheses imply that consciousness arose relatively early in vertebrate, or even invertebrate, evolution, and cast conscious experience as an intermediary between primitive reactions and cognitive processing. However, whereas Humphrey suggests that conscious sensation is vestigial, Dickinson and Balleine assign it an important continuing role in behavioral adaptation. In crude summary, Humphrey says that the function of consciousness *was* to alert the self to the body's reactions to sensory inputs; Dickinson and Balleine say that the function of consciousness *is* to alert the action system to the body's reactions to sensory inputs.

Macphail's analysis of the evolution of consciousness contrasts with Humphrey's and Dickinson and Balleine's in two principal respects. First, Macphail suggests that consciousness arises from the capacity to use language, and thus places the cognitive transition associated with consciousness much later in phylogenetic history. Second, Macphail's analysis implies that consciousness does not have, and never has had, an adaptive function. He argues that self-conception is necessary for conscious sensation, and that the intentionality of language is necessary for self-conception, but conscious sensation itself is not portrayed as being necessary, or even useful, for anything.

The chapters in this section may be regarded as lying on a continuum of optimism regarding the prospects for empirical investigation of consciousness. Heinrich, working in the framework of cognitive ethology, is the most optimistic. In his view, we cannot doubt that human and nonhuman animals are conscious, and, assuming that consciousness more commonly accompanies complex problem-solving activity than innate or conditioned responses, we can find out about the contents of animal consciousness through behavioral experiments. Thus, in contrast with the other contributors to this book, he could be said to regard cognitive processes as necessarily conscious. This contrast is most apparent when one compares Heinrich's and Dunbar's discussions of mental rehearsal, and Heinrich's analysis of action-outcome learning with that of Dickinson and Balleine.

Although it may not have been Humphrey's intention, his chapter represents the least optimistic view. It stresses the privacy of conscious experience; that it is conceivable that any behavior, including verbal behavior, could be performed with arbitrarily different qualia, or without any conscious experience at all. Humphrey pursues one implication of this traditional view of conscious experience, that it could not be subject to natural selection, but it would seem that an equally direct implication is that consciousness is inaccessible to empirical investigation in animals and humans.

Macphail and Clayton et al. are intermediate in their degree of optimism. Macphail argues that consciousness is present only in language users, and Clayton et al. assume that we cannot find out whether or not animals are conscious unless they use language. If, as Macphail suggests, humans are the only animals that use language (cf. Rumbaugh et al., this volume), both of these positions imply that it is only human consciousness that is subject to empirical investigation.

Clayton et al. are careful to point out that their evidence that scrub jays can remember what food items they have cached, when, and where, does not necessarily imply that these birds have autonoetic consciousness, a variety of consciousness claimed by Tulving to be characteristic of human episodic memory. Even if one extends this cautious approach to Heinrich's studies of insight and takes the data from both scrub jays and ravens to be evidence of cognitive but not necessarily conscious achievements, they are impressive. Combined with the evidence of relational learning in parrots and corvids (Mackintosh, this volume), they suggest that certain avian taxa have cognitive capacities similar to those of great apes (Dunbar, this volume; Rumbaugh et al., this volume; Tomasello, this volume).

13 The Privatization of Sensation

Nicholas Humphrey

D. H. Lawrence, the novelist, once remarked that if anyone presumes to ask why the midday sky is blue rather than red, we should not even attempt to give a scientific answer but should simply reply: "Because it is." And if one were to go still further, and to ask why his own conscious sensation when he looks at the midday sky is characterized by blue qualia rather than red qualia, I've no doubt that Lawrence, if he were still around—along with several contemporary philosophers of mind—would be just as adamant that the last place we should look for enlightenment is science.

But this is not my view. The poet William Empson wrote: "Critics are of two sorts: those who merely relieve themselves against the flower of beauty, and those, less continent, who afterwards scratch it up. I myself, I must confess, aspire to the second of these classes; unexplained beauty arouses an irritation in me" (Empson, 1961, p. 28). And equally, I'd say, unexplained subjective experience arouses an irritation in me. It is the irritation of someone who is an unabashed Darwinian: one who holds that the theory of evolution by natural selection has given us the licence to ask "why" questions about almost every aspect of the design of living nature, and, what's more, to expect that these "whys" will nearly always translate into scientifically accredited "wherefores."

Our default assumption, I believe, can and should be that living things are designed the way they are because this kind of design is—or has been in the past—biologically advantageous. And this will be so across the whole of nature, even when we come to ask deep questions about the way the human mind works, and even when what's at issue are the central facts of consciousness.

Why is it like this to have red light fall on our eyes? Why is it like this to have a salt taste in our mouths? Why is it like this to hear a trumpet sounding in our ears? I think these questions, as much as any, deserve our best attempt to provide Darwinian answers: answers, that is, in terms of the biological function that is being—or has been—served.

There are two levels at which the questions can be put. First we should ask about the biological function of our having sensations at all. Next, once we have an answer to this first question, we can proceed to the trickier question about the function of our sensations being of the special qualitative character they are.

No doubt the first will strike most people as the easy question, and the second as the hard one. But this first question may not be as easy as it seems. And, although I want to spend most of this paper discussing sensory quality, I realize I ought to begin at the beginning by asking: What, of biological importance, do we gain from having sensations at all?

To see why this seemingly easy question requires serious consideration and why the answer is not in fact self-evident, we have to take on board the elementary distinction between sensation and perception.

The remarkable fact that human beings—and presumably many other animals also—make use of their bodily senses in two quite different ways, was first brought to philosophical attention two hundred years ago by Thomas Reid. "The external senses," Reid wrote,

have a double province—to make us feel, and to make us perceive. They furnish us with a variety of sensations, some pleasant, others painful, and others indifferent; at the same time they give us a conception and an invincible belief of the existence of external objects.... Sensation, taken by itself, implies neither the conception nor belief of any external object. It supposes a sentient being, and a certain manner in which that being is affected; but it supposes no more. Perception implies a conviction and belief of something external—something different both from the mind that perceives, and the act of perception. Things so different in their nature ought to be distinguished.   (Reid, 1785, II, ch. 17 & 16)

For example, Reid said, we smell a rose, and two separate and parallel things happen: we feel the sweet smell at our own nostrils and we perceive the external presence of a rose. We hear a horn blowing from the valley below: we both feel the booming sound in our own ears and we perceive the external presence of a ship down in the Firth. In general we can and usually do use the evidence of sensory stimulation both to provide "a subject-centred affect-laden representation of what's happening to me," and to provide "an objective, affectively neutral representation of what's happening out there" (Humphrey, 1992).

Yet, while Reid insisted so firmly on this difference, he never, it seems, thought it necessary to ask the question that so clearly follows: Why do the senses have a double province? Do human beings really need both perception and sensation? If, as might well be argued—especially in the case of vision and hearing—what interests us in terms of our survival is not at all our personal relation to the stimulation at our body surface but only what this stimulation denotes about the outside world, why ever should we bother to represent "what is happening to me" as well as "what is happening out there"? Why should we not leave sensation out of it entirely and make do with perception on its own? Would not such insensate perception serve our biological needs perfectly well?

It is only in the last few years that psychologists have begun to face up to the genuine challenge of this question "why sensations?" There is certainly no agreement yet on what is the right Darwinian answer. However, there are now at least several possible answers in the offing. I (Humphrey, 1992), Anthony Marcel (1988), and Richard Gregory (1996) have all, in different ways, endorsed what is probably the strongest of these: namely, that sensations are required, in Gregory's felicitous wording, "to flag the present."

The idea here is that the main role of sensations is, in effect, to help keep perception honest. Both sensation and perception take sensory stimulation as their starting point. Yet, whereas sensation then proceeds to represent the stimulation more or less as given, perception takes off in a much more complex and risky way. Perception has to combine the evidence of stimulation with contextual information, memory, and rules so as to construct a hypothetical model of the external world as it exists independently of the observer. The danger is that, if this kind of construction is allowed simply to run free, without being continually tied into present-tense reality, the perceiver may become lost in a world of hypotheticals and counterfactuals.

What the perceiver needs is the capacity to run some kind of on-line reality check, testing his or her perceptual model for its currency and relevance, and in particular keeping tabs on where the self now stands. And this, so the argument goes, is precisely where low-level, unprocessed, sensation does in fact prove its value. As I summarized it earlier: "Sensation lends a here-ness and a now-ness and a me-ness to the experience of the world, of which pure perception in the absence of sensation is bereft" (Humphrey, 1992, p. 73).

I think we should be reasonably happy with this answer. The need to flag the present provides at least one compelling reason why natural selection should have chosen sensate human beings over insensate ones.

But we should be under no illusion about how far this answer takes us with the larger project. For it must be obvious that even if it can explain why sensations exist at all, it goes no way to explaining why sensations exist in the particular qualitative form they do.

The difficulty is this. Suppose sensations have indeed evolved to flag the present. Then surely it hardly matters precisely how they flag the present. Nothing would seem to dictate that, for example, the sensation by which each of us represents the presence of red light at our eye must have the particular red quality it actually does have. Surely this function could have been performed equally well by a sensation of green quality or some other quality completely.

Indeed, would not the same be true of any other functional role we attribute to sensations? For the fact is—isn't it?—that sensory quality is something private and ineffable, maybe of deep significance to each of us subjectively but of no consequence whatever to our standing in the outside world.

There is a long philosophical tradition that makes exactly this claim. John Locke originated it with his thought experiment about the undetectable "inverted spectrum" (Locke 1690, II, ch. 32). Imagine, said Locke, that "if by the different structure of our organs, it were so ordered, that the same object should produce in several men's minds different ideas at the same time; e.g., if the idea, that a violet produces in one man's mind by his eyes, were the same that a marigold produced in another man's, and vice versa." Then, Locke surmised, there would be no reason to think this difference in inner structure and the resulting difference in the inner experience of the quality of color would make any difference to outer behavior. In fact, he claimed, the difference in inner experience "could never be known: because one man's mind could not pass into another man's body."

Ludwig Wittgenstein later remarked: "The assumption would thus be possible—though unverifiable—that one section of mankind has one sensation of red and another section another" (Wittgenstein 1958, I, 272). Indeed, this unsettling possibility became one of the chief reasons why Wittgenstein himself decided to call a halt to any further talk about privately sensed qualities. And it is the reason, too, why other philosophers such as Daniel Dennett have been tempted to go even further, to argue that sensory qualia have no objective reality whatsoever (Dennett, 1988, although compare his more nuanced position of 1991).

Now, we need not go all the way with Wittgenstein or Dennett to realize that if even part of this argument about the privacy of qualia goes through, we may as well give up on our ambition to have a Darwinian explanation of them. For it must be obvious that nothing can possibly have evolved by natural selection unless it does in fact have some sort of major public effect—unless it has a measurably positive influence on survival and reproduction. If, as common sense, let alone philosophy, suggests, sensory quality really is for all practical purposes private, selection simply could never have gotten a purchase on it.

It appears that we cannot have it both ways. Either as Darwinists we continue, against the odds, to try to explain sensory quality as a product of selection, or we grudgingly accept the idea that sensations are just as private as they seem to be.

So, what is to be done? Which of these two strongly motivated positions must we give up?

I believe the answer is that actually we need not give up either. We can in fact hold both to the idea that sensory quality is private, as well as to the idea that it has been shaped by selection, provided we recognize that these two things have not been true at the same time: that, in the course of evolution, the privacy came only after the selection had occurred.

Here, in short, is the case that I would make. It may be true that the activity of sensing is today largely hidden from public view, and that the particular quality of sensations is not essential to the function they perform. It may be true, for example, that my sensation of red is directly known only to me, and that its particular redness is irrelevant to how it does its job. Yet it was not always so. In the evolutionary past the activity of sensing was a much more open one, and its every aspect mattered to survival. In the past my ancestors evolved to feel red this way because feeling it this way gave them a real biological advantage.

Now, in case this sounds like a highly peculiar way of looking at history, I should stress that it would not be so unusual for evolution to have worked like this. Again and again in other areas of biology it turns out that, as the function of an organ or behavior has shifted over evolutionary time, obsolete aspects of the original design have carried on down more or less unchanged.

For a simple example, consider the composition of our own blood. When our fish ancestors were evolving 400 million years ago in the Devonian seas, it was essential that the salt composition of their blood should closely resemble the external sea water, so that they would not lose water by osmosis across their gills. Once our ancestors moved on to the land and started breathing air, however, this particular feature of blood was no longer of critical importance. Nevertheless, because other aspects of vertebrate physiology had developed to fit in with it and any change would have been at least temporarily disadvantageous, well enough was left alone. The result is that human blood is still today more or less interchangeable with sea water.

This tendency toward what can be called "stylistic inertia" is evident at every level of evolution, not only in nature, but in culture as well. Clear examples occur in the development of language, manners, dress, and architectural design (as beautifully documented by Philip Steadman, 1979). But I would say that as nice a case as any is provided by the history of clocks and how their hands move.

Modern clocks evolved from sundials. In the northern hemisphere, where clocks began, the shadow of the sundial's vane moves around the dial in the "sunwise" direction that we now call "clockwise." Once sundials came to be replaced by clock-work mechanisms with moving hands, however, the reason for representing time by sunwise motion immediately vanished. Nevertheless, because by this stage people's habits of time-telling were already thoroughly ingrained, the result has been that nearly every clock on earth still uses sunwise motion.

But suppose now, for the sake of argument, we were to be faced with a modern clock, and, as inveterate Darwinians, we wanted to know why its hands move the way they do. As with sensations, there would be two levels at which the question could be posed.

If we were to ask about why the clock has hands at all, the answer would be relatively easy. Obviously the clock needs to have hands of some kind so as to have some way of representing the passage of time—just as we need to have sensations of some kind so as to have some way of representing stimulation at the body surface.

But if we ask about why the hands move clockwise as they do, the answer would have to go much deeper. Clearly the job of representing time could in fact nowadays be served equally well by rotationally inverted movement—just as the job of representing sensory stimulation could nowadays be served equally well by quality inverted sensations. In fact, as we've seen, this second question for the clock can only be answered by reference to ancestral history—just as I would argue for sensations.

When an analogy fits the case as well as this, I would say it cries out to be taken further. It strongly suggests there is some more profound basis for the resemblance than has at first appeared. In this case I think that, surprisingly, we really have struck gold. For it seems with this clock analogy we may be arriving at the crucial idea we need to unlock the mystery of what sensations are and how they have evolved.

A clock tells time by acting in a certain way, namely by moving its hands. This action has a certain style inherited from the past, a clockwise style, clockwisely.

The remarkable truth is, I believe, that a person also has sensations by acting in a certain way. And, yes, each sensory action also has its own inherited style—for example, a red style, redly.

I have no space here to explain the full reasoning behind this theory. But I can at least attempt to sketch in the main themes.

As Reid long ago recognized, sensations are not what people mostly think they are. Our language misleads us. We talk of "feeling" or "having" sensations—as if somehow sensations were the objects of our sensing, sense data, out there waiting for us to grasp them or observe them with our mind's eye. But analysis shows that this is a mistake. Sensations are no more the objects of sensing than, say, volitions are the objects of willing or intentions the objects of intending.

"The form of the expression, I feel pain," Reid wrote,

might seem to imply that the feeling is something distinct from the pain felt; yet in reality, there is no distinction. As thinking a thought is an expression which could signify no more than thinking, so feeling a pain signifies no more than being pained. What we have said of pain is applicable to every other mere sensation.   (Reid, 1764, p. 112)

But I believe Reid got only part way to the truth here. For my own view (developed in detail in Humphrey, 1992) is that the right expression is not so much "being pained" as "paining." That is to say, sensing is not a passive state at all, but a form of active engagement with a stimulus occurring at the body surface. When, for example,

I feel pain in my toe, or taste salt on my tongue, or equally when I have red sensation at my eye, I am in effect reaching out to the site of stimulation with a kind of evaluative response appropriate to the stimulus and the body part affected. What I experience as my sensation of "what is happening to me" is based not on the incoming information as such, but rather on the signals I myself issue to make the response happen.

This is how I feel about what's happening right now at my toe—I'm feeling painily about it.

This is how I feel about what's happening right now at this part of the field of my eye—I'm feeling redly about it.

Now, it is true that, today, these sensory responses are largely internal, covert, and private. But, or so at least I want to argue, it was not always so. Rather, these responses began their evolutionary life as full-fledged bodily behaviors that were unambiguously in the public domain—and, what is more, as behaviors with a real adaptive role.

If I try, as I shall do now, to sketch the evolutionary story in cartoon form, it is because I want the general logic to come through rather than to attempt an accurate history. And I must trust you will be prepared to join me at this level.

So let us return in imagination to the earliest of times and picture a primitive amoeba-like animal floating in the ancient seas.

This animal has a defining edge to it, a structural boundary. This boundary is crucial, serving both to hold the animal's own substance in and the rest of the world out, and as the vital frontier across which essential exchanges of matter and energy and information can take place.

Now, light falls on the animal, objects bump into it, pressure waves press against it, chemicals stick to it, and so on. No doubt some of these surface events are going to be a good thing for the animal, others bad. In order for the animal to survive it must have evolved the ability to sort out the good from the bad and to respond differently to them—reacting to this stimulus with an *ow*!, to that with an *ouch*!, to this with a *whowee*!

Thus, when, say, salt arrives at its skin, it detects it and makes a characteristic wriggle of activity—it wriggles saltily. When red light falls on it, it makes a different kind of wriggle—it wriggles redly. Presumably these are adaptive responses, selected because they are appropriate to the animal's particular needs. Wriggling saltily has been selected as the best response to salt, whereas wriggling sugarly, for example, would be the best response to sugar. Wriggling redly has been selected as the best response to red light, and wriggling bluely would be the best response to blue light.

Still, as yet, these responses are nothing other than responses, and there is no reason to suppose that the animal is in any way mentally aware of what is happening. Let us imagine, however, that, as this animal's life becomes more complex, the time comes when it will be advantageous for it to have some kind of inner knowledge of what is affecting it: a mental representation of the sensory stimulation at the surface of its body and how it feels about it. One of the reasons it may need this kind of representation may be precisely the one we discussed earlier, namely to be able to flag the present.

Now, one way of developing this capacity for representing sensory stimulation might be to start over again with a completely fresh analysis of the incoming information from the sense organs. But, as it happens, this would be to miss a trick. The fact is that all the requisite details about the stimulation—where the stimulus is occurring, what kind of stimulus it is, and how it should be dealt with—are already encoded in the command signals the animal issues when it makes the appropriate sensory response.

Hence, all the animal needs to do to sense "what's happening to me" is to pick up on these already occurring command signals. To sense the presence of salt at a certain location on its skin, it need only monitor its own signals for wriggling saltily at that location, or equally to sense the presence of red light it need only monitor its signals for wriggling redly.

Thus the result is that sensations do indeed evolve at first as corollaries of the animal's public bodily activity. And because, in these early days, the form of this activity is still being maintained by natural selection, it follows that the form of the animal's mental representation—its sensory "experience" or proto-experience, if you like—is also going to be determined in all its aspects by selection.

The story is of course by no means over. As this animal continues to develop and to change its lifestyle, the nature of the selection pressures is bound to alter. In particular, as the animal becomes more independent of its immediate environment, the making of sensory responses directly to the stimulus becomes of less and less relevance to its biological survival. In fact, there comes a time when wriggling saltily or redly at the point of stimulation no longer has any adaptive value at all.

Then why doesn't the animal simply give up on this kind of local responding altogether? The reason is that, even though it may no longer have any use for the sensory responses as such, it has by this time become heavily dependent on the secondary representational functions that these responses have acquired. And because the way it has been getting these representations in the past has been by monitoring its own command signals for sensory responses, it clearly cannot afford to stop issuing these command signals entirely.

Local response   Response becomes   Response
occurs at point   targeted on   becomes
of stimulation   incoming   "privatized" within
                          sensory nerve   the brain

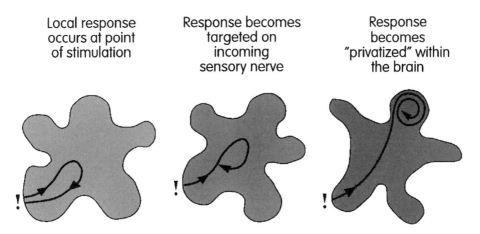

Figure 13.1

So, the situation now is this. In order to be able to represent "what's happening to me," the animal must continue to issue commands such as would produce an appropriate response at the right place on the body if they were to carry through into bodily behavior. But, given that the behavior is no longer wanted, it may be better if these commands remained virtual or as-if commands—in other words, commands which, while retaining their original intentional properties, do not in fact have any real effects.

The upshot is—or so I argue—that, over evolutionary time, there is a slow but remarkable change. The whole sensory activity gets "privatized": the command signals for sensory responses get short circuited before they reach the body surface, so that instead of reaching all the way out to the site of stimulation they now reach only to points closer and closer in on the incoming sensory nerve, until eventually the whole process becomes closed off from the outside world in an internal loop within the brain (figure 13.1).

Once this happens, the role of natural selection must of course sharply diminish. The sensory responses have lost all their original biological importance and have in fact disappeared from view. Therefore, selection is no longer involved in determining the form of these responses and a fortiori can no longer be involved in determining the quality of the representations based on them. The conclusion is that sensory experience has become privatized.

Note well, however, that this privacy has come about only at the very end, after natural selection has done its work to shape the sensory landscape. In fact, there is every reason to suppose that the forms of sensory responses and the corresponding experiences have already been more or less permanently fixed. And although, once selection becomes irrelevant, these forms may be liable to drift somewhat, they are likely always to reflect their evolutionary pedigree.

It is this pedigree that still colors private sensory experience right down to the present day. If today I feel the sensation red this way—as I know very well that I do—it is because I am descended from distant ancestors who were selected to feel it this same way long ago.

Here we are, then, with the solution that I promised. We can have it both ways. We can both make good on our ambition, as Darwinists, to explain sensory quality as a product of selection, and we can accept the common sense idea that sensations are as private as they seem to be—provided we recognize that these two things have not been true at the same time.

But the rewards of this Darwinian approach are greater still. For there remains to be told the story of how, after the privatization of sensory responses has taken place and the command signals have begun to loop back on themselves within the brain, there are likely to be dramatic consequences for sensory phenomenology. In particular, how the activity of sensing is destined to become self-sustaining and partly self-creating, so that sensory experiences get lifted into a time dimension of their own—into what I call the "thick time" of the subjective present (Humphrey, 1992, 1995). What is more, how the establishment of this time-loop is the key to the thing we value most about sensations: the fact that not only do they have quality, but that this quality comes across to us in the very special, self-intimating way that we call the *what it's like* of consciousness.

When did this transformation finally occur? Euan Macphail (this volume) argues that conscious sensations require the prior existence of a self. The philosopher Gottlob Frege made a similar claim, saying, "An experience is impossible without an experient. The inner world presupposes the person whose inner world it is" (Frege, 1967, p. 27). I agree with both these writers about the requirement that sensations have a self to whom they belong. But I think Macphail, in particular, goes much too far with his insistence that such a self can only emerge with language. My own view is that self-representations arise through action, and that the "feeling self" may actually be created by those very sensory activities that make up its experience.

This is, however, another story for another time. I will simply remark here, with Rudyard Kipling, contra Lawrence, that "Them that asks no questions isn't told a lie"—and no truths either.

Summary

It is the ambition of evolutionary psychology to explain how the basic features of human mental life came to be selected because of their contribution to biological survival. Counted among the most basic must be the subjective qualities of conscious sensory experience: the felt redness we experience on looking at a ripe tomato, the felt saltiness on tasting an anchovy, the felt pain on being pricked by a thorn. But, as many theorists acknowledge, with these qualia, the ambition of evolutionary psychology may have met its match. Everyone agrees that a trait can only contribute to an organism's biological survival in so far as it operates in the public domain. Yet almost everyone also agrees that the subjective quality of sensory experience is (at least for all practical purposes) private and without external influence. We must, it seems, either concede that the subjective quality of sensations cannot after all have been determined by selection (even if this is theoretically depressing), or else demonstrate that the quality of sensations is not as private as it seems to be (even if this is intuitively unconvincing). I believe neither of these solutions to the puzzle is the right one. I argue instead that the truth is that the quality of sensations has indeed been shaped by selection in the past, despite the fact that today it is effectively private. This situation has come about as a result of a remarkable evolutionary progression, whereby the primitive activity of sensing slowly became "privatized"—that is to say, removed from the domain of overt public behavior and transformed into a mental activity that is now, in humans, largely if not exclusively internal to the subject's mind.

Note

An earlier version of this chapter has appeared in "Toward a Science of Consciousness III. The Third Tucson Discussions and Debates" (Hameroff, S, Kaszniak, A, Chalmers, D, eds), Cambridge, MA: MIT Press, 1999.

References

Dennett DC (1988) Quining qualia. In: Consciousness in contemporary science (Marcel AJ, Bisiach E, ed), pp 42–77. Oxford: Clarendon Press.

Dennett DC (1991) Consciousness explained. New York: Little Brown.

Empson W (1961) Seven types of ambiguity. Harmondsworth Penguin, 3rd edition.

Frege G (1967) The thought: A logical inquiry. In: Philosophical logic (Strawson PF, ed). Oxford: Oxford University Press.

Gregory RL (1996) What do qualia do? Perception, 25: 377–378.

Humphrey N (1992) A history of the mind. London: Chatto & Windus.

Humphrey N (1995) The thick moment. In: The third culture (Brockman J, ed), pp 198–208. New York: Simon & Schuster.

Locke J (1690/1975) An essay concerning human understanding. Oxford: Clarendon Press.

Marcel AJ (1988) Phenomenal experience and functionalism. In: Consciousness in contemporary science (Marcel AJ, Bisiach E, ed), pp 121–158. Oxford: Clarendon Press.

Reid T (1764/1813) An inquiry into the human mind. Charlestown: Samuel Etheridge.

Reid T (1785/1813) Essays on the intellectual powers of man. Charlestown: Samuel Etheridge.

Steadman P (1979) The evolution of designs. Cambridge: Cambridge University Press.

Wittgenstein L (1958) Philosophical investigations. Oxford: Blackwell.

14 The Search for a Mental Rubicon

Euan M. Macphail

I approach the problem of consciousness as an experimental psychologist; my goal is to understand how a collection of nonconscious components—the cells of the body—can be assembled in such a way as to become conscious. I assume that the answer to this problem lies not in the uniting of the body with a nonphysical entity, but in the functional organization of the body, and of the nervous system in particular. The functional analysis of nervous systems is the subject matter of psychology, so I believe that it is once again proper (after the blind alley of stimulus-response behaviorism) for psychologists to concern themselves with consciousness.

I have persuaded myself at least that the argument I shall develop below proceeds in reasonably sensible steps. I make this somewhat defensive claim at the outset because I am well aware that the conclusion that I shall reach is not likely to be widely regarded as reasonable. To back up my claim of reasonableness, I shall organize this chapter so as to emphasize the steps that lead me progressively to so unreasonable a view.

Definition of Consciousness

The term "consciousness" has various uses, and I shall use it in different ways in different sections of this chapter, where the sense intended should be clear from the context. But the basic problem with which I am concerned—what is for me the problem of consciousness—is the capacity of any organism to sense or to feel something—anything. When I ask whether some organism is or is not conscious, this is the meaning I have in mind. It is, I believe, the same notion of consciousness Humphrey is concerned with in his chapter. The question is, then, whether it is valid to ascribe sensory "qualia" to a nonhuman organism. But rather than ask whether nonhumans experience such "neutral" qualia as redness or saltiness, I prefer to focus on the capacity to feel pleasure or pain or, more generally, on the capacity to prefer some states to others. This aspect of consciousness allows us to be somewhat more specific about what it would be to ascribe consciousness to an organism, as it is closely tied to some of our most basic ethical assumptions: most of us would agree that you can do neither right nor wrong to an organism that feels neither pleasure nor pain and has no preference for any one state over any other. So, to decide that an organism is conscious is to decide that it is an appropriate object of ethical discussion.

One further point of definition is that I shall assume that an organism is either conscious or not conscious. It may well be that there is sense in the idea that some animals might feel things more acutely than others (although what the metric of comparison might be would clearly be a difficult issue)—but the important issue is whether an animal feels *anything*. There is a difference in kind, a qualitative leap, between organisms that feel and those that do not—between conscious and nonconscious organisms.

Assumptions

I shall ignore the philosophical problems associated with the existence of "other minds," and adopt the effectively universal common sense assumption that adult humans are conscious; the restriction here to "adult" humans is intended to reflect only the widely accepted possibility that an embryonic child, undeniably human, might not yet have reached the stage of development at which feelings are experienced. And I shall assume that all nonliving entities—stones, rivers, the stars, and so on—are not conscious and that, of living beings, only species of the animal kingdom are potentially conscious: trees, mushrooms, protozoans, and so on are not conscious. Finally, I assume, along with my fellow scientists and, I hope, most of the Western world, that organisms are related to one another, and that we humans evolved from an apelike ancestor by the process of natural selection. This noncontroversial assumption does not imply, however, that I embrace what is now known as "evolutionary" psychology. It does not seem to me that to accept that animals are adapted to the demands of their particular ecological niches entails accepting that differences in cognitive "modules" should be anticipated. In fact my own interpretations (e.g., Macphail, 1996) of the phenomena of learning incline me to favor the general process view advocated in Bitterman's chapter rather than the cognitive modularity of Shettleworth's contribution.

Two Problems

Which Animals Are Conscious?

Although I shall assume that only animals are candidates for consciousness, I do not assume that all animals are conscious (here and elsewhere I shall, for brevity's sake, use "animals" to refer to nonhuman animals). This too is probably a widely held view: many of us might doubt that sponges feel anything, but are quite certain that, say, cats and dogs do. This brings me to my first problem: if not all animals are to be assumed conscious, how are we to decide which are, and which are not? This is clearly a critical issue, because unless we can decide which animals are conscious, and which are not, we shall be at a grave disadvantage in trying to decide which aspects of the development of nervous systems are associated with consciousness. In attempting to answer this question, I shall avoid any prejudging of the issue by abandoning the common sense assumption that cats and dogs feel pain and asking instead what criteria should be used for the demonstration of consciousness in non-humans. Once those criteria are settled, we can decide which animals are conscious.

What Is the Function of Feeling?

My second problem arises from another objection to my declining to assume consciousness in at least some animals. We humans evolved from nonhuman ancestors —from animals that must have had much in common with animals alive today. Our descent is quite evident in our behavior, which clearly has much in common with the behavior of animals, and particularly with the behavior of animals that are closely related to ourselves—the behavior, for example, of primates or of mammals in general. What is particularly pertinent here is that the way in which we react to pleasant and painful stimuli shows clear parallels to that seen in animals: we bask in the sun, and we yelp and run away when struck a violent blow. How could the idea that dogs and cats do not feel anything be reconciled with Darwin's account of evolution? Is it sensible to suppose that the same behavior, derived from a common ancestor, might be accompanied in one species by feelings but not in another?

My response to this has two parts. First, this is a question that must be faced by any account that supposes that some, but not all, animals, are conscious. Wherever we set the line between those that are conscious and those that are not, we are bound to find, on one side of that line, behaviors that are similar to those of related species on the other side of the line, and so similar behaviors that are supposed to be accompanied by feeling in one species but not in another. Second, the appropriate response to any question about divergence in evolution must be one that refers to the adaptive value of the novel character. In the present context, we should look for some novel environmental demand that is best met by behavior accompanied by feeling. This leads us to my second problem: what *is* the adaptive value of feelings?

The issue of the function of feeling is intimately connected with that of criteria for consciousness. For most observers, the responses of animals to potentially dangerous stimulation—noxious stimulation, of the sort that would cause pain in us—are compelling evidence of feelings in them. But there are real difficulties in accepting these forms of behavior as criteria of feelings. We could, for example, readily construct a machine that would yelp and withdraw from a blow—but no rational person would suppose that this in itself would be sufficient to create a conscious machine. And, of course, actors can simulate these reactions without experiencing the feelings that normally accompany them. Perhaps more to the point, major components of these reactions can be found in organisms that have been subjected to procedures that lead most of us to suppose that they are not capable of consciousness.

Most people will identify with a struggling worm. But as every boy who has baited a fish hook knows, if a worm is cut in two, the front half with its primitive brain seems not to mind as much as the back half, which writhes in "agony." But surely if the worm felt pain as we do, surely it would be the part with the brain that would do the agonising. The agony of the tail end is our agony, not the worm's; its writhing is a mechanical release phenomenon, the motor nerves in the tail end firing in volleys at being disconnected from their normal inhibition by the cephalic ganglion. (Jaynes, 1993, p. 6)

Similarly, spinal animals (including humans) whose spinal cord has been severed from the brain not only show vigorous reactions to noxious stimuli delivered to regions that have no nervous connections with the brain, but also show conditioned responses to initially ineffective stimuli that have been paired with noxious stimulation (Patterson et al., 1973; Ince et al., 1978).

Let us return now to the humble worm, and note that we are happy to accept that the hind part of the severed worm could show vigorous wriggling without feeling anything. The implication is, of course, that the wriggling of the intact animal might not be accompanied by feeling. Now we don't need to decide here whether or not the worm is feeling anything—the point is simply that it is clear that it is not absurd to suppose that an effective withdrawal response could occur without any feeling accompanying it. And this, of course, raises the question of function: if effective responses to noxious stimuli are possible in the absence of feeling, what is the adaptive value of adding feeling to those responses? If we cannot conceive an adaptive value, then it is hard to see how feelings could have evolved. It is easy to see that a multicellular animal should develop sensory systems that would classify external stimuli into potentially noxious and potentially beneficial stimuli, and that the output of those sensory systems should be linked to behavioral systems of approach and withdrawal. But I find it difficult, if not impossible, to see either how the evolution of feeling could enhance the effectiveness of those systems or, a more profound difficulty, how a mechanical system of nonconscious nerve cells could be transformed into a conscious system.

In what follows, I rely upon my inability to conceive a function for feelings as a reason for supposing that they must have evolved in conjunction with some other system that did convey selective advantage. By way of contrast, a more positive approach to function can be found in Humphrey's chapter, in which not only are sensations given a function, but their qualitative aspect also finds a role.

Behavioral Complexity as a Criterion?

However difficult it may be to conceive of any way in which consciousness might have evolved, the fact is, of course, that it did evolve—we humans are conscious. If we cannot use feelinglike behavior as evidence of consciousness in nonlinguistic organisms, then we must seek some other criterion. An initial step in this search is suggested by the fact that, in general, those animals—like mammals—that seem to us most likely to be conscious are more complex than those—worms, for example—that seem less likely. Increases of complexity are seen both in the size and in the organization of nervous systems. It does not seem plausible that increases simply in the numbers of nerve cells could result in the emergence of consciousness. We would not suppose that simply adding more and more components to a computer would make it conscious. The human spinal cord is far larger than the entire nervous systems of many small mammals, but we would not rule out consciousness in them simply because their nervous systems were smaller than the nonconscious human spinal cord. We might, then, look for a shift in the complexity of organization of the nervous system, a shift that would inevitably be reflected in a shift in behavioral complexity.

Although I am primarily concerned with the origin of feelings, it does not seem likely to me that we should find the criterion we need in those behaviors that are most closely associated in our minds with feelings. Effective systems of approach and withdrawal are found virtually universally among animals, and even if we extend the search to include emotional behavior, I doubt that we shall find a shift in complexity at a plausible stage of evolution: there is, for example, good evidence for the existence in the sea-hare *Aplysia* of a central state that closely resembles what we call fear (Walters et al., 1981). We should, then, look instead for a shift in cognition. It is surely our cognitive capacities rather than any developments in feelings and emotions that mark us off from most other animals, and perhaps we shall find some shift in cognition in some groups of animals that may offer a plausible criterion for the emergence of consciousness.

Are There Shifts in Cognition?

This is not the place for any attempt at a detailed survey of potential differences in cognition among various species. It has been my contention (Macphail, 1996) that there is currently little evidence of differences (and so no shifts in cognitive capacity) in what might be called general intelligence among nonhuman vertebrate species. My case has been that there are no tasks that differentiate among species as a consequence of differences in cognitive capacity rather than differences in such factors as motivation and perceptual or motor capacity. I have, accordingly, suggested that we should adopt the "null hypothesis"—namely, that all nonhuman vertebrates are of comparable intelligence (Macphail, 1985). This is, of course, a contentious claim that has met with considerable scepticism (see, for example, commentaries in Macphail, 1987). But it is also true that no specific claim for a difference in cognitive capacity has met with universal—or even very widespread—approval. Although most psychologists may well believe that there are differences in intellectual capacity among species, they cannot agree on what those differences are, nor on any one specific difference. For our present purposes, I do not rely on the validity of the null hypothesis: all I wish to argue is that, if there are indeed differences in cognition among nonhuman vertebrates, they are not sufficiently striking to rank as potential candidates for a shift in cognition that might mark a transition from nonconscious to conscious organisms.

There are, moreover, as emphasized in Bitterman's chapter, striking parallels between the general processes of vertebrate and invertebrate learning. My case is, then, that associative processes lie at the core of learning in both vertebrates and invertebrates, and that nowhere in nonhumans do we see any striking shift in cognitive capacity. I should add here that this conclusion is also supported from work on one of those cognitive capacities—learning about spatial relationships—that many suppose does involve processes over and above association formation. We find good evidence of sophisticated navigation not only in mammals and birds, but in bony fish (Braithwaite et al., 1996) and in invertebrates such as ants, bees, and wasps (Collett, 1996). It is in any case, of course, not easy to see a link between maps and consciousness, but I shall in a later section discuss work on proposed differences (that I shall reject) among nonhuman primate species on tasks that are directly related to consciousness.

The Emergence of Language

Although I have not been able to find convincing demonstrations of shifts in cognition among nonhuman animals, I have concluded (Macphail, 1982) that there is a major shift between nonhumans and humans, namely, the emergence of language in humans. The claim that humans possess a species-specific language acquisition device is contentious, but it is one that has been made by a number of scientists, both psychologists and linguists. I shall not attempt to review the voluminous and ever-growing body of research findings here, but my subsequent argument will assume that language is peculiar to humans, and that the critical feature of our language is the capacity to form sentences—to combine a noun phrase with a verb phrase.

Given the assumption that only humans possess language, two propositions stand out: first, humans are the only organisms that we *know* are conscious; second, humans are the only organisms that talk. But although the emergence of language is indisputably a striking shift in cognition, it is not obvious that there could be a link between language and consciousness so that the latter might be explained in terms of the former. It's a possibility that is clearly worth exploring, but before doing so, we should probe the cognitive shift a little more deeply.

Association Formation in Humans

Language clearly dominates the intellectual activities of humans: we use language either overtly in solving problems, or indirectly by using the educational experience we gain largely through the medium of language. My contention with regard to nonhumans is that their intellectual activity is dominated by association formation. A pertinent question is, then: has language been added to our ancestors' associative system, or has it replaced that system? Do we, in other words, still form associations in the same way that nonhumans do? Consideration of this issue again raises the function of consciousness: is it plausible to suppose that animals could learn but not be conscious?

The seemingly straightforward question of whether humans form associations as animals do is surprisingly difficult to answer. Although humans readily acquire responses when, for example, a tone and an airpuff to the eye are paired, it can be argued (e.g., Brewer, 1974) that these responses reflect the expectation that tones will be followed by puffs, and that this expectation is the outcome of an explicit hypothesis formed by the subject. It is not supposed that this cognitive process is the same as that involved in the incremental growth of associative strength seen in conditioning in animals. The acquisition of responding in tasks involving simple pairings of stimuli may, then, be interpreted as the outcome of a "higher" cognitive process and so as providing no evidence of our forming associations as animals do.

Evidence has, however, accumulated over recent decades to suggest that the nonhuman associative system is available to humans. This evidence derives from work on implicit learning, in which knowledge is acquired in the absence of any awareness of learning, and, accordingly, without the generation of explicit hypotheses. The tasks involved are generally complex, and one well-known example is the acquisition of artificial grammars (Reber, 1967, 1993). Studies using this technique have shown subjects appear to learn arbitrary "rules" governing the generation of strings of items (letters or symbols, for example) without knowing that they have done so, or having any explicit account available of what those rules might be. This procedure does not at first sight seem obviously to involve conditioning (conventionally conceived as learning engendered by the pairing of two discrete stimuli). But Reber (1993) argues that the subjects have in fact detected "covariations or contingencies" between events, and has pointed to the clear parallel between this property of the human "implicit" system and the associative learning that we see in animals. Experiments using other techniques have encouraged the view that human associative learning does employ a system comparable to the associative system of animals: blocking, for example, has been observed (Dickinson et al., 1984). Reber himself suggests that, paradoxically, we use the implicit system when faced with rather complex input that does not readily yield to simple hypotheses about the rules determining its structure. My account of implicit learning leans heavily on Reber's work, and his distinction between implicit and explicit systems is not universally accepted (for a critique of the distinction, see Shanks and St. John, 1994). But, just as I have assumed that animals cannot acquire language, so my argument henceforth will follow Reber in supposing that there is a human counterpart of the animal associative system and that it operates in implicit learning.

I conclude, therefore, that our acquisition of language has not ousted our ancestors' associative system, and that the two systems act in parallel. That, perhaps, is hardly surprising—we should not expect a system that is found throughout virtually all animals wholly to disappear in humans. What is more intriguing is that this is a system of whose operations we seem to be entirely unaware. It is not a conscious system. This might seem at first sight to suggest that associative learning—which, I argue, dominates cognition in animals—is not conscious in animals. But although the data on implicit learning argue that at least some forms of learning do not require consciousness, they do not force the inference that animal learning provides no evidence of consciousness. This is partly because it is clear that animal learning involves processes in addition to those used by humans in implicit learning tasks. Evidence for this is derived from further data on unconscious learning in humans, where the learning is unconscious as a consequence of brain damage.

Amnesia and the Implicit System

It is well known that damage to the hippocampus and its associated structures leads to anterograde amnesia in humans: patients suffering this form of amnesia do not recognize people or places that they have encountered subsequent to the trauma, and cannot consciously recall any events of their posttraumatic lives. But it is also the case that amnesics can acquire certain types of novel information: they can, for example, form conditioned responses and retain them over a relatively long period;

they can acquire new perceptual motor skills; and they can show efficient learning in those tasks in which humans without brain damage show implicit learning (Knowlton et al., 1992; Macphail, 1993). It makes sense, then, to suppose that the implicit associative learning system is one that is available to amnesics, a system independent of the hippocampal system. (Which precise structures are responsible for amnesic symptoms—and whether the hippocampus is involved at all—remains a controversial issue, but one that need not concern us here. I shall use "hippocampal system" to refer to the set of structures that are involved, acknowledging that it is possible that the hippocampus may not be one of them.) Although it has proved extremely difficult to characterize the role of the hippocampal system in nonhuman vertebrates, it is clear that it does play a crucial role in some learning tasks. It is therefore quite possible that in both animals and humans there is an associative system, independent of the hippocampal system, whose operations are not open to conscious inspection, and that there is in addition a learning system, dependent in vertebrates upon the hippocampal system, whose operations in humans we know are open to conscious access.

We can conclude, then, that the formation of associations does not necessarily require (and so cannot demonstrate) consciousness. A central issue now is whether those forms of learning that require hippocampal involvement in vertebrates, which are conscious in humans, are conscious in animals also. In the following section I tackle this question by considering the memory of human infants, where I find evidence that use of the hippocampal system does not necessarily involve consciousness.

Language and Consciousness

My discussion thus far has made out the case for the following propositions: first, it makes sense to look for a shift in cognition as a correlate of the emergence of consciousness; second, the only major shift that I can detect is the emergence in humans of language, a capacity that has not replaced the associative system of animals, but operates in parallel with it. These propositions invite further questions: first, what other evidence might be relevant to deciding whether there is a link between language and consciousness? Second, is it possible to conceive of a causal link between them? I shall begin by considering relevant evidence on infants.

Are Babies Conscious?

Animals are not alone in not talking: we humans do not acquire language until at least several months after birth. If we are interested in a potential link between language and consciousness, it makes sense that we should inquire into the nature of consciousness in babies. Do babies, for example, feel pleasure and pain? This is an issue that has come to the fore recently in medical circles, where the question has been extended to the consciousness of fetuses. It seems that until a decade or so ago most doctors believed that fetuses and newborn babies were not capable of feeling pain, and that this belief led to the use of either no anesthetics or very low doses of anesthetics when performing surgical procedures on them (Owens, 1984; Fitzgerald, 1998).

It is hardly necessary to note that when babies are subjected to potentially noxious stimuli—like the insertion of needles—they do respond, by crying, for example, as though they were unpleasant (Owens and Todt, 1984); recent work has found that following intrauterine procedures fetuses too may show increases in stress-related hormones (Giannakoulopoulos et al., 1994). Nevertheless, at least some of those working on the neurobiology of pain in infants are still inclined to doubt whether pain awareness develops until some months after birth (Fitzgerald, 1998). The problem is precisely the same as that of deciding whether or not an animal feels pain or pleasure: the responses do not guarantee consciousness, and would be equally effective whether or not they were accompanied by consciousness.

One reason for supposing that babies must feel pain is surely that we know that they will develop into adults who we are certain are conscious (in a way that, I contend, we cannot be certain about animals). But this does not help very much, because there must be a stage at which the embryo moves from unconsciousness to consciousness; at some point we must decide where that transition occurs, and, as is the case for animals, it may seem most likely that this transition should be marked by a transition in cognition. It might seem, however, that the fact that babies do eventually develop into language users should allow us another way of deciding whether babies feel anything—we could simply attempt to recall our prelinguistic lives and find out what we felt. But we all know that, despite the presumably dramatic and certainly novel events that occur in infancy, we have no recollection of them in adulthood. Freud first drew attention to the peculiarity of infantile amnesia, and I shall discuss its possible cause here because I believe that it may throw some light on the origins of consciousness.

Infantile Amnesia

Freud believed that the explanation for infantile amnesia was to be found in the suppression of well-formed memories. But the most popular account until recently was that infantile amnesia was a consequence of the inability of the immature nervous system to form stable memories. This account is now widely rejected because there are now a large number of reports showing good retention by young babies in a number of paradigms. Although the length of time over which retention is demonstrated increases as babies grow older, impressive retention is found in young babies. Rovee-Collier, for example, has used a procedure in which babies learn to kick in order to move a mobile attached by a ribbon to their ankles; when given a "reminder" (for example, seeing the mobile being moved 24 hours before being tested) three-month-old babies retain the learned kicking response for as much as four weeks (Rovee-Collier and Shyi, 1992). By using the deferred imitation technique—in which babies watch an adult modelling some particular way of playing with a toy— McDonough and Mandler (1994) have shown retention by 11-month-old babies over a 12-month period. As the offset of infantile amnesia occurs at somewhere between three and four years old, it is clear that stable memories can be laid down at a time when no memories will survive into adulthood.

It should be noted, however, that the types of procedure in which infants show good retention are generally comparable to the simple conditioning procedures used with rats: learning the kicking response looks very much like a simple case of instrumental conditioning. Conditioning, as we have seen, may be an implicit process, and so does not constitute compelling evidence of consciousness.

Infants Use the Hippocampal System   A more specific suggestion is that a particular type of learning is not possible in childhood, namely, learning served by the hippocampal system (Nadel and Zola-Morgan, 1984). This in turn, it is supposed, reflects the immaturity of the hippocampal system in infancy.

An implication of this proposal is that infants should show a pattern of memory impairment comparable to that shown by adult hippocampal amnesics. It has, however, become clear recently that this is not the case. Infants, unlike adult amnesics, succeed in a wide range of tests of recognition—of faces, voices, and so on. A counter argument here is that it is *conscious* recognition that fails in amnesics, and that we have no way of knowing whether infant "recognition" is conscious or not. There are, however, tasks that do not appear to require conscious recognition that infants can master and amnesics cannot: one of these is the deferred imitation task, outlined above (McDonough et al., 1995). The fact that infants succeed in deferred imitation argues that infantile amnesia is not to be attributed to immaturity of the hippocampal system. It does not, however, demonstrate conscious recall, and I have discussed elsewhere (Macphail, 1998) evidence that learning in infants is not accompanied by conscious recall.

Origins of Autobiographical Memory   The achievements of infants in learning and memory tasks indicate neither a general inability to remember over the long term nor a specific inability to use a particular neurological system. This encourages the search for a developmental change in cognition, a change of a sort that might be reflected in a failure to lay down the type of memory that can be recalled in adult life. Two influential reviews point to two potential candidates for such a change. The first suggests that the development of language is a critical prerequisite for the offset of infantile amnesia (Pillemer and White, 1989); the second, that the critical developmental change is the development of a concept of "self" (Howe and Courage, 1993). I shall suggest here that, in essence, both accounts are true because there is a causal link between the development of language and the emergence of a concept of self.

The notion that language plays a critical role in ending infantile amnesia appeals to the distinction that we have already seen between implicit and explicit learning. The essence of explicit learning is that it is verbalizable—we can demonstrate explicit knowledge by saying what it is that we know. Implicit learning, I have argued, relies upon a system that is critically involved (in humans and in animals) in associative learning, and is not open to conscious inspection by humans. The explicit system, accessed through the hippocampal system, does give rise to conscious, verbalizable experience. This might in itself provide the basis for an account of infantile amnesia were it not for the fact that, as we have already seen, the hippocampal system is active in infants: why, then, should the development of language not allow the recall and verbalization of experiences that involved hippocampal system activity but occurred at a prelinguistic stage?

An answer to these questions may be found in the suggestion that conscious memories require the development of a concept of self. The self concept is a cognitive structure that is a necessary prerequisite of autobiographical memory. Evidence from a variety of sources indicates that the self concept begins to emerge at about 18–24 months old—a time at which children begin to recognize themselves in mirrors and video recordings, and to use pronouns like "I," "me," and (a little later) "you" (Howe and Courage, 1997).

According to this account, without a self there is no principle of organization that would allow events to be committed to memory in such a way that they are remembered as happening to "me." The basic neurological systems responsible for the establishment of memories do not change suddenly, but there comes into existence a novel entity—the cognitive self—that for the first time allows memories to be placed in time and space relative to the remembering person. Explicit recall—conscious recall—is dependent upon the self concept, and before its development, the infant is not aware of his or her experiences as events that involved him or her. So, recall in adulthood of childhood experiences cannot go back further than (at the earliest) the point at which the self concept developed.

This account emphasizes, then, the basic continuity of fundamental processes of memory through infancy to childhood—and there is extensive evidence showing that factors influencing retention have similar effects in infancy as in later life (Howe and Courage, 1997; Rovee-Collier, 1997). There is, however, a change in the way in which experience is structured following the emergence of the self.

I shall, then, adopt the core of Howe and Courage's (1993) account, and suppose that the cause of infantile amnesia is to be found in the absence of a concept of self in infants. However, unlike Howe and Courage, I believe that there is a link between language and the self concept. I shall develop this topic in a later section, following a discussion of some implications of this view of infantile amnesia for consciousness in animals.

Infantile memories are implicit, not explicit, and there is no reason to suppose that the operation of the hippocampal system in them gives rise to conscious awareness of the events of their lives (and if it did, why would those events not yield some form of conscious recall at a later stage?). If the hippocampal system can operate without giving rise to explicit memories, then it might seem that we are left with no compelling reason to suppose that its operations in animals give rise to conscious experiences in them, either. Unless, of course, animals—or at least some animals—also develop a "cognitive" self.

Do Animals Develop a Concept of Self?

Two areas of primate research are clearly pertinent to this question: the mirror mark test of self-recognition, introduced by Gallup (1970), and studies exploring the idea that the great apes might possess a "theory of mind" (Premack and Woodruff, 1978). Some have used this work to support the idea that there is a mental Rubicon (Byrne, 1995) between the cognitive capacities of great apes and those of other animals. Clearly, this shift, if valid, could constitute a plausible candidate in the search for a shift that might lead to the development of consciousness. That work has been reviewed elsewhere (Heyes, 1998; Macphail, 1998), and I shall restrict myself here to restating my conclusion, which is that I remain unconvinced either that the mark test provides a proof of the existence of a self concept, or that there is solid experimental support for the possession by apes of a theory of mind.

One consequence of denying a self to animals is, of course, that according to this account animals do not possess explicit autobiographical memory: they are not capable of conscious recall. The idea that there is a major difference between human and animal recall has been advanced recently by Tulving and Markowitsch (1998), whose specific claim is that animals are not capable of the "mental time travel" involved in human episodic memory. This view is challenged in the chapter in this volume by Clayton et al., who argue that the ability of scrub jays to recall what was stored, and where, and when, demonstrates the existence in scrub jays of all the salient features of episodic memory except the involvement of "autonoetic consciousness," an involvement that seems impossible to demonstrate empirically. My own response to their data is that, despite the remarkable ingenuity of the work, I find the demonstration that all three features of a storing episode may contribute to a subsequent discrimination no more convincing as evidence that the birds show conscious recall—in this case, that they in some sense re-live the storing episode—than evidence that any single feature so contributes. One unfortunate result of the absence in animals of language is that they cannot provide what would be the only reliable evidence on how they use learned information.

Language and the Self

At this point I am compelled to move from interpretation of data to the much less comfortable realms of speculation. In the final two sections I shall attempt to argue, first, that there is a plausible link between language and the self, and second, that there is a link between the cognitive self and experience of any kind.

One of the principal reasons for denying true language to any animal has been the failure to produce a convincing demonstration of sentence production or comprehension by an animal. If we ask what is the basic process underlying sentence production—what is, in effect, the basic language process—we find that it is the ability to combine a noun phrase with a verb phrase. This is turn reflects the ability of a language user to refer to something, an object, say, and to say something about that object. Language users can conceive of one internal representation as being "about" another internal representation, and it is this aboutness relation that lies at the heart of our ability to use sentences.

It is conventional now to speak of associative learning as involving a connection between two internal representations in such a way that the activation of one tends to activate the other. But this is not the same as forming the aboutness relation between two representations: an animal may learn—in a sensory preconditioning task, for example—that a red light is associated with a green light. This is, of course, very different from entertaining the proposition that red *is* green, and I do not see how the mechanisms of association formation familiar to us from animal learning theory could lead to the production of "thoughts" having a subject-predicate form. This is not to deny that a connectionist account of language may be possible, but implies that a successful model will have to incorporate structures that are not themselves the product of associative learning (structures comparable to those that I suppose are innate in humans). And just as I do not see that associative learning could produce the subject-predicate "aboutness" relationship, so I find it difficult to see that any organism capable of that relationship should fail to acquire language.

The word "self" is used in many different ways; the sense in which I am using it is to refer to a cognitive structure that gradually develops over the first year or two of a child's life. A more primitive "presymbolic" (Howe and Courage, 1993) or "non-representational" (Neisser, 1994) self matures in many, if not all, animals early in life, and allows the animal's perceptual and motor systems to learn about, for example, the distinction between sensory events that are a consequence of motor commands and those that are independent of those commands and the likely consequences for the perceptual systems of activation of specific motor commands. The cognitive self builds upon this mechanistic self, the system that is both the originator of the commands and the recipient of the sensory input. A major initial step in the formation of the cognitive self may be assumed to be the conceptual identification of this executive system as having an existence discriminable from the motor and sensory systems. Central to this cognitive achievement—the conceptual identification of a "self"—must be the capacity to conceive propositions about this self: an organism cannot become self-conscious without the ability to conceive certain states as being states of itself rather than of some other entity.

My contention is, then, that self-consciousness—the ability to *conceive* of oneself as a specific entity, different from any other entity, depends upon the "aboutness" relation, which I believe is the basic prerequisite of language. Now this proposition is probably not universally contentious, and I imagine that the conclusions reached by this point will find a reasonable body of adherents. But although many might agree that worms, slugs, bees—perhaps fish—do not form a self concept, and might agree even that this could reflect an absence in them of any capacity for language, most would not agree that this carries any clear implication for the presence or absence of *any* form of consciousness—the ability to feel anything whatever.

From the Self to Consciousness

The proposals that I have made so far have the merit—if they have *any* merits—of parsimony. The only major evolutionary change that I envisage is the emergence during the transition from apes to humans of a capacity in humans (and perhaps in some hominid ancestor) to form aboutness relations among internal representations; that capacity leads to language, and to the formation of a cognitive self. Animals are capable of forming internal representations (although, as they do not use them to refer to entities, they might best be referred to as internal correlates), and the hippocampal memory system to which the cognitive self gains access is also found in (vertebrate) animals (and is operational in infants before the development of the cognitive self). The cognitive self is also intimately concerned with the short-term memory store to which it has access and over which it can exert a degree of control—by, for example, deliberate rehearsal.

The idea that a cognitive self may be a prerequisite of any form of experience has at its root the question, where is a given experiential event occurring? If, for example, we experience a pain in an arm, we do not suppose that the pain occurs *in* the arm. Centrally acting anaesthetic drugs that do not influence nervous activity in the arm may nevertheless abolish the pain. For the pain to be experienced, the person must be conscious—by which we mean self-conscious. We do not ask *what* is in pain, we ask *who* is in pain, and an appropriate answer must identify the "self" concerned; we do not concern ourselves that the isolated part of a spinal man might be in pain because we do not believe that that part has a self.

The intimate relationship between the self and memory provides another ground for the notion that the self is essential for experience. Suppose a drug was developed that had a profoundly amnestic effect so that a person's explicit memory stores were disabled under its influence. Physiological measures might reveal that the peripheral and central nervous activity normally associated with painful stimulation was not changed by the drug; and we might even suppose that painful stimuli elicited powerful withdrawal actions, perhaps "involuntary" vocalization. And suppose that this new drug had no unwelcome side effects—would a rational person accept the drug as an anaesthetic for a surgical operation? Presumably anyone having undergone the treatment would have no problem: he would, just like anyone undergoing a conventional general anaesthetic, have no recall of anything unpleasant. But does it make sense to suppose that pain is being experienced but is subsequently forgotten? It seems to me that we do not find this a sensible suggestion, and that this is because pain must be experienced by a self, a structure that operates through our explicit memory stores. If this self does not know anything about an experience—if the experience at no time entered either the short-term or the long-term explicit store—then it was not an experience of the self. And, as it could not be an experience of anything else, an event that does not register in an explicit memory store is not an experience at all.

There is, then, a case for the claim that a cognitive self is a prerequisite for experience of any kind. Given that there is a case for the claim that language is a prerequisite of the cognitive self, the possibility exists that only language-using humans who have developed sufficiently to have a self are conscious in the sense that they can feel anything, prefer any state to any other—are, in short, sentient beings and proper objects of ethical concern. It need hardly be added that this speculative possibility does not imply that we should now treat animals as though none of them were sentient. The basic argument of this chapter is that if we assume that not all animals are conscious, we should look for a shift in cognition as an index of the emergence of consciousness. But we cannot be certain that the emergence of language is the critical shift—cannot, of course, even be certain that some animals are not conscious. Where there is no certainty, our clear ethical obligation is to continue to assume in our treatment of animals that they are sentient.

Summary

The fact that animals such as dogs and cats respond similarly to humans to stimuli that afford us pleasure and pain suggests that they, like us, are conscious in the sense that they experience feelings. But animals less closely related to us, such as slugs and worms, also respond appropriately to nutritious and dangerous stimuli, and we can at least conceive their doing so without having feelings. If we assume that there was at some stage in evolution a transition from nonfeeling to feeling organisms, how could this have come about, and how could species with feelings be distinguished from species without feelings? A plausible proposal is that the transition reflected a shift in complexity of cognition; but the only strong current candidate for such a shift is the appearance of language in humans, a capacity that operates in parallel with the predominantly associative learning systems of nonhuman animals. Sentences require that something is said "about" the subject, and it is suggested that, first, the capacity for the "aboutness" relation is necessary for the construction of a self concept; and second, a self concept is necessary for the experience of feelings. Indirect support for these proposals is drawn from evidence that associative learning may proceed in humans without conscious awareness, and that babies do not form consciously accessible memories before they acquire language and construct a self.

References

Braithwaite VA, Armstrong JD, McAdam HM, Huntingford FA (1996) Can juvenile Atlantic salmon use multiple cue systems in spatial learning? Animal Behaviour, 51: 1409–1415.

Brewer WF (1974) There is no convincing evidence for operant and classical conditioning in human beings. In: Cognition and the symbolic processes (Weimer WB, Palermo DJ, ed), pp 1–42. Hillsdale, NJ: Lawrence Erlbaum Associates.

Byrne R (1995) The thinking ape: Evolutionary origins of intelligence. Oxford: Oxford University Press.

Collett TS (1996) Insect navigation en-route to the goal—multiple strategies for the use of landmarks. Journal of Experimental Biology, 199: 227–235.

Dickinson A, Shanks DR, Evenden J (1984) Judgment of act-outcome contingency: The role of selective attribution. Quarterly Journal of Experimental Psychology, 36A: 29–50.

Fitzgerald M (1998) The birth of pain. MRC News, Summer 1998: 20–23.

Gallup GG (1970) Chimpanzees: Self-recognition. Science, 167: 86–87.

Giannakoulopoulos X, Sepulveda W, Kourtis P, Glover V, Fisk NM (1994) Fetal plasma cortisol and ß-endorphin response to intrauterine needling. Lancet, 344: 77–81.

Heyes CM (1998) Theory of mind in nonhuman primates. Behavioral and Brain Sciences, 21: 101–134.

Howe ML, Courage ML (1993) On resolving the enigma of infantile amnesia. Psychological Bulletin, 113: 305–326.

Howe ML, Courage ML (1997) The emergence and early development of autobiographical memory. Psychological Review, 104: 499–523.

Ince LP, Brucker BS, Alba A (1978) Reflex conditioning in a spinal man. Journal of Comparative and Physiological Psychology, 92: 796–802.

Jaynes J (1993) The origin of consciousness in the breakdown of the bicameral mind. London: Penguin Books.

Knowlton BJ, Ramus SJ, Squire LR (1992) Intact artificial grammar learning in amnesia—dissociation of classification learning and explicit memory for specific instances. Psychological Science, 3: 172–179.

Macphail EM (1982) Brain and intelligence in vertebrates. Oxford: Clarendon Press.

Macphail EM (1985) Vertebrate intelligence: The null hypothesis. Philosphical Transactions of the Royal Society B, 308: 37–51.

Macphail EM (1987) The comparative psychology of intelligence. Behavioral and Brain Sciences, 10: 645–696.

Macphail EM (1993) The neuroscience of animal intelligence: From the seahare to the seahorse. New York: Columbia University Press.

Macphail EM (1996) Cognitive function in mammals—the evolutionary perspective. Cognitive Brain Research, 3: 279–290.

Macphail EM (1998) The evolution of consciousness. Oxford: Oxford University Press.

McDonough L, Mandler JM (1994) Very long-term recall in infants—infantile amnesia reconsidered. Memory, 2: 339–352.

McDonough L, Mandler JM, McKee RD, Squire LR (1995) The deferred imitation task as a nonverbal measure of declarative memory. Proceedings of the National Academy of Sciences of the USA, 92: 7580–7584.

Nadel L, Zola-Morgan S (1984) Infantile amnesia: A neurobiological perspective. In: Advances in the study of communication and affect, vol. 9. Infant memory: Its relation to normal and pathological memory in humans and other animals (Moscovitch M, ed), pp 145–172. New York: Plenum Press.

Neisser U (1994) Multiple systems—a new approach to cognitive theory. European Journal of Cognitive Psychology, 6: 225–241.

Owens ME (1984) Pain in infancy: Conceptual and methodological issues. Pain, 20: 213–230.

Owens ME, Todt EH (1984) Pain in infancy: Neonatal reaction to a heel lance. Pain, 20: 77–86.

Patterson MM, Cegavske CF, Thompson RF (1973) Effects of a classical conditioning paradigm on hindlimb flexor nerve response in immobilized spinal cats. Journal of Comparative and Physiological Psychology, 84: 88–97.

Pillemer DB, White SH (1989) Childhood events recalled by children and adults. In: Advances in child development and behaviour, vol. 21 (Reese HW, ed), pp 297–340. San Diego: Academic Press.

Premack D, Woodruff G (1978) Does the chimpanzee have a theory of mind? Behavioral and Brain Sciences, 1: 515–526.

Reber AS (1967) Implicit learning of artificial grammars. Journal of Verbal Learning and Verbal Behavior, 5: 855–863.

Reber AS (1993) Implicit learning and tacit knowledge: An essay on the cognitive unconscious. Oxford: Clarendon Press.

Rovee-Collier C (1997) Dissociations in infant memory: Rethinking the development of implicit and explicit memory. Psychological Review, 104: 467–498.

Rovee-Collier C, Shyi G (1992) A functional and cognitive analysis of infant long-term retention. In: Development of long-term retention (Howe ML, Brainerd CJ, Reyna VF, ed), pp 3–55. New York: Springer-Verlag.

Shanks DR, St. John MF (1994) Characteristics of dissociable human learning systems. Behavioral and Brain Sciences, 17: 367–447.

Tulving E, Markowitsch HJ (1998) Episodic and declarative memory: Role of the hippocampus. Hippocampus, 8: 198–204.

Walters ET, Carew TJ, Kandel ER (1981) Associative learning in *Aplysia*: Evidence for conditioned fear in an invertebrate. Science, 211: 504–506.

15 Declarative and Episodic-like Memory in Animals: Personal Musings of a Scrub Jay

Nicola S. Clayton, D. P. Griffiths, and Anthony Dickinson

Memory is a trick that evolution has invented to allow creatures to compress physical time. Owners of biological memory systems are capable of behaving more appropriately at a later time because of their experiences at an earlier time, a feat not possible for organisms without memory.
—Tulving, 1995a, p. 285

The acquisition of memories concerned with unique, personal past experiences and their subsequent recall has long been the subject of intensive investigation in humans. This type of memory is referred to as episodic memory (Tulving, 1972), to separate it from other forms of recall such as memories of facts about the world that have not been acquired through personal experience (Tulving, 1983). Another hallmark of episodic memory is that "it receives and stores information about temporally dated episodes or events, and temporal-spatial relations among these events" (Tulving, 1972, p. 385). Thus, episodic memory provides information not only about "what" event occurred, but also about "when" and "where" it happened. It is widely believed that the storage and subsequent recall of this "episodic" information is beyond the memory capabilities of nonhuman animals (Tulving, 1995b; Tulving and Markowitsch, 1998). However, recent work on memory for cache sites in food-storing jays provides a working model for testing episodic-like memory in animals (Clayton and Dickinson, 1999a) and suggests that many of the features of episodic memory may not be as exclusive to humans as previously thought.

In this chapter, we will begin by presenting a brief review outlining the critical features of episodic memory that distinguish it from other forms of memory, and why it is believed to be unique to humans. We will then present recent results that demonstrate that some species of birds can perform a food-caching and recovery memory task that depends on episodic-like memory, a type of memory recall that closely resembles episodic memory, in that it fulfills the purely behavioral criteria of requiring a trial-unique knowledge of what, where, and when the animal experienced a particular event in the past. Finally, we will discuss the similarities and differences between this system of recalling past experience and the contemporary definition of human episodic memory proposed by Tulving and Markowitsch (1998).

Definitions of Declarative, Semantic, and Episodic Memory

Memory in humans has been subdivided into several categories. The broadest distinction is between declarative and procedural memory. Procedural memory is characterized by its inaccessibility to conscious recall and is demonstrated by phenomena such as priming, motor learning of skills, and simple forms of classical conditioning (see Schacter et al., 1993; Squire et al., 1993 for a review). Tulving and Markowitsch (1998) offer a comprehensive description of declarative memory, the essence of which is that it supports the retrieval of information that can be characterized in propositional form (i.e., it can be described symbolically) and has truth value. This information can be used to guide inferences and generalizations, both to support reasoning and to control behavior: behavioral expression of the information retrieved, however, is optional rather than obligatory. In this chapter, we are concerned only with declarative memory.

Declarative memory is further subdivided into episodic and semantic components. There is some disagreement as to the nature of this division and the relationship between these two memory systems, both in terms of function and the neural structures involved. It is generally agreed, however, that episodic memory is concerned with the conscious recall of specific past experiences, whereas semantic memory is involved in the storage of factual knowledge about the world. The difference is often referred to in terms of remembering and knowing: episodic memory is concerned with remembering specific personal experiences, whereas semantic memory mediates what one knows about the world (Tulving, 1983). Remembering the rain falling outside the seminar room window at the last conference that you attended in England is an example of episodic memory, but knowing that it often rains in England is an example of semantic memory because it need not be acquired as a result of a personal experience of getting wet.

Human Episodic Memory

Tulving and Markowitsch's contemporary definition of episodic memory (1998) states that it is unique, possessing features that no other memory system does. An episodic memory system makes it possible to remember specific past experiences. Furthermore, episodic memory develops later than semantic memory in children (Pillemer and White, 1989; Perner and Ruffman, 1995), and is impaired sooner in old age (Herlitz and Forsell, 1996; Nilsson et al., 1997). It is known to be associated with selective and unique patterns of cortical activity (Fletcher et al., 1995; Nyberg et al., 1996a, 1996b, 1996c).

Tulving and Markowitsch (1998) also state that episodic memory is accompanied by a special kind of consciousness, which they term "autonoetic" consciousness. This is different from the "noetic" consciousness involved with the retrieval of declarative information. Such a distinction is based on the fact that human subjects can distinguish between recalling past personal experience and remembering an impersonal declarative fact. Because of this, the two types of consciousness can be defined operationally in terms of remembering and knowing: remembering a specific event requires autonoetic consciousness, whereas knowing a fact is noetic in nature. This feature, in combination with the others outlined above, lead Tulving and Marko-witsch (1998) to claim that episodic memory, as defined by these features, is not present in animals other than humans. This claim will be now be considered in greater detail in the light of recent advances in the study of episodic or "episodic-like" memory in animals.

Studying Declarative Memory in Animals

To date, most of the learning and memory experiments on animals have not dis-tinguished between episodic and semantic memory. Until recently, there was no evi-dence that animals could recall a specific past experience and respond appropriately, nor was there any reason to believe they would need such a memory system in the types of laboratory tasks on which they were tested. It is widely accepted, however, that animals are capable of declarative memory. For example, Tulving and Marko-witsch (1998, p. 202) state that animals "possess well-developed knowledge of the world (declarative memory systems), and are capable of acquiring vast amounts of flexibly expressible information." In terms of empirical evidence, there are a number of laboratory experiments describing declarative memory, particularly in primates (Gaffan, 1992; Zola-Morgan et al., 1995) and rodents (Dusek and Eichenbaum, 1997).

Perhaps the most compelling examples of this ability come from studies of the deployment of general knowledge in complex reasoning by great apes (e.g., Gillan et al., 1981). It is also clear, however, that even the humble rodent is capable of declarative-like memory. It was demonstrated that simple conditioned responses can be mediated by representations of their relationship to the reinforcer (Dickinson, 1980; see also Dickinson and Balleine, this volume). Even more persuasive evidence for declarative memory in the rat comes from Dusek and Eichenbaum's (1997) studies of transfer across conditional odor discriminations. Their rats were capable of inferring the appropriate responses to pairs of stimuli that have never been directly encountered together previously, based upon their knowledge of previous stimulus pairings.

Do Animals Have Episodic Memory?

Tulving and Markowitsch (1998) define episodic memory, at least in part, in terms of the conscious experience of recollection. This definition presents an insurmountable barrier to demonstrating this form of memory in animals because there are simply no agreed behavioral markers of conscious experience. Other attempts to define episodic memory without reference to consciousness do not resolve this problem. Morris and Frey (1997), for example, asserted that to show event memory (a synonym for episodic memory), an experiment needs to demonstrate the presence of recollective experience. More formally, "The task should distinguish between changes in behavior that occur because an animal remembers some prior event and changes that merely happen because some prior event has occurred" (p. 1495). This definition, however, again lacks an agreed behavioral measure of the experience of recollection.

This dilemma can be resolved to some degree by using the classic definition of episodic memory when referring to animals. In his original definition, Tulving (1972) identified episodic recall as the retrieval of information about "where" a unique event or episode took place, "what" occurred during the episode, and "when" the episode happened. The merit of this definition is that the simultaneous retrieval and integration of information about these three features of a single, unique experience may be demonstrated behaviorally in animals.

Although there are many laboratory procedures for investigating memory for discrete past episodes, these tasks require the animal to retrieve information about only a single feature of the episode (see Griffiths et al., 1999, for a review of possible examples of episodic memory in animals). For example, monkeys can be trained to choose between two complex objects on the basis of whether they are same as (delayed matching-to-sample, DMS) or different from (delayed non-matching-to-sample or oddity, DNMS) an object they were shown some time previously (e.g., Mishkin and Delacour, 1975). The monkey may have recalled episodically the events at the start of the trial. A simpler explanation, however, is that the monkey learned to choose—or avoid—the most familiar object (Griffiths et al., 1999).

A second possible example of episodic memory in animals came from Gaffan (1992). Monkeys learned to choose between two complex visual scenes on the basis of whether one of them contained a specific object at a particular location within the scene. This task appears to require retrieval of both spatial (where) and object (what) information. However, the discrimination was learned over many trials, and there is therefore no reason to believe that on any given trial the monkey's choice was controlled by the episodic recall of its choices and their outcomes on previous trials. The animals may have remembered the more general declarative information that a particular what-where configuration was associated with a reward.

In many studies that appear to demonstrate episodic-like recall in animals, the results observed can be more readily explained in terms of simple familiarity. There is a distinct difference between the feeling that a stimulus is familiar and an episodic recollection of where and when it has been seen before (Mandler, 1980; Aggleton and Brown, 1999). For example, a face can appear highly familiar without any recall of where and when one has previously met its owner. By only requiring the monkeys to recognize a stimulus, but not recollect where and when it was previously seen, these matching tasks are most readily solved by familiarity rather than episodic recall, and, indeed, the fact that monkeys learned more rapidly when novel objects are used supports this (Mishkin and Delacour, 1975).

The experiments outlined above suggest that most of the laboratory tasks used to date can be explained in terms other than episodic recall. A different approach to testing whether or not animals are capable of episodic memory is to consider cases in nature in which an animal might benefit from the capacity to remember unique episodes that occurred in the past (see Shettleworth, this volume, for a comprehensive review of adaptive specializations). These criteria are probably met by several behaviors. One potential example is the ability of brood parasitic species such as cowbirds and cuckoos to keep track of the current status of hosts' nests in which they lay their eggs, so that they can later return to the correct nest site at the appropriate time (e.g., Reboreda et al., 1996; Clayton et al., 1997). Another candidate for episodic recall by animals is the recovery of caches by food-storing birds and mammals (Vander Wall, 1990). Many species scatter hoard food throughout their winter territories when food is abundant only to retrieve them days, weeks, and even months later when food is scarce. A wealth of evidence from both the field and laboratory shows that memory plays a role in cache retrieval (reviewed by Shettleworth, 1995). In terms of purely behavioral criteria for episodic memory, the animal must be able to encode the information based on a single, personal experience that occurred in the past, and then accurately recall the information about what, where, and when a particular event occurred at a later date.

In birds, at least four features of food recovery suggest that episodic processes may play a role in the recovery of caches. First, information guiding recovery is based on a single past experience of when that bird stored food, suggesting that these birds remember information about a specific personal experience that occurred at one point in the past. Second, in terms of accuracy of memory, the retrieval pattern in at least some species reflects precise information about the spatial location of the cache (e.g., Balda and Kamil, 1992; Healy and Suhonen, 1996). Third, birds can recall not only the location of their caches but also their contents (Sherry, 1982, 1986; Clayton and Dickinson 1999b). Finally, many food-storing species cache insects and other perishable items in addition to seeds (Vander Wall, 1990); it therefore may be adaptive for them to encode and recall information about what has been cached when, as well as where. For example, European jays (*Garrulus glandarius*) cache perishable food at a lower frequency than nonperishable food and recover it more quickly (Clayton et al., 1996).

Figure 15.1
A black and white photograph of a jay, about to cache a wax worm in one of the caching trays.

Food-Caching Jays Can Remember What, Where, and When a Food Item Was Cached

Clayton and Dickinson (1998, 1999c) used the food-caching and recovery paradigm to examine whether or not scrub jays (*Aphelocoma coerulescens*) are capable of episodic-like memory by testing their ability to remember what, where, and when they have cached a particular foodstuff, based on a trial-unique experience of caching. The birds (divided into two groups, designated Degrade and Replenish) were allowed to recover perishable "wax worms" (wax moth larvae) and nonperishable peanuts that they had previously cached in visuospatially distinct sites in caching trays made out of ice cube trays and Lego bricks (figure 15.1).

In order to learn that worms degrade and become unpalatable over time, and therefore to avoid recovering these items when a relatively long time (124 hours) had elapsed between caching and recovery, jays in the Degrade group were given a series of pretraining trials in which they cached both food types in two different sand-filled storage trays, one food type per tray, before recovering them either four hours or 124 hours later (Clayton and Dickinson, 1999c). During the pretraining and training trials, birds could rely on the sight and smell of their caches as cues about where to search during cache recovery.

To test whether or not jays could remember what, where, and when the worms and peanuts had been cached in the absence of these cues, each individual received a pair of test trials in which all food items were removed prior to the recovery phase of each test trial and fresh sand was placed in the tray. The results of the test trials showed that birds in the Degrade group preferred to recover worms after the four-hour retention interval, but preferred to recover the peanuts and avoid the worms after the 124-hour retention interval (Clayton and Dickinson, subm.).

The preference for peanut caches on the 124-hour test trial could have been due to more rapid forgetting of worm vs. peanut caches. In order to test this possibility, birds in the Degrade group were compared to that of a second, Replenish group that never had the opportunity to learn that worms decay over time. Birds in the Replenish group received the same treatments during pretraining, training, and test as those in the Degrade group except that the old wax worms were removed immediately after the caching phase and replaced by fresh ones just before the start of the cache recovery phase. Birds in the Replenish group always preferred to recover worm caches, irrespective of the time since caching (four hours vs. 124 hours). Thus the preference to recover worms after four hours but to recover peanuts after 124 hours is shown only by the Degrade group, and therefore does not reflect a genetic predisposition to recover particular foods at particular times, but instead arose as a result of learning (Clayton and Dickinson, subm.).

Once they had been trained and tested on caching different food in different trays, the same birds were then given a pair of training trials in which they were required to cache peanuts in one side of a single tray during one caching phase and wax worms in the opposite side of the same tray during the other caching phase 120 hours later (Clayton and Dickinson, 1998). To ensure that the birds had access to only one side of the storage tray during each caching phase, the other side of the tray was covered with a Plexiglass strip that was secured with bulldog clips so that it could easily be swapped between caching phases. It was removed during the recovery phase so that birds could recover their caches from both sides of the caching tray four hours after the second caching phase. Thus at the time of recovery the birds had cached one food type four hours ago and the other food type 124 hours ago. On P/W trials birds cache peanuts first and then worms, whereas on W/P trials birds cache the two food types in the reverse order. Different, novel trays were used on each trial, and the trays were placed in different spatial locations within the cage to ensure that the cache sites were trial-unique.

The design is shown in figure 15.2a for birds in the Degrade group. If jays can remember what and where they stored the food items, they should search in the caching sites in which worms had recently been cached four hours earlier because

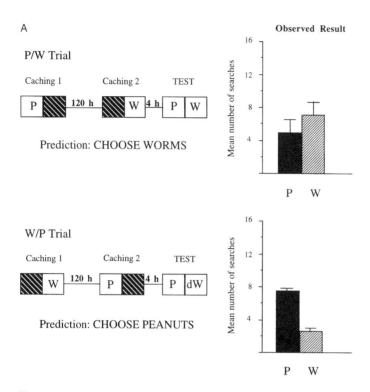

Figure 15.2
The experimental design, predictions, and observed results for birds in the Degrade (a) and Replenish (b) groups in Experiment 1. During the caching phases birds were prevented from storing food items in the shaded halves of the tray by a cover (unavailable cache sites), while being free to cache in the open, non-shaded halves (available cache sites). P, peanuts; W, fresh wax worms; dW, decayed wax worms; and ( ), food items pilfered on test. In P/W trials birds cached peanuts first, followed by worms 120 h later. The test phase followed 4 h after the end of the second caching phase. In W/P trials the order in which worms and peanuts were cached is reversed. The histograms show the mean number of searches to the peanut and worm sides of the storage trays (error bars: [√MSe/n] for these contrasts) during the recovery phase of P/W and W/P test trials.

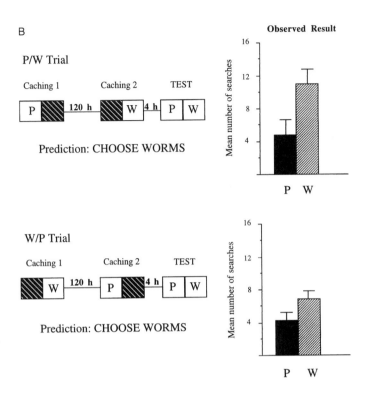

Figure 15.2 (continued)

they prefer fresh wax worms over peanuts. For episodic memory, the critical result is the performance of birds in W/P trials: If the birds can also recall the relative time at which they cached peanuts and worms, then during the recovery phase for trials when worms had been cached 124 hours earlier, they should search in the caching sites in which they had stored peanuts rather than worms because the worms would have decayed and become unpalatable by that time.

Figure 15.2a summarizes the results of the test trials: Eighty percent of birds in the Degrade group searched the worm side of the caching tray first on the P/W trial, whereas all birds inspected the peanut side first on the W/P trial. A similar pattern was seen for the total number of searches made during cache recovery. These results suggest that the birds remembered not only where the worms were stored but also information about the relative time between caching and recovery because they searched preferentially in the worm side of the tray when the worms had been cached four hours earlier, but preferred to search in the peanut side when the worms had been cached 124 hours prior to the recovery test.

The preference for peanut caches on the W/P test trial could also have been due to more rapid forgetting of worm vs. peanut caches. In order to test this possibility, birds in the Degrade group were compared again to those in the Replenish group that never had the opportunity to learn that worms decay over time. As shown in figure 15.2b, all birds in the Replenish group searched first in the worm side of the caching tray on both W/P and P/W trials.

Comparing the results of birds in the Degrade and Replenish groups on both types of test trial (i.e., with two trays or with different sides of the same tray) shows that (a) the peanut-side preference shown by the Degrade group was not simply due to differential forgetting of worm caches; and (b) that the preference to search for worms four hours after caching and for peanuts 124 hours after caching does not reflect a genetic predisposition because this strategy was only adopted by birds in the Degrade group, which had the opportunity to learn that worms decay over time.

In terms of evidence for episodic-like memory, the critical result is the reversal of cache recovery preference shown by the Degrade group during P/W versus W/P test trials. The switch in preference from the worm side on the P/W trial to the peanut side on the W/P trial shown by birds in the Degrade group requires the birds to recognize a particular cache site in terms of both its contents and the relative time that has elapsed between caching and recovery. This result can only be explained by recall of information about what items (peanuts or worms) were cached; where each type of item was stored (left or right side); and when (four hours or 124 hours) the worms were cached. Furthermore, the information was formed on the basis of a single, trial-unique personal experience. The results of Experiment 1 therefore suggest that the cache recovery pattern of scrub jays relies on episodic-like memory (Clayton and Dickinson, 1998). Moreover, this result cannot be explained by the simple rule "search in the side of the tray in which food was stored most recently, regardless of food type" because during training and testing with two different trays (Clayton and Dickinson, subm.) the birds were also capable of remembering what had been cached, where, and when. Because both food types were cached at the same time, at four hours and 124 hours ago, using a rule about recency would not allow the birds to solve this version of the task.

Food-Caching Jays Can also Remember Sites from which They Have Recovered Their Caches and Update Their Memories Accordingly

Having demonstrated that birds can remember what, where, and when a food item has been cached, in a second experiment we examined a further aspect of the recall

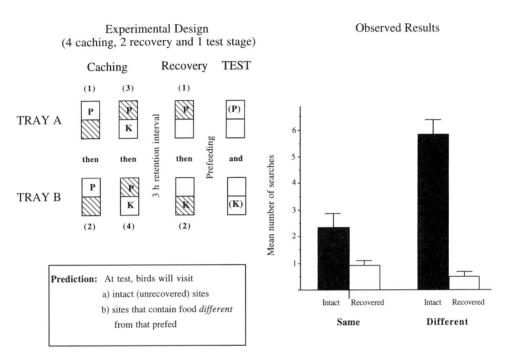

Figure 15.3
The experimental design, predictions, and observed results for Experiment 2. The shaded areas represent the covered halves of the trays (unavailable cache sites) and nonshaded areas the open halves of the trays (available cache sites). P, peanuts; K, dog food kibbles; and ( ), food items pilfered on test. The histogram shows the mean number of searches to the two caching trays as a function of whether the food items remaining in the tray after recovery were the same as or different from the type of food prefed before the test. The number of searches are shown separately for the intact (unrecovered) and recovered side of each caching tray. The error bars are $\sqrt{(MSe/N)}$ for the contrast between searches to the same and different trays for each side.

of specific past experiences during cache recovery, namely whether or not they can remember not only which sites have been depleted by cache recovery but also which type of food item has been recovered (Clayton and Dickinson, 1999a). Experiment 2 consisted of four caching phases and two recovery phases followed by a recovery test phase (figure 15.3). Birds cached three peanuts in the left-hand sides, and three dog-food kibbles in the right-hand sides, of two visuospatially distinct storing trays, and then recovered all the peanuts from one tray and all the kibbles from the other tray three hours later. This meant that at the end of these recovery phases, one tray contained only kibbles and the other tray contained only peanuts. During each of these caching or recovery phases the birds had access to only half a tray at a time, as

Plexiglas strips covered the other side of each tray. Finally, during the recovery test birds were presented simultaneously with both caching trays.

As in Experiment 1, the items remaining in the trays after the recovery phases were removed prior to this test. This ensured that no extraneous cues were present and therefore the birds had to rely on memory about what they had cached and what they had recovered from the left- and right-hand sides of each tray. If birds can recall not only the type of food cached in each of the sites, but also those recovered from each site, and can integrate these two sources of information, then during the test birds should direct more searches to the tray that should still contain their preferred food. Rather than relying on the intrinsic preference for one food over another as in Experiment 1, Clayton and Dickinson (1999a) manipulated the relative preference of the foods at recovery by prefeeding the birds with one of the two food types because prefeeding selectively reduces the value of that food in terms of both eating and caching (Clayton and Dickinson, 1999b). Birds that were prefed powdered kibbles should therefore search more in the tray that still contained peanuts whereas birds that had been prefed powdered peanuts should preferentially search in the sites where they had cached but not recovered the kibbles. The important feature of this design is that the pattern of test choices cannot easily be explained in terms of avoiding recently visited storing trays. Because cache sites in both trays are visited during the recovery phases, both trays should be equally affected by any tendency to avoid recently visited locations.

The trays can be categorized in terms of whether they contained food items that were the *same* as or *different* from the prefed food at the end of the two recovery phases. If birds in the experiment can also remember what they have cached where, then after prefeeding on one food type these birds should preferentially search in the different tray. Additionally, the two sides of the tray can be distinguished by whether those items had been *recovered* during the recovery phases or whether the caches remained *intact* (i.e., unrecovered). If birds can remember not only about the caching episodes but also about what happened during the two recovery phases, and integrate all of that information, then they should preferentially search in the intact side of the different tray. These predictions were upheld. Nine of the twelve birds searched first in the intact side of the different tray. Furthermore, birds made many more searches to the intact side of the different tray than to the intact side of the same tray. The number of searches in the recovered sides were low for both trays (figure 15.3). Furthermore, the birds were highly accurate in directing their searches to the specific sites within each tray where they had cached food items during the recovery test.

Three main conclusions can be drawn from Experiment 2. First, scrub jays encode information about the type of food they store in cache sites. Without this knowledge they could not have directed their searches selectively to the different tray, that is, the tray that should still have contained the non-prefed food. Second, the birds can update their memory of whether or not a caching location currently contains a food item following recovery in a way that cannot be explained in terms of the familiarity of the location because they cached and recovered from both trays. Finally, the birds must be capable of integrating information of the content of a cache at recovery with information about the specific location of the cache. Without the capacity for such integration, the birds could not have directed their searches selectively to the intact sides of the tray, let alone to the particular cache sites in which they had stored the food items.

Episodic-like Memory in Jays: An Analogue of Human Episodic Memory?

The results of Experiments 1 and 2 show that jays (a) remember what, where, and when a particular past event occurred; and (b) what behavior to direct at the trays at what time—when to store food and when to recover, despite the contextual cues (other than time) being the same. Experiment 2 further shows that jays can differentiate between memories of caching and recovering, and update their information about the current status of a cache based on whether or not they had recovered the cache that they had stored prior to the recovery test.

These results fulfill most of the criteria for episodic memory as defined by Tulving and Markowitsch (1998). The one major absence, in terms of their definition, is that there is no evidence that the birds are using autonoetic consciousness in their recall of past events: this is probably untestable in animals because this state has no obvious manifestation in nonlinguistic behavior. It is this feature that presently makes "episodic" memory a uniquely human phenomenon, and probably always will.

Tulving and Markowitsch (1998) argue that although it is impossible to prove the absence of episodic memory in animals because a universal negative cannot be disproved, it is equally difficult to demonstrate a difference between declarative (semantic) and episodic memory in nonhuman animals. It seems, therefore, that the above results, and indeed many demonstrations of episodic memory, can be considered in the declarative terms suggested by Eichenbaum (1997). Consider a situation like the food-storing experiment above: the birds remember a series of facts about an object (the food item), a place (where they stored it), a time (how long it was since they stored the item), and an action (caching versus cache recovery) that allow them to subsequently recall that information and execute the appropriate behavior. Each of these items could be considered individually as a semantic fact, because on their own they would not allow the recall of the specific episode of caching a food item. When all these facts are integrated, it results in the animal possessing enough information to isolate what was cached and what was recovered, where, and how long ago: functionally, the animal has enough information to recall the episode of caching a specific item. The question is whether any of the information that the animal used was essential on its own to allow the animal to isolate the specific episode of storing that item. If you consider an ability to judge time elapsed and to recall context as examples of declarative memory, then the answer seems to be no. There are many well-documented examples of animals judging time (e.g., Biebach et al., 1989) and remembering context (e.g., Kim and Fanselow, 1992) individually, so it seems that these factors can indeed be considered as declarative in nature.

This in turn raises the question of how much does an animal have to show that it has learned about a specific event to suggest that it can recall that particular episode, and not just a series of semantic facts? The issue then becomes one of asking how much information about an event an animal needs to remember for a memory to be classed as episodic as opposed to the summation of a series of semantic facts.

When considered in these terms, the results of the food-storing study can be used to support a declarative theory of episodic memory. The only reason that the results do not fit within Tulving's theory of episodic memory is that there is no evidence of the involvement of autonoetic consciousness. As the question of animal consciousness in episodic recall is seemingly an unanswerable one, it seems that Tulving's assertion that episodic memory is unique to humans cannot be refuted, and animal examples of episodic memory will continue to be considered as analogs of human episodic memory at best (cf. Gaffan, 1992; Tulving and Markowitsch, 1998).

It seems, therefore, that we have a choice: either take autonoetic consciousness to be an essential feature of episodic memory, in which case we can never definitively know whether animals possess episodic capabilities (and therefore cannot challenge Tulving's claim that they do not), or characterize episodic memory in terms of the information encoded. If we adopt the latter approach, it seems that the results of the scrub jay experiments do indeed demonstrate the phenomenon of episodic memory in animals.

References

Aggleton JP, Brown MW (1999) Episodic memory, amnesia and the hippocampal-anterior thalamic axis. Behavioral and Brain Sciences, in press.

Balda RP, Kamil AC (1992) Long-term spatial memory in Clark's nutcrackers, Nucifraga columbiana. Animal Behaviour, 44: 761–769.

Biebach H, Gordjin M, Krebs JR (1989) Time-and-place learning by garden warblers (Sylvia borin). Animal Behaviour, 37: 353–360.

Clayton NS, Dickinson AD (1998) What, where and when: Evidence for episodic-like memory during cache recovery by scrub jays. Nature, 395: 272–274.

Clayton NS, Dickinson AD (1999a) Memory for the content of caches by scrub jays. Journal of Experimental Psychology: Animal Behavior Processes, 25: 82–91.

Clayton NS, Dickinson AD (1999b) Motivational control of food storing in the scrub jay Aphelocoma coerulescens. Animal Behaviour, 57: 435–444.

Clayton NS, Dickinson AD (1999c) Scrub jays (Aphelocoma coerulescens) remember when as well as where and what food items they cached. Journal of Comparative Psychology, 113: 403–416.

Clayton NS, Mellor R, Jackson A (1996) Seasonal patterns of food storing in the European jay (Garrulus glandarius). Ibis, 138: 250–255.

Clayton NS, Reboreda JC, Kacelnik A (1997) Seasonal changes of hippocampal volume in parasitic cowbirds. Behavioural Processes, 41: 237–243.

Dickinson A (1980) Contemporary animal learning theory. Cambridge: Cambridge University Press.

Dusek JA, Eichenbaum H (1997) The hippocampus and memory for orderly stimulus relations. Proceedings of the National Academy of Science USA, 94: 7109–7114.

Eichenbaum H (1997) How does the brain organise memories? Science, 277: 330–332.

Fletcher PC, Dolan RJ, Frith CD (1995) The functional anatomy of memory. Experimentia (Basel), 51: 1197–1207.

Gaffan D (1992) Amnesia for complex naturalistic scenes and for objects following fornix transection in the rhesus monkey. European Journal of Neuroscience, 4: 381–388.

Gillan DJ, Premack D, Woodruff G (1981) Reasoning in the chimpanzee: I. Analogical reasoning. Journal of Experimental Psychology: Animal Behavior Processes, 7: 1–17.

Griffiths DP, Dickinson A, Clayton NS (1999) Declarative and episodic memory: What can animals remember about their past? Trends in Cognitive Sciences, 3: 74–80.

Healy SD, Suhonen J (1996) Memory for locations of stored food in willow tits and marsh tits. Behavior, 133: 71–80.

Herlitz A, Forsell Y (1996) Episodic memory deficit in elderly adults with suspected delusional disorder. Acta Psychiatry Scandinavia, 93: 355–361.

Kim JJ, Fanselow MS (1992) Modality-specific retrograde amnesia of fear. Science, 256: 675–677.

Mandler G (1980) Recognising: The judgement of previous experience. Psychological Review, 87: 252–271.

Mishkin M, Delacour J (1975) An analysis of short-term visual memory in the monkey. Journal of Experimental Psychology: Animal Behavior Processes, 1: 326–334.

Morris RGM, Frey U (1997) Hippocampal synaptic plasticity: Role in spatial learning or the automatic recording of attended experience? Philosphical Transactions of the Royal Society B, 352: 1489–1503.

Nilsson L-G, Backman L, Erngrund K, Nyberg L (1997) The Betula prospective cohort study: Memory, health and aging. Aging and Cognition, 1: 1–36.

Nyberg L, Cabeza R, Tulving E (1996a) PET studies of encoding and retrieval: The HERA model. Psychonomic Bulletin and Review, 3: 135–148.

Nyberg L, McIntosh AR, Cabeza R, Habib R, Houle S, Tulving E (1996b) General and specific brain regions involved in encoding and retrieval of events: What, where, and when. Proceedings of the National Academy of Sciences of the USA, 93: 11280–11285.

Nyberg L, McIntosh AR, Houle S, Nilsson L-G, Tulving E (1996c) Activation of medial temporal structures during episodic memory retrieval. Nature, 380: 715–717.

Perner J, Ruffman T (1995) Episodic memory and autonoetic consciousness: Developmental evidence and a theory of childhood amnesia. Journal of Experimental Child Psychology, 59: 516–548.

Pillemer DB, White SH (1989) Childhood events recalled by children and adults. In: Advances in child development and behaviour, vol. 21 (Reese HW, ed), pp 297–340. San Diego: Academic Press.

Reboreda JC, Clayton NS, Kacelnik A (1996) Species and sex differences in hippocampus size between parasitic and non-parasitic cowbirds. Neuroreport, 7: 505–508.

Schacter DL, Chiu CY, Ochsner KN (1993) Implicit memory: A selective review. Annual Review of Neuroscience, 16: 159–182.

Sherry DF (1982) Food storage, memory and marsh tits. Animal Behaviour, 30: 631–633.

Sherry DF (1986) Food storage by black-capped chickadees: Memory for the location of contents of caches. Animal Behaviour, 32: 451–464.

Shettleworth SJ (1995) Memory in food-storing birds: From the field to the Skinner box. In: Behavioural brain research in naturalistic and semi-naturalistic settings (Alleva E, Fasolo H-P, Nadel L, ed), pp 158–179. Dordrecht: Kluwer Academic Publishers.

Squire LR, Knowlton B, Musen G (1993) The structure and organization of memory. Annual Review of Psychology, 44: 453–496.

Tulving E (1972) Episodic and semantic memory. In: Organization of Memory (Tulving E, Donaldson W, ed), pp 381–403. New York: Academic Press.

Tulving E (1983) Elements of episodic memory. Oxford: Clarendon Press.

Tulving E (1995a) Introduction (chapter VI: Memory). In: The cognitive neurosciences (Gazzaniga MS, ed), pp 751–753. Cambridge, MA: MIT Press.

Tulving E (1995b) Organization of memory: Quo Vadis? In: The cognitive neurosciences (Gazzaniga MS, ed), pp 839–847. Cambridge, MA: MIT Press.

Tulving E, Markowitsch HJ (1998) Episodic and declarative memory: Role of the hippocampus. Hippocampus, 8: 198–204.

Vander Wall SB (1990) Food hoarding in animals. Chicago: University of Chicago Press.

Zola-Morgan S, Squire LR, Ramus SJ (1995) The role of the hippocampus in declarative memory: A reply to Nadel. Hippocampus, 5: 235–239.

16 Testing Insight in Ravens

Bernd Heinrich

My aim in this chapter is to describe a set of five interrelated experiments and observations that in their entirety appear to demonstrate insight in common ravens, *Corvus corax*. By insight I refer to mental visualization that can be used to determine alternate choices in solving a specific problem whose solution is not wholly pre-programmed. I mean not only the mental visualization of some feature of the world that is relevant to the animal, such as a nest site or food item, or such; I mean also that the animal is conscious, capable of building mental scenarios, so that alternative choices or motor patterns are expressed or suppressed depending on their probable outcome, either before or after such outcome has been experienced. Thus, insight would either reduce or eliminate potentially lengthy and costly trial-and-error learning in a predictably inconstant environment.

Consciousness is a prerequisite for both insight and intelligence (reflecting appropriateness or depth of insight). It is awareness derived from the ability to project images backwards (memory) or forward (insight) in a progression. There is an enormous literature on animal consciousness and intelligence. Opinions on the presence vs. absence of consciousness in animals and its role in behavior differ greatly (Griffin, 1992), as Griffin's recent (1998) review article citing over 120 references attests. Additionally, books on these topics are proliferating (Balda et al., 1998; Dukas, 1998; Shettleworth, 1998), making any attempt by me to recapitulate the arguments and the diversity of views and definitions redundant.

I shall specify only what I perceive to be the major problem involved in testing for insight. If insight is operationally defined as the expression of behavior that provides the solution to a problem, then there is the major difficulty of excluding prewired behavior that is not, but could be, insightful. In contrast to procedures for demonstrating learning, which require excluding only innate behavior (and where the possible role of insight is routinely ignored), demonstrating insight requires excluding both learning and innate programming regardless of whether insight is involved or not. This is a difficult task because everything that an animal does potentially includes insight and learned responses, neither of which can be simply excised. There is, furthermore, no apparent limit to the complexity of animal behavior that can be innate or learned, provided it relates to the *same* predictable conditions or problems the animal has faced over long enough evolutionary time (Shettleworth, this volume). The only way to minimize the effects of innate and learned components of behavior, to maximize the possibility of demonstrating insight, is to restrict experimental examination to problems that the animal has not encountered as a selective force in evolution or thorough individual experience.

Among the few attempts to demonstrate insight, Köhler (1927) examined chimpanzee's indirect access to food. However, the ape's possible use of insight is debated (see Gould and Gould, 1994, p. 76–81). Insight has also been invoked to explain the behavior of various small birds in reaching food on string (Bierens de Haan, 1933; Thorpe, 1943, 1963) although, as discussed elsewhere (Heinrich, 1996), the behavior that was observed could most economically be explained by mechanisms other than insight (Altevogt, 1953; Vince, 1958, 1961; Dücker and Rensch, 1977). However, the absence of demonstrating insight by these methods, at that task, in those species, says nothing about the presence/absence of insight in animal behavior more generally. Insight, even where it is possible to surmount the procedural difficulties of demonstrating it, presumably differs enormously from one species, individual, problem, and perhaps specific instance to the next. Each instance must be evaluated independently.

The raven's social as well as ecological environment is characterized by unpredictability. In this environment there is the potential of unleashing an escalation in the evolution of capacity to anticipate the behavior of conspecifics (Dunbar, this volume). Once such a general capacity has evolved, it could presumably be co-opted to apply to some other features of the environment.

This scenario is currently our best bet for the evolution of insight in hominids, and the same principles, if correct, should apply elsewhere. Ravens may be a non-mammalian example.

Several features of the raven's life history and ecology are comparable to those of the hominids'. As elaborated in detail elsewhere (Heinrich, 1999b), in many parts of their present and aboriginal range, ravens have a symbiotic relationship with wolves, *Canis lupus*, relying on them to kill and open carcasses for them. The birds' intimate relationship with this potentially dangerous carnivore is apparently a long-evolved one, because ravens have innate exploratory (Heinrich, 1995) and play behavior (Heinrich and Smolker, 1998) that allows them to access, and to then learn, the responses of wolves and other carnivores. Furthermore, if given a choice, ravens show a strong tendency to feed alongside, *with* wolves, rather than at open meat unattended by wolves (Heinrich, 1999a).

Given their distribution and diet (Ratcliffe, 1997), ravens are perhaps the world's most behaviorally flexible birds. Their circumpolar distribution extends from the arctic tundra and taiga, south into the highest mountains, deserts, forests, agricultural lands, and urban environments. Their diet includes not only meat from carcasses killed by wolves and a variety of other carnivores, but also fruits and grains. Ravens hunt various small mammals, birds, fish, reptiles, amphibians, and insects. Ravens' foraging behavior involves not only choosing what they will eat and how to catch it, but commonly also requires social interactions with each other and with other animals. All these factors are predictably correlated with increased brain size (Carlier and Lefebvre, 1996; Lefebvre et al., 1997).

In almost all of their geographic range, for at least part of the year, ravens are scavengers closely associated with mammalian hunters. However, their flexibility allows alternatives. In eastern Oregon, ravens do not feed directly from large carcasses but rather steal meat from intermediaries, primarily magpies, *Pica pica*, and golden eagles, *Aguila rapax*, who do feed directly from the carcasses. Ravens chase them and steal from them (Heinrich, 1999a). In contrast, in New England where there are neither wolves nor magpies, ravens feed at carcasses that they fear (apparently because they are unattended by wolves) in large crowds of individuals that are recruited (Marzluff et al., 1996) and then share the carcass. Numerous complex social interactions ensue in the competition among the recruited birds (Heinrich and Pepper, 1998) and with the resident birds that defend carcasses (Heinrich, 1988). Ravens form mutual alliances that depend on individual recognition (Heinrich, 1999a). I speculate that in ravens the sum of inter- and intra-specific social complexity, combined with geographical and seasonal complexity, is probably unprecedented for any bird.

Anecdotes about behavioral flexibility in ravens are legion. In one example, one of a pair of ravens feigned a wing injury, apparently to invite attack to lure a swan off its nest so the raven's mate could rush in to grab an egg (personal communication, Dieter Wallenschläger, Univ. Potsdam). Mates routinely share food (personal observation). In another unusual anecdote, a raven removed smaller pieces of fat off a large, untransportable piece of suet, by hacking a groove in dozens of consecutive blows with the bill in a precise line, in effect slicing a large transportable chunk off the immovable block of fat (Heinrich, 1999c). Ravens have also been seen throwing objects at nest intruders (see Heinrich, 1998b) and working in teams to distract predators and feigning death (summarized in Heinrich, 1999a). However, the possibility has never been excluded that some of these behaviors are either extremely complex, innate, and automatic responses, or the result of individuals' learning experience. The experiments I shall here describe were designed to address these two points. I tested performance of a behavior that the birds did not have opportunity to perform before, and that is not observed in the wild.

To examine the problem-solving abilities of ravens, I presented them with food suspended on a long string. Because ravens, like parrots and parids, have the innate capacity to grasp objects with their bills and feet, I expected that they would be *physically* capable of pulling up the meat. My question was: Do they have the mental capacity to reach down and grasp the string attached to the meat with their bill, pull the string up, place the pulled-up loop of string onto their perch, press a foot on the pulled-up loop to clasp it against the perch, then let go with their bill while continuing to bear down with one foot on the string and reaching down to pull up another loop of string to continue the exact sequence at least five times until the meat could be grasped by the bill directly? Each of the steps in this behavior could potentially be innate and/or learned and mindlessly executed, but the solution to reaching the meat consisted not of a single behavior but of assembling a series of specifically relevant behaviors into a novel repetitive sequence that solved a problem they had not previously encountered. In addition, the birds' choices were tested given string of the color with which they had previously been rewarded vs. other colors, as well as with crossed strings. Furthermore, I indirectly examined grip strength to test for stepping on vs. holding on. I also tested the tendency to fly off with attached vs. unattached meat. The results of some of these experiments, can, I think, only be explained in terms of insight on the part of the subjects.

Preliminary Studies

I provided meat on white string within three meters of a solidly frozen cow carcass in the snow (near Mount Blue State Park in Weld, Maine), where approximately 50 wild ravens were feeding. Due to the low temperature ($-30\,°C$), the meat from the cow could only be laboriously chipped off in tiny pieces, so birds competed for any loose meat. However, when the ravens saw the string they acted highly alarmed, and left. When they later returned to the carcass they were again highly agitated, flying off in fright. For the next several days they avoided the immediate area of the meat on string, although they continued to chip on the frozen cow nearby. As also indicated later with other not fully acclimated birds, fear of food on string was a big problem in these experiments; ravens have many strong "irrational" fears (summarized in Heinrich, 1999a).

Two groups of 14 and 13 wild-caught birds held temporarily in a 7,000 cubic meters aviary, were examined after they had been in captivity for over a year. As in the wild, all the birds showed fright when I examined their response to meat on string. One bird in the first group did approach a string after two hours, jumping up and down on the perch about one meter from it. On the next day when I again provided food to the hungry birds only on string, the same bird again approached the string and this time pulled the meat up in <1 minute on its first try, staying in place to consume it (Heinrich, 1996). Three more of the 14 birds in this group pulled up meat during six more days of one-hour trials per day. Most of the other birds did not even approach the meat on string. In the second group of 13 wild-caught birds, three individuals approached the meat after 1.5 hour, and succeeded in pulling it up after one or several minutes of contacting the string. No bird from either group ever approached a string without meat.

Recently fledged ravens are not yet neophobic (Heinrich, 1998a; Heinrich et al., 1996) and would not be expected to fear string. Predictably, four young, two months out of the nest and of fully adult appearance, all quickly approached strings with meat. They dripped saliva from their bills as they looked down onto the food while making loud, almost constant "begging" yells. All of the birds repeatedly pecked at the strings, yanked at them, and occasionally reached down and pulled them up. However, even after an hour, none had succeeded in accessing any meat. After this initial trial, these birds were not exposed to string or meat on a string for two years. At the end of that time, two of these birds were retested; they pulled up the meat "immediately" (several seconds). A third bird from same group pulled the meat up in five minutes. The fourth bird failed to pull up meat in the five-minute period that I observed it. Instead, it jumped up from the ground and tried to rip the meat off the string, grasping it in its bill.

Study 1

The first ravens I examined systematically for string-pulling behavior were five two-year-old hand-reared birds. The birds were kept in a group in aviaries ranging in size from 90 cubic meters to 7,000 cubic meters. The aviaries contained roosting sheds, natural ground cover, and horizontal poles and small trees for perches. (Several of the hand-reared ravens later nested and reared their young within the aviaries). The birds were identified either by uniquely colored and numbered plastic patagial wing tags and/or U.S. Fish and Wildlife aluminum leg rings. In December 1990, these birds were presented for the first time with food on a string. They had not seen string before. I provided two or more 70 centimeters long strings with meat, presented to the whole group at the same time.

Two of the five birds flew up at the meat from below, grasping it directly in their first one-hour experimental period; they continued the same fly-up behavior on subsequent trials over the next six days. They could not rip the meat I used off (hard, air-dried salami), and I presumed they got no meat or only tiny bits by this method. One bird approached the string from the perch, briefly pecked and yanked, then abandoned all further attempts to reach the meat until six hours later, when he again hesitatingly approached the string in the same way. This time he completed the whole string-pulling sequence, accessing the meat within seconds. Having pulled it up he could hold it in his feet and hack off pieces to eat. However, I chased him off before he had a chance to eat and he instantly (<10 seconds) flew back and repeated the sequence. For reasons explained later, the chase-off-pull-up sequence was repeated several (five) times, each following the other by seconds, until I allowed him to feed on the pulled-up meat. In four of the five ravens of this group that ultimately succeeded in accessing food on the string, the transition from either ignoring the food or merely yanking on the string to consistent success occurred in one trial (not timed but estimated to be less than a minute).

The string-pulling itself was only the first part of the experiment. The major experiments showing insight were done with those birds that pulled up meat. Insight implies the ability to see into relationships. Was the sequence of steps leading to successfully reaching meat understood by the ravens, or was it merely a stimulus-response phenomenon? I made testable predictions to distinguish insight from rote learning.

Overload

The birds could either yank on the string because they expected the attached meat to come up or they could learn by trial and error that pulling on the string caused meat to come up. I tested these alternatives by giving birds the choice of a string with 200 grams of meat (that they could pull up) vs. a string loaded with 2 kilograms of meat (which was too heavy to lift). I presumed that when confronted with this choice the birds would first test both strings and then learn by trial and error that the second load was too heavy to pull up. Thereafter I expected that they would only try to pull up the light load. Alternately, if they used insight they might determine that the heavy load was too heavy to lift just by visual examination, and then not even to try to lift the heavy meat from the beginning.

On the first trial, three string-pulling birds made eight pulling attempts, and all eight were on the string with the *small* piece of meat. None pulled even once on the string with the two kilograms of meat, although one bird jumped at the large meat directly. When the large piece of meat was let onto the ground, all three birds immediately approached the meat and fed from it in preference to the small, hanging piece of meat. These results are consistent with, but do not prove, insight.

The Initial String Tug and Insight

If the ravens merely associated meat with string they should attempt to get meat by yanks of the appropriate heft on any arbitrary string near bait. On the other hand, if they understood the functional significance of their actions, then they should only pull string with meat attached to it but not string that provides the same heft but that does not hold meat. Such is normally the case, except that these birds were trained not to look first before contacting string.

Until the birds had pulled up meat, two or more strings had always been provided simultaneously, and *all* of the available strings held meat. That is, the birds that pulled up meat were presumably trained to expect all strings to hold meat. As indicated previously, all the birds in this group were always tested together and there was therefore often competition among them to be first at the string. Subsequently, when these birds were provided with two strings simultaneously (within 15 centimeters of each other) where one was with and the other was without meat (but with an equal weight of rock), they again rushed in as before, but contacted the two strings randomly. However, they never pulled a "wrong" string up, always quickly switching to the correct string (the one with meat) after an initial tug or two on the wrong string. After each making 10–20 errors, the birds looked before pulling and confined their initial pulls to the correct string. They were now ready for the experiment.

Given that I had made it necessary for the birds to *look*, to make sure that they not only pulled up but also *contacted* the correct string first, I asked them what mental concept they used in their choice. By crossing strings (Heinrich, 1996), one with meat and the other without meat but with an equal weight of rock, the string attached to the perch above the meat was no longer the correct one to pull up. The birds had before only pulled on the string above the meat, but they may have performed the identical behavior on the basis of two different mental concepts: namely, pulling on the string above meat, or pulling on the string attached to meat. The crossed-string experiment could distinguish between the two alternatives.

Three birds never once tugged on the correct (meat bearing) string on their first trials in a total of their first 79 string-pulling tugs with crossed string (Heinrich, 1996). That is, they looked down, saw the meat, and contacted "string above meat," which is what they had *learned* through numerous previous trials. That mental concept took precedence over what they next experienced during numerous negative conditioning trials. In contrast, the fourth bird overwhelmingly (17 vs. 4) first contacted the correct string, the one attached over the rock, in a situation it had not previously encountered. Although this test, as such, did not prove insight, it proved individual mental involvement, namely what the birds thought was "correct."

Novel Stimuli

If the birds understood the functional aspects of their successful string-pulling, then they should attend preferentially to relevant stimuli, ignoring irrelevant ones that may always have been present in the training situation. I used the same kind of string (light brown twine) in all of the experiments described above. That is, the birds should have been conditioned to expect food on *that* kind of string. To find out if they attended to relevant stimuli, as opposed to conditioned stimuli, I continued to use the same twine as a control, but now put the meat onto new, dark green woven string. Instead of their performance (in their initial tug or contact with string) deteriorating, they now showed greatly improved performance: 32 of 33 initial trials were on the correct, green string. (Presumably it was easier for them to see the connection to the meat when the two strings were a different color than when they were the same color, as always before).

Fly-offs: Knowing Functional Connections

Before (or after) pulling up meat on a string the birds could have a mental picture of the string as making a physical connection between their perch and the food. Alternately, they could simply associate meat and string, without formulating any mental scenario of a functional connection between the two. To distinguish between the two possibilities, I capitalized on the birds' behavior of normally flying away when given a piece of meat, to eat it in isolation away from conspecifics who normally tried to get it. Given their fear of string, their tendency to fly off immediately with meat should be even greater after they had pulled up meat, than if that meat was not associated with string. However, if they knew that the meat they had pulled up continued to be physically tied to the branch, then they should be inhibited from trying to fly off with it; they should eat in place, or if shooed away they should drop the meat before departing. They would, of course, learn after a few trials that trying to fly off with tied-on meat is likely to be nonproductive (unless they tear off bits). The critical test, however, was what they would do on their first trials before having had a chance to gain experience.

I examined the fly-off response in these birds and in two American crows. Unlike the ravens, the crows never showed fear of the string. They immediately went to the string and pecked it, but subsequently ignored meat attached to string that was left dangling in their aviary for a month. I then placed the meat (still attached to string) onto the horizontal perch to which it was attached. The crows now almost instantly grabbed it, and tried to fly off with it. They responded identically in five and nine trials respectively, before learning to drop the meat before flying off (Heinrich, 1996). The one raven of the five that was with the crows and that had *not* pulled up meat once stole meat that another bird had pulled up. She then tried to fly off with it. It was jerked out of her bill after about 0.5 meter off her perch, and after that she did not come near food on string again. The above results with the two crows and the one raven are in accord with what would be expected in classical trial and error learning, reinforcing the idea that the following results could not be explained by trail and error learning.

The other four ravens that pulled up meat in hundreds of trials, without any exception, did something new. In the first half-dozen pull-ups that the birds did, I sought to prevent them from eating. (I wanted to see if they would continue to pull up the string when they could not be rewarded by eating the food, but only by the mental concepts of having successfully completed the task that should get them closer to eating.) As soon as they held food in the bill I feigned an aggressive move toward them. From the first pull-up, and all subsequent ones, they never tried to fly off with the meat. They always dropped the meat before flying off, then came back within several seconds to pull it up again, at which point I repeated the shoo-off. After several trials, the birds still dropped the meat, although it became increasingly more difficult for me to shoo them away. I sometimes had to resort to physical force to shove them off the branch. When I stopped shooing them away, they invariably ate the meat in place, where they had pulled it up.

Study 2

These birds, like the previous group, were housed in the same large aviaries built into the woods where they had access to the same natural objects normally found in woodland. In addition, like the others, they had daily social interactions with me. These birds were hand-reared and tested at the age of nine months (Heinrich, 1999b). With this group I sought to correct the three complications observed in the previous group. The first complication was the fear of strings. The second was dominance interactions. In the previous group, subordinate birds were prevented from approaching the string as dominants tried to steal the meat as soon as subordinates began trying to pull it up. Subordinates subsequently left the vicinity of meat on a string whenever a dominant approached. The third complication was possible observational learning.

Each individual of this group of six birds (from three different nests) was given access to meat on string, one at a time, separated from the other birds by an opaque partition. Prior to the tests, I attempted to habituate the birds to string; strings were pulled taut and tied at both ends between branches, or were left dangling along the wire screening of the aviary walls for four months. Thus, the birds had an opportunity to see string, but they had no reason and no opportunity to pull it up as required in the test. None had seen food attached to string prior to the test.

Pull-ups

When presented with food dangled on string, all but one of the six birds approached the string with food within several seconds or minutes when allowed into the experimental part of the aviary. The sixth bird remained shy of food on string despite my attempts at conditioning. It refused to perch where the food was suspended, even though this site had previously been a favored perch. This bird never attempted to pull up meat, and it only (in hundreds of trials) attempted to get the meat from the string by flying directly at it and grabbing and holding on, and dangling.

The five birds that attempted to reach the food from above, by perching where it was suspended, all succeeded within four to seven minutes after first contact with the string. All five birds tried a number of techniques to get the meat in the following approximate order: (1) pecking at the string where it was attached (none pecked control string without food attached) as if trying to sever the string; (2) grabbing the top of the string and violently twisting it from side to side as if trying to break it off; (3) reaching down to pull up a loop of string, then yanking it sideways. Within five minutes, each of the five birds had stepped on a pulled-up loop of string, and within two more minutes they all did repetitive pull-up-step-down sequences that allowed them to reach the meat in approximately 10–20 seconds. The string and branch were both smooth, and the weight of the meat caused the string to slip, so sometimes a dozen separate loop-pulls were required before the birds reached the meat.

Two patterns of pull-ups were seen. In one pattern, the direct pull-up, the bird stayed in place. It moved its feet up and down as it stepped on successive pulled-up loops of string. In this method the bird often placed its foot tentatively up and down several times before finally firmly planting it in the loop. In the second pattern, the side-step, the bird pulled the string taut laterally, then placed its foot on the furthest point of the pulled-up length of string that was stretched along the perch. Most birds alternated between these two methods even in the same pull-up of meat, while others used one or the other method almost exclusively.

Reverse Pull-up

I provided the same birds with a set-up where they had to pull *down* on string (that was looped up and then down behind a wire partition) to get meat to come up to their perch. The one bird that had not done pull-ups ignored the string and meat, but all five of the other birds showed almost no hesitation in approaching the string, pulling down, stepping on the pulled-down string, and so on, until reaching the meat. I presumed their behavior could be explained most economically by a transfer of learning, rather than insight. They may have had insight, but previous string pulling had been explicitly rewarded and it was now also a learned behavior.

Grip Strength

The birds could either merely passively step onto the pulled-up loop of string or they could deliberately hold the string down firmly to try to prevent slippage. I increased the weight of the meat from 20 to 180 grams to increase slippage, reasoning that birds who pulled up 20 grams food would now fail if they continued merely to step onto the string, as opposed to attending to the relevant variable of holding it tightly to the branch. All of the birds continued to get the meat as before, and two of the five continued to reach the meat by the pull-ups at the same speed as before, indicating that they knew why they were stepping on the string (Heinrich, 1999b).

Fly-offs

In this group I repeated the fly-off experiments, but more systematically, using a more specific protocol. As indicated, each of the birds was tested independently in visual isolation from the others. In the first trial, prior to any string-pulling experiments, I tied a piece of meat onto string, as was used in subsequent string-pulling experiments. I then laid the meat with the attached string onto the horizontal bar (the string-pulling perch). The string was *not* attached to the perch, and almost invariably each of the birds immediately grabbed the meat with attached string and flew off with it, trailing the string (Heinrich, 1999b). These results showed that string, as such, did not prevent fly-offs. However, as with the previous group, no bird *spontaneously* flew off with meat that it had itself pulled up. I again resorted to shooing them away from the perch after they had pulled up meat and before they had a chance to eat it. In these experiments some of the birds did occasionally fly off with meat in bill when I aggressively shooed them. Nevertheless, the rare fly-offs with meat showed no tendency to decrease, as would be expected from learning. I was using semifrozen squirrel or calf meat, which was not as solid as the old dried salami used previously, and I speculate that after numerous trials (when the birds were not allowed to eat) they may have tried to get some meat by ripping it off.

Discussion

In these studies I examined how ravens access food on string, comparing the roles of innate programming, learning, and insight as possible alternatives. Innate programming and learning stretch credulity as the sole explanations for the empirical data, as does random chance. Programming cannot account for dozens of discrete behavioral steps that solve a specific problem that (1) is not encountered in the wild, (2) appears within minutes of exposure to the problem, (3) often differs in its specific details from one individual to the next, and (4) is updated and altered in progress in accordance with an apparent goal. The simplest remaining alternative hypothesis is that the birds had anticipated at least some consequences of behavior before overtly executing them. This explanation is not, however, only a deduction from the string-pulling behavior as such. It was confirmed in additional tests relating to the same problem. I hasten to add, however, that I am not proposing that the birds necessarily contemplate meat on string, have an "aha" experience, and then proceed to execute a plan. My results did not address that possibility; I do not know if a raven's first step onto string was premeditated (although the approach of primarily knowledgeable birds to the feared situation suggests that it might be). The data indicate that the ravens' behavior changed markedly within several seconds of doing so: insight could have occurred just before or after achieving the partial solution of first stepping on a loop of pulled-up string.

My approach and my conclusions on insight, and the consciousness that is required of it, differ fundamentally from those presented by Macphail (this volume). He appeals to basic empirical data that I also find compelling, though irrelevant to the role of possible insight. In his review of learning, Macphail (1982) proposes that in fish, reptiles, birds, and primates (and presumably also insects, see Bitterman, this volume) there is no evidence of qualitative differences in learning. I would be highly surprised if there were! After all, learning is presumably as basic a mechanism in nervous systems as are action potentials in neurons. Associative processes are presumably relevant in learning in both vertebrates and invertebrates, but that does not warrant the extrapolation that there are no differences in consciousness and intelligence among these groups of organisms. Insight, where it occurs, though a physical property as is nervous conduction, is an emergent property that presumably arises in a continuum out of the complexity of billions of interconnected neurons acting in concert with one another.

Macphail defines consciousness as "the capacity of any organism to feel something—anything," particularly the capacity to feel pleasure or pain. It goes without saying that we don't know if a dog feels pain just because it yelps if we kick it, that one can program a robot to recoil from a hot stove, and that an earthworm's movements may have nothing to do with pain. How might we know? I propose we can learn a great deal about the design of animals from comparative biology, and from the powerful vision that an evolutionary perspective provides. From the evolutionary perspective, the capacity of organisms to feel "something—anything" is not a question, nor is it something in need of "discovery" or refutation. The relevant questions are, *what* do specific animals feel, and *how* and *why* do they feel?

We know that to associate pleasure or pain with specific stimuli allows us humans to seek that which aids survival and reproduction while avoiding that which does not. I assume these are primitive traits (relative to reasoned responses) that presuppose situations where choice is possible. Thus, from the evolutionary perspective, a clam that has for hundreds of millions of years lived at constant temperatures in an ocean where it never chooses the temperature where it may reside presumably has no capacity to feel pain in the boiling pot, because it does not and never did have any need for making vital choices relative to temperature. Similarly, a small insect with a hard exoskeleton faces no decisions that effect it being bruised; hence it is not likely to feel mechanical injury. A dog (wolf) might yelp when it feels the pain of a kick because it is a social animal who provides feedback to its kin or pack members. On the other hand, a bird might give no expression of pain when harmed, because such expression might indicate vulnerability and tip off predators to attack it. Yet there are adaptive reasons to suppose it *feels* pain nevertheless.

Adaptive scenarios involving choice presuppose memory, and possibly insight. For example, the pain of pressing on a sharp object, coupled with memory, would reduce our likelihood of repeating the behavior. But by coupling the memory with *insight*, the mere pressing on a pebble would preclude us from jumping on any pointed object in the first place. Evolutionary perspective that encompasses the larger picture will begin to help us sort out of the otherwise conflicting interrelatedness of feelings, consciousness, memory, learning, innateness, insight, and intelligence. Failing to distinguish species and their evolutionary history will inevitably lead us to seeing only the residual common denominators: learning, nervous conduction, and so on. In other words, it may filter out that which is, in our present discourse, the primary topic of interest.

My perspective as a Darwinian biologist and a physiologist also biases my thoughts as regards components of the still unknown neurological mechanism of insight, associated consciousness, and sensations and emotions. The results and conclusions on insight in ravens are in accord with the mechanisms proposed by Dickinson (this volume), even though his definition of consciousness is not mental representation of scenarios, but rather the medium that assigns value to intentioned representations of potential goals. That is, his definition includes representations of potential goals. It differs from mine in including also part of what I consider the *mechanism* for actuating specific choices. We both propose that insight evolved because it supports goal-directed behavior; a raven with memory and insight can be internally rewarded with the first step in a long, complex sequence of behavioral acts that will bring it food, and so it can assign "relative value" to different choices and then proceed with the best choice, without overtly trying all the others. These ideas are also congruent with Humphrey (this volume), who asks why we have sensations at all, and who argues that sensations give us "an invincible belief in the existence of

external objects." The pleasurable sensation that a hungry raven presumably identifies with a specific piece of meat on a string (that it hasn't yet eaten) is presumably
retrieved from memory and/or generated from past learning and programming. Precisely what that sensation is, is private, arbitrary, and irrelevant. However, the question is not *what* it is, but that it exists and that it is different from that associated
with, for example, an inedible piece of some other substance. In sum, reflexes can be
exerted without conscious perceptions, but sensory perceptions and insight are
required where *choice* is necessary.

From an economic evolutionary perspective it can be predicted that most behavior
would be reflexive, automatic, and unconscious, wherever possible. A reflex behavior, and learning at its simplest level, requires two neurons and an interconnecting
synapse. To achieve insight and the underlying consciousness probably requires
billions of neurons, each with possibly tens of thousands of synapses. In an insect,
when specific neural motor patterns are active, then muscles innervated by these
neurons are active as well (Heinrich and Kammer, 1973), and when the neurons
innervating (for example) the flight muscles are inactive, then the respective muscles,
too, are inactive. On the other hand, when we think (mentally visualize) about a leap
over an obstacle, then the areas of the brain involved with that consciousness or
memory become active and stay active for as long as we think about that behavior,
even while the neurons innervating the leg muscles themselves remain largely inactive. I speculate that the above facts imply that we have massive monitoring of neural patterns, in possibly reverberating circuits, that can proceed indefinitely while
output to the muscles (i.e., behavior) is simultaneously suppressed (except sometimes
being partially released when we are asleep, in dreams).

Monitoring is presumably a general physiological property of any integrated system, where one part must "know" (at least unconsciously) what the other is doing so
that the animal can act as a unit rather than have one part proceed independently of
another. The more novel the required movements, such as trying to do a previously
impractical back flip or those movements required to get meat by pulling up string,
the more consciousness we must invoke to generate and sort out alternative motor
patterns to be ultimately used.

All behavior is ultimately reducible to muscle motor patterns that are centrally
encoded and only optionally released. The mere encoding of precise motor patterns
requires relatively little neural mass; after all, a dragonfly superbly coordinates its
four wings, six legs, and various mouthparts, with a brain no larger than a pinhead.
The raven's relatively massive brain cannot be required merely for superb coordination of two legs and two wings. A major difference between the dragonfly and the
raven is that the latter can make numerous choices, after evaluating options inter-

nally, as my studies have shown. That is, the raven can move its body parts in other than stereotyped, reflexive ways.

Consciousness and insight on the appropriateness of various options would be particularly useful when there is need to anticipate another's moves. For example, a raven feeding at a carcass among wolves could potentially learn by trial and error how to get meat without getting bitten. But how many wolf bites can a raven afford and still survive? If the raven could project the wolf's movements, in effect forming a mental scenario of its bodily motions relative to its own, it could play out an interaction before it occurs. It could then avoid the first mistake, the one that could be fatal. Once consciousness has been selected to serve in unpredictable circumstances where reflexes no longer suffice, it could be co-opted for use in other circumstances, in the same way that an insects' wings, originally adapted for flight, are now secondarily used also for armor, camouflage, sexual signaling, and shading.

I suspect we'll never find the neural basis of insight or consciousness by focusing on individual neurons. The more we dissect or reduce a complex phenomenon to its component parts, the more we destroy or look past what we are trying to find. Consciousness is likely to reveal itself only in the infinite interconnections of neurons, which cannot and will never be unraveled one and all.

Some believe that consciousness, and the thinking derived from it, requires linguistic ability. According to that view, only humans are conscious beings. This narrow view ignores both our everyday experience and the powerful insight that evolution affords. It confuses cause with effect. Language only became possible after we achieved a critically high threshold of consciousness. However, who of us thinks through the intricacies of doing a swan dive, or throwing a spear into a retreating deer, in words? We can and do transpose thought into words, but that is because of an evolutionary history, not for ease of thinking; we are social animals. Using language allowed us to transfer useful mental images into our helper's and associate's minds. It was words, then, that enormously amplified our capacity to think, to store and to transfer knowledge, to build culture, and most of all, to form alliances. It was "the word" that, for us, became the ultimate shield and weapon.

Summary

This chapter reviewed observations and experiments with captive ravens of different ages to test insight. The birds were confronted with the problem of food dangled on a string. Juvenile birds did not reach the meat by pull-ups but (unsuccessfully) tried a variety of other methods. Intermediate-age (near one year) birds also tried a variety of methods, but were successful in pulling up meat within four to seven minutes.

Some of the older birds reached suspended meat by pulling it up within a minute after first contacting string. A major confounding factor that affected the behavior, particularly of older and wild birds, was fear of food on string. I conducted five different tests on those birds that pulled up meat, to test what they knew. All five tests showed that some, but not all, birds had acquired new responses without learning trials. I conclude that trial-and-error learning alone cannot explain the birds' behavior. The results are consistent with the hypothesis that ravens anticipate consequences of some novel motor patterns before committing them to action. I speculate on possible components of underlying neurological mechanisms and on the basis of how and why consciousness evolved. Consciousness only makes sense for unpredictable situations in an environment where proximate choice is possible or necessary.

References

Altevogt R (1953) Über das "Schöpfen" einiger Vogelarten. Behavior, 6: 147–152.

Balda RP, Pepperburg IM, Kamil AC, ed (1998). Animal cognition in nature. New York: Academic Press.

Bierens DeHaan JA (1933) Der Stieglitz als Schöpfer. Journal für Ornithologie, 1: 22.

Carlier P, Lefebvre L (1996) Differences in individual learning between group-foraging and territorial zenaida doves. Behavior, 133: 15–16.

Dücker G, Rensch B (1977) The solution of patterned string problems by birds. Behavior, 62: 164–173.

Dukas R, ed (1998). Cognitive ecology. Chicago: University of Chicago Press.

Gould JL, Gould CG (1994) The animal mind. New York: W.H. Freeman.

Griffin DR (1992) Animal minds. Chicago: The University of Chicago Press.

Griffin DR (1998) From cognition to consciousness. Animal Cognition, 1: 3–16.

Heinrich B (1988) Winter foraging at carcasses by three sympatric corvids, with emphasis on recruitment by the raven, Corvus corax. Behavioral Ecology and Sociobiology, 23: 141–156.

Heinrich B (1995) Neophilia and exploration in juvenile common ravens, Corvus corax. Animal Behaviour, 50: 695–704.

Heinrich B (1996) An experimental investigation of insight in common ravens, Corvus corax. Auk, 112: 994–1003.

Heinrich B (1998a) Why do ravens fear their food? The Condor, 90: 950–952.

Heinrich B (1998b) Raven tool use? The Condor, 90: 270–271.

Heinrich B (1999a) Mind of the Raven. New York: Harper-Collins.

Heinrich B. (1999b). Young raven's response to novel problems. (MS).

Heinrich B (1999c) Planning to facilitate caching: Possible suet cutting by a common raven. Wilson Bulletin, 111: 276–278.

Heinrich B, Kammer A (1973) Activation of the fibillar muscles in the bumblebee during warm-up, stabilization of thoracic temperature and flight. Journal of Experimental Biology, 58: 677–688.

Heinrich B, Marzluff J, Adams W (1996) Fear and food recognition in naive common ravens. Auk, 112: 499–503.

Heinrich B, Pepper J (1998) Influence of competitors on caching behaviour in common ravens, Corvus corax. Animal Behaviour, 56: 1083–1090.

Heinrich B, Smolker R (1998) Play in common ravens (Corvus corax). In: Animal play (Bekoff M, Byers JA, ed), pp 27–44. Cambridge: Cambridge University Press.

Köhler W (1927) The mentality of apes. New York: Harcourt Brace.

Koyama NF, Dunbar RIM (1996) Anticipation of conflict of chimpanzees. Primates, 37: 79–86.

Lefebvre L, Whittle P, Lascaris E, Finkelstein A (1997) Feeding innovations and forebrain size in birds. Animal Behaviour, 53: 549–560.

Macphail EM (1982) Brain and intelligence in vertebrates. Oxford: Clarendon Press.

Marzluff JM, Heinrich B, Marzluff CS (1996) Roosts are mobile information centers. Animal Behaviour, 51: 89–103.

Ratcliffe D (1997) The raven. San Diego: Academic Press.

Shettleworth SJ (1998) Cognition, evolution, and behavior. New York: Oxford University Press.

Thorpe WH (1943) A type of insight learning in birds. British Birds, 37: 29–31.

Thorpe WH (1963) Learning and instinct in animals. London: Methuen & Co.

Vince MA (1958) String-pulling in birds. II. Differences related to age in green finches, chaffinches, and canaries. Animal Behaviour, 6: 53–59.

Vince MA (1961) "String-pulling" in birds. III. The successful responses in green finches and canaries. Behavior, 17: 103–129.

Addendum

The *critical* reverse pull-up tests (with the string looped up, then dangling down) were not performed until the winter of 1999–2000, just prior to reading the proofs of this manuscript. A cohort of four hand-reared ravens then reached the age of 9–10 months, like the similarly aged and similarly treated previous group that had been assayed for this test after already having performed the direct pull-up. Thus, in this group, the possible effect of transfer learning was eliminated.

I speculated that these latter birds would probably not pull up meat because the unintuitive problem of pulling *down* to get meat to come *up* might not be understood by them. That is, I presumed their logic is limited, and the test might distinguish between two possibilities: the birds could contact any string *near* food without having expectation of how to access the food, vs. pulling on string because they see a logical connection between the string and the food, thus allowing them to use the string as a tool.

As I had predicted, none of the four birds paid any overt attention to the looped string near food, even though they all approached closely to it and looked at the food repeatedly. None made any attempt to peck at, pull or yank on the string connected to the food. Nevertheless, none hesitated to take food placed onto the perch next to the string. These results then are another independent confirmation of the hypothesis that the birds are aware of the problem as previously described. That is, it is the logical connections that motivate the birds, not string as such.

V CULTURE

Each of the three chapters in this section uses the selection theoretic framework (Heyes, this volume) in its analysis of the evolution of cognition. Whereas Wilson et al. focus on humans, Lefebvre and Richerson and Boyd consider a range of taxa and combine selection theoretic analysis with phylogenetic, comparative, and more broadly ecological approaches. All three contributions emphasize that behavior and cognition are shaped by cultural evolution in addition to natural selection operating at the genetic level. In other words, they stress that an important determinant of the what/when rules of cognition (if not its how rules) are processes of variation and selective retention acting, not on genetic variants, but on behavioral and cognitive units.

The questions at issue in this section, and in Tomasello's discussion of culture in this volume, concern the nature of the cognitive capacities necessary to sustain cultural evolution, and the role of phylogenetic evolution in generating these capacities. On the one hand, Lefebvre assumes that a range of social learning processes are sufficient to allow information to pass between group members in a fashion analogous to genetic transmission, and presents compelling evidence that, at least among avian taxa, neither the phylogenetic origins nor the how rules of these social learning processes are distinct from those of individual learning. At the other extreme, Tomasello proposes that there is only one kind of social learning that will support cultural evolution, intentional imitation, and that this is a phylogenetically evolved cognitive capacity, an adaptation for cultural exchange, with distinctive how rules, and present only in humans. Thus, Tomasello believes that transmission fidelity sufficient for cultural evolution is achieved only when an observer copies the body movements of a model, guided by inferences about the model's intentions. In contrast, Lefebvre allows that information may be transmitted with sufficient fidelity for cultural evolution when, for example, a model's behavior attracts an observer's attention to an environmental object, but the observer learns for itself how to manipulate the object.

Richerson and Boyd's position is closer to Tomasello's than Lefebvre's, but their analysis has features in common with both. Ultimately they agree with Tomasello that, among nonlinguistic social learning processes, imitation based on theory of mind is likely to provide the highest fidelity in cultural transmission, and imply that this cognitive capacity has distinctive how rules and is phylogenetically evolved. Also, their "strategic modeling" suggests, in contrast with Lefebvre's data, that individual and social learning are phylogenetically distinct, with the latter having been favored by selection pressure arising from climatic change. However, consistent with Lefebvre's assumption that a range of social learning processes can support cultural evolution, Richerson and Boyd argue that social learning generally has been favored by natural selection because of its role in cultural transmission, and caution against the tendency among evolutionary psychologists to assume that adaptations are phylogenetically, rather than culturally, generated.

It is tempting to try to resolve this debate by supposing that Lefebvre's findings apply only to nonimitative social learning in birds, and that while this kind of learning may not be distinctive, phylogenetically or in terms of its how rules, neither does it support cultural evolution of the sort found in humans. Lefebvre himself acknowledges that his analysis may not apply to imitation, and such a view would leave the way clear to accept Tomasello's and Richerson and Boyd's suggestion that *real*, cumulative culture depends on being able to infer mental states and to copy body movements.

In spite of its appeal, this compromise is problematic. Some of the best recent evidence of motor imitation (copying body movements, not vocalizations) in animals comes from avian taxa (e.g., Akins and Zentall, 1996; Lefebvre et al., 1997; Campbell, Heyes, and Goldsmith, 1999), suggesting, according to the compromise, either that birds can infer the intentions of others and exhibit humanlike culture, or, as argued by Heyes (this volume), that imitation need not involve the attribution of intention. If the latter is true, a question arises: Why might we expect intentional imitation, body movement copying based on inferences about the model's goal or purpose, to support more faithful transmission of information than nonintentional imitation? In both cases, information is transmitted about how to do something (e.g., how to open a nut or to fashion a clay pot), and it is not clear that acquisition of additional information about the model's purpose in performing act would increase the fidelity with which the information about technique was received by the current observer, or passed on from that individual to the next observer in the cultural chain. Indeed, if/when imitation depends on the attribution of intentions to the model, one might expect transmission fidelity to be eroded to the extent that the model's motives differ from those of the observer.

The chapter by Wilson et al. contains, in addition to specific insights concerning human cultural evolution, a perspective that may help resolve the broader debate about social learning and imitation. Their principal theme is the role of gossip in group-level cultural evolution. They argue that gossip is a means of social control, preventing members of human social groups from deviating from approved patterns of thought and behavior, and thereby allowing such groups to act as units in cultural evolution. This proposal, which is accompanied by original data exemplifying methods that could be used to investigate the hypothesis, complements Richerson and Boyd's focus on individual-level cultural evolution, and together they indicate the potential power of these evolutionary processes in shaping cognition.

The significance of Wilson et al.'s analysis with respect to the imitation debate lies in its concern with psychological mechanisms that promote retention, rather than initial acquisition, of cultural attributes. In contrast with those who study imitation, Wilson et al. look for the cognitive source of the evolutionary properties of culture, not primarily in the processes through which an individual originally "catches" information from a conspecific, but in processes that prevent individuals from subsequently and self-interestedly changing or discarding this information. If one accepts that such retention processes are important in ensuring that human cultural transmission is faithful enough to support cultural evolution, some of the pressure is released from the imitation debate. According to this view, transmission fidelity does not depend exclusively on imitation or any other process of information acquisition. Consequently, it would not be surprising if imitation occurred in taxa, such as birds, where cumulative culture is limited or absent, and if intentional imitation were associated with the same or lower transmission fidelity than nonintentional imitation.

References

Akins CK, Zentall TR (1996) Imitative learning in male Japanese quail using the two-action method. Journal of Comparative Psychology, 110: 316–320.

Campbell FM, Heyes CM, Goldsmith A (1999) Stimulus learning and response learning by observation in the European starling, in a two-object/two-action test. Animal Behaviour, 58: 151–158.

Lefebvre L, Templeton J, Brown K, Koelle M (1997) Carib grackles imitate conspecific and zenaida dove tutors. Behaviour, 134: 1003–1017.

17 Feeding Innovations and Their Cultural Transmission in Bird Populations

Louis Lefebvre

Behavioral novelty can originate and spread in animal populations in two ways: mutant alleles on loci affecting behavior can increase in frequency over successive generations if the genetic mutation increases the inclusive fitness of its bearers; alternatively, an innovation, whether of genetic origin or not, can spread to and beyond the descendant network of its originator through cultural transmission. The origin and spread of genetic change is intensively studied by molecular and population biologists, but our understanding of the origin and spread of cultural innovations in animals is much more limited.

The study of culture (and of its replication mechanism at the individual level, social learning) is by no means confined to the spread of innovations; some traditional, noninnovative behaviors are thought to be socially transmitted (e.g., song, migration routes, predation skills), but most examples of cultural transmission in the field feature novel behaviors, often in the feeding repertoire. Laboratory studies of social learning also focus primarily on innovations, because controls and null hypotheses are easier to set up for new behaviors that are likely to be absent in the absence of a tutor to learn them from.

Cultural transmission (defined in the broad biological sense; Tomasello, this volume), and in particular its most sophisticated learning mechanism, motor imitation, is thought to have appeared relatively recently in evolutionary history and is also presumed to require a complex neural substrate. Research has therefore focused on higher vertebrates, mostly birds and mammals. Within these two classes, taxonomic groups clearly vary in social learning probability: herbivorous mammals such as horses (Baer et al., 1983; Baker and Crawford, 1986; Nicol, pers. comm.) or cows (Veissier, 1993) appear not to show even the simplest stimulus forms of social learning, whereas apes use complex motor imitation to a much greater extent than the closely related monkeys (Visalberghi and Fragaszy, 1990; see however Bugnyar and Huber, 1997).

In some cases, this taxonomic variation may simply reflect phylogenetic inertia and exaptation: for instance, the innovative and imitative skills of hominoids may have as much to do with their common descent from a large-brained ancestor as it has to their current specialization on embedded foods (Russon et al., 1998; see, however, Tomasello, this volume, for a view that distinguishes human and chimpanzee culture). In other cases, detailed comparative analysis may suggest ecological, structural, and life history correlates leading to predictions on the selective context in which innovation and cultural transmission contribute most to reproductive success.

The correlates in this evolutionary view can be summarized in schematic form (figure 17.1). First, variation in the spatial and temporal distribution of resources should be associated with variation in the animal's exploitation strategy. For example, high altitude and harsh winter conditions are thought to favor food caching (Balda et al., 1996); spatial and temporal clumping of high-density, unpredictable food favors group foraging over territorial defence (Brown, 1964); a high variance in the abundance of different food types favors opportunistic generalism over conservative specialization (Gray, 1981).

In turn, variation in exploitation strategy (and/or life history traits) should be associated with variation in cognition and learning (Rozin and Schull, 1988; Shettleworth, 1993): storing will require more spatial memory to retrieve the hidden food (Sherry and Schacter, 1987); group foraging may favor learning from others in the group (Klopfer, 1959); opportunistic generalism should be associated with exploration and sampling and favor discrimination learning skills to monitor the positive and negative consequences of encounters with new foods (Rozin and Kalat, 1971); site fidelity favors imitation over individual elaboration of song (Kroodsma and Verner, 1978); precocial mobility (Lorenz, 1935) and optimal outbreeding (Bateson, 1980) favor parental imprinting in Galliformes and Anseriformes.

An exploitation strategy like opportunistic generalism may have additional intervening effects on learning and cognition: it may increase and diversify the tendency for animals to explore their environment (Gray, 1981), interact with new stimuli (neophobia; Greenberg, 1983, 1984, 1989, 1990), taste new foods (Daly et al., 1982), or feed in the vicinity of potentially dangerous species that are normally avoided (e.g., pigeons near humans, Lefebvre, 1996; ravens near wolves, Heinrich, this volume). In some cases, these intervening variables can affect the results of comparative learning tests, leading to difficulties in the interpretation of apparent interspecific differences in cognition and learning (Macphail, 1982, 1985).

Third, a larger and/or more complex neural substrate should be associated with each of these skills (Sherry and Schacter, 1987): a larger hippocampus to store more spatial memory (Sherry et al., 1989; Krebs et al., 1989); a larger neocortex to process more varied and rapidly changing information about food types (Clutton-Brock and Harvey, 1980) or group members (Dunbar, 1992, this volume); a larger high vocal center (HVC) in oscine species with larger repertoires (DeVoogd et al., 1993) and in males of species with stronger sexual dimorphism in song (Brenowitz and Kroodsma, 1996).

Fourth, development of these neural structures should normally be associated with a slower pace in life history traits such as time of gestation (Sacher and Staffeldt, 1974), fledging (Portmann, 1946; Bennett and Harvey, 1985), and weaning, as well

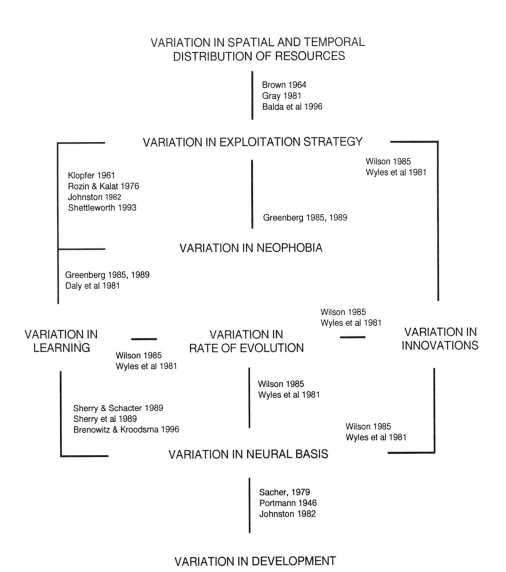

Figure 17.1
Ecological, structural, and life history variables correlated with variation in innovations, neophobia, and learning. Authors mentioned near each link are those most relevant to this part of the framework.

as age of first reproduction. This reproductive delay is a significant cost to behavioral flexibility and large neural structures (Johnston, 1982), as, compared to fast developers, the number of lifetime descendants will be lower.

Finally, the rate of fixation of structural mutations may accelerate when allelic variants come into rapid contact with a wider array of selective contexts (Wyles et al., 1981; Wilson, 1985). According to Wilson, this may occur when larger, more complex neural structures lead to a higher rate of behavioral novelty (one operational definition of cognition) and a faster rate of transmission of these innovations to large numbers of individuals through social learning.

This broad evolutionary framework seems to account for at least three specialized forms of learning: spatial memory (linked to food storing and home range size and based in the hippocampus, Clayton et al., this volume), parental imprinting (linked to precocial mobility in Galliformes and Anseriformes and based in the left intermediate region of the medial hyperstriatum ventrale (IMHV), Horn, 1990; Bateson, this volume), and song imitation (linked to vocal complexity in oscines and based in the HVC, Nottebohm et al., 1990). In all three cases, a localized neural structure is associated with the learning specialization; in two cases, spatial memory and song imitation, similar interspecific variation has been demonstrated both in the neural substrate and the learning ability.

Attempts to apply this evolutionary framework to the cultural transmission of feeding innovations in birds have produced three clear results: (1) feeding innovations show coherent variation among avian taxa in different parts of the world, a variation associated with forebrain size; (2) social learning of new feeding behaviors varies with opportunism and social organization, but this variation appears to be accompanied by a parallel variation in individual learning and neophobia, suggesting that social learning (at least in its nonimitative, nonacoustic forms) may not be as specialized as spatial learning, song imitation, or imprinting; (3) there is no one-to-one relationship between social learning potential, as assessed experimentally in isolated animals, and cultural transmission of feeding innovations in more natural populations. This chapter reviews a set of studies on these three questions in birds.

Variation in Feeding Innovations

The most obvious exploitation strategy thought to be linked to innovation and learning is opportunistic generalism. This strategy is easy to define in relative terms: most biologists would agree that gulls are more opportunistic and generalized than are, for example, the closely related sandpipers. Quantifying the strategy for the purpose of broad comparative studies is much more difficult, however. A diversity index of diet is possible in some cases, but unlikely to be available for large numbers of taxa. This is where the observational skills of professional and amateur ornithologists are useful. If the sighting and reporting of rare species has long been a feature of bird clubs and journals, so has the description of new or unusual feeding behaviors. In countries of Anglo-Saxon tradition in particular, the short note sections of ornithology journals contain large numbers of such reports by professionals or experienced amateurs. We collated over 1000 of these notes by exhaustively scanning ornithology journals covering northwestern Europe, North America, India, Australia, and New Zealand (Lefebvre et al., 1997b, 1998). A consistent pattern emerges from the comparison of these zones: feeding innovations tend to be concentrated in a similar, restricted set of avian taxa, leading to high interzone correlations in the number of innovations per taxon. Orders or parvorders with high innovation frequencies include Ciconiida (e.g., herons), Charadriida (e.g., gulls), Accipitrida (e.g., hawks), Falconida (falcons), Psittaciformes (parrots), Piciformes (e.g., woodpeckers), Passerida (songbirds), and Corvida (crows). Innovations are rare in the orders Anseriformes (ducks and geese), Galliformes (pheasants and partridges), Apodiformes (swifts), and Columbiformes (pigeons and doves).

The taxonomic trends appear clear and robust, but there may be several problems with data of this type. First, they are anecdotal, a data-gathering technique that carries some risk of over-interpretation (Byrne and Whiten, 1988). To alleviate this, we simply tabulated totals per taxon from the exhaustive reviews and avoided all speculations on mechanisms and cognitive complexity. The second problem is that our inclusion procedure may sometimes depend on subjective judgements: a case where the author does not textually state that a behavior is new or unusual may or may not be added to our corpus by a given reader, depending on his or her experience. We dealt with this problem by using readers blind to the general trend and to the hypothesis linking opportunism and forebrain size. We also calculated inter-reader reliability, using two people to review the same journal, blind to each other's decisions; even if the readers differ on a certain number of cases, the distribution of innovations per taxon is nevertheless very similar (Lefebvre et al., 1998).

In collecting our anecdotes, we often had to rely on the judgements of amateur ornithologists. Do they report the same trends as do academic researchers with university affiliations? We dealt with this problem by splitting a 50-year data set from the Australian journal *Emu* into two historical periods, 1941–1968 and 1969–1996. These periods differ in their editorial policy and their reliance on amateur vs. institutionally based ornithologists: until 1969, the short notes section of *Emu* was called "Stray Feathers" and was often written by amateur contributors giving private addresses; as of 1969, the reports are more conservatively called "Short Notes" and "Short Communications," and contributors provide institutional addresses. If subjective preferences guide the choice of birds to watch, these should conceivably be stronger in the more amateur "Stray Feathers" period. This is not so: the distribution of innovations per order is highly correlated in the two historical periods, suggesting that taxa preferred by amateur bird-watchers do not bias the data (Lefebvre et al., 1998).

If, as we think, variation in innovation rate really does reflect a fundamental property of avian taxa, does the variation fit into the evolutionary framework outlined in figure 17.1? The most obvious link to test is the one between opportunism and neural substrate. Multiple regressions reveal a positive link between forebrain size and innovation frequency in our four regional data sets, whether or not we factor in species number per taxon, an obvious confound that will inflate the number of observed cases in taxa with large numbers of species (e.g., Passerida). This association between forebrain size and innovation frequency could be the result of both independent evolution and common descent (Felsenstein, 1985). A large forebrain may very well be associated with a high innovation frequency in Australian parrots, North American woodpeckers, and European Corvida as a result of independent evolutionary events, as these groups are phyletically distant; however, a similar association in Falconida and Accipitrida, on the one hand, and in Corvida and Passerida, on the other, could be caused by descent from a common ancestor in each of these pairs of related parvorders (Sibley and Ahlquist, 1990). In Australasia, independent contrasts (Purvis and Rambaut, 1995) that factor in genetic similarity between parvorders suggest that common ancestry is partially responsible for the association between innovation rate and forebrain size (Lefebvre et al., 1998). This is not so for other areas of the world, however, and the forebrain/innovation link is independent of phylogeny when all geographical zones are pooled using weighted averages. The trend is also independent of brain size differences between precocial and altricial birds (Lefebvre et al., 1998), a confounding variable that accounts for some of the links between ecology and neuroanatomy (Bennett and Harvey, 1985).

Variation in Social Learning

Opportunism as an Ecological Predictor

Opportunism, in addition to its effect on innovations, is also associated with taxonomic variation in social learning. Sasvari (1979, 1985a) has compared three Parus and two Turdus species on the speed with which they learn by observing a conspecific find food using a novel technique. The species vary in an important correlate of opportunism, the tendency to colonize urban habitats. Results of the social learning test are consistent with variation in urbanization: blackbirds learn more quickly from a conspecific than does the less opportunistic song thrush, while marsh tits learn more slowly than do blue tits, who in turn learn more slowly than do great tits. Sasvari (1985b) has also compared the same species on their ability to learn on their own, without a conspecific tutor. Results of this study parallel those on social learning: song thrushes again learn more slowly than blackbirds, while great tits and blue tits learn faster than marsh tits. Klopfer (1961) has similarly compared the opportunistic great tit with the more conservative greenfinch: as predicted, great tits are better at avoidance learning in social conditions (learning in pairs), but they are also slightly better at learning nonsocially (Lefebvre and Giraldeau, 1996).

The link outlined earlier between opportunism and forebrain size is relevant to interspecific trends in social and individual learning. Among the species studied by Sasvari (1979, 1985a, b), blackbirds have a larger telencephalon (regressed against body weight) than do song thrushes; great tits and blue tits have a larger telencephalon than do marsh tits. The telencephalon of the great tit is also larger than that of the greenfinch (telencephalon and body weight data for great tits, blue tits, blackbirds, and songthrushes taken from Portmann, 1947; telecephalon volume for marsh tits and greenfinches taken from DeVoogd et al., 1993 and transformed to weight based on brain weight/volume relationship in Boire, 1989; body weight for greenfinch and marsh tit taken from Dunning, 1993).

Social Foraging as an Ecological Predictor

Social foraging has been examined as a second, obvious correlate of social learning. Again, all studies to date have come up with the same conclusion: social learning covaries with individual learning, and, in cases where this variable has been examined, neophobia. A series of comparative experiments in our laboratory shows a common trend for all these variables in group-feeding and territorial columbids: group-foraging feral pigeons learn very readily from a conspecific, while territorial zenaida doves do not (Lefebvre et al., 1996); group-foraging zenaida doves also learn much better from conspecifics than do territorial ones (Dolman et al., 1996). Group-foraging pigeons learn individually much faster than do territorial doves (Lefebvre et al., 1996), while group-foraging doves learn slightly faster than do territorial doves (Carlier and Lefebvre, 1996; Seferta, 1998). Furthermore, differences in neophobia in captivity are in the same direction as differences in learning: pigeons are more rapid than gregarious doves, who are in turn more rapid than territorial doves at simply feeding from a new dish (Seferta, 1998). Whittle (1996) found a similar pattern of covariance among neophobia, individual learning, and social learning in two domesticated species of finches that differ in the amount of aggressive interference they use when feeding. Cutthroat finches feed much more aggressively than do zebra finches, but show similar latencies to learn alone, to learn from a conspecific, and to simply feed from a new seed container. Using multiple regressions, Seferta (1998) showed that in both Whittle's experiments on finches and in her own work with columbids, individual variation in the simple latency to feed in a familiar or a new apparatus predicts latency to individual learning, which in turn predicts latency to social learning.

These results could have important consequences for evolutionary views of learning and cognition: if inter-specific, inter-population and inter-individual variance in learning is partially (in some cases, entirely?) due to intervening variables like neophobia and latency to feed in captivity, then maybe these traits have undergone selection in addition to (or even in lieu of?) some learning abilities. The standard practice in animal psychology of removing these variables a priori through habituation and taming may have lead comparative workers to either disregard their importance or treat them as confounding nuisances.

A challenge to the view that social and individual learning covary is presented by the elegant comparative work on corvids (reviewed by Balda et al., 1996). In spatial learning tests, Clarks' nutcrackers consistently outperform Pinyon jays, who in turn outperform Mexican jays. These results parallel species' differences in reliance on cached food in the field, which are probably linked to differences in seasonal food availability. More importantly for our purposes, Bednekoff and Balda (1996a, b) report a second set of ecologically correlated learning differences that are opposite to the ones found for caching and spatial memory: they show that Clark's nutcracker is poorer than the Mexican jay, which is in turn poorer than the Pinyon jay in remembering sites where they have observed conspecifics caching food. These observational learning differences parallel differences in the social structure of the species: Pinyon jays are more social than Mexican jays, who are in turn more social than Clark's nutcracker (Balda et al., 1996).

Balda et al. (1996) interpret these results as evidence for divergent specialization in social and individual components of spatial learning problems; the corvid data thus seem at variance with the comparative work described above, which suggest no specialization for social learning. However, the interspecific differences reported for observational learning of cache sites parallel those found by Olson et al. (1995) on a nonspatial, nonsocial operant task. In this experiment, the relative order of performance of the three species was the same as it was in the observational learning task of Bednekoff and Balda: Pinyon jays first, Mexican jays second, and Clark's nut-cracker third. These trends have a striking parallel in the other well-studied family of food caching birds, Paridae: marsh tits are better than great tits at spatial memory problems (Healy and Krebs, 1992), but poorer both on a social task and a non-spatial operant task (Sasvari, 1979, 1985a, b).

Overall, the comparative work thus suggests that spatial memory is specialized, but social learning is not (Lefebvre and Giraldeau, 1996). The prediction that adaptive specialization should lead to different interspecific trends for different learning abilities represents a strong, falsifiable test of the modularity concept (Shettleworth, this volume). The prediction is implicit in Sherry and Schacter's (1987) idea of trade-offs in memory systems and is routinely used in the literature on neural substrates. The association between size of the HVC and size of the song repertoire in oscines (DeVoogd et al., 1993), or that between spatial memory and size of the hippocampus (Sherry et al., 1989; Krebs et al., 1989), is always calculated with respect to the rest of the telencephalon, which implies that something, somewhere in the telencephalon, has become relatively smaller in the taxa that have evolved a relatively larger hippocampus or HVC.

If both Corvidae and Paridae have different interspecific trends for spatial memory (Clark's nutcracker being the best corvid among those tested and marsh tits being the best parid) and for nonspatial, individual learning (Clark's nutcracker being the worst corvid and marsh tits the worst parid), this is strong comparative evidence for modularity. Conversely though, if interspecific differences are the same on social and individual tasks in four sets of studies using six different avian families (Columbidae, Corvidae, Muscicapidae, Paridae, Fringillidae, and Passeridae), then only two conclusions follow: either these forms of learning are nonmodular or, as suggested by Richerson and Boyd (this volume), there could be both general purpose and special purpose modules for learning. Birds sexually selected for complex accoustic signalling could thus have a special purpose module for song imitation localized in telencephalic nuclei like HVC; birds naturally selected for the storing of surplus food could have a special purpose module for remembering the spatial and temporal information required for retrieval (Clayton et al., this volume). In contrast, a hungry bird searching for environmental predictors of hidden food could be using a single, general purpose module when it forages in an unfamiliar place (neophobia), when it tries out new food types or handling behaviors (feeding innovations), when it uses others as cues for finding food (nonimitative social learning), and when it associates contingencies in the physical environment and/or consequences of its actions to modify its foraging behavior (individual learning). The idea that individual learning and nonimitative forms of social learning covary is further supported by the strong consensus among psychologists that the two modes share the same processes (Heyes, 1994; Heyes and Galef, 1998).

Social Foraging and Identity of Tutors

Ecological context does not seem to have specialized effects on how much social learning there will be (contrary, for instance, to how much spatial memory will be required), but from whom this learning will occur. Studies of an opportunistic avian guild in Barbados show that the direction of social learning is associated with the type of inter- and intraspecific foraging competition in the field. Territorial zenaida doves are extremely aggressive toward conspecifics, yet often feed in mixed species aggregations where Carib grackles (*Quiscalus lugubris*) are the most prominent heterospecifics (Dolman et al., 1996). If these doves learn very poorly from conspecific tutors, they in contrast learn very readily from grackles (Dolman et al., 1996). Gregarious doves in turn learn very poorly from grackles, who mob them but seldom feed in their company on the cereal and legume spillage that causes group-feeding in the localized harbor population of doves (Carlier and Lefebvre, 1996; Dolman et al., 1996). Grackles, who do not compete aggressively either with other grackles or with territorial doves, learn as readily from either tutor type (Lefebvre et al., 1997a), as do zenaida doves caught at a site where feeding occurs both with conspecifics and grackles (Carlier and Lefebvre, 1997).

The association between social foraging mode and tutor identity may or may not be based on divergent selection for different learning rules (Sherry and Schacter, 1987): watching one tutor species rather than another in an experiment could be a simple effect of reinforcement history in the field, with some species, depending on local context, acting as reliable predictors of food or reliable predictors of attacks (mobbing grackles in the case of gregarious harbor doves, neighboring conspecifics in the case of territorial doves). For zenaida doves, this "learned tutor attention" hypothesis is all the more plausible because territorial and gregarious populations are geographically adjacent and intermixing, which excludes genetic isolation (Carlier and Lefebvre, 1997). Zenaida dove social behavior is also flexible and driven by feeding economics (Brown, 1964): experimental increases in food clumping and predictability lead to rapid increases in defence by otherwise group-feeding harbor doves (Goldberg, 1998). Seen in this light, the comparative work on zenaida doves and grackles does not warrant a "who" rule that would need to be added to the "what/when" and "how" rules envisioned by Heyes (this volume); social cues, like nonsocial ones, appear to be simple environmental predictors of positive or negative outcomes.

Does Variation in Social Learning Correspond to Variation in Cultural Transmission?

All the experiments described above involve a caged innovator placed in front of a single naive observer. This may be the ideal situation for working out the mechanisms and preferential pathways for social learning potential: species that fail to learn in these controlled conditions are unlikely to show much cultural transmission in the field (e.g., vervet monkeys, Cambefort, 1981; Lefebvre and Palameta, 1988). In contrast, positive results from captivity may be less relevant to the field than negative ones: in some cases, animals capable of social learning in a cage may not use this potential very often in the real world.

Our ecological framework points to scramble competition and group living as key correlates of social and individual learning ability. When moving from the single cage to the field, however, two important things change: the dynamics of group living modify the obligate one-to-one relationship between the caged innovator and its naïve observer. Secondly, "old" feeding behaviors are available to the observer in the field in addition to the new behavior used by the innovator; in a cage setting, the observer's only alternatives are to learn or go hungry. In genetic transmission, differential reproductive success associated with a mutant allele is routinely compared to that of extant alleles to predict the spread of new variants. Does the same logic apply to cultural transmission, that is, that the net benefit of a feeding innovation must exceed that of established behaviors if the cultural equivalent of natural selection is to occur? Note here that for behaviors other than feeding (e.g., communication signals), cultural transmission may not always be constrained by this net benefit rule. For example, transmission of vocal innovations in songbirds may follow a neutral allele model and be simply based on copying errors that appear and go extinct with few or no fitness consequences. In other cases, the benefit of the innovation may be linked to mating rather than maintenance, and the appropriate genetic analogy may be sexual rather than natural selection: a bird that sings a larger imitated repertoire may be subject to the same cost-benefit tradeoff as one that grows longer feathers or brighter colours, that is, an increased mating success offsets increased energetic and predation costs.

Beyond the risks of exploring novel stimuli (Fagen, 1981), feeding innovations yield direct payoffs to the innovator. For example, drinking cream in winter has obvious benefits for a tit. Tits often hunt for insects by looking under strips of bark; stripping open a milk bottle cap is probably only an extension of this searching technique, but with the added risk of approaching human dwellings, since bottles are only accessible to tits on doorsteps. As far as the naïve observer is concerned, however, there are several additional components to the cost-benefit tradeoff of learning:

first, the observer, contrary to the innovator, avoids the risks of exploring new stimuli. Second, when the observer adopts the innovation, it theoretically obtains the same benefit as the innovator. The payoffs of established alternatives to the innovation also enter into the tradeoff: an observer tit searching for insects must weigh the relative payoff of this option against that of opening bottles. For the innovator, these alternatives probably differ: the simple fact that it was exploring the new stimuli that led to the innovation suggests that payoffs to established alternatives were lower. Finally, the actions of the innovator may produce exploitable, indirect benefits for others: in the tit example, cream may be accessible from an opened bottle, so that naïve birds obtain similar benefits to those of the innovator even if they do not learn the opening technique.

This situation has been extensively modeled and is known as a producer-scrounger game (Giraldeau and Caraco, 2000). It is an ideal set-up for studying the costs and benefits of cultural learning in groups, because the frequency dependence of group dynamics determines the relative payoffs of learning the innovation vs. staying with established alternatives. When a single animal brings a scroungeable innovation into a group, the producer-scrounger game effectively becomes a learn vs. nonlearn game, with the innovation theoretically spreading until its frequency reaches the equilibrium point where the mean payoffs to learning and nonlearning are the same. This is illustrated by the following example in pigeons: if the mean number of birds who can scrounge from innovation 1 (e.g., pretraining a single bird to open tubes) is double that of birds who can scrounge from innovation 2 (e.g., pretraining a single bird to open boxes), then the transmission curve of innovation 2 should asymptote at twice the level of that of innovation 1. This is exactly what we get in aviary flocks of pigeons. Learning by naïve birds follows logistic functions that have the predicted differences in their asymptotes (Lefebvre and Hatch, in prep).

There are several reasons for this frequency dependent limit placed on learning (summarized in table 17.1). Many of them have been worked out in cage and aviary experiments with pigeons. Social learning is slowed down by the simple presence of nonperforming bystanders around a rewarded tutor (Lefebvre and Giraldeau, 1994). A single naïve bird foraging with a single innovator will not be subject to this effect, nor will it be distracted by the movements of other scroungers (Lefebvre and Helder, 1997), nor will it need to scramble compete with them, nor will it need to learn which of its many flock mates is a producer worth following (Giraldeau and Lefebvre, 1987). When tested alone, it is therefore not surprising that a single naïve bird that scrounges in the presence of its tutor shows it learned the new technique, whereas birds who scrounge in groups do not (Lefebvre and Helder, 1997). To these effects can be added the simple relative rewards of the tutor performing its innovation and

Table 17.1
Summary of innovator and observer variables affecting transmission in pigeons

Observer(s)	ONE		SEVERAL	
	eats	does not	eat	do not
Innovator(s)				
eats	GT+/−	PL+ GL2+	LHe−−	LG−
	LHe+	GT+ LG+		
ONE				
does	GL2−−	GT+/−	(−?)	(−?)
not	GT−	PL−		
eat	(+?)	LG++	GL1+/− GL2−	(?)
			L− LHa−, +/−	
SEVERAL				
do not	(−?)	(?)	(−?)	(−?)

PL, Palameta and Lefebvre 1985; L, Lefebvre 1986; GL1, Giraldeau and Lefebvre 1986; GL2, Giraldeau and Lefebvre 1987; GT, Giraldeau and Templeton 1990; LG, Lefebvre and Giraldeau 1994; LHe, Lefebvre and Helder 1997; LHa, Lefebvre and Hatch in prep.; cases in parentheses are hypothetical

the observer watching it: if the tutor gets little or no food from the new technique while the observer is rewarded simply for being caged in front of the tutor, the naïve bird does not learn (Giraldeau and Lefebvre, 1987; Giraldeau and Templeton, 1991); nor does it learn if it simply sees an unrewarded tutor pecking at a paper-covered food box (Palameta and Lefebvre, 1985).

Because the aviary allows group dynamics and the relative payoffs of alternatives to operate, it is more realistic than the single cage. Because the aviary group is confined, however, it differs from field conditions in a crucial way: the open, variable structure of many animal groups cannot have its normal effects on cultural transmission. In open, urban flocks of pigeons (Lefebvre, 1985), the transmission curve for a new feeding technique does not decelerate to a simple asymptote like it does in a closed aviary flock. Instead, transmission keeps occurring at a rate that reflects the constant immigration of new naïve birds and emigration of knowledgeable ones that yielded scroungeable food discoveries for the previously nonlearning birds.

Conclusion

Innovation, social learning, and cultural transmission can be seen as nongenetic analogues of mutation, replication, and natural selection. Just as these three components of genetic transmission involve very different mechanisms and functional determinants, the three components of nongenetic transmission need not necessarily covary (Heyes, 1993). Wilson (1985; Wyles et al., 1981), however, has suggested that large-brained animals who innovate frequently, as well as learn and transmit these innovations rapidly, may undergo faster evolution as a consequence of their higher rate of encounter with a wider variety of selective conditions. Because in this view innovation and cultural transmission have a common neural basis and a common evolutionary impact, it is tempting to read into Wilson's suggestion the possibility that they have co-evolved. A first step in testing this idea would be to show that the phyletic distribution of the two traits is correlated, filling a crucial link in the evolutionary framework suggested in figure 17.1.

Such a broad, predictive, comparative approach would complement the ones described by Shettleworth (this volume) and Richerson and Boyd (this volume). In some cases, however, the approaches may lead to contradictions: for the moment, the comparative data show no specialized divergence between social and individual learning, even if mathematical models and examples from other learning systems both suggest that they should be traded off. The contradictions can be reconciled if we accept Richerson and Boyd's concept (this volume) of special purpose and general purpose heuristics. If we do this, however, we need to be aware that the modularity concept becomes less falsifiable when broad modules are invoked a posteriori to replace a failed prediction of strict specialization. Secondly, the tradeoffs envisioned in other approaches may operate on short time scales, but not long ones. For example, a bird cannot simultaneously look upwards to follow others around and look down at the ground to search for food; producer-scrounger games thus assume that the two options they model are mutually exclusive within very short time scales (Giraldeau and Caraco, 2000). However, over a longer time frame, for example in different food-finding problems, the same individual can switch from following others to searching on its own and may in fact be selected for this flexibility on the basis of skill pool advantages (Giraldeau, 1984; Giraldeau and Lefebvre, 1986). Furthermore, in any social situation that favors learning from others, frequency dependence may automatically make individual learning more useful, not less, if too many copiers converge on the same solution and reduce the mean payoff of social learning below the equilibrium point of the different options. For all these reasons, social and individual forms of learning may be less incompatible than is sometimes assumed and may instead both be part of a broad system for dealing with novelty.

Summary

Innovation, social learning, and cultural transmission can be seen as nongenetic analogues of mutation, replication, and natural selection. In birds, the innovation rate for feeding behaviors varies between taxonomic groups; this variation is correlated with the relative size of the telencephalon. Learning new feeding behaviors by observing conspecifics is associated with opportunism and the social foraging mode. Interspecific differences in social learning parallel differences in individual learning and neophobia; this suggests that nonimitative social learning may not, contrary to spatial memory and song imitation, have gone through an evolutionary process of divergent specialization. Because of group dynamics and frequency dependent payoffs, innovations that are easily learned in the one-to-one context of a social learning experiment may show little or no cultural transmission in a more naturalistic setting.

References

Baer KL, Potter GD, Friend TH, Beaver BV (1983) Observation effects on learning in horses. Applied Animal Behaviour Science, 11: 123–129.

Baker AEM, Crawford BH (1986) Observational learning in horses. Applied Animal Behaviour Science, 15: 7–13.

Balda RP, Kamil AC, Bednekoff PA (1996) Predicting cognitive capacity from natural history, examples from four species of corvids. Current Ornithology, 13: 33–66.

Bateson PPG (1980) Optimal outbreeding and the development of sexual preferences in Japanese quail. Zeitschrift für Tierpsychologie, 53: 231–244.

Bednekoff PA, Balda RP (1996a) Social caching and observational spatial memory in pinyon jays. Behaviour, 133: 807–826.

Bednekoff PA, Balda RP (1996b) Observational spatial memory in Clark's nutcrackers and Mexican jays. Animal Behaviour, 52: 833–839.

Bennett PM, Harvey PH (1985) Relative brain size and ecology in birds. Journal of Zoology London, 207: 151–169.

Boire D (1989) Comparaison quantitative de l'encéphale, de ses grandes subdivisions et de relais visuels, trijumaux et accoustiques chez 28 espèces d'oiseaux. Ph.D. dissertation, Université de Montréal, Canada.

Brenowitz EA, Kroodsma DE (1996) The neuroethology of birdsong. In: Ecology and evolution of acoustic communication in birds (Kroodsma DE, Miller EH, ed), pp 285–304. New York: Cornell University Press.

Brown JL (1964) The evolution of diversity in avian territorial systems. Wilson Bulletin, 49: 160–169.

Bugnyar T, Huber L (1997) Push or pull: An experimental study on imitation in marmosets. Animal Behaviour, 54: 817–831.

Byrne RW, Whiten A (1988) Machiavellian intelligence. Social expertise and the evolution of intellect in monkeys, apes, and humans. New York: Oxford University Press.

Cambefort JP (1981) Comparative study of culturally transmitted patterns of feeding habits in the chacma baboon (Papio ursinus) and the vervet monkey (Cercopithecus aethiops). Folia Primatologica, 36: 243–263.

Carlier P, Lefebvre L (1996) Differences in individual learning between group-foraging and territorial zenaida doves. Behaviour, 133: 15–16.

Carlier P, Lefebvre L (1997) Ecological differences in social learning between adjacent, mixing, populations of zenaida doves. Ethology, 103: 772–784.

Clutton-Brock TH, Harvey PH (1980) Primates, brain and ecology. Journal of Zoology London, 190: 309–323.

Daly M, Rauschenberger J, Behrends P (1982) Food-aversion learning in kangaroo rats: A specialist-generalist comparison. Animal Learning and Behavior, 10: 314–320.

DeVoogd TJ, Krebs JR, Healy SD, Purvis A (1993) Relations between song repetoire size and the volume of brain nuclei related to song: Comparative evolutionary analyses amongst oscine birds. Proceedings of the Royal Society, London, B, 254: 75–82.

Dolman C, Templeton J, Lefebvre L (1996) Mode of foraging competition is related to tutor preference in Zenaida aurita. Journal of Comparative Psychology, 110: 45–54.

Dunbar RIM (1992) Neocortex size as a constraint on group size in primates. Journal of Human Evolution, 20: 469–493.

Dunning JB (1993) CRC handbook of avian body masses. Boca Raton: CRC Press.

Fagen RM (1981) Animal play behavior. New York: Oxford University Press.

Felsentein J (1985) Phylogenies and the comparative method. American Naturalist, 125: 1–15.

Giraldeau LA (1984) Group foraging: The skill pool effect and frequency-dependent learning. American Naturalist, 124: 72–79.

Giraldeau LA, Caraco T (2000) Social foraging theory. Princeton: Princeton University Press.

Giraldeau LA, Lefebvre L (1986) Exchangeable producer-scrounger roles in a captive flock of feral pigeons. Animal Behaviour, 34: 797–803.

Giraldeau LA, Lefebvre L (1987) Scrounging prevents cultural transmission of food-finding behaviour in pigeons: A case for the skill pool effect. Animal Behaviour, 35: 387–394.

Giraldeau LA, Templeton J (1991) Food scrounging and diffusion of foraging skills in pigeons, Columba livia: The importance of tutor and observer rewards. Ethology, 89: 63–72.

Goldberg J (1998). Variation in food defence as a function of ecological conditions in zenaida doves. M.Sc. thesis, McGill University.

Gray L (1981) Genetic and experiential differences affecting foraging behavior. In: Foraging behavior (Kamil AC, Sargent TD, ed), pp 455–473. New York: Garland STM Press.

Greenberg R (1983) The role of neophobia in determining the foraging specialization of some migratory warblers. American Naturalist, 98: 444–453.

Greenberg R (1984) Differences in feeding neophobia in the tropical migrant wood warblers, Dendroica castanea and D. pensylvanica. Journal of Comparative Psychology, 98: 131–136.

Greenberg R (1989) Neophobia, aversion to open space, and ecological plasticity in song and swamp sparrows. Canadian Journal of Zoology, 67: 1194–1199.

Greenberg R (1990) Feeding neophobia and ecological plasticity: A test of the hypothesis with captive sparrows. Animal Behaviour, 39: 375–379.

Healy SD, Krebs JR (1992) Comparing spatial memory in two species of tits: Recalling a single positive location. Animal Learning and Behavior, 20: 121–126.

Heyes CM (1993) Imitation, culture and cognition. Animal Behaviour, 46: 999–1010.

Heyes CM (1994) Social learning in animals: Categories and mechanisms. Biological Review, 69: 207–231.

Heyes CM, Galef Jr. BG (1998) The Napoli social learning conference. International Journal of Comparative Psychology, 11: 73–92.

Horn G (1990) Neural bases of recognition memory investigated through an analysis of imprinting. Philosophical Transactions of the Royal Society B, 329: 133–142.

Johnston TD (1982) The selective costs and benefits of learning: An evolutionary analysis. Advances in the Study of Behavior, 12: 65–106.

Klopfer PH (1959) Social interactions in discrimination learning with special reference to feeding behavior in birds. Behaviour, 14: 282–299.

Klopfer PH (1961) Observational learning in birds: The establishment of behavioral modes. Behaviour, 17: 71–80.

Krebs JR, Sherry DF, Healy SD, Perry VH, Vaccarino AL (1989) Hippocampal specialization in food-storing birds. Proceedings of the National Academy of Sciences USA, 86: 1388–1392.

Kroodsma DE, Verner J (1978) Complex singing behaviours among Cistothorus wrens. Auk, 95: 703–716.

Lefebvre L (1985) Stability of flock composition in urban pigeons. Auk, 102: 886–888.

Lefebvre L (1986) Cultural diffusion of a novel food-finding behaviour in urban pigeons: An experimental field test. Ethology, 71: 295–304.

Lefebvre L (1996) Ecological correlates of social learning: Problems and solutions for the comparative method. Behavioural Processes, 35: 163–171.

Lefebvre L, Gaxiola A, Dawson S, Timmermans S, Rozsa L, Kabai P (1998) Feeding innovations and forebrain size in Australasian birds. Behaviour, 135: 1077–1097.

Lefebvre L, Giraldeau LA (1994) Cultural transmission in pigeons is affected by the number of tutors and bystanders present. Animal Behaviour, 47: 331–337.

Lefebvre L, Giraldeau LA (1996) Is social learning an adaptive specialisation? In: Social learning in animals: The roots of culture (Heyes CM, Galef Jr BG, ed), pp 107–128. New York: Academic Press.

Lefebvre L, Hatch KK (in prep.) Cultural transmission and scrounging in kin-structured flocks of pigeons.

Lefebvre L, Helder R (1997) Scrounger numbers and the inhibition of learning in pigeons. Behavioural Processes, 40: 201–207.

Lefebvre L, Palameta B (1988) Mechanisms, ecology and population diffusion of socially learned, food-finding behaviour in feral pigeons. In: Social learning: Psychological and biological perspectives (Zentall TR, Galef Jr BG, ed), pp 141–164. Hillsdale, NJ: Erlbaum.

Lefebvre L, Palameta B, Hatch KK (1996) Is group-living associated with social learning? A comparative test of a gregarious and a territorial columbid. Behaviour, 133: 241–261.

Lefebvre L, Templeton J, Brown K, Koelle M (1997a) Carib grackles imitate conspecific and zenaida dove tutors. Behaviour, 134: 1003–1017.

Lefebvre L, Whittle P, Lascaris E, Finkelstein A (1997b) Feeding innovations and forebrain size in birds. Animal Behaviour, 53: 549–560.

Lorenz K (1935) Der Kumpan in der Umwelt des Vogels. Journal of Ornithology, 83: 137–213.

Macphail EM (1982) Brain and intelligence in vertebrates. Oxford: Clarendon Press.

Macphail EM (1985) Vertebrate intelligence: The null hypothesis. Philosphical Transactions of the Royal Society B, 308: 37–51.

Nottebohm F, Alvarez-Buylla A, Cynx JK, Ling CY, Nottebohm M, Suter R, Tolles A, Williams H (1990) Song learning in birds: The relation between perception and production. Philosphical Transactions of the Royal Society B, 329: 115–124.

Olson DJ, Kamil AC, Balda RP, Nims PJ (1995) Performance of four seed-caching corvid species in operant tests of nonspatial and spatial memory. Journal of Comparative Psychology, 109: 173–181.

Palameta B, Lefebvre L (1985) The social transmission of a food-finding technique: What is learned? Animal Behaviour, 33: 892–896.

Portmann A (1946) Etudes sur la cérébralisation des oiseaux. I. Alauda, 14: 2–20.

Portmann A (1947) Etudes sur la cérébralisation des oiseaux. II. Les indices intra-cérébraux. Alauda, 15: 1–15.

Purvis A, Rambaut A (1995) Comparative analysis by independent contrasts (CAIC): An Apple Macintosh application for analysing comparative data. Computer Applications in the Biosciences, 11: 247–251.

Rozin P, Kalat JW (1971) Specific hungers and poison avoidance as adaptive specialisations of learning. Psychological Review, 78: 459–486.

Rozin P, Schull J (1988) The adaptive-evolutionary point of view in experimental psychology. In: Steven's handbook of experimental psychology (Atkinson RC, Hernnstein RJ, Lindzey G, Luce RD, ed), pp 503–546. New York: Wiley.

Russon AE, Mitchell RW, Lefebvre L, Abravanel E (1998) The comparative evolution of imitation. In: Piaget, evolution and intelligence (Langer J, Killen M, ed), pp 103–143. Hillsdale, NJ: Erlbaum.

Sacher GA, Staffeldt EF (1974) Relation of gestation time to brain weight for placental mammals: Implications for the theory of vertebrate growth. American Naturalist, 108: 593–616.

Sasvari L (1979) Observational learning in great, blue and marsh tits. Animal Behaviour, 37: 767–771.

Sasvari L (1985a) Different observational learning capacity in juvenile and adult individuals of congeneric bird species. Zeitschrift für Tierpsychologie, 69: 293–304.

Sasvari L (1985b) Keypeck conditioning with reinforcements in two different locations in thrush, tit and sparrow species. Behavioural Processes, 11: 245–252.

Seferta A (1998) The role of intervening variables in learning differences between group-foraging and territorial columbids. M.Sc. thesis, McGill University.

Sherry DF, Schacter DL (1987) The evolution of multiple memory systems. Psychological Review, 94: 439–454.

Sherry DF, Vaccarino AL, Buckenham K, Herz RS (1989) The hippocampal complex of food-storing birds. Brain, Behavior and Evolution, 34: 308–317.

Shettleworth SJ (1993) Where is the comparison in comparative cognition? Alternative research programs. Psychological Science, 4: 179–184.

Sibley CG, Ahlquist JE (1990) Phylogeny and classification of birds: A study in molecular evolution. New Haven: Yale University Press.

Veissier I (1993) Observational learning in cattle. Applied Animal Behaviour Science, 35: 235–243.

Visalberghi E, Fragaszy DM (1990) Do monkeys ape? In: Language and intelligence in monkeys and apes: Comparative developmental perspectives (Parker S, Gibson KK, ed), pp 247–273. Cambridge: Cambridge University Press.

Whittle PJ (1996). The relationship between scramble competition and social learning: A novel approach to testing adaptive specialisation theory. M.Sc. thesis, McGill University.

Wilson AC (1985) The molecular basis of evolution. Scientific American, 253: 164–173.

Wyles JS, Kunkel JG, Wilson AC (1981) Birds, behaviour and anatomical evolution. Proceedings of the National Academy of Sciences USA, 80: 4394–4397.

18 Climate, Culture, and the Evolution of Cognition

Peter J. Richerson and Robert Boyd

What are the causes of the evolution of complex cognition? Discussions of the evolution of cognition sometimes seem to assume that more complex cognition is a fundamental advance over less complex cognition, as evidenced by a broad trend toward larger brains in evolutionary history. Evolutionary biologists are suspicious of such explanations because they picture natural selection as a process leading to adaptation to local environments, not to progressive trends. Cognitive adaptations will have costs, and more complex cognition will evolve only when its local utility outweighs them.

In this chapter, we argue that Cenozoic trends in cognitive complexity represent adaptations to an increasingly variable environment. The main support for this hypothesis is a correlation between environmental deterioration and brain size increase in many mammalian lineages.

We would also like to understand the sorts of cognitive mechanisms that were favored in building more complex cognitions. The problem is difficult because little data exists on the adaptive tradeoffs and synergies between different cognitive strategies for adapting to variable environments. Animals might use information rich, innate decision-making abilities, individual learning, social learning, and, at least in humans, complex culture, alone or in various combinations, to create sophisticated cognitive systems.

We begin with a discussion of the correlated trends in environmental deterioration and brain size evolution and then turn to the problem of what sorts of cognitive strategies might have served as the impetus for brain enlargement.

Plio-Pleistocene Climate Deterioration

The deterioration of climates during the last few million years should have dramatically increased selection for traits increasing animals' abilities to cope with more variable environments. These traits include more complex cognition. Using a variety of indirect measures of past temperature, rainfall, ice volume, and the like, mostly from cores of ocean sediments, lake sediments, and ice caps, paleoclimatologists have constructed a stunning picture of climate deterioration over the last 14 million years (Lamb, 1977; Schneider and Londer, 1984; Dawson, 1992; Partridge et al., 1995). The Earth's mean temperature has dropped several degrees and the amplitudes of fluctuations in rainfall and temperature have increased. For reasons that are as yet ill understood, glaciers wax and wane in concert with changes in ocean circulation, carbon dioxide, methane, and dust content of the atmosphere, and changes in average precipitation and the distribution of precipitation. The resulting pattern of fluctuation in climate is very complex. As the deterioration has proceeded, different cyclical patterns of glacial advance and retreat involving all these variables have dominated the pattern. A 21,700-year cycle dominated the early part of the period, a 41,000-year cycle between about 3 and 1 million years ago, and a 95,800-year cycle the last million years.

This cyclic variation is very slow with respect to the generation time of animals, and is not likely to have directly driven the evolution of adaptations for phenotypic flexibility. However, increased variance on the time scales of the major glacial advances and retreats also seems to be correlated with great variance at much shorter time scales. For the last 120,000 years, quite high-resolution data are available from ice cores taken from the deep ice sheets of Greenland and Antarctica. Resolution of events lasting only a little more than a decade is possible in ice 90,000 years old, improving to monthly after 3,000 years ago. During the last glacial period, ice core data shows that the climate was highly variable on time scales of centuries to millennia (GRIP, 1993; Lehman, 1993; Ditlevsen et al., 1996). Even when the climate was in the grip of the ice, there were brief spikelike ameliorations of about a thousand years' duration in which the climate temporarily reached near interglacial warmth. The intense variability of the last glacial period carries right down to the limits of the nearly 10-year resolution of the ice core data. Sharp excursions lasting a century or less occur in estimated temperatures, atmospheric dust, and greenhouse gases. Comparison of the rapid variation during this period with older climates is not yet possible. However, an internal comparison is possible. The Holocene (the last relatively warm, ice-free 10,000 years) has been a period of very stable climate, at least by the standards of the last glacial epoch. At the decadal scale, the last glacial climates were much more variable than climates in the Holocene. Holocene weather extremes have had quite significant effects on organisms (Lamb, 1977). It is hard to imagine the impact of the much greater variation that was probably characteristic of most if not all of the Pleistocene. Floods, droughts, windstorms, and the like, which we experience once a century, might have occurred once a decade. Tropical organisms did not escape the impact of climate variation; temperature and especially rainfall were highly variable at low latitudes (Broecker, 1996). During most periods in the Pleistocene, plants and animals must generally have lived under conditions of rapid, chaotic, and ongoing reorganization of ecological communities as species' ranges adjusted to the noisy variation in climate. Thus, since the late Miocene, organisms have had to cope with increasing variability in many environmental parameters at time scales on which strategies for phenotypic flexibility would be highly adaptive.

Brain Size Evolution in the Neogene

Mammals show clear signs of responding to climate deterioration by developing more complex cognition. Jerison's (1973) classic study of the evolution of brain size documents major trends toward increasing brain size in many mammalian lineages that persist up through the Pleistocene. The time trends are complex. There is a progressive increase in average encephalization (brain size relative to body size) throughout the Cenozoic. However, many relatively small-brained mammals persist to the present even in orders where some species have evolved large brains. The *diversity* of brain size increases toward the present. Mammals continue to evolve under strong selective pressure to minimize brain size (see section on cognitive economics, below), and those that can effectively cope with climatic deterioration by range changes or noncognitive adaptations do so. Other lineages evolve the means to exploit the temporal and spatial variability of the environment by using behavioral flexibility. The latter, we suppose, pay for the cost of encephalization by exploiting the ephemeral niches that less flexible, smaller brained species leave under-exploited.

Humans anchor the tail of the distribution of brain sizes in mammals; we are the largest brained member of the largest brained mammalian order. This fact supports a Darwinian hypothesis. Large gaps between species are hard to account for by the processes of organic evolution. That we are part of a larger trend suggests that a general selective process such as we propose really is operating. Nevertheless, there is some evidence that human culture is more than just a more sophisticated form of typical animal cognitive strategies. More on this vexing issue below.

The largest increase in encephalization per unit time by far is the shift from Miocene and Pliocene species to modern ones, coinciding with the Pleistocene climate deterioration. In the last 2.5 million years, encephalization increases were somewhat larger than during the steps from Archaic to Paleogene and Paleogene to Neogene, each of which represent tens of millions of years of evolution.

General Purpose Versus Special Purpose Mechanisms

To understand how evolution might have shaped cognitive adaptations to variable environments we need to know something about the elementary properties of mental machinery. Psychologists interested in the evolution of cognition have generated two classes of hypotheses about the nature of minds. A long-standing idea is that cognitively sophisticated mammals and birds have evolved powerful and relatively general purpose mental strategies that culminate in human intelligence and culture. These flexible general purpose strategies replace more rigidly innate ones as cognitive sophistication increases. For example, Donald Campbell (1965, 1975) emphasizes the general similarities of all knowledge acquiring processes ranging from organic evolution to modern science. He argues that even a quite fallible cognitive apparatus could nevertheless obtain workable mental representations of a complex variable environment by trial and error methods, much as natural selection shapes random mutations into organic adaptations. Bitterman's (this volume) empirical argument that simple and complex cognitions use rather similar learning strategies is a kindred proposal. Jerison (1973) argues that the main region of enlargement of bird and mammal brains in the Cenozoic has been the forebrain, whose structures serve rather general coordinating functions. He believes that it is possible to speak of intelligence abstracted from the particular cognition of each species, which he characterizes as the ability to construct perceptual maps of the world and use them to guide behavior adaptively. Edelman's (1987) theory of neuronal group selection is based on the argument that developmental processes cannot specify the fine details of the development of complex brains and hence that a lot of environmental feedback is necessary just to form the basic categories that complex cognition needs to work. This argument is consistent with the observation that animals with more complex cognition require longer juvenile periods with lots of "play" to provide the somatic selection of the fine details of synaptic structure. In Edelman's argument, a large measure of phenotypic flexibility comes as a result of the developmental constraints on the organization of complex brains by innate programming. If cognition is to be complex, it must be built using structures that are underdetermined at birth.

Against general purpose hypotheses, there has long been the suspicion that animal intelligence can only be understood in relationship to the habitat in which the species lives (Hinde, 1970: 659–663). Natural selection is a mechanism for adapting the individuals of a species to particular environmental challenges. It will favor brains and behaviors specialized for the niche of the species. There is no reason to think that it will favor some general capacity that we can operationalize as intelligence across species. A recent school of evolutionary psychologists has applied this logic to the human case (Barkow et al., 1992; Pinker, 1997; Shettleworth, this volume). The brain, they argue, even the human brain, is not a general problem-solving device, but a collection of modules directed at solving the particular challenges posed by the environments in which the human species evolved. General problem-solving devices are hopelessly clumsy. To work at all, a mental problem-solving device must make a number of assumptions about the structure of its world, assumptions that are likely to hold only locally. Jack of all trades, master of none. Human brains, for example, are adapted to life in small-scale hunting and gathering societies of the Pleistocene. They will guide behavior within such societies with considerable precision but behave unpredictably in other situations. These authors are quite suspicious of the idea that culture alone forms the basis for human behavioral flexibility. As Tooby and Cosmides (1992) put it, what some take to be cultural traditions transmitted to relatively passive imitators in each new generation could actually be partly, or even mainly, "evoked culture," innate information that leads to similar behavior in parents and offspring simply because they live in similar environments. In this model, human cognition is complex because we have many content rich, special purpose, innate algorithms, however much we also depend upon transmitted culture.

This debate should not be trivialized by erecting straw protagonists. On the one hand, it is not sensible for defenders of cognitive generalism to ignore that the brain is a complex organ with many specialized parts, without which no mental computations would be possible. No doubt, much of any animal's mental apparatus is keyed to solve niche-specific problems, as is abundantly clear from brain comparative anatomy (Krubitzer, 1995) and from performance on learning tasks (Garcia and Koelling, 1966; Poli, 1986). Learning devices can be only *relatively* general; all of them must depend upon an array of innate processing devices to interpret raw sense data and evaluate whether it should be treated as significant (an actual or potential reinforcer). The more general a learning rule is, the weaker it is liable to be.

On the other hand, one function of all brains is to deal with the unforeseeable. The dimensionality of the environment is very large even for narrow specialists, and even larger for weedy, succeeds-everywhere species like humans. Being preprogrammed to respond adaptively to a large variety of environmental contingencies may be costly or impossible. If efficient learning heuristics exist that obviate the need for large amounts of innate information, they will be favored by selection.

When the situation is sufficiently novel, like most of the situations that rats and pigeons face in Skinner Boxes, every species is forced to rely upon what is, in effect, a very general learning capability. An extreme version of the special purpose modules hypothesis would predict that animals should behave completely randomly in environments as novel as they usually face in the laboratory. The fact that adaptive behavior emerges at all in such circumstances is a clear disproof of such an extreme position. Likewise, humans cannot be too tightly specialized for living in small hunting and gathering societies under Pleistocene conditions. We are highly successful in the Holocene using far different social and subsistence systems.

A Role for Social Learning in Variable Environments

Our own hypothesis is that culture plays a large role in the evolution of human cognitive complexity. The case for a role for social learning in other animals is weaker and more controversial, but well worth entertaining. Social learning and culture furnish a menu of heuristics for adapting to temporally and spatially variable environments. Learning devices will only be favored when environments are variable in time or space in difficult to predict ways. Social learning is a device for multiplying the power of individual learning. Systems of phenotypic adaptation have costs. In the case of learning, an individual will have to expend time and energy, incur some risks in trials that may be associated with costly errors, and support the neurological machinery necessary to learn. Social learning can economize on the trial and error part of learning. If kids learn from Mom, they can avoid repeating her mistakes. "Copy Mom" is a simple heuristic that may save one a lot of effort and be almost as effective as learning for oneself, provided the environment in one's own generation is pretty much like Mom's. Suppose the ability to somehow copy Mom is combined with a simple check of the current environment that warns one if the environment has changed significantly. If it has, one learns for oneself. This strategy allows social learners to avoid some learning costs but rely on learning when necessary.

We have constructed a series of mathematical models designed to test the cogency of these ideas (Boyd and Richerson, 1985, 1989, 1995, 1996; see also Cavalli-Sforza and Feldman, 1973; Pulliam and Dunford, 1980). The formal theory supports the story. When information is costly to obtain and when there is some statistical resemblance between models' and learners' environments, social learning is potentially adaptive. Selection will favor individual learners who add social learning to their repertoire so long as copying is fairly accurate and the extra overhead cost of the capacity to copy is not too high. In some circumstances, the models suggest that social learning will be quite important relative to individual learning. It can be a great advantage compared to a system that relies on genes only to transmit information and individual learning to adapt to the variation. Selection will also favor heuristics that bias social learning in adaptive directions. When the behavior of models is variable, individuals that try to choose the best model by using simple heuristics like "copy dominants" or "go with the majority," or by using complex cognitive analyses, are more likely to do well than those who blindly copy. Contrariwise, if it is easy for individuals to learn the right thing to do by themselves, or if environments vary little, then social learning is of no utility.

A basic advantage common to many of the model systems that we have studied is that a system linking an ability to make adaptive decisions to an ability to copy speeds up the evolutionary process. Both natural selection and the biasing decisions that individuals make act on socially learned variation. The faster rate of evolution tracks a variable environment more faithfully, providing a fitness return to social learning.

Our models of cultural evolution are much like the learning model Bitterman describes in this volume. In fact, one of our most basic models adds social learning to a model of individual learning virtually identical to his in order to investigate the inheritance-of-acquired-variation feature of social learning. Such models are quite simple and meant to be quite general. We expect that they will apply, at least approximately, to most examples of social learning likely to be found in nature.

Social learning strategies could represent a component of general purpose learning systems. Social learning is potentially an adaptive supplement to a weak, relatively general purpose learning rule. (We accept the argument that the more general a learning rule is the weaker it has to be.) However, we have modeled several different kinds of rules for social learning. These would qualify as different modules in Shettleworth's terms (this volume). The same rule, with different inputs and different parameter settings, can be implemented as a component of many narrowly specialized modules. Psychological evidence suggests that human culture involves numerous subsystems and variants that use a variety of patterns of transmission and a variety of biasing heuristics (Boyd and Richerson, 1985). Although all nonhuman social learning systems are, as far as we know, much simpler than human culture, they probably obey a similar evolutionary logic and vary adaptively from species to species (Chou and Richerson, 1992; Laland et al., 1996).

In no system of social learning have fitness effects yet been estimated; the adaptiveness of simple social learning warrants skepticism. Rogers (1989, see also Boyd and Richerson, 1995) constructed a plausible model in which two genotypes were possible, individual learners and social learners. In his model, the social learning genotype can invade because social learners save on the cost of learning for themselves. However, at the equilibrium frequency of social learners, the fitness of the two types is equal. Social learners are parasites on the learning efforts of individual learners. Social learning only raises the average fitness of individuals if individual learners also benefit from social learning. The well-studied system of social learning of food preference in rats is plausibly an example of adaptive social learning (Galef, 1996), but the parasitic hypothesis is not yet ruled out. Lefebvre's (this volume) data indicating a positive correlation of individual and social learning suggests an adaptive combination of social and individual learning, although his data on scrounging in aviaries shows that pigeons are perfectly willing to parasitize the efforts of others. We will be surprised if no cases of social learning corresponding to Rogers' model ever turn up.

The complex cognition of humans is one of the great scientific puzzles. Our conquest of *the* ultimate cognitive niche seems to explain our extraordinary success as a species (Tooby and Devore, 1987). Why then has the human cognitive niche remained empty for all but a tiny slice of the history of life on earth, finally to be filled by a single lineage? Human culture, but not the social learning of most other animals, involves the use of imitation, teaching, and language to transmit complex adaptations subject to progressive improvement. In the human system, socially learned constructs can be far more sophisticated than even the most inspired individual could possibly hope to invent. Is complex culture the essence of our complex cognition, or merely a subsidiary part?

The Problem of Cognitive Economics

To understand how selection for complex cognition proceeds, we need to know the costs, benefits, tradeoffs, and synergies involved in using elementary cognitive strategies in compound architectures to adapt efficiently to variable environments. In our models we have merely assumed costs, accuracies, and other psychological properties of learning and social learning. We here sketch the kinds of knowledge necessary to incorporate cognitive principles directly into evolutionary models.

Learning and decision making require larger sensory and nervous systems in proportion to their sophistication, and large nervous systems are costly (Eisenberg, 1981: 235–236). Martin (1981) reports that mammalian brains vary over about a 25-fold range, controlling for body size. Aiello and Wheeler (1995) report that human brains account for 16 percent of our basal metabolism. Average mammals have to allocate only about 3 percent of basal metabolism to their brains, and many marsupials get by with less than 1 percent. These differences are large enough to generate significant evolutionary tradeoffs. In addition to metabolic requirements, there are other significant costs of big brains, such as increased difficulty at birth, greater vulnerability to head trauma, increased potential for developmental snafus, and the time and trouble necessary to fill these large brains with usable information. On the cost side, selection will favor as small a nervous system as possible.

If our hypothesis is correct, animals with complex cognition foot the cost of a large brain by adapting more swiftly and accurately to variable environments. Exactly how do they do it? Given just three generic forms of adaptation to variable environments—innate information, individual learning, and social learning—and two kinds of mental devices—more general and less general purpose—the possible architectures for minds are quite numerous. What sorts of tradeoffs will govern the nature of structures that selection might favor? What is the overhead cost of having a large repertoire of innate special purpose rules? Innate rules will consume genes and brain tissue with algorithms that may be rarely called upon. The gene-to-mind translation during development may be difficult for complex innate rules. If so, acquiring information from the environment using learning or social learning may be favored. Are there situations where a (relative) jack-of-all-trades learning rule can out-compete a bevy of specialized rules? What is the penalty paid in efficiency for a measure of generality in learning? Are there efficient heuristics that minds can use to gain a measure of generality without paying the full cost of a general purpose learning device? Relatively general purpose heuristics might work well enough over a wide enough range of environmental variation to be almost as good as several sophisticated special purpose algorithms, each costing as much brain tissue as the general heuristic (see Gigerenzer and Goldstein, 1996, on simple but powerful heuristics).

Hypothesis building here is complicated because we cannot assume that individual learning, social learning, and innate knowledge are simply competing processes. For example, more powerful or more general learning algorithms may generally require more innate information (Tooby and Cosmides, 1992). More sophisticated associative learning will typically require more sense data to make finer discriminations of stimuli. Sophisticated sense systems depend upon powerful, specialized, innate algorithms to make useful information from a mass of raw data from the sensory transducers (Spelke, 1990; Shettleworth, this volume). Hypothesis building is also complicated because we have no rules describing the efficiency of a compound system of some more and some less specialized modules. For example, a central general purpose associative learning device might be the most efficient processor for such sophisticated sensory data because redundant implementation of the same learning algorithm in many modules might be costly. Intense modularity in parts of the mind may favor general purpose, shared, central devices in other parts. Bitterman's (this volume) data are consistent with there being a central associative learning processor that is similar by homology across most of the animal kingdom. However, his data are also consistent with several or many encapsulated special purpose associative learning devices that have converged on a relatively few efficient association algorithms. Shettleworth's (this volume) argument for modularity by analogy with perception has appeal. If the cost of implementing an association algorithm is small relative to the cost of sending sensory data large distances across the brain, selection will favor association algorithms in many modules. However, the modularity of perception is surely driven in part by the fact that the different sense organs must transduce very different physical data. Bitterman's (this volume) data show that, once reduced to a more abstract form, many kinds of sense data can be operated on by the same learning algorithm, which might be implemented centrally or modularly. The same sorts of issues will govern the incorporation of social learning into an evolving cognitive system.

There may be evolutionary complications to consider. For example, seldom-used special purpose rules (or the extreme seldom-used ranges of frequently exercised rules) will be subject to very weak selection. More general purpose structures have the advantage that they will be used frequently and hence be well adapted to the prevailing range of environmental uncertainty. If they work to any approximation outside this range, selection can readily act to improve them. Narrowly special purpose algorithms could have the disadvantage that they can be "caught out" by a sudden environmental change, exhibiting no even marginally useful variation for selection to seize upon, whereas more general purpose individual and social learning strategies can expose variation to selection in such cases (Laland et al., 1996). On the other hand, we might imagine that there is a reservoir of variation in outmoded special purpose algorithms, on which selection has lost its purchase, that furnishes the necessary variation in suddenly changed circumstances.

The high dimensionality of the variation of Pleistocene environments puts a sharp point on the innate information vs. learning/social learning modes of phenotypic flexibility. Mightn't the need for enough information to cope with such complex change by largely innate means exhaust the capacity of the genome to store and express it? Recall Edelman's (1987) neuronal group selection hypothesis in this context. Immelman (1975) suggests that animals use imprinting to identify their parents and acquire a concept of their species because it is not feasible to store a picture of the species in the genes or to move the information from genes to the brain during development. It may be more economical to use the visual system to acquire the picture after birth or hatching by using the simple heuristic that the first living thing one sees is Mom and a member of one's own species. In a highly uncertain world, wouldn't selection favor a repertoire of heuristics designed to learn as rapidly and efficiently as possible?

As far as we understand, psychologists are not yet in a position to give us the engineering principles of mind design the way that students of biological mechanics now can for muscle and bone. If these principles turn out to favor complex, mixed designs with synergistic, nonlinear relationships between parts, the mind design problem will be quite formidable. We want to avoid asking silly questions analogous to "which is more important to the function of a modern PC, the hardware or the software?" However, in our present state of ignorance, we do run the risk of asking just such questions!

With due care, perhaps we can make a little progress. In this chapter, we use a method frequently used by evolutionary biologists, dubbed "strategic modeling" by Tooby and Devore (1987). In strategic modeling, we begin with the tasks that the environment sets for an organism and attempt to deduce how natural selection should have shaped the species' adaptation to its niche. Often, evolutionary biologists frame hypotheses in terms of mathematical models of alternative adaptations that predict, for instance, what foraging or mate choice strategy organisms with a given general biology should pursue in a particular environment. This is just the sort of modeling we have undertaken in our studies of social learning and culture. We ask: how should organisms cope with different kinds of spatially and temporally variable environments?

Social Learning Versus Individual Learning Versus Innate Programming?

Increases in brain size could signal adaptation to variable environments via individual learning, social learning, or more sophisticated innate programming. Our mathematical models suggest that the three systems work together. Most likely increases in brain size to support more sophisticated learning or social learning will also require at least some more innate programming. There is likely an optimal balance of innate and acquired information dictated by the structure of environmental variability. Given the tight cost/benefit constraints imposed on brains, at the margin we would expect to find a tradeoff between social learning, individual learning, and innate programming. For example, those species that exploit the most variable niches should emphasize individual learning, whereas those that live in more highly autocorrelated environments should devote more of their nervous systems to social learning.

Lefebvre (this volume) reviews studies designed to test the hypothesis that social and opportunistic species should be able to learn socially more easily than the more conservative species, and the conservative species should be better individual learners. Surprisingly, the prediction fails. Species that are good social learners are also good individual learners. One explanation for these results is that the synergy between these systems is strong. Perhaps the information-evaluating neural circuits used in social and individual learning are partly or largely shared. Once animals become social, the potential for social learning arises. The two learning systems may share the overhead of maintaining the memory storage system and much of the machinery for evaluating the results of experience. If so, the benefits in quality or rate of information gained may be large relative to the cost of small bits of specialized nervous tissue devoted separately to each capacity. If members of the social group tend to be kin, investments in individual learning may also be favored because sharing the results by social learning will increase inclusive fitness. On the other hand, Lefebvre notes that not all learning abilities are positively correlated. Further, the correlation may be due to some quite simple factor, such as low neophobia, not a more cognitively sophisticated adaptation.

The hypothesis that the brain tissue tradeoff between social and individual learning is small resonates with what we know of the mechanisms of social learning in most species. Galef (1988, 1996), Laland et al. (1996), and Heyes and Dawson (1990) argue that the most common forms of social learning result from very simple mechanisms that piggyback on individual learning. In social species, naïve animals follow more experienced parents, nestmates, or flock members as they traverse the environment. The experienced animals select highly nonrandom paths through the environment. They thus expose naïve individuals to a highly selected set of stimuli that then lead to acquisition of behaviors by ordinary mechanisms of reinforcement. Social experience acts, essentially, to speed up and make less random the individual learning process, requiring little additional, specialized, mental capacity. Social learning, by making individual learning more accurate without requiring much new neural machinery, tips the selective balance between the high cost of brain tissue and advantages of flexibility in favor of more flexibility. As the quality of information stored on a mental map increases, it makes sense to enlarge the scale of maps to take advantage of that fact. Eventually, diminishing returns to map accuracy will limit brain size.

Once again, we must take a skeptical view of this adaptive hypothesis until experimental and field investigations produce better data on the adaptive consequences of social learning. Aside from Roger's parasitic scenario, the simplicity of social learning in most species and its close relationship to individual learning invites the hypothesis that most social learning is a byproduct of individual learning that is not sufficiently important to be shaped by natural selection. Human imitation, by contrast, is so complex as to suggest that it must have arisen under the influence of selection.

Eisenberg's (1981, ch 23) review of a large set of data on the encephalization of living mammals suggests that high encephalization is associated with extended association with parents, late sexual maturity, extreme iteroparity, and long potential life span. These life cycle attributes all seem to favor social learning (but also any other form of time-consuming skill acquisition). We would not expect this trend if individual and social learning were a small component of encephalization relative to innate, information rich modules. Under the latter hypothesis, animals with a minimal opportunity to take advantage of parental experience and parental protection while learning for themselves ought to be able to adapt to variable environments with a rich repertoire of innate algorithms. Eisenberg's data suggest that large brains are not normally favored in the absence of social learning and/or social facilitation of individual learning. The study of any species that run counter to Eisenberg's correlation might prove very rewarding. Large-brained species with a small period of juvenile dependence should have a complex cognition built disproportionately of innate information. Similarly, small-brained social species with prolonged juvenile dependence or other social contact may depend relatively heavily on simple learning and social learning strategies. Lefebvre and Palameta (1988) provide a long list of animals in which social learning has been more or less convincingly documented. Recently, Dugatkin (1996) and Laland and Williams (1997) have demonstrated social learning in guppies. Even marginally social species may come under selection for behaviors that enhance social learning, as in the well known case of mother housecats who bring partially disabled prey to their kittens for practice of killing behavior (Caro and Hauser, 1992).

Some examples of nonhuman social learning are clearly specialized, such as birdsong imitation, but the question is open for other examples. Aspects of the social learning system in other cases do show signs of adaptive specialization, illustrating the idea that learning and social learning systems are only general purpose *relative* to a completely innate system. For example, Terkel (1996) and Chou (1989, personal communication) obtained evidence from laboratory studies of black rats that the main mode of social learning is from mother to pups. This is quite unlike the situation in the case of Norway rats, where Galef (1988, 1996) and coworkers have shown quite conclusively that mothers have no special influence on pups. In the black rat, socially learned behaviors seem to be fixed after a juvenile learning period, whereas Norway rats continually update their diet preferences (the best-studied trait) based upon individually acquired and social cues. Black rats seem to be adapted to a more slowly changing environment than Norway rats. Terkel studied a rat population that has adapted to open pinecones in an exotic pine plantation in Israel, a novel and short-lived niche by most standards, but one that will persist for many rat generations. Norway rats are the classic rats of garbage dumps, where the sorts of foods available change on a weekly basis.

Human Versus Other Animals' Culture

The human species' position at the large-brained tail of the distribution of late Cenozoic encephalization suggests the hypothesis that our system of social learning is merely a hypertrophied version of a common mammalian system based substantially on the synergy between individual learning and simple systems of social learning. However, two lines of evidence suggest that there is more to the story.

First, human cultural traditions are often very complex. Subsistence systems, artistic productions, languages, and the like are so complex that they must be built up over many generations by the incremental, marginal modifications of many innovators (Basalla, 1988). We are utterly dependent on learning such complex traditions to function normally.

Second, this difference between humans and other animals in the complexity of socially learned behaviors is mirrored in a major difference in mode of social learning. As we saw above, the bulk of animal social learning seems to be dependent mostly on the same techniques used in individual learning, supplemented at the margin by a bit of teaching and imitation. Experimental psychologists have devoted much effort to trying to settle the question of whether nonhuman animals can learn by "true imitation" or not (Galef, 1988). True imitation is learning a behavior by seeing it done. True imitation is presumably more complex cognitively than merely using conspecifics' behavior as a source of cues to stimuli that it might be interesting to experience. Although there are some rather good experiments indicating some capacity for true imitation in several socially learning species (Heyes, 1996; Moore, 1996; Zentall, 1996), head-to-head comparisons of children's and chimpanzee's abilities to imitate show that children begin to exceed chimpanzees' capabilities at about three years of age (Whiten and Custance, 1996; Tomasello, 1996, this volume). The lesson to date from comparative studies of social learning suggests that simple mechanisms of social learning are much more common and more important than imitation, even in our close relatives and other highly encephalized species.

Why Is Complex Culture Rare?

One hypothesis is that an intrinsic evolutionary impediment exists, hampering the evolution of a capacity for complex traditions. We show elsewhere that, under some sensible cognitive-economic assumptions, a capacity for complex cumulative culture cannot be favored by selection when rare (Boyd and Richerson, 1996). The mathematical result is quite intuitive. Suppose that to acquire a complex tradition efficiently, imitation is required. Suppose that efficient imitation requires considerable costly, or complex, cognitive machinery, such as a theory of mind/imitation module (Cheney and Seyfarth, 1990: 277–230; Tomasello, this volume). If so, there will be a coevolutionary failure of capacity for complex traditions to evolve. The capacity would be a great fitness advantage, but only if there are cultural traditions to take advantage of. But, obviously, there cannot be complex traditions without the cognitive machinery necessary to support them. A rare individual who has a mutation coding for an enlarged capacity to imitate will find no complex traditions to learn, and will be handicapped by an investment in nervous tissue that cannot function. The hypothesis depends upon there being a certain lumpiness in the evolution of the mind. If even a small amount of imitation requires an expensive or complex bit of mental machinery, or if the initial step in the evolution of complex traits does not result in particularly useful traditions, then there will be no smooth evolutionary path from simple social learning to complex culture.

If such an impediment to the evolution of complex traditions existed, evolution must have traveled a roundabout path to get the frequency of the imitation capacity high enough to begin to bring it under positive selection for its tradition-supporting function. Some suggest that primate intelligence was originally an adaptation to manage a complex social life (Humphrey, 1976; Byrne and Whiten, 1988; Kummer et al., 1997; Dunbar, 1992, this volume). Perhaps in our lineage the complexities of managing the sexual division of labor, or some similar social problem, favored the evolution of a sophisticated theory of mind capacity. Such a capacity might incidentally make efficient imitation possible, launching the evolution of elementary complex traditions. Once elementary complex traditions exist, the threshold is crossed. As the evolving traditions become too complex to imitate easily, they will begin to drive the evolution of still more sophisticated imitation. This sort of stickiness in the evolutionary processes is presumably what gives evolution its commonly contingent, historical character (Boyd and Richerson, 1992).

Conclusion

The evolution of complex cognition is a complex problem. It is not entirely clear what selective regimes favor complex cognition. The geologically recent increase in the encephalization of many mammalian lineages suggests that complex cognition is an adaptation to a common, widespread, complex feature of the environment. The most obvious candidate for this selective factor is the deterioration of the earth's climate since the late Miocene, culminating in the exceedingly noisy Pleistocene glacial climates.

In principle, complex cognition can accomplish a system of phenotypic flexibility by using information-rich innate rules or by using more open individual and social learning. Presumably, the three forms of phenotypic flexibility are partly competing, partly mutually supporting mechanisms that selection tunes to the patterns of environmental variation in particular species' niches. Because of the cost of brain tissue, the tuning of cognitive capacities will take place in the face of a strong tendency to minimize brain size. However, using strategic modeling to infer the optimal structure for complex cognitive systems from evolutionary first principles is handicapped by the very scanty information on tradeoffs and constraints that govern various sorts of cognitive information processing strategies. For example, we do not understand how expensive it is to encode complex innate information-rich computational algorithms relative to coping with variable environments with relatively simple, but still relatively efficient, learning heuristics. Psychologists and neurobiologists might usefully concentrate on such questions.

Human cognition raises the ante for strategic modeling because of its apparently unique complexity and yet great adaptive utility. We can get modest but real leverage on the problem by investigating other species with cognitive complexity approaching ours, which in addition to great apes may include some other monkeys, some cetaceans, parrots, and corvids (Moore, 1996; Heinrich, this volume; Clayton et al., this volume). Our interpretation of the evidence is that human cognition mainly evolved to acquire and manage cumulative cultural traditions. This capacity probably cannot be favored when rare, even in circumstances where it would be quite successful if it did evolve. Thus, its evolution likely required, as a preadaptation, the advanced cognition achieved by many mammalian lineages in the last few million years. *In addition*, it required an adaptive breakthrough, such as the acquisition of a capacity for imitation as a byproduct of the evolution of a theory of mind capacity for social purposes.

References

Aiello LC, Wheeler P (1995) The expensive tissue hypothesis: The brain and the digestive system in human and primate evolution. Current Anthropology, 36: 199–221.

Barkow JH, Cosmides L, Tooby J (1992) The adapted mind: Evolutionary psychology and the generation of culture. Oxford: Oxford University Press.

Basalla G (1988) The evolution of technology. Cambridge: Cambridge University Press.

Boyd R, Richerson PJ (1985) Culture and the evolutionary process. Chicago: Chicago University Press.

Boyd R, Richerson PJ (1989) Social learning as an adaptation. Lectures on Mathematics in the Life Sciences, 20: 1–26.

Boyd R, Richerson PJ (1992) How microevolutionary processes give rise to history. In: History and evolution (Nitecki MH, Nitecki DV, ed), pp 179–209. Albany: State University of New York Press.

Boyd R, Richerson PJ (1995) Why does culture increase human adaptability? Ethology and Sociobiology, 16: 125–143.

Boyd R, Richerson PJ (1996) Why culture is common but cultural evolution is rare. Proceedings of the British Academy, 88: 77–93.

Broecker WS (1996) Glacial climate in the tropics. Science, 272: 1902–1903.

Byrne RW, Whiten A (1988) Machiavellian intelligence. Social expertise and the evolution of intellect in monkeys, apes, and humans. New York: Oxford University Press.

Campbell DT (1965) Variation and selective retention in sociocultural evolution. In: Social change in developing areas: A reinterpretation of evolutionary theory (Barringer HR, Blanksten GI, Mack RW, ed), pp 19–49. Cambridge, MA: Schenkman.

Campbell DT (1975) On the conflicts between biological and social evolution and between psychology and moral tradition. American Psychologist, 30: 1103–1126.

Caro T, Hauser M (1992) Is there teaching in nonhuman animals? Quarterly Review of Biology, 67: 151–174.

Cavalli-Sforza LL, Feldman MW (1973) Models for cultural inheritance. I. Group mean and within group variation. Theoretical Population Biology, 4: 42–55.

Cheney DL, Seyfarth RM (1990) How monkeys see the world: Inside the mind of another species. Chicago: University of Chicago Press.

Chou L-S (1989). Social Transmission of Food Selection by Rats. Ph.D. Dissertation, University of California, Davis.

Chou L, Richerson PJ (1992) Multiple models in social trasmission among Norway rats, *Rattus norvegicus*. Animal Behaviour, 44: 337–344.

Dawson AG (1992) Ice Age Earth: Late Quaternary geology and climate. London: Routledge.

Ditlevsen PD, Svensmark H, Johnsen S (1996) Contrasting atmospheric and climate dynamics of the last-glacial and Holocene periods. Nature, 379: 810–812.

Dugatkin LA (1996) Copying and mate choice. In: Social learning in animals: The roots of culture (Heyes CM, Galef Jr BG, ed), pp 85–105. San Diego: Academic Press.

Dunbar RIM (1992) Neocortex size as a constraint on group size in primates. Journal of Human Evolution, 20: 469–493.

Edelman GM (1987) Neural Darwinism: The theory of neuronal group selection. New York: Basic Books.

Eisenberg JF (1981) The mammalian radiations: An analysis of trends in evolution, adaptation, and behavior. Chicago: University of Chicago Press.

Galef Jr BG (1988) Imitation in animals: History, definition, and interpretation of data from the psychological laboratory. In: Social learning: Psychological and biological perspectives (Zentall TR, Galef Jr. BG, ed), pp 3–28. Hillsdale, N.J.: Erlbaum.

Galef Jr BG (1996) Social enhancement of food preferences in Norway rats: A brief review. In: Social learning in animals: The roots of culture (Heyes CM , Galef Jr BG, ed), pp 49–64. San Diego: Academic Press.

Garcia J, Koelling R (1966) Relation of cue to consequence in avoidance learning. Psychonomic Science, 4: 123–124.

Gigerenzer G, Goldstein DG (1996) Reasoning the fast and frugal way: Models of bounded rationality. Psychological Review, 103: 650–669.

GRIP (Greenland Ice-core Project Members) (1993) Climate instability during the last interglacial period recorded in the GRIP ice core. Nature, 364: 203–207.

Heyes CM (1996) Introduction: Identifying and defining imitation. In: Social learning in animals: The roots of culture (Heyes CM, Galef Jr BG, ed), pp 211–220. San Diego: Academic Press.

Heyes CM, Dawson GR (1990) A demonstration of observational learning using a bidirectional control. Quarterly Journal of Experimental Psychology, 42B: 59–71.

Hinde RA (1970) Animal behaviour: A synthesis of ethology and comparative psychology. New York: McGraw Hill.

Humphrey NK (1976) The social function of intellect. In: Growing points in ethology (Bateson PPG, Hinde RA, ed), pp 303–317. Cambridge: Cambridge University Press.

Immelman K (1975) Ecological significance of imprinting and early learning. Annual Review of Ecology and Systematics, 6: 15–37.

Jerison HJ (1973) Evolution of the brain and intelligence. New York: Academic Press.

Krubitzer L (1995) The organization of neocortex in mammals: Are species differences really so different? Trends in Neurosciences, 18: 408–417.

Kummer H, Daston L, Gigerenzer G, Silk JB (1997) The social intelligence hypothesis. In: Human by nature: Between biology and the social sciences (Weingart P, Mitchell SD, Richerson PJ, Maasen S, ed), pp 159–179. Mahwah, NJ: Erlbaum.

Laland KN, Richerson PJ, Boyd R (1996) Developing a theory of animal social learning. In: Social learning in animals: The roots of culture (Heyes CM, Galef Jr BG, ed), pp 129–154. San Diego: Academic Press.

Laland KN, Williams K (1997) Shoaling generates social learning of foraging information in guppies. Animal Behaviour, 53: 1161–1169.

Lamb HH (1977) Climatic history and the future. Princeton: Princeton University Press.

Lefebvre L, Palameta B (1988) Mechanisms, ecology and population diffusion of socially learned, food-finding behaviour in feral pigeons. In: Social learning: Psychological and biological perspectives (Zentall TR, Galef Jr BG, ed), pp 141–164. Hillsdale, NJ: Erlbaum.

Lehman S (1993) Climate change: Ice sheets, wayward winds and sea change. Nature, 365: 108–109.

Martin RD (1981) Relative brain size and basal metabolic rate in terrestrial vertebrates. Nature, 293: 57–60.

Moore BR (1996) The evolution of imitative learning. In: Social learning in animals: The roots of culture (Heyes CM, Galef Jr BG, ed), pp 245–265. San Diego: Academic Press.

Partridge TC, Bond GC, Hartnady CJH, deMenocal PB, Ruddiman WF (1995) Climatic effects of late Neogene tectonism and vulcanism. In: Paleoclimate and evolution with emphasis on human origins (Vrba ES, Denton GH, Partridge TC, Burckle LH, ed), pp 8–23. New Haven: Yale University Press.

Pinker S (1997) How the mind works. New York: Norton.

Poli MD (1986) Species-specific differences in animal learning. In: Intelligence and evolutionary biology (Jerison H, Jerison I, ed), pp 277–297. Berlin: Springer.

Pulliam HR, Dunford C (1980) Programmed to learn: An essay on the evolution of culture. New York: Columbia University Press.

Rogers AR (1989) Does biology constrain culture? American Anthropologist, 90: 819–831.

Schneider SH, Londer R (1984) The coevolution of climate and life. San Francisco: Sierra Club Books.

Spelke ES (1990) Principles of object perception. Cognitive Science, 14: 29–56.

Terkel J (1996) Cultural transmission of feeding behavior in the black rat (*Rattus rattus*). In: Social learning in animals: The roots of culture (Heyes CM, Galef Jr BG, ed), pp 17–47. San Diego: Academic Press.

Tomasello M (1996) Do apes ape? In: Social learning in animals: The roots of culture (Heyes CM, Galef Jr BG, ed), pp 319–346. New York: Academic Press.

Tooby J, Cosmides L (1992) Psychological foundations of culture. In: The adapted mind: Evolutionary psychology and the generation of culture (Barkow JH, Cosmides L, Tooby J, ed), pp 19–136. Oxford: Oxford University Press.

Tooby J, DeVore I (1987) The reconstruction of hominid behavioral evolution through strategic modeling. In: The evolution of human behavior: Primate models (Kinzey WG, ed), pp 183–237. Albany: State University of New York Press.

Whiten A, Custance D (1996) Studies of imitation in chimpanzees and children. In: Social learning in animals: The roots of culture (Heyes CM, Galef Jr BG, ed), pp 291–318. San Diego: Academic Press.

Zentall T (1996) An anlysis of imitative learning in animals. In: Social learning in animals: The roots of culture (Heyes CM, Galef Jr BG, ed), pp 221–243. San Diego: Academic Press.

19 Gossip and Other Aspects of Language as Group-Level Adaptations

David Sloan Wilson, Carolyn Wilczynski, Alexandra Wells, and Laura Weiser

Gossip has a strange status in everyday life. On the one hand, people in all cultures gossip with an appetite that rivals their interest in food and sex. On the other hand, gossip is often denigrated and trivialized with terms such as "small talk" and "tittle-tattle." Gossiping is thought to be undignified and the information conveyed by gossip is regarded as unreliable and self-serving.

The academic study of gossip mirrors its ambivalent status in everyday life. Ethnographers seldom fail to mention gossip as a pervasive activity in cultures around the world. A few authors have stressed the need to study gossip as an important part of human nature (e.g., Gluckman, 1963; Haviland, 1977; Merry, 1984; Barkow, 1992; Levin and Arluke, 1994; Goodman and Ben-Ze-ev, 1994; Dunbar, 1996), but their call has not been heeded. The scientific literature on gossip remains miniscule (in addition to the above cited papers, see Roberts, 1964; Paine, 1967, 1968, 1970a, b; Gluckman, 1968; Abrahams, 1970; Bleek, 1976; Cox, 1970; Handelman, 1973; Wilson, 1974; Besnier, 1989, 1990; de Raad and Calje, 1990; Dunbar et al., 1997; Walker and Blaine, 1991; Eder and Enke, 1991; Nevo et al., 1993; Harrington and Bielby, 1995).

Gossip's perennial neglect can be traced to at least two factors, the first of which is conceptual. Gossip is frequently interpreted by ethnographers as benefitting the group: for example, by communicating the values of the group, punishing those who violate social norms, or defining the boundaries of group membership (e.g., Gluckman, 1963). However, many scientists reject group-level explanations, insisting that all adaptations must be explained in terms of individual or genetic self-interest. The issue of group vs. individual welfare needs to be clarified before gossip can be properly understood.

The second factor is methodological. Gossip is usually confined to familiar associates and stops in the presence of outsiders, including scientists studying gossip. Numerous anthropologists have observed that understanding and partaking in gossip is a sure sign of acceptance by the people who are being studied (e.g., Haviland, 1977). Even then, however, it would be difficult to study gossip experimentally without betraying the trust that is required to be a member of a gossip community. These methodological difficulties must be solved before the study of gossip can move beyond the descriptive stage.

In this paper we will attempt to alleviate both of these limiting factors. First we will discuss gossip in the light of multilevel selection theory, which shows how group-interest and self-interest can be understood within a single conceptual framework.

Then we will present a method for studying gossip by using fictional gossip episodes whose elements can be systematically varied.

Gossip is fascinating in its own right, but it is also just the tip of the larger iceberg of language in general. Language, like gossip, has often been explained in terms of its group-level benefits, yet this kind of explanation has been avoided by many scientists who have adopted an individualistic perspective. We will therefore attempt to point out the implications of multilevel selection theory for the general study of language, in addition to the more specific study of gossip.

Multilevel Selection, Altruism, and Social Control

Seeing groups as adaptive units in their own right and seeing groups as a byproduct of individual self-interest are two longstanding perspectives that exist across scientific disciplines and in everyday thought. For example, Gluckman's (1963) group-level perspective on gossip was criticized by Paine (1967), who claimed that individuals gossip, not groups, and they gossip for their own benefit. This argument took place without any reference to evolution and ended in a stalemate. That is the usual outcome of clashes between the two perspectives, at least outside evolutionary biology. The two sides merely agree to disagree and their interaction does not lead to productive research.

In evolutionary biology, the conflict between the two perspectives came into sharp focus because both made claims about adaptation and natural selection. Darwin realized that many traits that would benefit the whole group would actually decrease the fitness of the individuals expressing the traits, compared to other individuals in the same group. The classic example is altruism, which benefits others at the expense of the self. Darwin realized that, despite the disadvantage of altruism within groups, groups of altruists would have an advantage over groups of selfish individuals in intergroup competition. In short, evolutionary biology provides a theoretical foundation for *both* perspectives and shows how they can be related to each other. Groups can evolve into adaptive units in their own right, but only by a process of between-group selection that outweighs the often opposing process of within-group selection.

Modern evolutionary biologists have refined Darwin's formulation of the problem but they have not altered its basic structure. Thus, the question of whether gossip or any other set of traits can be explained as group-serving rather than self-serving depends on whether group selection has been a significant force and the degree to which it has been opposed by selection at other levels. In the 1960s, a consensus emerged that group selection is so weak that it can be ignored for most traits, which therefore must be explained in terms of their individual-level (or gene-level) benefits. Since then, most evolutionary biologists and social scientists inspired by evolution have avoided group-level explanations at all costs. With respect to gossip, Gluckman (1963) would be branded a "naive group selectionist" and Paine (1967) would be regarded as on the right track.

Despite it's rock-solid appearance, it is almost certain that the earlier consensus was wrong. Group selection is a significant evolutionary force and probably was especially important throughout human evolution. Justifying this statement requires a book-length treatment (Sober and Wilson, 1998; see also Richerson and Boyd, this volume). Here, we will discuss only a few points that facilitate our study of gossip from a multilevel perspective.

One important development that challenges the earlier consensus is the interpretation of individual organisms as higher-level units of selection. The history of life on earth is increasingly viewed as a series of major transitions in which previously independent lower-level units coalesced into functionally integrated higher-level units (Maynard Smith and Szathmary, 1995). These coalescing events involve the same problems of altruism and selfishness that Darwin envisioned for individuals in social groups. For example, a group of genes might collectively benefit by coordinating their activities, but some genes might also "cheat" by using shared resources to replicate faster than other genes in the same cell. According to Maynard Smith and Szathmary, this problem is solved by the evolution of mechanisms that prevent the possibility of cheating. For example, if the genes form into a string (a chromosome) that replicates as a unit, the differential reproduction of genes within the cell is no longer possible. Higher-level selection (more coordinated cells outcompeting less coordinated cells) can now proceed in the absence of opposing within-group selection (some genes replicating faster than others within cells).

This scenario illustrates an important trend in modern evolutionary thought, in which higher-level organization is explained on the basis of *social control* rather than *altruism*. An entire lexicon of words describing social control in human life has been borrowed to explain the interactions of genes and other subunits of individual organisms: "sheriff" genes, "parliaments" of genes, "rules of fairness," and so on. These mechanisms suppress within-group selfishness without themselves being overtly altruistic, but they still require group selection to evolve. A sheriff gene imposes harmony for the whole group, including alternative "freeloader" genes that do not suppress "outlaw" genes. In fact, if there is any cost to suppressing outlaw genes, the sheriff gene itself qualifies as altruistic by imposing harmony for everyone at its own expense. The evolution of social control is a multilevel selection problem similar to the evolution of altruism, but selection pressures within groups are weak when the costs of imposing social control are low, allowing between-group selection to proceed unopposed (Sober and Wilson, 1998, ch 4).

An example of social control from the social insects will pave the way for our study of gossip. Altruism and the intricate coordination of social insect colonies has traditionally been explained on the basis of kin selection (Hamilton, 1964). However, it turns out that members of a colony are often less related than previously thought because the colony has multiple queens or a single queen has mated with multiple males. For example, honey bee queens routinely mate with ten or more males, resulting in multiple patrilines among the workers of a single hive. In such a genetically diverse colony, a gene that causes workers to lay unfertilized eggs (which develop into males) would be favored by within-colony selection, even if it disrupted the well-being of the colony as a whole. This kind of "cheating" has been looked for but rarely observed, in part because workers who try to lay eggs are attacked by other workers and their eggs are eaten (reviewed by Seeley, 1995). This response to cheating is called "policing," borrowing yet another term from the lexicon of human social control. We therefore must consider the evolution of two sets of behaviors: the original act of cheating and its altruistic alternative ("lay eggs" vs. "refrain from laying eggs"), and the act of policing and its alternative ("attack egg layers and eat their eggs" vs. "do nothing to prevent egg laying"). Policing can itself be considered altruistic if it involves costs that are not shared by its do-nothing alternative. The population structure of honeybee colonies is not sufficient for "refrain" to evolve by itself, but it is sufficient for "attack/refrain" to evolve as a package. The adaptive organization of social insect colonies, like the adaptive organization of individual organisms, relies on social control mechanisms to buttress the behaviors that would be considered overtly altruistic if they were performed in the absence of social control.

Policing in Human Social Groups

Comparing human groups to single organisms and social insect colonies would be regarded by many as the ultimate in "naive group selectionism." Nevertheless, this conditioned reaction, based on a consensus that is now over thirty years old, needs to be questioned in the light of the developments outlined above. It is true that the members of human groups are often weakly or entirely unrelated to each other, but genetic relatedness is only one of many factors that must be considered from the multilevel perspective. Other factors, including social control mechanisms, have probably made group selection a strong force throughout human evolution. Once again, this statement requires a book-length treatment to justify (Sober and Wilson, 1998), but it will probably be considered obvious in retrospect. After all, if metaphorical sheriffs, police, and parliaments can turn groups of genes and insects into well-functioning units, why can't real sheriffs, police, parliaments, and their ancient counterparts do the same for human groups?

To see this more vividly, imagine that you are a honey bee worker who is tempted to lay your own eggs. The problem is that you are *never alone* and you are fully aware that if you try to lay eggs in the presence of others, you will be attacked and your eggs will be eaten. Furthermore, if you see another worker lay eggs, you are filled with righteous indignation and join in the attack. Attacking another worker might be dangerous if it was a one-on-one confrontation, but not when it is many-on-one. You therefore prudently refrain from laying eggs and devote your time to making the colony run as a smoothly functioning unit. Your payoff for being a solid citizen may be substantial, but it is not measured by comparing your fitness with that of other members of your colony. Rather, it is measured by comparing your well-running colony with other colonies that do not function so well. Your behaviors are *group-serving*, not *self-serving*.

Now imagine that you are a member of a human group who is tempted to benefit yourself at the expense of your neighbors. The possibilities are endless: you can avoid sharing the food that you procure, avoid the effort of procuring food while sponging off more altruistic suckers, spend more effort having babies than caring for them, and on and on. The uses of language for self-serving purposes are also endless: you can denigrate your rivals, tell lies and withhold vital information when it serves your purposes, and on and on and on. The trouble is that you are almost *never alone* and your selfish efforts are always in danger of being detected. Furthermore, when you observe selfishness in others you are filled with righteous indignation and join in the attack. Righteous indignation can be dangerous if it results in a one-on-one confrontation, but less so if the confrontation is many-on-one. Seeing that the odds are stacked against you, you wisely decide to avoid the temptations of selfishness and join the group effort. Your payoff as a solid citizen may be considerable, but it is not to be measured by comparing your fitness with that of other members of your group. Rather, it must be measured by the performance of your group, compared to other groups. Your efforts are *group-serving*, not *self-serving*.

We indulge in this imagery with reluctance because it can be mistaken for a claim about the mental processes that actually guide behavior. It would be absurd to suppose that honey bees actually think about how to behave as we have described above. It may be equally wrong to suppose that *people* think about how to behave as we have described above. Perhaps all people are scheming Machiavellians who are quick to cheat when they can get away with it, but perhaps something closer to genuine psychological altruism also exists (Wilson et al., 1996, 1998; Sober and Wilson,

1998). The evolution of the psychological mechanisms that motivate behavior is an important subject in its own right, but it does not concern us here. Our point is to show that social control mechanisms can promote group-serving behaviors and suppress self-serving behaviors in human groups in much the same way as in social insect colonies, despite the large differences in genetic relatedness. The comparison between human groups, social insect colonies, and single organisms is not so far-fetched after all.

Two Meanings of Gossip

Now we are in a position to approach gossip from a multilevel perspective. The word gossip is often used to describe the use of language for self-serving purposes. For example, a person who spreads information (true or false) that tarnishes the reputation of a rival is clearly gossiping. Another common meaning of the word gossip, emphasized by observers of cultures around the world, is the use of language to control all kinds of self-serving behavior in others, including the self-serving use of language. In short, the single word "gossip" refers *both* to self-serving uses of language *and* to the use of language to police the self-serving behaviors of others.

For gossip to function as an efficient social control mechanism, self-serving behaviors must be detectable and punishable at low cost to those who impose the punishment. These conditions do not invariably exist; when absent, we should find groups in which selfishness is rampant, including the self-serving use of language, and efforts to promote group-interest are feeble and ineffective. However, it is also likely that these three conditions *do* exist in *some* human groups and may have been especially prevalent in the small, face-to-face groups that existed throughout our evolutionary history. Social behavior in these groups should be organized to promote the common good.

Three examples out of hundreds that could be cited from the ethnographic literature will illustrate how gossip often serves as an effective policing device. The first comes from the Melanesian island of Lesu (Powdermaker, 1933, p. 323):

There is much talk in the village because Tsengali's pig has broken into Murri's garden. Murri displays no particular anger but Tsengali is much annoyed because of all the talk that the incident has occasioned. So he announces that he will give a pig to Murri to stop the talk. But Murri tells him that this would be foolish "to eat a pig for nothing." Instead, Murri declares that the incident has ended, and that there should be no talk.

This example involves an act of negligence rather than willful selfishness, but it nevertheless triggered a surge of gossip in the community. Acts like these are virtually certain to be detected in a close-knit society like the Lesu, satisfying the first condition outlined above. The gossip clearly damages the offender's reputation, which he is willing to go to great lengths to salvage. If one's reputation stands for more tangible costs and benefits, then the second condition is satisfied. Finally, the cost of imposing the punishment appears negligible. Those who gossiped presumably would have talked about something else and the person who suffered most from the negligent act probably increased his reputation by acting gracious and good-natured. Gossip appears to be such an effective mechanism of social control in this example that it almost has a machinelike quality: a tiny rupture in social organization instantly leads to a gossip response, which ends as abruptly as it began when the rupture is repaired.

Our second example comes from a Norwegian fishing village studied by Paine (1970b), the anthropologist who criticized Gluckman's (1963) group-level perspective on gossip. Despite his emphasis on self-interest, Paine's field work shows how gossip makes it difficult for individuals to pursue their self-interest without regard to the rest of the community. The fishing village studied by Paine included an entrepreneur who attempted to increase his own wealth by starting new businesses. This person tried to form alliances by talking privately with individuals and asking them not to divulge the contents of their conversation. In fact, this person's house was unusual for including a room in which it was *possible* to have a private conversation! His secretive methods of talking aroused the entire community, whose public talk caused the entrepreneur to become isolated: "In the end, he had to keep his own company" (p. 177). Paine also described a shopkeeper who went bankrupt for betraying confidences and a man who achieved high status by fostering an open form of communication that involved the entire community. Once again, the three conditions of detecting transgressions, and the high-cost punishment that can be imposed at low cost to the punishers, appear to be satisfied in this example.

A recent study of cattle ranchers in California (Ellickson, 1991) shows that gossip can function as strongly in modern life as in more traditional societies. Order was maintained through informal social norms and almost never by resorting to formal legal channels. The first response to a neighbor who refused to mend fences (both literally and figuratively) was "truthful negative gossip" (e.g., p. 57).

The mildest form of self-help is truthful negative gossip. This usually works because only the extreme deviants are immune from the general obsession with neighborliness.... People tend to know one another, and they value their reputations in the community. Some ranching families have lived in the area for several generations and include members who plan to stay indefinitely. Members of these families seem particularly intent on maintaining their reputations as good neighbors. Should one of them not promptly and courteously retrieve a stray, he might fear that any resulting gossip would permanently besmirch the family name.

The dynamics of social control in this example are almost identical to our first example from Melanesia. The general thesis of Ellickson's book is that small groups of people establish and maintain social norms that promote the common good. Many evolutionary biologists might object to this "benefit of the group" perspective, but effective social control mechanisms show how it can be justified.

These examples illustrate what has always seemed obvious to observers of human societies around the world. People tend to be passionate about maintaining their reputations, which in turn depends on being solid citizens, as defined by the social norms of the community. The breakdown of social organization is quickly detected by other members of the group and communicated by gossip. Offenders must repair the damage and make amends to salvage their reputation. In a perceptive review, Merry (1984) emphasizes that gossip and loss of reputation by themselves are not effective social control mechanisms, but must stand for more tangible forms of punishment that will take place if the offenders fail to mend their ways. Talk is "empty" in the absence of real social control, but when social groups have the means to truly punish their members, gossip and reputation are usually sufficient to maintain social order without heavy-handed punishment actually occurring.

We need to emphasize once again that these conditions do *not* invariably exist in human social groups. The purpose of multilevel selection theory is not to show that all groups are adaptive but to recognize adaptations where they exist, at all levels of the biological hierarchy. It is easy to imagine social environments (especially in modern life) in which antisocial behaviors are difficult to detect and even when detected are difficult to punish without great cost to those attempting to enforce social norms. The concept of group-interest should have little predictive value in these cases. Nevertheless, it would be a great mistake to extend this conclusion to all human social groups, which is what many scientists do when they categorically reject arguments based on "the good of the group." Multilevel selection theory combines the group and individual perspectives into a single predictive framework in which gossip plays at least two central roles: as a form of antisocial behavior, and as a means of controlling all forms of antisocial behavior.

Other Group-Serving Functions of Language

The word "gossip" defies precise definition. We have already identified two fundamentally different meanings, and others may also exist. Many uses of language do not qualify as gossip in any sense of the word. If group selection has been a significant force in human evolution, we need to think about language in general from the group-level perspective. To state the conjecture boldly, suppose that human groups have evolved into "superorganisms" with a "group mind." The components of the group mind are connected not by neurons but by language. How must language be structured for a group to have a mind? The purpose of indulging in this fantasy of group-level functionalism is not because it is literally true but because it may be *partially* true, depending on the degree to which language has evolved by group selection. Group-level adaptations must be imagined before their existence can be tested (Wilson, 1997; Sober and Wilson, 1998, ch 3).

Individual minds are often portrayed by evolutionary psychologists as a collection of special purpose mechanisms that evolved to solve the major adaptive problems confronted in ancestral environments (see Bitterman, this volume; Lefebvre, this volume; Richerson and Boyd, this volume; Shettleworth, this volume). If this view is true for individual minds, it should be equally true for group minds. Language must be *multifunctional* to adaptively coordinate the activities of human groups. It also must be richly *context sensitive* for the different functions to be performed through a common medium. Finally, just as most individual cognition takes place without conscious awareness, people should routinely participate as components of the group mind without being aware of what they are doing. *People should talk in ways that they do not talk about.* These are three major predictions that emerge easily by viewing language from the group-level perspective.

What are some of the specific functions of the group mind, beyond the policing function that we have already discussed? One possibility is the gathering and transmission of accurate information (see also Lefebvre, this volume; Richerson and Boyd, this volume). Groups with many eyes and ears that evaluate the quality of information would fare better than other kinds of groups. It might seem that these predictions are manifestly false, because gossip is commonly thought to be a notoriously unreliable source of information. However, this criticism ignores the importance of context-sensitivity that we emphasized above. Accurate knowledge is not adaptive in *all* contexts. Even outrageously false beliefs can be adaptive if they cause the believers to behave adaptively in the real world (Wilson, 1990, 1995). To evaluate the claim that language functions to gather and transmit accurate information, we must study the use of language in contexts in which it is adaptive to know the facts of the matter.

This discussion obviously fails to do justice to the large and complicated subject of language, but perhaps it is sufficient to show how language can be approached from the multilevel perspective. Of course, it is not enough to have a conceptual framework that generates interesting predictions. We must also have an empirical methodology for testing the predictions.

Testing Predictions about Gossip and Other Forms of Talk

Psychological research includes the use of simple paper-and-pencil tests that can be administered to hundreds of subjects in only a few minutes. These tests have limitations and should be used in conjunction with more naturalistic methods, but they are undeniably an important tool for testing predictions about human nature. They have been used successfully by evolutionary psychologists to explore subjects ranging from mate choice (Buss, 1994), to social exchange (Cosmides and Tooby, 1992), to sex differences in spatial abilities (Silverman and Philips, 1998). Curiously, these methods have not been used to study gossip. We therefore conducted a series of experiments involving fictional gossip episodes whose elements can be systematically varied.

Our main hypothesis was that response to gossip should be *context sensitive*. People should condemn gossip when it is self-serving but not when it is used for social control. They should attend to the quality of information when it is important to know the facts of the matter but not otherwise. Our first experiment consisted of two versions of the following story.

Jane and Susan are waiting outside their biology class for the final grades to be posted. They have been best friends since high school. Both are hard-working students, well liked and trusted by their friends. They take their classes very seriously and each are working part-time jobs to supplement their academic scholarships. The grade in this class is particularly important, because the medical schools they have applied to have high standards. When the grades are posted, they see that they have just missed the cut-off for a grade that the schools find acceptable.

Jane: "This would be easier to take if I didn't know that a group of students cheated."

Susan: "Really? What do you mean?"

Jane: "They asked me if I wanted to join them! They stole a copy of the exam from the office the night before!"

In this version, the two gossipers are described as good people who had much to lose from cheating by others, a clear violation of a social norm. In the second version, the same story was followed by a more self-serving dialogue:

Jane: "I bet we would have gotten a better grade if we sucked up to the professor the way those students in the front row did."

Susan: "Really? What do you mean?"

Jane: "Oh you know, always asking questions and pretending they're interested."

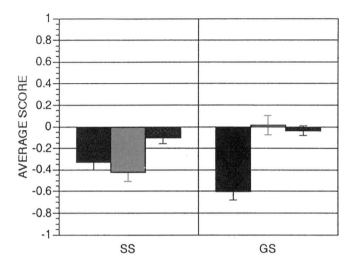

Figure 19.1
Average subject approval rating of the target (black histogram), the speaker (light-shaded histogram), and the listener (dark-shaded histogram), for fictional gossip episodes in which the speaker is self-serving (SS) or responding to the violation of a social norm (group-serving, or GS) Male and female scores were not statistically significant and are combined for analysis.

Although some people might regard asking questions in class as a violation of a social norm, we assumed that most would interpret Jane's comments as blaming others for her own poor performance. Eighty-four undergraduate students (23 males, 61 females) read one version of the story and were asked to indicate the degree to which they approved of the speaker, the listener, and the target of the gossip on a scale from "highly disapprove" (−1) to "highly approve" (+1). Figure 19.1 shows that response to negative gossip is indeed context-sensitive, as we had predicted. Self-serving gossip damaged the reputation of the gossiper even more than the target of the gossip. When the gossip was about a rule-breaking event, the target was judged extremely harshly but the evaluation of the speaker was neutral. The difference in the evaluation of the speaker between the two treatments is highly significant (ANOVA, df = 1, SS = 16.29, F = 12.83, p = .0006).

Our second experiment consisted of five fictional gossip episodes patterned after Ellickson's study of cattle ranchers. Each version was divided into two parts, corresponding to the events leading up to the gossip and the gossip itself. The first version was intended to represent the "truthful negative gossip" that ranchers actually employ against their neighbors who refuse to mend fences.

Part 1. Shasta County, California, is cattle ranching country. The ranches have been passed from father to son for many generations and the ranchers almost always settle their disputes among themselves rather than using formal legal procedures. The Jim Turner ranch is well known for its careless management. In 1967, some of Jim Turner's cattle broke their fence and started grazing the land of one of Jim's neighbors, Tom Stark. Tom's first response was to call Jim's ranch to inform him of the problem, but his calls were not answered. Tom's second response was to visit the Turner ranch in person. Jim met Tom at the door and said he would retrieve the cattle but did not invite Tom inside. A week after the incident began, the cattle were still not retrieved.

Part 2. The next day, Tom sat down with a group of other ranchers at a local diner and felt like airing his complaint against Jim. They had the following conversation.

Tom: Jim Turner is at it again.

Another rancher: What do you mean?

Tom: His cattle broke my fence and have been grazing my land for a week and he hasn't done anything about it!

Ellickson's emphasis on *truthful* negative gossip suggests that false or gratuitous negative gossip might damage the reputation of the gossiper, even when provoked by the violation of a norm. We tested this hypothesis in a second version of the story by adding a single sentence to Tom's final speech: "I'll bet he spends too much time getting drunk to think about mending fences!"

It might seem that the most honorable form of policing would take place *in the presence of the rule-breaker*. We tested this hypothesis in a third version by changing part 2 of the story as follows:

Part 2. The next day, Tom sat down with a group of other ranchers that included Jim Turner at a local diner and felt like airing his complaint against Jim. He began the following conversation.

Tom: Jim, perhaps you would like to explain to all of us here why you haven't done anything about your cattle that broke my fence and have been grazing my land for a week.

Another possible course of action for Tom would be to remain silent. This might seem especially noble, but it would also leave the problem unresolved. Boyd and Richerson (1992) have shown that effective policing requires what they call *higher-order punishment*, in which failure to enforce social norms itself violates the norms and is subject to punishment. We therefore predicted that at least some subjects would judge Tom harshly for *failing* to gossip, which we tested in a fourth version of the story by altering part 2 as follows:

Part 2. The next day, Tom sat down with a group of other ranchers at a local diner and felt like airing his complaint against Jim, but decided to remain silent.

These four versions examined differences in how a person might respond to a norm-breaking event. The fifth version altered the story to make the gossip self-serving, although the specific content of the gossip remained truthful.

Part 1. Shasta County, California is cattle ranching country. The ranches have been passed from father to son for many generations and the ranchers almost always settle their disputes among themselves rather than using formal legal procedures. In 1967, some of Jim Turner's cattle broke their fence and started grazing the land of one of Jim's neighbors, Tom Stark. Tom's first response was to call Jim's ranch to inform him of the problem, but his calls were not answered. Tom's second response was to visit the Turner ranch in person, where he discovered that Jim was out of town and his ranch manager was in the hospital with a broken leg. Jim apologized to Tom, retrieved his cattle, and mended the fence as soon as he returned from his trip, a week after the incident began.

Part 2. Several months later, both Jim and Tom ran for the office of county sheriff. Tom had the following conversation with some other ranchers at a local diner.

Tom: Jim's a good man but sometimes he does things that a neighbor just shouldn't do.

Another rancher: What do you mean?

Tom: Why, his cattle broke their fence and grazed my land for a whole week before he did anything about it!

One hundred and ninety-five undergraduate students (78 males, 117 females) read a single version of the story and were asked to indicate the degree to which they approved of Tom Stark's conduct during part 2 on a scale from "highly disapprove" (-1) to "highly approve" $(+1)$. The subjects were also asked to provide written comments on their reaction to the story. An important interaction with gender emerged in this study, so results for males and females are shown separately in figure 19.2. Confirming the results of the previous study, self-serving gossip was judged far more harshly than gossiping in response to the violation of a social norm (compare SSG with the other four treatments in figure 19.2; for the comparison between SSG and TNG, $n = 79$, $df = 1$, $SS = 184.51$, $F = 49.09$, $p = .80$ E-09). A typical verbal comment on the truthful negative gossip version was: "He had a right to complain to others." A typical comment for the self-serving gossip version was "Tom's conduct in part 2 was completely inappropriate—he only told part of the story of what occurred."

In addition, subjects reacted to the details of gossip in response to the violation of a social norm. Supplementing truthful negative gossip with a single pejorative sentence significantly decreased the reputation of the gossiper (compare TNG with FNG in figure 19.2; $n = 82$, $df = 1$, $SS = 21.98$, $F = 5.32$, $p = .023$). The verbal comments left little doubt that the subjects were holding the gossiper to a high moral standard. One wrote, "The way that Tom responded in part 2 was certainly less than appro-

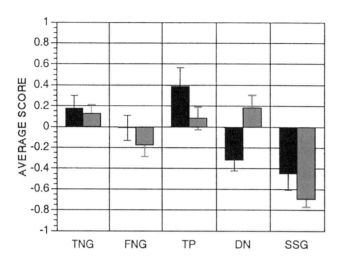

Figure 19.2
Average approval rating by male subjects (black histogram) and female subjects (shaded histogram) for five gossip scenarios: TNG, truthful negative gossip in response to a norm violation; FNG, false negative gossip in response to a norm violation; TP, speaking with the transgressor present in response to a norm violation; DN, remaining silent (doing nothing) in response to the norm violation; SSG, self-serving gossip episode.

priate, since he had no grounds to base his claim of drunkenness. The fact that he voiced his opinion to the other ranchers, however, could serve to help bring Jim back into the right through pressure of his peers." It would be hard to improve upon this comment as a statement of our own hypothesis!

Discussing the problem in the presence of the transgressor was *not* rated more highly than discussing it in his absence (compare TNG with TP; $n = 85$, $df = 1$, $SS = .097$, $F = .019$, $p = .89$). Some subjects did feel that it was better not to "talk behind someone's back," but others felt that raising the issue to his face in front of others was too confrontational and might escalate the conflict.

Remaining silent was strongly disapproved by male subjects but not by female subjects (compare TNG with RS; $n = 84$, $df = 1$, $SS_{TRT} = 15.51$, $SS_{SEX} = 16.95$, $SS_{TRT \times SEX} = 25.31$, $F_{TRT} = 3.67$, $F_{SEX} = 4.01$, $F_{TRT \times SEX} = 5.99$, $p_{TRT} = .058$, $p_{SEX} = .048$, $p_{TRT \times SEX} = .016$). A typical comment from a female was "Tom Stark did the right thing [in part 1], although he didn't say anything in part 2 when most people would have. The problem is between Tom and Jim, no one else, but if Jim still does not cooperate, then either the law should be informed or Tom should tell the other ranchers to ask for their opinions or help in how to deal with Jim." Even this person thought that talk would eventually be appropriate to deal with the problem. A typical male response was "Plain and simple he should have told about the problem to warn other ranchers about Jim Turner." For this person and for many other subjects, *failing* to gossip violated a social norm.

To summarize, our second experiment confirmed and extended the results of our first experiment, even though it occurred in a completely different social setting (male cattle ranchers vs. female undergraduate students). Self-serving gossip was judged highly inappropriate. Gossiping to enforce a social norm was judged appropriate, but only when done in a responsible manner. Approval of truthful negative gossip equalled or exceeded all the other courses of action, including remaining silent.

Our third experiment examined context sensitivity with respect to the quality of information with eight versions of the following story.

Pat and Adrian are both teaching assistants for Professor Wright's physics class. Professor Wright is a brilliant scientist whose involvement with his work has given him the reputation of an "absent minded professor." He relies on his TA's to keep his class in good running order. After an exam, Pat approaches Adrian for advice.

Pat: A student cheated on the exam. Do you think that I should tell Professor Wright?

Adrian: How do you know that he cheated?

Pat: I saw him do it.

This story describes a situation in which it is clearly important to know the facts of the matter. Four versions of the story were prepared in which Pat was an eyewitness to the event ("I saw him do it"), a trusted friend reported the event ("A very good friend of mine told me that he saw him do it and I know that he wouldn't lie about something like that"), two unknown students reported the event independently ("Two different students approached me after the exam and told me that they saw him do it"), or one unknown student reported the event ("Another student told me that he saw him do it"). If people are sensitive to the quality of information, they should regard an eyewitness account as more believable than hearsay. When evidence is based on hearsay, they should be sensitive to the number and trustworthiness of the sources. To create a context in which the quality of information is not important, the dialogue part of the story was changed as follows:

Pat: Did you hear that Professor Wright came to work with his pants on inside out?

Adrian: No way! How do you know that?

Pat: I saw him myself!

The quality of information was also varied for this version of the story, leading to a total of eight treatments. After reading the story, subjects were asked to rate the credibility of the information on a scale from "highly unbelievable" (-1) to "highly believable" ($+1$). As predicted, sensitivity to the quality of information was context dependent (figure 19.3). The four versions of the cheating story were ranked with respect to credibility in the order eyewitness account (S) > Two unknown sources (2) > One trusted source (T) > One unknown source (1). The difference between the versions was highly significant (ANOVA, df = 3, SS = 8.79, F = 8.96, p = .00003). A multiple comparison of means showed that the major difference was between the eyewitness account and other accounts, which were not statistically different from each other. When the professor was being caricatured, subjects regarded the story as moderately credible but were completely insensitive to the quality of information, with no significant differences among the four versions.

All paper-and-pencil tests in psychological research must be interpreted with caution and cross-checked with other methods to confirm that they correspond to behavior in the real world. Our results are preliminary, but they suggest that people respond to fictional gossip events much as they would respond to gossip in their own lives (e.g., our cattle rancher study compares well with the behavior of actual cattle

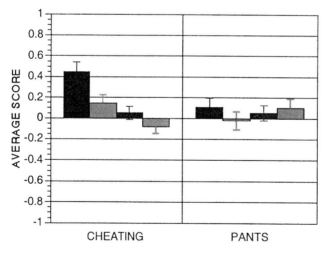

Figure 19.3
Average subject rating for credibility of the information for four versions of two episodes; one in which it is important to know the facts of the matter (Cheating) and one in which it is not (Pants). The four versions are eye-witness account (black histogram), two hearsay accounts (moderately shaded histogram), one hearsay account from a trusted person (darkly shaded histogram), and one hearsay account (lightly shaded histogram). Male and female scores were not statistically significant and are combined for analysis.

ranchers as reported by Ellickson, 1991). If so, then it will be possible to make rapid empirical progress toward understanding the contours of gossip in particular and language in general from a multilevel perspective.

Summary

We have tried to provide both a conceptual framework and an empirical methodology for studying gossip. Our starting point was the longstanding conflict between group and individual-level perspectives that exists, independently, in biology and the social sciences. We showed that effective social control mechanisms allow groups to evolve into adaptive units and that gossip has been reported to function as a social control mechanism in cultures around the world. Methodologically, we explored the use of simple paper-and-pencil tests that have been widely used to study other subjects in psychology but not gossip. We showed that people are easily engaged by fictional gossip episodes whose elements can be systematically varied. They highly disapprove of self-serving gossip but approve of gossiping in response to norm violations, as long as the gossip is conducted in a responsible manner. Indeed, in some contexts, failing to gossip can be more hazardous than gossiping to one's reputation. The results of our experiments agree with descriptive accounts of gossip around the world and show how gossip can function as a social control mechanism without damaging the reputation of the gossiper.

Our study of gossip led to the more general study of language from a multilevel perspective. Language is among the most communal of human faculties, yet the individualistic perspective dominant in the study of human evolution has retarded the study of language as something that evolved to benefit whole groups. We boldly asked what language would look like as the medium of a group mind and predicted context dependent sensitivity to the quality of information. Our prediction was supported by a single experiment. Obviously, we have only scratched the surface of a very large set of subjects, but perhaps sufficiently to show that our conceptual framework, coupled with our simple methods, offers a fertile interplay between hypothesis formation and testing.

References

Abrahams RD (1970) A performance-centered approach to gossip. Man, 5: 290–301.

Barkow JH (1992) Beneath new culture is old psychology. In: The adapted mind: Evolutionary psychology and the evolution of culture (Barkow JH, Cosmides L, Tooby J, ed), pp 627–638. Oxford: Oxford University Press.

Besnier N (1989) Information withholding as a manipulative and collusive strategy in Nukulaelae gossip. Language in Society, 18: 315–341.

Besnier N (1990) Conflict management, gossip, and affective meaning on Nukulaelae. In: Disentangling: Conflict discourse in Pacific societies (Watson-Gegeo KA, White GA, ed), pp 290–334. Stanford, CA: Stanford University Press.

Bleek W (1976) Witchcraft, gossip, and death: A social drama. Man, 11: 526–541.

Boyd R, Richerson PJ (1992) Punishment allows the evolution of cooperation (or anything else) in sizable groups. Ethology and Sociobiology, 13: 171–195.

Buss DM (1994) The evolution of desire. New York: Basic Books.

Cosmides L, Tooby J (1992) Cognitive adaptations for social exchange. In: The adapted mind (Barkow J, Cosmides L, Tooby J, ed), pp 163–225. New York: Academic Press.

Cox BA (1970) What is Hopi gossip about? Information management and Hopi factions. Man, 5: 88–98.

de Raad B, Calje H (1990) Personality in the context of conversation: Person-talk scenarios replicated. European Journal of Personality, 4: 19–36.

Dunbar RIM (1996) Grooming, gossip and the evolution of language. Cambridge, MA: Harvard University Press.

Dunbar RIM, Duncan NDC, Marriott A (1997) Human conversational behavior. Human Nature, 8: 231–246.

Eder D, Enke JL (1991) The structure of gossip: Opportunities and constraints on collective expression among adolescents. American Sociological Review, 56: 494–508.

Ellickson RC (1991) Order without law. Cambridge, MA: Harvard University Press.

Gluckman M (1963) Gossip and scandal. Current Anthropology, 4: 307–316.

Gluckman M (1968) Psychological, sociological and anthropological explanations of witchcraft and gossip: A clarification. Man, 3: 20–34.

Goodman RF, Ben-Ze'ev A (1994) Good gossip. Lawrence: University of Kansas Press.

Hamilton WD (1964) The genetical evolution of social behavior: I and II. Journal of Theoretical Biology, 7: 1–52.

Handelman D (1973) Gossip in encounters: The transmission of information in a bounded social setting. Man, 8: 210–227.

Harrington CL, Bielby DD (1995) Where did you hear that? Technology and the social organization of gossip. Sociological Quarterly, 36: 607–628.

Haviland JB (1977) Gossip, reputation and knowledge in Zinacantan. Chicago: Chicago University Press.

Levin J, Arluke A (1994) Gossip: The inside scoop. New York: Plenum Press.

Maynard Smith J, Szathmáry E (1995) The major transitions in evolution. Oxford: W. H. Freeman.

Merry SE (1984) Rethinking gossip and scandal. In: Toward a general theory of social control: Fundamentals (Black D, ed), pp 271–302. Orlando, FL.: Academic Press.

Nevo O, Nevo B, Derech-Zehavi A (1993) The development of the tendency to gossip questionnaire: Construct and concurrent validation for a sample of Israeli college students. Educational and Psychological Measurement, 53: 973–981.

Paine R (1967) What is gossip about? An alternative hypothesis. Man, 2: 278–285.

Paine R (1968) Gossip and transaction. Man, 3: 305–308.

Paine R (1970a) Lappish decisions, partnerships, information management, and sanctions—a nomadic pastoralist adaptation. Ethnology, 9: 52–67.

Paine R (1970b) Informal communication and information management. Canadian Review of Sociology and Anthropology, 7: 172–188.

Powdermaker H (1933) Life in Lesu: The study of a Melanesian society in New Ireland. Foreward by Dr. Clark Wissler. New York: Norton.

Roberts JM (1964) The self-management of cultures. In: Explorations of cultural anthropology: Essays in honor of George Peter Murdock (Goodenough WH, ed), pp 433–454. New York: McGraw-Hill.

Seeley T (1995) The wisdom of the hive. Cambridge, MA: Harvard University Press.

Silverman I, Phillips K (1998) The evolutionary psychology of spatial sex differences. In: Handbook of evolutionary psychology (Crawford C, Krebs DL, ed), pp 595–612. Mahwah, NJ: Erlbaum.

Sober E, Wilson DS (1998) Unto others: The evolution and psychology of unselfish behavior. Cambridge, MA: Harvard University Press.

Walker CJ, Blaine B (1991) The virulence of dread rumors: A field experiment. Language and Communication, 11: 291–297.

Wilson DS (1990) Species of thought: A comment on evolutionary epistemology. Biology and Philosophy, 5: 37–62.

Wilson DS (1995) Language as a community of interacting belief systems: A case study involving conduct towards self and others. Biology and Philosophy, 10: 77–97.

Wilson DS (1997) Incorporating group selection into the adaptationist program: A case study involving human decision making. In: Evolutionary social psychology (Simpson J, Kendrick D, ed), pp 345–386. Mahwah, NJ: Erlbaum.

Wilson DS, Near D, Miller RR (1996) Machiavellianism: A synthesis of the evolutionary and psychological literatures. Psychological Bulletin, 199: 285–299.

Wilson DS, Near DC, Miller RR (1998) Individual differences in Machiavellianism as a mix of cooperative and exploitative strategies. Evolution and Human Behavior, 19: 203–212.

Wilson PJ (1974) Filcher of good names: An enquiry into anthropology and gossip. Man, 9: 93–102.

Contributors

Bernard W. Balleine
Department of Psychology
University of California, Los Angeles
Los Angeles, California

Patrick Bateson
Sub-Department of Animal Behaviour
University of Cambridge
Cambridge, England

Michael J. Beran
Language Research Center
Georgia State University
Atlanta, Georgia

M. E. Bitterman
Békésy Laboratory of Neurobiology
University of Hawaii
Honolulu, Hawaii

Robert Boyd
Department of Anthropology
University of California, Los Angeles
Los Angeles, California

Nicola S. Clayton
Section of Neurobiology, Physiology
and Behavior
University of California, Davis
Davis, California

Juan D. Delius
Department of Psychology
University of Konstanz
Konstanz, Germany

Anthony Dickinson
Department of Experimental
Psychology
University of Cambridge
Cambridge, England

Robin I. M. Dunbar
ESRC Research Centre in Economic
Learning and Social Evolution
School of Biological Sciences
University of Liverpool
Liverpool, England

D. P. Griffiths
Section of Neurobiology, Physiology
and Behavior
University of California, Davis
Davis, California

Bernd Heinrich
Department of Biology
University of Vermont
Burlington, Vermont

Cecilia Heyes
Department of Psychology
University College London
London, England

William A. Hillix
Language Research Center
Georgia State University
Atlanta, Georgia

Ludwig Huber
Institute of Zoology
University of Vienna
Vienna, Austria

Nicholas Humphrey
Centre for Philosophy of Natural and
Social Sciences
London School of Economics
London, England

Masako Jitsumori
Department of Cognitive and
Information Sciences
Chiba University
Chiba, Japan

Louis Lefebvre
Department of Biology
McGill University
Montreal, Quebec, Canada

Nicholas J. Mackintosh
Department of Experimental
Psychology
University of Cambridge
Cambridge, England

Euan M. Macphail
Department of Psychology
University of York
York, England

Peter J. Richerson
Department of Environmental Science
and Policy
University of California, Davis
Davis, California

Duane M. Rumbaugh
Language Research Center
Georgia State University
Atlanta, Georgia

Sara J. Shettleworth
Department of Psychology
University of Toronto
Toronto, Ontario, Canada

Martina Siemann
Department of Psychology
University of Konstanz
Konstanz, Germany

Kim Sterelny
Department of Philosophy
Victoria University of Wellington
Wellington, New Zealand

Michael Tomasello
Max Planck Institute for Evolutionary
Anthropology
Leipzig, Germany

Alexandra Wells
Department of Biological Sciences
Binghamton University
Binghamton, New York

Laura Weiser
Department of Biological Sciences
Binghamton University
Binghamton, New York

Carolyn Wilczynski
Department of Biological Sciences
Binghamton University
Binghamton, New York

David Sloan Wilson
Department of Biological Sciences
Binghamton University
Binghamton, New York

Species Index

Author Index

Subject Index